SCOTLAND:
THE MAKING AND UNMAKING OF THE NATION
c.1100–1707

SCOTLAND
THE MAKING AND
UNMAKING OF
THE NATION
c.1100 – 1707

VOLUME 3 : READINGS:
C.1100 – 1500

Edited by
Bob Harris and Alan R MacDonald

DUNDEE UNIVERSITY PRESS

and

THE OPEN UNIVERSITY IN SCOTLAND

First published in Great Britain in 2006 by
Dundee University Press

University of Dundee
Dundee DD1 4HN

www.dundee.ac.uk/dup

ISBN 10: 1-84586-005-5
ISBN 13: 978-1-84586-005-9

British Library Cataloguing-in-Publication Data
A catalogue record for this book is available on request from the British Library

Typeset by HewerText UK Ltd, Edinburgh
Printed and bound by Bell & Bain Ltd, Glasgow

Contents

PREFACE   vii

ACKNOWLEDGEMENTS   xi

1 'Prospects of the Advancement of Knowledge in
   Early Scottish History'   1
   AO Anderson

2 'Generic Element Variation, with Special Reference to
   Eastern Scotland'   8
   S Taylor

3 'Gold into Lead? The State of Early Medieval Scottish History'   18
   Richard D Oram

4 'Robert Bruce: The Turn of the Tide'   31
   GWS Barrow

5 'The Exercise of Power'   49
   JM Brown

6 'Crown and Nobility in Late Medieval Britain'   66
   A Grant

7 'Scotland's "Celtic Fringe" in the Late Middle Ages: The
   Macdonald Lords of the Isles and the Kingdom of Scotland'   74
   A Grant

8 'The Papacy and Scotland in the Fifteenth Century'   96
   DER Watt

9 'The Flemish Dimension of the Auld Alliance'   113
   A Stevenson

10 'New Solutions to Old Problems: The Stewarts and the Alliance'   128
    N Macdougall

11 'Power to the People? The Myth of the Medieval Burgh
    Community'   136
    EP Dennison

12 'Aberdeen before 1800: The Medieval Market, c.1400–1550'   144
    E Gemmill and N Mayhew

13 'The People in the Towns'   156
    EP Dennison and GG Simpson

14 'The Scottish Medieval Pottery Industry: A Pilot Study'   162
    DW Hall

15   'Dogs, Cats and Horses in the Scottish Medieval Town'   168
     C Smith
16   'The Nobility'   191
     A Grant
17   'Early Church Architecture in Scotland'   209
     E Fernie
18   'St Rule's Church, St Andrews, and Early Stone-Built Churches
     in Scotland'   217
     N Cameron
19   'Introduction' (in his *Literary Practice and Social Change
     in Britain 1380–1530*)   224
     L Patterson
20   'The Ideology of Blood: Blind Hary's Wallace'   228
     RJ Goldstein
21   '*Scotichronicon*'s First Readers'   233
     S Mapstone
22   'Politics and Poetry in Fifteenth and Sixteenth Century Scotland' 239
     RJ Lyall

Preface

This volume and the series of which it is a part represent the completion of a project which began in the mid-1990s to facilitate the study of Scottish History in Scotland and beyond. A milestone was reached in 1998 with the launch of a module in Modern Scottish History – Modern Scottish History: 1707 to the Present. This module, and the five volumes which accompany it, have won consistently high praise from the students who have taken it, as well as strong commendation from many professional academics. Appropriately perhaps, with the project's completion in 2007, the 300th anniversary of the parliamentary union with England, anyone who wishes to will be able to study Scottish history from c.1100 to the present day by distance learning.

In 1998, the editors said that it was a particularly appropriate moment to bring Scottish history to a new and wider readership and audience. This reflected, in the first place, the outcome of the 1997 Referendum, but also the evident depth of contemporary interest, expressed in a large variety of ways, in the Scottish past. It is no less true today. Indeed, if anything, the need and desirability of doing so is only greater with the first flush of post-devolution excitement over and the place of Scottish history in universities and schools not necessarily any stronger than it was a few years ago. And while popular history books are being written and published, and since 2003 History Scotland has been available on newsagents' shelves, long-established myths and preconceptions about the Scottish past still exert a very firm grip on general opinion, and even on those who really should know better. Scottish history and Scotland deserve better than this.

These volumes aim to present recent academic research to a wide readership. As such, they should be of interest to anyone with an interest in knowing about the Scottish past as well as the essential historical background to many present-day concerns and issues. They also provide a way for readers to develop their own skills as students of history, focusing on issues relating to the use (and abuse) of primary sources and the conceptual questions and challenges raised by specific topics. While we have left out some of the overtly pedagogical material which was included in the Modern Scottish History volumes, there is still plenty of discussion on sources and methods for interested readers to follow up.

The potential scope of these volumes is enormous, and this despite the fact that the sources and scholarship for the medieval and early modern periods are considerably less abundant than for the modern one. Any decision we might have taken about how to present the history of periods as long as c.1100–c.1500 and c.1500–1707 would have involved some awkward compromises. Volumes 1 and 2, comprising new essays by expert authors, start with a number of broadly chronological chapters, furnishing readers with a basic narrative. These chapters are followed by a range of more thematic ones. All the chapters are designed to offer a reasonably comprehensive introduction to recent work and, as importantly, a context or contexts for further reading and investigation. There is some overlap between the chronological and thematic chapters, which offers scope for comparison between authors and for looking again at topics and themes from alternative perspectives. Some themes span the two volumes – for example, the Highland–Lowland divide, urbanisation, Scottish identity, Anglo-Scottish relations – so they can be traced over the 'long durée' and across conventional period divisions. There are no separate chapters on gender. Rather this theme has been deliberately blended in with other themes and topics. Some will find this not to their taste, but the aim is to present an inclusive, broad vision of the Scottish past, not one which segregates particular experiences. We have also chosen to include greater coverage of areas of cultural history than in the modern volumes. In part, this reflects recent trends in the writing of history – the so-called 'cultural turn' in historical studies – but also the wealth of scholarship which exists on such topics. It may also reflect something of an emancipation of scholars from the primacy of documentary sources, but then this is no new thing for medievalists. Throughout both volumes a key theme which emerges, in terms of how we study the Scottish past, and also the patterns and meanings present in this past, is the importance of Scottish relationships and involvement in a broader European past. Let's hope the anniversary of the Union does not mask or detract from this theme, and the great strides which have been made in recent decades to recover this dimension of the Scottish past. Volumes 3 and 4 contain selected readings to accompany the topic/theme volumes, and should prove a great resource for those wishing to explore further a particular subject. Volume 5 is a collection of primary sources for the history of Scotland from c.1100 to 1707 designed to accompany the other volumes. It makes accessible documents of both local and national importance, quite a few of which have been specially transcribed for this volume. All students of history should want to read primary sources for the uniquely rich insight they furnish into the past. We also hope that they may encourage some readers to make their own forays into local archives.

This book represents a further product of the University of Dundee–Open University collaboration to offer modules in Scottish history to distance-learning students. The modules are offered at honours level for undergraduates. However, all the volumes are designed to be used, singly or as a series, by anyone with an interest in Scottish history. Our hope is that they will inspire and deepen enthusiasm for the investigation of the Scottish past, perhaps even encouraging some to examine aspects of their own community history based on themes covered in the volumes.

From the outset, this project has depended on the efforts and enthusiasm of many people, and there are several major debts to acknowledge. Financial support for the development of these volumes was provided initially from the strategic fund of the Faculty of Arts and Social Sciences at the University of Dundee under the guidance of the then dean, Professor Huw Jones. His successor, Professor Christopher A. Whatley, has been a constant supporter, and has contributed his expertise to these volumes, as well as being an editor and contributor to the Modern Scottish History

volumes. The Strathmartine Trust generously provided further vital financial support to facilitate the production of these volumes. Within the Open University,
invaluable supporting roles have been played by Peter Syme, Director of the Open
University in Scotland, and Ian Donnachie, Reader in History at the Open University
in Scotland. It is the shared commitment of individuals in both institutions,
stimulated by the success and quality of the Modern Scottish History course, which
has driven forward the continued development of the project. John Tuckwell, who
published the Modern Scottish History volumes, and who commissioned the present
volumes, has been a sage and encouraging adviser to the editorial team. The authors
produced their contributions to agreed formats and, for the most part, to agreed
deadlines. While they are responsible for what they have written, they have also been
supported by other members of the writing team and our editors. Particular thanks
are also due to Sharon Adams for sterling support to the editors at a crucial stage, to
Mrs Johanne Phillips, the former secretary and administrator of the Modern Scottish
History course, and to Mrs Helen Carmichael and Mrs Sara Reid, secretaries in the
Department of History, University of Dundee for their administrative support.
Thanks are also due to Jen Petrie who typed many of the texts for inclusion in the
articles and documents volumes.

Finally, a word about the title of these volumes – *Scotland the Making and
Unmaking of the Nation* – is perhaps required. Some may be tempted to see this as
betraying a nationalist bias in the editors, with 1707 being deliberately framed as a
moment of national erasure and shame. It is certainly designed to provoke, but bear
in mind this preface was written by an English-born British historian who knows
very well that Scotland's history, like all histories, is wonderfully resistant to simple
generalizations. If it were otherwise, its study would not be so rewarding.

USING THIS BOOK

The chapters in Volumes 1 and 2 include lists of books and articles for further
reading. These lists are intended simply as guides to those who wish to follow up
issues and topics covered in the volumes. They are not intended as obligatory further
reading.

Bob Harris, Professor of British History, University of Dundee

Acknowledgements

Grateful acknowledgement is made to the following sources for permission to reproduce material in this volume.

S Taylor 1997 'Generic Element Variation, with Special Reference to Eastern Scotland', *Nomina* by permission of the editor of *Nomina*; Richard D Oram 2000 'Gold into Lead? The State of Early Medieval Scottish History' *in* T Brotherstone and D Ditchburn (eds), *Freedom and Authority: Essays in Honour of Grant G. Simpson*, Tuckwell Press; GWS Barrow 1988 'The Turn of the Tide', Chapter 11 of his *Robert Bruce and the Community of the Realm of Scotland*, by permission of Edinburgh University Press, www.eup.ed.ac.uk; JM Brown 1977 'The Exercise of Power', *in Scottish Society in the Fifteenth Century*, Edward Arnold; A Grant 1987 'Crown and Nobility in Late Medieval Britain', *in* RA Mason (ed), *Scotland and England, 1286–1815*, John Donald; A Grant 1988 'Scotland's "Celtic Fringe" in the Late Middle Ages: The MacDonald Lords of the Isles and the Kingdom of Scotland', *in* RR Davies (ed), *The British Isles 1100–1500. Comparisons, Contrasts and Connections*, John Donald; DER Watt 1984 'The Papacy and Scotland in the Fifteenth century', *in* RB Dobson (ed), *The Church, Politics and Patronage in the Fifteenth Century*, Sutton Publishing Ltd; A Stevenson 1996 'The Flemish Dimension of the Auld Alliance', *in* GG Simpson (ed), *Scotland and the Low Countries, 1124–1994*, Tuckwell Press; N Macdougall 2001 'New Solutions to Old Problems: The Stewarts and the Auld Alliance, *in his An Antidote to the English: The Auld Alliance, 1295–1560*, Tuckwell Press; A Grant 1991 'The Nobility', Chapter 5 of his *Independence and Nationhood: Scotland 1306–1469*, by permission of Edinburgh University Press, www.eup.ed.ac.uk; IB Blanchard, E Gemmill, N Mayhew and ID Whyte 2002, 'The Economy: Town and Country', *in* EP Dennison *et al* (eds), *Aberdeen Before 1800. A New History*, Tuckwell Press; EP Dennison 1998 'Power to the People? The Myth of the Medieval Burgh Community', *in* S Foster *et al* (eds), *Scottish Power Centres*, by permission of Ross Samson; EP Dennison and GG Simpson 2000 'Scotland', in D Palliser (ed), *The Cambridge Urban History of Britain, Volume 1 600–1540*, Cambridge University Press; DW Hall 1998 'The Scottish Medieval Pottery Industry: A Pilot Study', *Tayside and Fife Archaeological Journal* 4, by permission of *Tayside and Fife Archaeological Journal*; C Smith 1998 'Dogs, Cats and Horses in the Scottish Medieval Town', *Proceedings of the Society of Antiquaries of Scotland*, by permission of the Society of Antiquaries of Scotland; E Fernie 1986 'Early Church Architecture in Scotland', *Proceedings of the Society of Antiquaries of Scotland*, by permission of the Society of Antiquaries of Scotland; N Cameron 1994 'St Rule's Church, St Andrews, and Early Stone-Built Churches in Scotland', *Proceedings of the Society of Antiquaries of Scotland*, by permission of the Society of Antiquaries of Scotland; L Patterson 1990 'Introduction' *in* his

Literary Practice and Social Change in Britain 1380–1530, by permission University of California Press L. Paterson/*Literary Practice and Social Change*/ 1990/The Regents of the University of California; RJ Goldstein 1993 'The Ideology of Blood: Blind Hary's Wallace', *in* his *The Matter of Scotland: Historical Narrative in Medieval Scotland*, by permission of the University of Nebraska Press. Copyright 1993 by the University of Nebraska Press; S Mapstone 1999 '*Scotichronicon*'s First Readers', *in* BE Crawford (ed), *Church, Chronicle and Learning in Medieval and Early Modern Scotland*, Mercat Press; RJ Lyall 1976 'Politics and Poetry in Fifteenth and Sixteenth Century Scotland', *Scottish Literary Journal*, by permission of the Association for Scottish Literary Studies.

Prospects of the Advancement of Knowledge in Early Scottish History

Extracted from AO Anderson 1940 'A Lecture by Alan Orr Anderson to the Anthropological Section of the British Association, 1st September 1939', Dundee (Paul & Matthew), 3, 7–16.

The materials for the history of Scotland before the end of the thirteenth century have been the principal subject of my life study, carried on under the life-long difficulty of defective sight. I have still some work in hand, but I cannot expect to be able to do very much more, and I welcome this opportunity of passing on what appear to me to be important injunctions, in the hope that they may be heard by future historians of Scotland.

As history advances, it must modify the views that have been taught to the public, and so the attitude of the public to history is not entirely negligible. History is a matter neither of dogma nor of doctrine. It is also not a matter of art. The public should be trained to understand this, in the schools and after, and not to assume that it already knows, or can by inner consciousness decide, what historical research ought to find.

I appeal to the Scottish public especially not to allow history to be subordinated to politics.

I appeal also to teachers and others who demand a narrative in advance of historical knowledge, not to let their need of a narrative distort or embellish historical truth.

I appeal to research historians to remember that although the principles of historical method, the principles that is of the sound use of historical evidence, are to a great extent axiomatic, they are nevertheless very often not followed by writers of Scottish historical narrative.

Research work in this field is not greatly encouraged. Although two University foundations were made for it by bequest, one, for history and language, has been restricted to language; and the other, for ancient history and palaeography, has been diverted to later history and later palaeography. I wish to point out to the Universities that still much work remains to be done in this early period of Scottish history: the period that extends to 1291, or a little later . . .

The Picts, who invaded Roman Britain, are first located in North Britain in the beginning of the fourth century AD. In the end of the fourth century they are said to consist of two nations; so it appears that the name was already a geographical one, not confined to one people, about the time when Ninian became bishop of the Picts.

About the middle of the fifth century, St Patrick wrote of apostate Picts, who with Scots, apparently also from North Britain, invaded Ireland. By calling them "apostate" he appears to locate Picts within the bishopric of Ninian.

I would suggest to those who may investigate this matter further that if there had been a tributary border-state, called by the Romans "the province of the Picts", or something like it, that would sufficiently explain the origin of the titles "bishop of the Picts" and "king of the Picts", without necessarily involving that the name Pict was at that time applicable to one race only.

Some time after the departure of the Romans from Britain we find a *regnum Pictorum*, and thenceforward the name "Pict" was applied to any inhabitant of that kingdom, of whatever origin. There are traces of Roman influence within this kingdom. As Professor W J Watson has shown, the name of the county of Mearns is a pre-Irish, P-Celtic, word meaning the district of a *maer* or steward, the title being derived from the Latin *major*; and the same title appears in the various district-offices of *mormaer*, which means originally sea-steward, and indicates the duty of defence of shipping and the shore. These mormaers played an important part in the kingdom of the Picts. It is to be noted that the o of *mormaer* is short; *mor-* is not *mor* "great". This fact has been pointed out by Professor Watson, but its significance has not yet been generally grasped.

The language of the kingdom of the Picts appears to have been in general P-Celtic; just as remains show that the language of Gaul was generally P-Celtic.

Irish-speaking settlers came from Ireland to Argyllshire in the fifth century; and they came also, very little later, to Gowrie and Strathearn, and later into Fife. Their eastern kingdom received the name of *monid*, "mountain", perhaps to distinguish it from Argyll, the "shore of the Gaels". *Monid* was a British or Pictish word, and from it the modern Gaelic *monadh* is derived. The Irish pushed into Angus and Atholl, and through the Great Glen into Moray; a remnant of the Picts, perhaps in Aberdeenshire, was subdued, and the Irish dynasty, language and law, prevailed. This happened in the ninth century. But the law was presumably not that of ninth century Ireland, but that of the Ireland that the immigrants had left, in the fifth to seventh centuries. The idea that they brought with them the tanistry of fourteenth-century Ireland is fantastic, and yet that has been implied recently by several writers who should have known better.

The language of the Irish settlers was Q-Celtic, and the direct ancestor of modern Scottish Gaelic; but it must be remembered that Old Irish resembles modern Gaelic no more than Anglo-Saxon resembles modern English. Those who attempt, with a knowledge of modern Gaelic only, to solve linguistic problems of the sixth to the thirteenth centuries cannot succeed. It is necessary to have studied Old and Middle Irish, on sound philological lines. That can be done nowadays, I believe, in three Scottish Universities.

Nevertheless, a few years ago, after a lecture that I gave on the Picts, within Dundee University College buildings, I was rebuked by a man who said that no one imagined that P-Celtic was spoken in Gaul, or elsewhere than in Britain. He would not have made this extraordinary assertion if he had consulted any authority on

Celtic speech; since the facts appear in all Celtic grammarians of repute, from Zeuss to Thurneysen and Morris Jones. This sort of self-complacent ignorance is a serious obstacle to the advancement of knowledge.

Another essential subject for the would-be historian of early Scotland is palaeography, the study (in this case) of manuscripts of the twelfth to the fourteenth centuries. This subject needs exact observation, patience, training, and constant practise; it is less easily studied in Scotland. It is necessary for the establishment of texts; for separating additions from original material; and sometimes for dating writings, and detecting forgery. It is also essential for textual emendation.

Errors resulting from ignorance of manuscripts are harmful, and apt to be ludicrous. A manuscript bearing on Scottish history is wrongly dated in the Cottonian catalogue. I was criticized for making no mention of this manuscript in my Early Sources of Scottish History; but a slight knowledge of palaeography would have shown the critic that the writing was not of the reign of Edward I, as he thought, and that the subject-matter was quite outside the period of my Early Sources.

Epigraphy also comes into our subject. I will give as an instance the inscription of the Drostan Stone, in St Vigeans Church near Arbroath. The stone is somewhat worn, and a few of its letters are not clearly legible. These letters must be determined before we can establish the meaning of the inscription. A cast of the stone is in the Antiquarian Museum in Edinburgh; but in the cast, at least one letter has been touched up. It does not look like *e* on the stone, but has been made to look like *e* on the cast. It was the practice of J Romilly Allen, on whose work we still rely for information with regard to Scottish sculptured stones, when casts were made, to touch them up, so that they might be more intelligible.

Also E W B Nicholson, a Librarian of Bodley, published in his Keltic Researches a photograph of the inscription, in which the letters are made to appear as they do not appear on the stone. The photograph has been touched up by hand.

I protest against such practices, and against the custom of chalking sculptured stones before photographing them, and of touching-up rubbings of stone inscriptions.

Sound methods of use of historical material are equally and unescapably necessary.

Apart from the possible discovery of unknown sources (which, however apparently trivial, might have important bearing on doubtful points), early Scottish history can advance by the truer and more complete interpretation of sources; and by the adoption of sounder methods of use of existing sources.

Early editions of historical texts have often been inaccurate, for one reason or another, and even in recent years texts have been published with errors of transcription.

The first essential is to establish with certainty the exact words of the sources that we use. Published historical texts ought to reproduce the original in every letter, and should distinguish between the original writing and later additions to the manuscript. Emendations should be offered when they are so probable that they may be regarded as certainly correct, or when they are supported by some other writings or by the course of established events.

We must not use as evidence an uncorrected text that is shown to be corrupt, for instance by flaws in the metre of verse-compositions; but metre sometimes provides a clue to the correct reading. The Prophecy of Berchan is an outstanding example. Extreme caution must be used in emending corrupt texts. It has been customary to make in literary texts bold emendations that are inadmissible in historical sources. A corrupt passage that needs bold emendation remains at best of doubtful value.

For interpreting the language of a source, we need knowledge of language, and also knowledge of the circumstances to which the words refer. Interpretation of language is always more or less conjectural; and in order that we may choose the best conjecture, we need to have the widest possible knowledge of the kindred facts. History is not bounded by statistics; we must not simply argue from the general to the particular; history is not constructed out of common sense. We must have imagination, to think of every possible interpretation of the evidence, before we can be sure that we have found the true interpretation.

The problem of discriminating between better and worse evidence, and between what is evidence and what is not, is even more fundamental, and, perhaps, even more one for which the widest possible knowledge of related facts is needed. There are, however, elementary principles, which are, or ought to be, universally accepted, but which are by no means universally put into practice.

The fundamental principles of historical method are axiomatic, and some of you will think that what I have to say is too elementary to need saying. I reply that in my experience it does need to be said, and to be impressed upon those who undertake to do historical work. The need is shown in books and articles, and in discussions and correspondence that I have had with many people during many years. Too little distinction, or no distinction at all, is made between inferences from good evidence and inferences from sources that are not evidence. The latest book published on early Scottish history shows no improvement in this respect, and yet it has been received with high praise.

It is also customary not to distinguish between deductions from evidence, and conjectures for which there is no direct evidence. Every conjectural statement should be expressed conjecturally. He who is determined to write history in literary form should avoid the early history of Scotland.

The fundamental principles may be regarded as a matter of simple honesty. We wish not to repeat lies about past times, any more than about the present time. We must not admit as evidence in favour of our theories anything that is not evidence; nor as confirmation, anything that merely does not contradict. In repeating doubtful matters we must always repeat the doubt.

Sound training in historical method ought to be of value to the public, since it would dissuade people from believing and spreading false reports. But it is doubtful whether balanced judgement can be taught to those who do not wish to acquire it.

History is dependent upon the accident of survival of satisfactory evidence; and sound historical method compels us to confine our investigations to evidence that is satisfactory. The principle is elementary, and not in dispute. But it is not in fact strictly followed. There is a facile tendency to regard as evidence everything that has been written. To regard every written word as a footprint in the sands of time is utterly wrong; and that is what many people seem to do when they say that we must examine *all* the evidence. In fact, when early sources do not exist, later sources should not be called "late evidence". It is of course true that we must use all the evidence. But it is even truer to say that we must use nothing but the evidence. We cannot assume that all the written evidence has survived; nor that enough evidence for a true verdict ever was written. Of tradition I shall speak later.

History is not based on assumptions, but is a study of evidence; its verdicts are provisional, depending upon the sufficiency of the evidence. It is the first duty of the historian to examine carefully what is offered to him as evidence, and to reject what should no be accepted as evidence.

He must reject it entirely; refusing to be influenced by it, and refusing to interpret the evidence in accordance with it, or to take it as confirmation of an earlier source.

The mere accident that some writing survives does not make that writing evidence. History must be based exclusively on writings that are evidence.

An outstanding example is the problem of Anglo-Scottish relations. It was pointed out long ago by Peter Hume Brown that after the affairs that followed the arbitration of 1291 the accounts written on either side were partisan statements which added nothing to the evidence; and that in studying the history of early Anglo-Scottish relations, we must confine our attention to sources that were written not later than 1291. This is true, with trivial exceptions. The statements of the opposing cases are based almost entirely upon existing sources, and are not evidence.

We are better able now to reach a decision than Edward I was in his time.

But the bias of Edward's later years still affects us. There is still an English case and a Scottish case; and the truth is between the two, if we allow ourselves to see it. Hume Brown thought that the Scots did accept English overlordship, before and after the Norman Conquest, but he warned me that this fact was so unpopular in Scotland that it was better not to say much about it. My views have been published in Early Sources of Scottish History, and elsewhere, and they are much disliked by non-historians.

When it can be shown that a writing, contemporary with its subject, is not intended simply to record, but has the purpose of giving a theoretical or conjectural interpretation, or a partisan statement of a case, it is difficult to accept is evidence, unless we have also contemporary writings in support of the other side of the matter; we can then profitably study the two accounts together. We are too familiar with political propaganda at the present day to need a reminder that partisan statements in medieval times might have been almost equally untrue.

Official statements are to be regarded as statements of a case, but official copies of documents must be accepted, if the copies were published undisputed within the knowledge of the other parties at the time when the documents were written, and in circumstances that would have permitted the truth of the copies to be challenged.

The valuation of writings as evidence is a question too intricate for discussion in a short lecture. I wish however to say some things about questions that arise in early Scottish history.

The theorizing of historians three of four generations after the event is no more evidence of fact than is the theorizing of modern writers; Boece and Buchanan, for instance, are not to be accepted as evidence for early history, any more than W F Skene.

It has been repeatedly stated that John of Fordun's attitude to his sources is that of an historian interpreting evidence conjecturally, not that of a chronicler, repeating sources faithfully. But the consequences of this undoubted fact have not yet been fully grasped. Writers of history still quote Fordun as a source for the thirteenth century and earlier; without giving any warning that their source is unsound. Through constant repetition, Fordun's guesses are thought to be accepted fact. Instances in which his guesses are or may be correct are pointed to as confirmation of his supposed historical value. But lucky guessing is neither evidence nor history. It would be surprising if all Fordun's guesses were wrong. The only concern that we need have with Fordun and other late writers for the history of the thirteenth century and earlier is to find whether any of their statements have a written source behind them.

The additions to Fordun, attributed to Bower, for the twelfth and thirteenth centuries, are of a somewhat different character. Many of them were probably taken from written sources; and in those cases, they are not negligible. But they are based upon sources of uncertain age and merit; they are entered very confusedly, with regard to date, order or events, and identity of persons, and it is often impossible to draw from them the information that they were intended to give.

The Breviary of Aberdeen is an instance of a work still farther removed from the times for which it is too often accepted as a source. It has been accepted even by writers who admit that they ought not to accept it.

Repetitions by other writers do not confirm the original statement, any more than a rumour confirms the story from which it sprang.

Even contemporary accounts must in general be in part at least of a traditionary nature, but accounts that are not contemporary and not based upon earlier written accounts are of low value as evidence.

If a later writer derives his account from an earlier writer, the original account is to be preferred. If a later writer deliberately alters the original account, his alterations are not to be accepted, unless he can be shown to have had more direct sources of information than the original writer had.

A late writer has value only in so far as he reproduces correctly the accounts that he has received from others. If those were written by competent witnesses and he represents them faithfully his account is of value. If he edits them and fits them into a narrative constructed by himself, the whole work must be regarded as belonging to the time of the narrator. In the case of Icelandic sagas, they have high value as indications of tradition, but when they combine different sources into a new narrative, they must be regarded as works of the time of the narrator.

Tradition as a source of history has been greatly overvalued, and is still greatly overvalued in Scotland. In countless instances, a so-called tradition has been traced back to some written source, which it generally perverts, or to some circumstance that suggested it. Any statement or suggestion, written or unwritten, serious or jocular, may be the basis of a tradition. The rule in dealing with tradition is that if a so-called tradition could have been derived from a written account it must be regarded as having been derived from that account; and if it could have been suggested by any circumstance, it probably was suggested by that circumstance. The resulting tradition does not confirm its source.

The evidence that may be accepted is often too slight for any narrative to be based on it. When there is not enough acceptable evidence, we should not fall back upon accounts that are not evidence; no verdict ought to be expected of us, and none should be given.

Unless we reject everything to which credence should not be given, history ceases to exist, and we get instead something that is more misleading than a historical novel.

What I wish to impress upon you with the utmost conviction is that it is quite impossible for history to advance if we do not confine the investigation to what is evidence, rejecting entirely what is not evidence; and unless we use the evidence with absolute impartiality. If we follow these sound principles, our narrative will be vitally altered, and perhaps considerably reduced, but nothing that is historically true will be lost.

Generic-Element Variation, with Special Reference to Eastern Scotland

S Taylor 1997, *Nomina* 20, 5–22

The title of this article is not, I admit, the most gripping, even for dedicated toponymists. I had considered the more lurid title of 'Nightmare on Distribution Map', but I decided to go for the sober descriptive rather than the Hollywood-style alarmist. Although there are in what follows certain alarming consequences for place-name scholars everywhere, it is not, I hope, a negative contribution, and the consequences take on a nightmarish aspect only if we fail to acknowledge them.

I will start by briefly defining my terms. A generic element, or simply a generic, is that part of a place-name which tells us the general type of place we are dealing with, be it a hill, a river, a farm, a wood or any other general feature. This is opposed to what I will call the specific, the element which defines the generic, and allows us to distinguish between hundreds or thousands of other places with the same generic.

In 'Nottingham', for example, the generic is *ham*, while the specific answers the question 'Which *ham*?' The answer is 'Notting' – that is 'Snot's people's *ham*'. It is a general rule that while in the Germanic languages such as English, German or Scots, the specific comes before the generic, as in 'Nottingham', in the Celtic languages the order is usually reversed, with the generic first and the specific second. Take for example 'Inverness', where the generic is 'Inver', from the Gaelic *inbhir* 'river- or burn-mouth'; while the specific is the river-name 'Ness'. In both the Celtic and the Germanic systems, it is the specific which carries the stress, which accounts for the fact that so many Scottish, Irish, Welsh and Cornish place-names have an unstressed first element: eg Inver*ness*, Ar*magh*, Caer*narvon*, and Pol*perro*.

It must be emphasised that, despite the very technical-sounding title of this article, I am not here concerned with terminology. I have chosen the terms 'generic' and 'specific' as convenient descriptive terms.[1] I could have called the specific the 'defining element' or the 'qualifying element' – or I could simply have called them first and second elements.[2] It is possible that in the light of the phenomenon I am about to discuss it may be desirable to rethink our terminology relating to place-name elements, but such terminological redefinition is not the purpose of this article.[3]

I first became aware of a certain instability in generic elements while I was working on the settlement-names of Fife, a large peninsula of over 50 parishes which lies between the Firths of Forth and Tay. Appendix 2 includes the examples from Fife which started me thinking on this whole phenomenon: Balgeddie, Ballantagar, Baltilly, Bantuscall, Moncoutiemyre and Mountquhanie all provide excellent examples, showing variation between three Gaelic generics: *pett, baile, mòine*. (For the meanings of these and other elements see Appendix 4.)

Then, as I ventured furth of Fife, westwards through the Central Belt and northwards into Perthshire, Angus, the Mearns and Aberdeenshire, I became aware of a quite dizzying array of other variations, examples of which I have included in Appendices 1 and 2: variations such as (in Appendix 1) *Both-/Bal-* (Balfron); *Pol-/Bal-* (Balgownie); *Davoch-/Dal-* (Davochmaluag); and *Bad-/Pit-* (Pitfodels); and (in Appendix 2) *pett-/baile-* (Baldinny); *ath-/baile-* (Balgillo); **cair-/*coid-* (Cathcart); and **dol-/cinn-* (Kinbattoch).

Appendices 1 and 2 constitute two distinct groups. The first of these (Appendix 1) I have called 'Substitution'. In this group the variation in the generic is explicable simply by the confusion of one element with another: often a more unusual or less familiar element is confused with, and/or replaced by, a more commonly used, familiar one. This is frequently helped along by phonological factors. The shift from *Bad-* to *Pit-* would be an example. There is not a complete package of sound-changes in Gaelic or Scots which would produce this change, but they do have a general phonological similarity: both are monosyllables starting with a labial stop and finishing with a dental stop. Coupled with this is the fact that they always occur in unstressed position, thus increasing the likelihood of vowel confusion. What clinches the change from *Bad-* to *Pit-*, however, is the fact that *bad* is a relatively rare generic, while *pett* is one of the commonest. A combination of these factors means that we need look no further for an explanation of this change.

The same mix of factors is also behind the change of *Pol-* to *Bal-*, *Both-* to *Bal-*, and *Davoch-* to *Dal-*. It is probably also behind the changes from *Blair-* to *Bal-*, as in Belfatton.

There are also examples, usually purely to do with the written or printed word, where a common generic has replaced a rare one, but where phonology has played little or no part. This is a result of what can be termed onomastic assimilation. An example would be Catochil (in Abernethy parish, Perthshire), a farm in the Ochil hills on the Perthshire–Fife border. It appears as such when it is first recorded as *Cathehil* in 1295 (see Appendix 1). *Cat-* is almost unique as a generic in eastern Scottish place-names. Watson suggests it is related to the Welsh *cat* meaning 'piece, bit';[4] however, according to the *Geiriadur Prifysgol Cymru* (sv), this may be a loanword from English *cut*, which would immediately disqualify it as a candidate. It is much more likely to be from the Pictish cognate of Welsh *coed* 'a wood',[5] which usually occurs in stressed syllables as *Keith*, but can be reduced in unstressed syllables to *Cat-* etc (for example Cathcart, Renfrewshire, in Appendix 2). Whatever its origin its very rarity has made it prey to various substitutions, the first being in 1519, where it is written *Kintochil* with the common generic *Kin-* from Gaelic *cinn* '(at the) end of' substituted for *Ca-*, while the *t* from *Cat-* has been retained. And on J. Stobie's map of Perthshire of 1783, it appears as *Pitogle*. Someone involved in the making of this map thought this *Cat-* must be a mistake and put our old friend *Pit-* in its place. That these were purely literary developments is clear from the fact that that name is still Catochil.

Onomastic assimilation is no respecter of languages, and crosses from one language-group to another with insouciance. There is a farm in Strathmiglo parish (Fife) called Raecruick, a Scots name meaning something like 'sheltered land in a (river-)bend', the river in question being the Eden.[6] On J. Ainslie's map of Fife of 1775, and only here, it appears as *Balcruick*.

This phenomenon, which I have termed 'Substitution', relates to changes which are most likely to have happened in a period after the various elements had ceased to be understood as actual words or lexical items. In fact, it can be argued that these changes could come about only when meaning was lost, or had ceased to be important. Conditions were ideal for this throughout eastern lowland Scotland in the later middle ages, when the language in which most of the place-names were coined, Scottish Gaelic, was replaced by Scots. This process began in Fife in the later twelfth century, and was complete in most of the lowland areas by 1400.

I will argue that the phenomenon of 'Variation', which supplies the title, and the main theme, for this article, can only have come about when people still understood the meanings of the elements involved. It must therefore date from a time before the loss of Gaelic, and so is a much earlier phenomenon, unrelated to 'Substitution'.

A brief comparison of the examples in Appendices 1 and 2 is enough to indicate that there are two different processes at work here, and that in Appendix 2 we are not simply dealing with the various processes of assimilation I have described above. *Moncouty*, *Pitcouty* and *Balcouty* are phonologically distinct, as are *Bantuscall* and *Pittuscal*. *Ban-* is in fact an organic development from the falling together of *baile* with the following definite article of an original *Baile an t-soisgeil* 'estate of the Gospel'.[7] Furthermore, there is no obvious chronological development perceivable from one element to another, with the variant forms coming and going in random fashion (see for example Baltryne and Cathcart in Appendix 2). This is in contrast to the chronological progression which is the more usual pattern where 'Substitution' or assimilation is concerned, with the rarer original element found in the earliest forms, and the substituted more common element in the later ones.

The question then arises as to why, in the names in Appendix 2, should there be two, or even three, parallel forms that refer to the same place. The answer I would give is that in fact they did *not* originally refer to the same place. Names such as *Balcouty*, *Moncouty* and *Pitcouty* referred to different places, or at least to different parts or aspects of the same place. They ended up becoming interchangeable only after the lexical meanings had become lost or unimportant.

The process is best illustrated with names which contain Gaelic *mòine* 'bog, peat-bog'. In the parish of Monimail there is a farm called Ballantagar (see Appendix 2). In 1619 we have a reference to the 'glebe and kirklands of the vicarage of Monimail, commonly called *Montagart*'. We find the same variation between *mòine* and *baile* in Mountquhanie, also in Appendix 2. Not only is it fair to conclude from this that these two forms of the same place-name once referred to different places, or at least different parts of the same place; but also that this differentiation was a matter of the utmost importance to those using these names, since you confuse a peat-bog with a farm at your peril.

There is beside Mountquhanie House a large, flat area through which flows the Motray Water, and this is most probably the *mòine* referred to in the name. In the early sixteenth century this boggy area was called the 'Myre of Star'; it had its own name, as the original Gaelic names were no longer exact enough. Having lost their lexical meaning, they were now being used indiscriminately to refer to the estate itself. By having a new name for the bog, which was at least partly in Scots, the language of sixteenth-century Fife, this meant that everyone, and not just Gaelic-speakers, would avoid ending up in the *glaur* or mud.

When it comes to *pett* and *baile* things become somewhat more problematical, since it is generally accepted that they meant roughly the same thing. It is my contention, however, that they were once as readily distinguishable to those who first coined these names as 'myre' and 'farm-steading' are to us today.

The Gaelic word *pett* was borrowed from Pictish. It is related to the Gaulish word which was taken into Low Latin as *petia* and has, through French, given us our word 'piece'. It is found in modern Welsh as *peth*, meaning 'thing'.[8] So its basic meaning as a toponym was 'portion' or 'piece'. In the later ninth and early tenth century, Gaelic became the language of the kingdom of Alba, which had been newly formed from the kingdoms of the Picts in the east and of the Scots in the west. This new kingdom was forged by a Gaelic-speaking dynasty founded by Cinaed MacAlpin (Kenneth son of Alpin) in the 840s. It is now generally accepted that the MacAlpin dynasty took over much of the administrative and fiscal machinery of Pictland, and it is no doubt in this context that the element *pett* was also borrowed. Geoffrey Barrow has argued that by the twelfth century, when the documentary record effectively begins in Scotland, *Pit*-names are borne by estates dependent on a shire- or thanage-centre,[9] and 'dependent estate' is probably not far from its meaning already in the ninth century. It might be more useful, rather than thinking of *pett* as a piece or portion of land, to think of it as a piece of a larger administrative unit. This larger unit is usually called a 'shire', an Anglo-Saxon word, but one which was being used even in Gaelic-speaking Scotland by the eleventh century. This 'shires' were roughly parish-sized, with a shire-centre from which collection of tribute and render was organised for the king or overlord. A more neutral translation of pett, and one which begs fewer questions, would be 'holding'.[10]

As a formative place-name element *pett* seems to have been on the wane by the eleventh century, when the bulk of Gaelic settlement in Lothian and Strathclyde probably took place. This would account for its rarity in these areas, which did not become part of the Gaelic-speaking kingdom of Alba of Scotland until the late tenth and eleventh centuries.

Baile in contrast to *pett* belongs very much to the Gaelic-Irish world. Its etymology is unclear, but when it first appears in place-names around 1100, it means 'estate, farm, vill', in both Ireland and Scotland. It has, however, in both languages, come to mean 'town' or 'village'.

It also occurs in early Irish literature, where it seems to mean 'homestead, place of habitation'. For example in the early legend *Tochmarc Emire* ('The Wooing of Emer') emissaries are sent to find a wife for Cu Chulainn 'i nnách dunad no I nnách prímbali i nHerind' ('in any fort or *prímbale* in Ireland'), where *prímbale* is translated 'superior homestead' by Flanagan. And in 1011 the Annals of Ulster record the burning of a fort (*dun*) and the breaking down or demolition of its *baile* (translated as 'town').[11] This also strongly suggests an actual building or buildings. These and other examples are usefully brought together by Flanagan.[12]

I would argue from this that in place-names in Alba *baile* originally had the more specialised meaning of an actual habitation, at least when it applies to a dependent estate. It referred perhaps to the main place of habitation, or a habitational nucleus. On the other hand, during the first centuries of the kingdom of Alba, from the ninth to the eleventh century, *pett* referred to the full estate as part of a wider network of lordship and administrative and fiscal organisation.

The basic model which I am proposing here can be summed up as follows. There existed originally a core simplex name, which cannot usefully be defined as either a specific or a generic. This core simplex name referred in general terms to an estate or area of land perceived as some kind of an entity. To this simplex could then be added elements defining the particular aspect of that entity which the speaker wished to single out. In this early period, *Pitcouty* would have referred to the whole estate of *Couty* as an administrative or fiscal unit; *Balcouty* would have referred to some part of it, perhaps the habitative centre, or the early equivalent of the *big hoose*; while *Moncouty* referred to the bog-lands of the estate, source of valuable peats and heather, that part which later became known as the Myre.

It is clear from the names in Appendix 2 that such bolt-on specifics are not confined to *pett*, *baile* and *mòine*. They can involve the interchange between a range of generics such as *dol*, *cinn*, *tulach* and *dùn*.

As soon as these bolt-on specifics ceased to be understood, that is, as soon as Gaelic had been ousted by Scots, they often continued in use, but started to be used indiscriminately and at random, a randomness that is seen in the way in which the specifics waver and interchange throughout the centuries, finally coming to rest in one form or another, without any apparent underlying pattern. Some in fact still have not completely stabilised. The village of Pitroddie in the Carse of Gowrie east of Perth is still often referred to locally as Baltroddie, and this fluctuation is clearly seen from its earliest occurrence in the written record in 1265, when it appears as *Baltrodi* (see Appendix 2). You can perhaps begin to see where my alternative title, 'Nightmare on Distribution Map', came from!

The feudalisation, or, better, the 'Europeanization',[13] of Scotland in the twelfth century brought with it further complications in this model, at least in respect to *Pit*- and *Bal*- names. I have discussed this more fully elsewhere.[14] Suffice it to say here that *baile* seems to have become the indigenous word for the estate which appears in Latin documents as *villa*, with all its tenurial overtones, while *pett*, if not already obsolete or obsolescent, did not play any active role in the naming of newly formed, or re-formed, estates of the twelfth and thirteenth centuries.

A further implication of my basic model of core simplex with detachable generics is that the core simplex name might, in certain circumstances, be used on its own. In fact there is some evidence of this, for which see Appendix 3.

Amongst the lands given to the church of the Holy Trinity, Dunfermline, by Malcolm III and Margaret was the estate of *Lauer*, which appears in the early thirteenth century as both *Liver(s)* and *Petliuer*, and is today known as Pitliver, in Dunfermline parish (Fife). We can see how loose and detachable the element *pett* was when we consider the early thirteenth-century figure William of Pitliver. He witnessed seven Dunfermline Abbey charters; in three of them he is styled 'of *Pitliver*', in the other four 'of *Liver(s)*'.[15]

There is also Pittowie in Crail parish (Fife), which contains Gaelic *toll* 'hollow'. This appears from the twelfth to the fourteenth century as *Pittollie* or *Pittowie*; in the fifteenth century as *Tolly*, then in the seventeenth century as both *Tolly* and *Pittollie* (see Appendix 3).

A useful parallel from contemporary usage may be the following; the place-name Mountquhanie can today be used as a core simplex, or with such bolt-on terms as Mountquhanie Estate or Mountquhanie House. However, the name on the map, and in general local usage, is simply Mountquhanie, unless the speaker wants to stress a particular aspect of the place, or the management of the place, in the case of the word 'Estate'.

This last consideration in fact gets us further into the 'Nightmare on Distribution Map', with the thought that if there are some place-names which can exist quite happily with or without a generic, then might not, theoretically, all estates, at least of a similar status, behave the same way?

In this part of Scotland we have many farm-names which consist of a simplex only, and I would argue, on the basis of the above, that in fact these, too – at least those which formed estates dependent on a shire-centre – could equally well have survived with a generic such as *Pit-* or *Bal-*. The large estate of Cash in Strathmiglo parish (Fife) probably derives from Gaelic *caise* 'cheese'.[16] In Banffshire it is probably the specific in the obsolete place-name *Pitcash* (now Georgetown) near Tomintoul, Kirkmichael parish. On the analogy with Pitliver and Pittowie there is at least the possibility that during the Gaelic-speaking period the estate of Cash could have been referred to as both **Pett a'chaise* and **Baile a'chaise*, as well as simply *Caise*. It may have been purely chance that dictated that it has come down to us without any generic. On the other hand there may have been a good reason connected with its early administrative or tenurial status. If this is the case, then we have to start thinking in terms of explaining not merely the presence of differing generics but also their complete absence.

Cornwall offers yet more examples of variation, with strong echoes of the situation in Scotland, especially in relation to *pett* and *baile*; but in its English rather than its Cornish name-stock. Oliver Padel notes that the Old English element *land* is often used interchangeably with Old English *tun*, to denote respectively the lands of the manor and its centre. Thus you find pairs such as Blisland and *Bliston*; and Callington and *Calilond*. This phenomenon is also found in Devon, in such pairs as Hartland and *Hertitona*. Padel adds, 'It seems to be mere chance which of the pairs has survived to become the modern name, though forms with *tun* have done so more often.'[17] These words echo the randomness which may be detected in the survival of one form or another of place-names in eastern Scotland. It behoves place-name scholars everywhere to take a close look at this phenomenon and to determine whether this is indeed randomness, or whether it does in fact have a pattern behind it. If not; if it genuinely is chance alone which determines whether a place-name in certain countries or regions comes down with one generic or another, or even with no generic at all, then my 'Nightmare on Distribution Map' threatens to become a reality.

NOTES

1 They are taken from G. S. Stewart, *Names on the Globe* (New York, 1975), pp. 20–25, where they are fully defined. They are also used by W. F. H. Nicolaisen, *Scottish Place-Names* (London, 1976).

2 K. Cameron, *English Place-Names* (London, 1963) used 'first element' and 'second element', as well as 'defining element'. A. H. Smith, *English Place-Name Elements*, 2 vols, English Place-Name Society, 25–26 (Cambridge, 1956), I, liii, uses 'first element' and 'final element'. J. Field, *English Field-Names. A Dictionary* (Newton Abbot, 1972), p. xiv, in his discussion of field-names, uses 'qualifier' for the specific and 'denominative component' for the generic.

3 Padel has suggested a more precise way of classifying usages in Celtic place-names, based on 'generic' and 'qualifier': O. J. Padel, *Cornish Place-Name Elements*, English Place-Name Society, vol. 56–57 (Nottingham, 1985), pp. xiv–xvii, especially p. xvi.

4 W. J. Watson, *The History of the Celtic Place-Names of Scotland* (Edinburgh, 1926), p. 209

5 I am grateful to Oliver Padel for this suggestion.

6 It first appears as *Raacruik* 1580, and consistently as *Re-* or *Rae-* thereafter, apart from the one occurrence of *Bal-* in 1775. The bend which gave rise to the name disappeared when the Eden was straightened in the improvements of the early nineteenth century.

7 The meaning would be 'estate belonging to the church' or 'estate whose revenues were dedicated to the production of a Gospel'.

8 Watson, *Celtic Place-Names of Scotland*, p. 408.

9 G. W. S. Barrow, *The Kingdom of the Scots* (London, 1973), pp. 59–60

10 I am grateful to Dauvit Broun for this suggestion.

11 The fort was *Dun Echdach*, now Duneight, Co Down: *The Annals of Ulster (to AD 1131)*, edited by S. Mac Airt and G. Mac Niocaill, I (Dublin, 1983), pp. 442 –43, and E Hogan, *Onomasticon Goedelicum* (Dublin, 1910), p. 383.

12 D. Flanagan, 'Common elements in Irish place-names: *baile*', *Bulletin of the Ulster Place-Name Society*, 2nd series, I (1978), 8–13; see also L. Price, 'A note on the use of the word *baile* in place-names', *Celtica*, 6 (1963), 119–26.

13 As defined in R. Bartlett, *The Making of Europe* (London, 1994), pp. 269–70.

14 R. S. Taylor, 'Some early Scottish place-names and Queen Margaret', *Scottish Language*, 13 (1994), 1–17 (at 3–5).

15 See Appendix 3; also Taylor, 'Some early Scottish place-names', 13.

16 Barrow, *Kingdom of the Scots*, p. 278.

17 O. J. Padel, *A Popular Dictionary of Cornish Place-Names* (Penzance, 1988), p. 199. I am grateful to Dr Dauvit Broun for drawing my attention to this reference; also for his comments on a draft of this article.

18 See Watson, *Celtic Place-Names of Scotland*, pp. 366 –67

19 See K. H. Jackson, *The Gaelic Notes in the Book of Deer* (Cambridge, 1972) pp. 68–69.

20 For a fuller discussion of this element see S. Taylor, 'Place-names and the early Church in eastern Scotland', in *Scotland in Dark Age Britain*, edited by B. E. Crawford (St Andrews, 1996), pp. 93–110.

APPENDIX 1: GENERIC-ELEMENT SUBSTITUTION

Balfron (parish, Stirlingshire) *Both-* ~ *Bal-*
  Buthbren 1233; *Buthbrene* 1303; *Balfran* c 1609 (? Cumbric or Pictish **pren* 'tree')
Balfunning (Drymen parish, Stirlingshire) *Both-* ~ *Bal-*
  Boquhyning 1502; *Bathfynnainy*; *Batfynneing* 1549
Balgownie (Old Machar parish, Aberdeenshire) *Pol-* ~ *Bal-*
  Palgoueny 1256; *pons de Polgowny* 1400; *Polgony* vel *Balgony* 1595 (Gaelic *goh=bha* 'smith')
Balmoral (Crathie and Braemar parish, Aberdeenshire) *Both-* ~ *Bal-*
  Bou[t]hmorale 1451; *Balmorain* 1481
Balquhidder (parish, Perthshire) *Both-* ~ *Bal-*
  Bu[t]hfyder c 1268; *Buthfuder* 1275; *Buffydir* c 1275 (? St Peter)
Belfatton (Lonmay parish, Aberdeenshire) *Blair-* ~ *Bal-*
  Blairquhatoun 1588; *Belfatton* 1695; *Blairfatton* 1732
Catochil (Abernethy parish, Perthshire) *Cat-* ~ *Pit-*
  Cathehill 1295; *Catoichill* 1508; *Kintochill* 1519; *Pitogle* 1783
Davochmaluag or **Dochmaluag** (Fodderty parish, Ross & Cromarty) *Davoch-* ~ *Dal-*
  Dalfmalawage 1497; *Dalmalook* 1584 (*Davoch* of St Moluag)
Dochcarty (Fodderty parish, Ross & Cromarty) *Davoch-* ~ *Dal-*
  Dalcarty & *Davachcarty* 1541
Pitdelphin (Strachan parish, Kincardineshire) *Bad-* ~ *Pit-*
  Badelphin 1592; *Badelphin* 1612 (*bad* + ? personal name *Elfin*, a by-form of *Alpin*)
Pitfodels (Peterculter parish, Aberdeenshire) *Bad-* ~ *Pit-*
  Badfothel 1157 etc; *Badfodalis* 1440; *Petfodellis* 1488

APPENDIX 2: GENERIC-ELEMENT VARIATION

Baldinny (Kettins parish, Angus) *pett-* ~ *baile-*
  Petdynny 1528; *Petdynny* 1547; *Badiny* 1590s
Balgeddie (Leslie parish, Fife) *pett-* ~ *bile-*
  Pitgeddy 1521; *Balgedy* 1539; *Petgeddie* 1542 *et passim* to 1663; *Balgeddy* 1640s (Gaelic *gead* 'strip of arable land')
Balgillo (Monifieth parish, Angus) *ath-* ~ *baile-*
  ? *Hadgillin* 1173 x 1178
Balkemback (Tealing parish, Angus) *pett-* ~ *baile-*
  Petkemmok 1512; *Petcammo* 1513; *Pethcammo* 1542; *Balkemmak* 1557; *Petkemmok* 1561

Ballantagar (Monimail parish, Fife) *mòine- ~ baile-*
  Glebam et terras ecclesiasticas vicariae de *Monymaill*, vulgo vocatas *Montagart* et *Brewland* 1619 (Gaelic *an t-sagairt*, 'of the priest')
Baltilly (Ceres parish, Fife) *baile- ~ pett-*
  Baltaly 1410; *Baltuly* 1474, 1497, 1510; *Bawtuly* 1490; *Baltullie* 1517; *Pittillie* 1612; *Pittullye* alias *Batullye* 1623; *Pittuloch* 1640s (Gaelic *tulach*, 'hillock', 'mound')
Baltryne (Fordoun parish, Kincardineshire) *pett- ~ baile-*
  Baltryne 1507; *Pitdryne* 1553; *Petrynnie* 1580; *Pitrinnie* 1603; *Baltryne* 1603, 1608; *Petreny* 1616 (second element obscure)
Bantaskin (Falkirk parish, Stirlingshire) *pett- ~ baile-*
  Pettintoscale 1450. *Pettyntoskale* 1451; *Pettintoskane* 1546 (Gaelic *an t-soisgeil*, 'of the Gospel')
Bantuscall (obsolete, Kettle parish, Fife) *pett- ~ baile-*
  Pettuscal 1590; *Bantuscall* 1594; *Bantuscall* 1616; *Bantuscall* 1648 (Gaelic *an t-soisgeil*, 'of the Gospel')
Barlanark (Old Monklands parish, Lanarkshire) *pett- ~ bàrr-*
  Pethelenerke c 1120; *Barlanarc* 1172
Cathcart (parish, Renfrewshire) **cair- ~ coid-*
  Kerkert 1158; *Katkert* c 1170; *Chatkert* 1296; *Kerthkert* 1451; *Cathcort* 1590s; *Carcarth* c 1650 (Cumbric 'fort' or 'wood' [on the River] Cart)[21]
Dilspro (obsolete, Old Machar parish, Aberdeenshire) *pett- ~ dail-*
  Petsprottis (or *–ccis*) 1157; *Petsprot* (or *–c*) 1359; *Dilspro* 1543; *Dalspro* 1594
Inchfuir (Kilmuir Easter parish, Ross & Cromarty) *innis- ~ pett-*
  Inchfure 1463; *Petfure* 1479; *inchfure* alias *Pitfure* 1539 (Gaelic loan-word from Pictish **pur* 'crop-land')
Kinbattoch (former parish, now in Towie parish, Aberdeenshire) **dol- ~ cinn- (~ cill-)*
  Dolbethok 1211; *Dolbethoc* c 1240; *Kybethoc* c 1250; *Kinbethoc'* c 1250; *Kynbethok* c 1275; *Kynebethoc* 1366; *Kelbethok* 1507; *Kilbethok* 1513
(Pictish **dol* 'haugh, (water-)meadow'; also Gaelic *cinn* '(at the) end of' (with occasional late assimilation to *cill* 'church') + female personal (saint's?) name *Bethoc*; also the name of Malcolm II's daughter, mother of Duncan I (Duncan I died 1040)
Moncoutyemyre (obsolete, Kettle parish, Fife) *mòine- ~ pett- ~ baile-*
  Moncowtymyre 1486; *Moncoutemyre* 1542' *(marresia) lie Pitco[u]tiemyre* 1594; *Balcutymyir* 1599; *Moncutemyre* 1608; *(marresia) Pitcoutie-myre* 1616; *Balcuitiemyre* 1630; *(marresia) Pitcoutsmyre* vel *Pitcoutiemyre* 1648
Mountquhanie (Kilmany parish, Fife) *mòine- ~ both-[?] ~ baile-*
  Munchany 1217, *Munfanyn* 1294; *Mo[n]wanyn* 1294–95; *Munquhany* 1465, *Buchquhane* (x2) 1530, *Monquhany* 1541; (to Balfour of) *Balquhany* the lands and barony of *Monquhany* 1548
Pitroddie (Kilspindie parish, Perthshire) *baile- ~ pett-*
  (Walter de) *Baltrodyn* 1259; *Baltrody* 1374, *Baltrody* 1474; (barony of) *Baltrody*, (mains lands of) *Petrody* 1559; (barony of) *Pitreddie* 16th (Gaelic *trod* 'quarrel, combat')
Tullibody (medieval parish, now in Alloa parish, Clackmannanshire) *dùn- ~ tulach-*
  Dunbodeuin 1147; *Dumbodelin* 1147; *Tulibodeuin* 1163; *Tuligodevin* c 1185 (Pictish or Gaelic *both* 'church; + ?)
Tullochcurran (Kirkmichael parish, Perthshire) *pett- ~ tulach-*
  Petcarene 1232; *Tulahourene* 1232; *Tulicuran* 1470

APPENDIX 3: FORMS WITH NO GENERIC

Barevan (medieval parish, now in Cawdor parish, Nairnshire) *bàrr-*
   (church of) *Evein* 1225; (lands of) *Estirewin* 1494; (church of) *Braaven* 1593
Dreggie (Cromdale, Inverallan & Advie parish, Morayshire) *cill* or *coille Kildreke* c 1360
Pitliver (Dunfermline parish, Fife) *pett*
   Lauer c 1128; *Lauer* c 1166; *Petliuer* 1227, c 1230 (x2); *Liuer* 1230 x 36; *Livers* c 1230;
   Liuers 1231; *Petlyuer* 1451; *Pitleuir* 1557 x 1585 (Gaelic *leabhar* 'book', in this context
   'Gospel book')
Pitmurchie (Lumphanan parish, Aberdeenshire) *pett ?*
   Morchory 1250; *Pitmorche* 1470
Pittowie (Crail parish, Fife) *pett*
   Petollin 1153 x 1178; *Pitolly* 1312; *Tolly* 1452; *Pittowie* 1642; *Tollie* 1646 (Gaelic *toll*
   'hole, hollow')

APPENDIX 4: GAELIC, CUMBRIC AND PICTISH ELEMENTS (WITH APPROXIMATE MEANINGS)

àth (Gaelic) 'ford'
bad (Gaelic) 'spot, clump'
baile (Gaelic) 'estate'
bàrr (Gaelic) 'top'
blàr (Gaelic) 'field'; ? 'clearing in wood'
both (Gaelic, Cumbric and [?] Pictish) 'bothy, sheiling'; 'church' (Gaelicisation of Cumbric
   and [?] Pictish **bod* 'dwelling')
*cair (Cumbric and Pictish) 'fort'
cill (Gaelic) 'church'
cinn (Gaelic) 'head, end; (at the) end of'
*coid (Cumbric and Pictish) 'wood'
coille (Gaelic) 'wood'
dabhach (Gaelic) 'davoch' (measurement of arable land roughly equivalent to a carucate;
   probably borrowed from Pictish)
dail 'haugh, water-meadow' (borrowing into Gaelic of Pictish **dol*)
dùn (Gaelic) 'hill, fortified hill, fort'
innis (Gaelic) 'island, haugh'
mòine (Gaelic) 'bog, peat-bog'
pett (borrowing into Gaelic from Pictish) 'estate'
poll (Gaelic) 'pool, sluggish stream'
tulach (Gaelic) 'hillock; (?) habitational mound'

Gold into Lead? The State of Early Medieval Scottish History

Richard D Oram 2000 in T Brotherstone and D Ditchburn (eds), *Freedom and Authority: Essays in Honour of Grant G. Simpson*, East Linton (Tuckwell Press), 32–43.

Like Scotland itself in 1286, research on the period before the Wars of Independence appears to face a bleak future. We stand at a historical crossroads. This is not solely a consequence of the retirement of the leading academic figures in the field. It is a situation which has beckoned for many years as changes in the secondary education system influence new generations of university students. To compound the problems, advances in general medieval studies question the constructs and paradigms upon which most interpretations of medieval Scottish society are founded.[1] Each of these factors by itself would have a major impact: together they represent a formidable challenge when the subject is scarcely capable of response. This is not too pessimistic a note. Research on Scotland before the fourteenth century in the Scottish universities is atrophying. Furthermore, with no full-time lecturer in twelfth- and thirteenth-century studies at any of the Scottish universities, a reversal of that trend appears unlikely. It is not too extreme to claim that Scottish history – at least that of the twelfth and thirteenth centuries – again faces a 'strange death'.[2]

Marinell Ash's account of the 'strange death' of Scottish history in the late nineteenth century holds a bitter irony at present.[3] After three decades of growth we risk losing all that has been gained as no new generation of research students emerges to build upon past achievements. The current trend towards development of post-1300 – or more particularly post-1500 – postgraduate research is compounding the problem, for the next generation of research supervisors lies in the present postgraduate community. Whilst there are encouraging signs for the early and later medieval periods, the prognosis for the central middle ages is gloomy. In retrospect, this situation can be attributed to inherent flaws in the system which generated the great advance in scholarship over the last thirty years.

Historiography has travelled far since the 1900s when Lawrie and Anderson produced sourcebooks of charters and annals, thereby stimulating textual criticism which had languished since the demise of the Sir Walter Scott-inspired historical publishing clubs.[4] The study of medieval Scottish history remained, however, introspective and isolationist and, down to the 1950s, the little work which was published was largely a 'succession of historical kailyards'.[5] This trend was broken in 1956 by the publication of Geoffrey Barrow's *Feudal Britain*.[6] Although not Scottish history *per se*, *Feudal Britain* represented the first successful attempt to escape the kailyard and move into a wider British context and relevance. By dismantling spatial barriers which compartmentalised the component parts of Britain, just as temporal barriers between 'medieval' and 'modern' were being eroded by contemporary research, Barrow demonstrated that developments in one area of these islands could impact on other, far-removed areas. The approach was hardly new: Patrick Tytler had used English sources to elucidate Scottish circumstances as long ago as the 1830s.[7] What was different was that *Feudal Britain*'s general survey of the British Isles took an integrationist approach which moved beyond older, one-dimensional histories of Scotland.

Yet, the publication of *Feudal Britain* proved to be a false dawn for Scottish historiography. Unremarkable by today's standards, its approach was revolutionary for its time, and in an academic world dominated by exponents of traditional, compartmentalised medieval history it made few converts. Indeed, it was not until the 1980s that its pioneering outlook was re-adopted by historians of the twelfth and thirteenth centuries in any significant way. The result was that in the component parts of the British Isles, historians were 'happy enough to cultivate their gardens in isolation' and rarely crossed boundaries to keep abreast of current developments or explore areas of mutual historical contact other than where 'foreign' evidence supported their own theses.[8] Such selectivity of approach led merely to the cultivation of more kailyards.

In part the failure of *Feudal Britain* was due to its author, who subsequently abandoned his synthetic approach to medieval Scottish studies. Whilst Barrow can hardly be labelled isolationist, there was a singular failure to inculcate the broad perspective of *Feudal Britain* within the Scottish universities. Moreover, Barrow himself moved away from the broad-brush approach to 'British' history which made *Feudal Britain* outstanding. However, the still-birth of this first attempt since 1521 to produce 'a genuinely even-handed study of medieval Britain' must be counterbalanced against the revolution in Scottish historiography underway by the 1960s.[9] This produced a radical remodelling of Scottish medieval historical research and the formulation of the principal paradigms which were to govern the subject into the early 1990s. Whilst the opportunity was lost to break the moulds into which were set the four respective national histories, the sacrifice of a distinctively Scottish contribution to 'British History' saw instead a revitalisation and redirection of Scottish medieval studies.

Central to this was a revival in charter scholarship. Many primary sources had been published before 1914 but had received minimal editorial treatment. Moreover, with the exception of monastic cartularies published by the historical clubs, most printed sources comprised later medieval and early modern material. New research into the pre-1300 period required provision of soundly edited sources as a basic tool. This regeneration of documentary analysis underpinned the pioneering work of the 'new wave' of scholars – Barrow, A. A. M. Duncan, Grant Simpson and their fellows – and represented the first significant advance since Anderson and

Lawrie. The focus for this initiative lay in the *Regesta Regum Scottorum* series, the first two volumes of which were both edited by Barrow.[10] The project had a profound impact on the evolving historiography of the period and the scholarship which underpinned these volumes confirmed the twelfth and thirteenth centuries as Barrow's fief, within which few others presumed to tread.[11]

The principal development from this charter scholarship was the formulation of the 'Barrovian' thesis of the 'feudalisation' of Scotland. Barrow used his familiarity with the charter evidence to examine land-holding based on hereditary tenures, and to elaborate his earlier research on military aspects of the system which developed after 1124. Barrow saw knight-service and the provision of the personnel to perform that obligation as central to the colonising venture which accompanied the introduction of the new tenures. The impact of Anglo-Norman colonisation after *c*.1100 had been explored before, most notably by R. L. G. Ritchie, but the weight of documentary research behind the essays which prefaced the *Acts of Malcolm IV* produced *prima facie* evidence for the scale of the transformation wrought by these incomers and their royal patrons.[12] Backed by the fruits of the new scholarship, arguments for the construction of a 'feudal system' and a sea change in the structure of society could be advanced with confidence: 'Feudal Scotland' became the central tenet of the new historiography.

Given the enormous influence which this thesis gained, it is surprising that Barrow did not publish a monograph articulating his ideas on the subject until the 1980s. Instead, the origin of the 'Barrovian' thesis lay in essays, such as 'The earls of Fife in the twelfth century'; and its more sophisticated exposition first appeared in 'The beginnings of feudalism in Scotland' – published in the same year as *Feudal Britain*.[13] The introductions to the first two volumes of the *Regesta* presented the thesis as it pertained to the reigns of Malcolm IV and William; and publication of a collection of earlier essays in 1973 brought together disparate strands which came the nearest yet to an articulation of the construct of Scottish military feudalism.[14] It was not, however, until publication of *The Anglo-Norman Era in Scottish History* and *Kingship and Unity* that the mature thesis was presented.[15] While, however, *The Anglo-Norman Era in Scottish History* was a masterly exposition of charter scholarship, it is in *Kingship and Unity* that the governing principles of the theory of the 'feudalisation' of Scotland are expounded in a tightly argued and deceptively simple presentation.

In both volumes Barrow re-staked his 'British history' credentials through an exploration of English (and French) contributions to the development of Scotland. One important theme which emerged in *The Anglo-Norman Era* was the equation of the Scots common law with the contemporary system in England. From this developed the argument that the 'feudal' society expounded in Scottish legal treatises such as *Regiam Majestatem* was directly modelled on the 'classic feudal' institutions established in England after 1066.[16] England was the intermediary through which the 'continental, west European phenomenon' of military feudalism reached Scotland, and it was a wholesale importation of an already highly evolved system.[17] What the Scots imported (along with the colonists to put it into practice) transformed the relationship between a ruler and his greater nobles from one which depended upon traditional exercise of his kingly role, into one which emphasised the proprietary controls governing relationships between landlords and tenants.

The depth to which this thesis penetrated the consciousness of researchers is testimony to the presentational skill of its proponent. 'Barrovian' feudalism – particularly the military aspects of the system which were seen as having strengthened the Scottish crown – lies at the heart of most general histories of Scotland produced between about 1970 and 1990; and it influenced a host of other work which took the 'feudalisation' of Scottish society as a pivotal theme.[18] Moreover, the social reconstructionalism which is an inevitable concomitant of such theoretical constructs imbedded itself deeply in the consciousness af archaeologists.[19] An alien system founded upon the principle of grants of land to foreign colonists in return for service, imposed on Scotland from above by its kings, is a convenient model for explaining the appearance of new phenomena in the archaeological landscape.

Cogent though this construct was, it did not meet with universal acceptance. Before the articulation of the mature thesis, Duncan advanced alternative interpretations of feudalism in the central Middle Ages. These questioned the basis of relationships between lords and men, which Barrow considered dependent on tenure. Wrestling with indications that property was transferred by sale or by gift, Duncan argued that relationships based on tenure (central to Barrow's thesis) were coincidental to, rather than dependent on, mutual bonds of obligation arising from such tenure. To him, the relationship stemmed from the power and status of the lord and the fact that the knight's lands lay within the territorial sphere of his influence.[20] In effect, Duncan challenged the tidy 'feudal pyramid' which the charter scholarship of the new historiography appeared to reveal, questioning the idea of the neat system of tenure and service, which the formulaic recitation of the documents had fossilised. Where a feudal system existed it was as a mere fig leaf to cover the blushing modesty of a reality far removed from the Barrovian ideal. 'It existed,' wrote Duncan, 'as a form to enable two basic kinds of transaction to take place: sale of land outright, and irredeemable loan of land at a fixed rate of interest, the feu duty.'[21] The charters, viewed as evidence for the spread of feudalism and of the practical workings of the hierarchy of tenures could now be dismissed as legal safeguards for the respective interests of donors (or vendors) and recipients (or purchasers). The proliferation of secular documentation after about 1170 was neither an accident of survival, nor evidence for an acceleration of knight-service infeftments. It was, instead, a symptom of the increasingly easy alienation of land and the need to record transactions in a form which preserved the spirit of the donor's or vendor's intentions.

It is an irony of charter-based historiography of the period from 1100 to 1300 that such opposed views should spring from different analyses of the same evidence. The root of the differences, however, as revealed to great effect by Grant Simpson in his unpublished study of mainly thirteenth-century non-eleemosynary grants (presented to the Conference of Scottish Medieval Historical Research at Pitlochry in January 1986) lies in the skewing of the evidence marshalled by Barrow. Simpson demonstrated the pitfalls of concentration on the *acta* of the topmost strata of society which moved in a rarefied atmosphere of feudal purity, pointing instead to the parchment records of activity at lower levels amongst individuals directly touched by a messy reality on the ground. His was not a world where feus and knight-service pre-dominated, but rather one in which money governed the relationships between men.

Arguments concerning relationships between lords and men in the 'new' kingdom which emerged after 1124 are more blurred than might be expected after thirty years of research. Indeed, there is a widening gulf between Barrow and his opponents, rather than any convergence of views. Nevertheless, it remains a debate where little heat and less light has been generated with which either to fire the enthusiasm of students or to illuminate them; and this despite the centrality which the under-standing of lordship, the means of its exercise, and the structure of relationships between sorts of men holds not just for studies in pre-Wars of Independence Scotland, but for the whole of the medieval and early modern periods. Feudalism has become, as Jenny Wormald observed, a wall of uncertain composition which obscures understanding of what preceded it and also of what followed.[22] The wall of polite silence which greeted Grant Simpson in 1986, and the apparent rejection of Duncan's reappraisal of the evidence, means that 'Barrovian feudalism' still, apparently, holds the ring in Scotland. Sooner or later, however, its adherents will have to engage with Susan Reynolds's monumental assault on the orthodox ideas about European feudalism.

Unconsciously interlinked with arguments for social transformation through the introduction of 'off-the-peg' feudalism runs acceptance of continuity from the pre-feudal past. There is no conflict between these two strands, for they combined to form the hybrid construct which was medieval Scottish society. Nevertheless, there was little attempt to quantify the scale or significance of the contribution which 'continuity' made to the whole.[23] It is a paradox of this peculiar situation that while there was no question in the minds of scholars that what was being recorded in the mid-twelfth century was change, there was no significant effort to determine the nature of the earlier structures which were experiencing that transformation. In part, the charter-based nature of the scholarship militated against such examination, for the documents furnish *prima facie* evidence for widespread innovation but only residual traces of continuity.

Despite efforts to set evidence for novelty alongside that for continuity, much analysis has merely emphasised that the pre-feudal past was transformed. It has avoided wrestling with the problem of how old and new were accommodated together.[24] This reflected an implicit view that in areas that mattered, although old and new intermingled, it was the new that was dominant and allowed Scotland to escape the limitations of the Celtic past.[25] The tunnel vision of the new charter scholarship, dealing as it was with the raw evidence for change, produced still greater marginalisation of arguments for continuity. This is manifest in the first volume of the *Regesta* series, where brief commentaries on native traditions are submerged by detailed analysis of the new mechanisms which evolved, conveying the image of an abandonment of earlier forms in a scramble to 'modernise'.[26]

The historical uncertainties of the pre-'feudal' past remained unexplored ground until the later 1970s. Stimulus for this stemmed from two major studies of early medieval Scotland by Marjorie Anderson and, more relevant in the present context, by John Bannerman.[27] Concerned essentially with pre-Kenneth MacAlpin Argyll, Bannerman's essays, and particularly his detailed study of the *Senchus fer nAlban*, offered insight into social structures in the unified Scoto-Pictish kingdom. This appeared in synthetic form in *The Making of the Kingdom*, but the telling comments made there against the conventional view of the years 1058 to 1124 as a transitional period between the Celtic past are blunted by the narrative.[28] The conclusion, that 'it may be doubted whether the innovations read into meagre evidence were important either in quantity or quality or, indeed, whether many of them took place in this period at all', heightens the image of dichotomy between the reigns of David I and his predecessors.[29] While Edgar and Alexander I may have been 'content with the framework of the old Scottish state' and the structures inherited from it, that old Scottish state still ends symbolically with consideration of the two kings at the close of Duncan's sixth chapter.

For Duncan and Barrow the reign of David I constituted the moment of change to a brave new world dominated by Anglo-Norman influences.[30] This outlook in Barrow's work in particular cannot be attributed to distortion by his feudal spectacles, for quite simply he was exploring the positive imagery of the new world preserved within the parchment record, rather than the negative reflection of the old. For example, in 'The pattern of lordship and feudal settlement in Cumbria', twelfth-century lordships were projected against a background of Celtic continuity.[31] 'Badenoch and Strathspey, 1130–1312' took a similar approach, where analysis of the 'feudalisation' of the region produced a masterly display of his ability to draw out the evidence from a fragmentary record.[32] Discussion of native continuity, prefaced by the comment that 'in spite of lordships, fiefs and castles much of the *ancien régime* remained in the thirteenth and fourteenth centuries and even beyond', becomes a frustratingly brief coda which scarcely addresses the issues of the nature and level of survival.[33] His treatment of the same forms of evidence in 'The lost Gaidhealtachd of medieval Scotland' emphasises this deliberate bias in his work: continuity is largely taken for granted in an exposition of the dynamics of change.[34]

A consequence of this promotion of 'innovation' by Barrow was understatement of the underlying conservatism and resilience of Celtic Scotland in work influenced by him. The reaction when it came was not anti-Barrovian, but took as its focus his theme of continuity rather than that of change. The result has been more far-reaching than this simple shift in emphasis might suggest: 'feudalisation' now appears as a thin veneer which clouds observation of the material below. Again, the constraints of charter scholarship can be seen to have pushed research in one particular direction, drawing the eye to the changing colonial world where charters were essential records of title to property in circumstances where local lordship was in a state of flux. The newcomers needed security of title by charter, but native lords turned to parchment only once they entered the land market of the later twelfth and thirteenth centuries or where they began to deal with the crown and the new colonial elites.

Against the traditional 'feudalising' image of the earl of Fife receiving his earldom as a feu (i.e. change) stands the 'anti-feudal' posture of the earl of Strathearn (i.e. continuity). Cynthia Neville showed the crown's inability – or reluctance – to force the pace of change in Strathearn, with colonisation prevented by a native ruler whose centres of power were fixed in upland zones and rested on the support of a native nobility, a pattern which survived into the mid-fifteenth century.[35] Clearly this is a native landowner perceiving no necessity for newfangled tenures in his earldom, but where new land came into the possession of the Strathearn family, title was confirmed by charter: new circumstances demanded new responses.[36] Much the same occurred in Galloway, where traditional historiography has presented a confrontational relationship between native lords and feudal colonists, focusing on an 'enforced infeudation' and the destruction of the native nobility.[37] Trappings of change were important to the lords of Galloway, but they moved between the old and new worlds with ease and for all their Anglo-Normanised urbanity continued as native lords who depended on the support of the native community for much of their power.[38] In Galloway the brilliance of the few recorded instances of feudal colonisation has blinded historians to the continuing dominance of native aristo-crats.[39]

The most valuable contributions to this trend lie in the festschrift presented to Barrow.[40] Amongst the themes explored by the essays in that volume is 'the interplay between Celtic and feudal influences'.[41] This is 'Barrovian', but its emphasis has switched from concentration on feudal innovation to exploration of the Celtic legacy. In particular, Bannerman's study of 'MacDuff of Fife', by addressing the strong survival of a kin-based, Celtic social structure at the apex of which stood the figure of the earl, demonstrates the superficiality of 'feudalisation' in the first of the native earldoms touched by the mechanisms of feudalism.[42] Whilst Barrow was drawn to the 'feudal' significance of the re-grant to the earl, Bannerman indicated that this infeftment scarcely affected how the earl and his kin functioned within Fife.[43] Indeed, the role which was fulfilled by the MacDuffs as late as the 1290s was that of mormaer of a Celtic province rather than feudal lord of a great feu.[44]

This radical redirection has occasioned a comparative unresponsiveness in Scottish medievalists to recent developments in 'British' historiography. A redefini-tion of domestic issues has resulted, for example, in a signal failure amongst Scottish-based historians to contribute in any significant way to the new wave of 'British History' influenced by Rees Davies and Robin Frame.[45] This failure is all the more surprising considering the long-established tradition of Anglo-Scottish studies amongst Scottish historians. The direction of this Anglo-Scottish research, however, has been largely moulded by conventional perspectives which, like Tytler in the 1830s, simply used English sources to illuminate Scottish problems. It is rarely that Scottish historians stepped back from the traditional lines of demarcation to take the wide-angled view prescribed by Frame, producing instead dimly perceived keyhole glimpses of themes within a restricted field of politically oriented study.[46] The latter and preferred approach was essentially that taken by Barrow in *The Anglo-Norman Era*, narrowly focused on aristocratic relationships and governmental development, rather than his broadly-based comparative studies of the *Feudal Britain* tradition. While this saw major advances in understanding of the political relationship between Scotland and England, of Anglo-Scottish cross-border landholding, and of the processes at work in the colonising ventures (characterised by the outstanding work of Keith Stringer), the seminal comparative studies of social structures and institutions produced by Barrow failed to germinate and produce a parallel area of growth.[47]

The self-satisfied assumption that this tradition of research into Anglo-Scottish themes indicates an openness of mind and willingness to embrace 'British History' in contrast to the narcissistic introspection which is often characteristic of English historians is a further facet of the malaise which afflicts Scottish historical research. It is, moreover, self-deception, for, with the notable exceptions of Barrow and Stringer, much recent work is strongly Scoto-centric and gives scant consideration to underlying political and social stresses in England – and elsewhere in Britain – which might affect the Scottish position. This is evident, for example, in the only academic book devoted to the reign of a thirteenth-century Scottish monarch (Alexander III) to be produced in the last thirty years.[48] With the exception of Nicholas Mayhew's essay on the state of the Scottish economy under Alexander, there is an astonishing failure to consider the impact of the relationship with Scotland's southern neighbour on domestic politics.[49] Indeed, it has taken a non-historian, Roy Owen, in his overview of the reign of William the Lion, to underscore the potential in a broader exploration of Scotland's international relationships.[50]

A similarly one-dimensional approach has blighted understanding of Anglo-Scottish relations in the period from 1000 to 1174. Lynch, in a search for 'the over-arching continuities which give coherence' to free-standing episodes in Scottish history, recognised the continuity of policy towards northern England from the tenth to the twelfth centuries, but failed to address the interplay of responses between Scottish and English kings.[51] This is a consequence of the constraints of a single-volume history, but is also symptomatic of the research upon which his narrative is based. The influence of William Kapelle's study of the transformation of northern English society runs throughout Lynch's analysis, underscoring the failure of Scottish historians of the period to attempt parallel studies for their side of the border.[52] England, as Kapelle demonstrated, was more than an occasional reservoir of inspiration or colonising manpower upon which Scottish rulers could draw: co-operation and collaboration rather than confrontation underpinned the establishment of the pre-1135 Anglo-Scottish frontier.[53]

Significantly, all important – and recent – advances in this context are the work of historians based outwith Scotland. For example, Judith Green has produced a wide-ranging study of Anglo-Scottish relations from 1066 to the Treaty of Falaise, in which she explores the mutual attempts and responses of Scottish and English kings to fill the political vacuum in Northumbria. In particular, she stressed David I's relationship with Henry I before and after his accession in 1124 and the part which the stability which arose from this played in the consolidation of Norman control in northern England and in the origins of cross-border landholding, commonly understated in conventional Scottish interpretations.[54] The most significant contribution, however, is Stringer's reassessment of the reign of King Stephen, where the traditional image of David's involvement in the English civil war has been overturned.[55] Viewed from a Scottish perspective, this was a side-issue whose only lasting consequence was to compromise Scottish independence. The short-lived nature of David's conquests and failure to recognise the degree of his control over them led to a dismissive attitude towards David's 'Scoto-Northumbrian' realm. But Stringer has argued cogently that David's conquests were 'firmly absorbed into the Scottish kingdom', and that 'David ruled them in complete independence of Stephen'.[56] The implications are far-reaching for our understanding of Anglo-Scottish relations from 1157 to 1237, but the integration into the Scottish realm which Stringer posits speaks of the survival of ancient bonds and the forging of new social, cultural and economic links. The need for a Kapelle-style analysis of southern Scotland is now all the more pressing, but equally, perhaps, here we can see most clearly – and explore – the mechanisms at work which were used to bind together the extended realm which David and his heirs established. The question arises, however, of who will undertake such work: where are the Competitors who would rescue Scottish history 'and remede that stad is in perplexytie'?

There is no gainsaying the remarkable achievement of the last thirty years. Few academic subjects have experienced such a renaissance in the truest sense of that word, nor seen such rapid and comprehensive reconstruction of its research base. The achievement is all the more remarkable if the smallness of the group of scholars who carried it through is considered, and in particular that the revolution in our understanding of the period from 1124 to 1296 was largely the product of one man's efforts. Geoffrey Barrow and his fellows effectively resuscitated medieval Scottish history, gave it a philosophy and ethos which established it as a credible independent academic subject. They furnished it with the construct and paradigms which underpinned research. But it is in the very smallness of the group involved that many of its most life-threatening defects originate. In the drive to create a 'new' history there was a need for closeness and co-operation: without consensus there would have been no revolution. But consensus can also stifle debate and the cosy closeness of co-operation can lead to blandness. This absence of radical discussion and the domination of specialist spheres within the subject has led to stagnation. Without debate there can be no stimulus for advance.

To survive, Scottish medieval historical research needs to move on, to find new impetus and direction. 'Dark Age' studies have perhaps shown the way forward in the willingness of researchers in that field to look beyond traditional temporal and spatial barriers and to embrace the products of related disciplines. This has two dimensions, the multi-disciplinary synthesis represented, for example, in Barbara Crawford's *Scandinavian Scotland*, and the supranational scope which is a characteristic of both that volume and the work of the Committee for Dark Age Studies and the Early Medieval Research Group.[57] The potential for developing similar research on the central Middle Ages has already been demonstrated by Robert Bartlett, whose identification of common themes and responses on a Europe-wide platform has revealed the parochialism of traditional 'national' histories. It is not only Scottish history that has cultivated its own kailyards for too long.[58] At the other extreme, however, there is a need to scrutinise the kailyard ever more closely. Local studies have illustrated starkly the fallacious complacency which has allowed the presentation as 'national' history of generalised results founded on the research of a narrow-based group into what can be seen increasingly as an unrepresentative region. In a scramble to establish its credentials as a viable independent subject, Scottish medieval research leaped for the maturity of 'big idea' history without first passing through an adolescence that would equip it with the experience for survival.

There can be no turning back of the clock, nor should there be. While many interpretations of pre-fourteenth-century Scotland are long past their sell-by date, the charter scholarship upon which interpretation was built remains as fresh and valid as ever. Nevertheless, internal inconsistencies in the traditional image of pre-Wars of Independence Scotland, and in the theses from which this image has been constructed, can no longer be glossed over by generalisations. There is an urgent need for these issues to be re-examined and debated – not least because historiographical developments beyond Scotland have tarnished the gold of the new Scottish historiography of the 1960s to reveal a leaden burden in shabby packaging. This must be jettisoned if scholarship is to advance significantly and if Scottish history is to play any part in the development of medieval studies in general. The legacy of the charter scholarship of the 1960s must not be the present tottering structure, falling down under the weight of its own contradictions. Rather, it must lie in the panoply of edited tools with which the structure can be rebuilt from the foundations. It is an inheritance which could be truly golden. We can but pray that it does not fail through default of heirs.

NOTES

Abbreviations used in the notes
PSAS   *Proceedings of the Society of Antiquaries of Scotland*
RRS   *Regesta Regum Scottorum*
SHR   *Scottish Historical Review*
TDGAS   *Transactions of the Dumfriesshire and Galloway Natural History and Antiquarian Society*

 1 E.g. E. A. R. Brown, 'The tyranny of a construct: feudalism and historians of medieval Europe', *American Historical Review*, lxxix (1974), 1063–88; S. Reynolds, *Fiefs and Vassals: The Medieval Evidence Reinterpreted* (Oxford, 1994).
 2 The scarcity of entries for Scottish topics falling into the 1100–1300 period in the Institute of Historical Research's lists of theses in progress underscores this point.
 3 M. Ash, *The Strange Death of Scottish History* (Edinburgh, 1980).

 4 A. C. Lawrie, *Early Scottish Charters* (1905); A. O. Anderson, *Scottish Annals from English Chroniclers AD500 to 1286* (London, 1908); idem, *Early Sources of Scottish History AD500–1286* (Edinburgh, 1922).

 5 Ash, *Strange Death of Scottish History*, 152.

 6 G. W. S. Barrow, *Feudal Britain: The Completion of the Medieval Kingdoms, 1066–1314* (London, 1956).

 7 Ash, *Strange Death of Scottish History*, 100–15.

 8 R. Frame, *The Political Development of the British Isles 1100–1400* (Oxford, 1990), 1.

 9 A. Grant and K. J. Stringer, eds., *Medieval Scotland: Crown, Lordship and Community* (Edinburgh, 1993), p. xiv.

10 *RRS*, vols. I and II.

11 See the comments in Duncan, *Kingdom*, 651–2.

12 R. L. G. Ritchie, *The Normans in Scotland* (Edinburgh, 1954).

13 G. W. S. Barrow, 'The earls of Fife in the twelfth century', *PSAS*, lxxxvii (1952–3), 51–62; G. W. S. Barrow, 'The beginnings of feudalism in Scotland', *Bulletin of the Institute of Historical Research*, xxix (1956), 1–31.

14 G. W. S. Barrow, *The Kingdom of the Scots: Government, Church and Society from the Eleventh to the Fourteenth Century* (London, 1973).

15 G. W. S. Barrow, *The Anglo-Norman Era in Scottish History* (Oxford, 1980); G. W. S. Barrow, *Kingship and Unity: Scotland 1000–1306* (London, 1981).

16 T. M. Cooper, ed., *Regiam Majestatem and Quoniam Attachiamenta* (Stair Society, 1947); Barrow, *Anglo-Norman Era*, 118–20. See also H. L. MacQueen, *Common Law and Feudal Society in Medieval Scotland* (Edinburgh, 1993); and idem, 'Canon law, custom and legislation: law in the reign of Alexander II', in R. D. Oram, ed., *Scotland in the Reign of Alexander II* (forthcoming).

17 Barrow, *Kingship and Unity*, 43–4.

18 E.g. R. Mitchison, *A History of Scotland* (London, 1970), esp. ch. 2. More recent work, such as R. A. McDonald's *Kingdom of the Isles: Scotland's Western Seaboard, c.1100–c.1336* (East Linton, 1997) takes a Barrovian line to explain the relationship between Somerled and the Scots in terms of an 'anti-feudal' reaction by a Celtic traditionalist.

19 The influence of basic theories of the feudalisation of Scottish society on archaeological studies of aristocratic settlement can be seen in, e.g., C. J. Tabraham, 'Norman settlement in Upper Clydesdale: recent archaeological fieldwork', *TDGAS*, liii (1977–8), 114–28; idem, 'Norman settlement in Galloway: recent fieldwork in the Stewartry', in D. Breeze, ed., *Studies in Scottish Antiquity* (Edinburgh, 1984), 87–124; P. A. Yeoman *et al.*, 'Excavations at Castlehill of Strachan, 1980–81', *PSAS*, cxiv (1984), 315–64.

20 Duncan, *Kingdom*, 407–8.

21 Ibid., 408.

22 J. Wormald, *Lords and Men in Scotland: Bonds of Manrent, 1442–1603* (Edinburgh, 1985), 10.

23 Barrow, *Feudal Britain*, 224.

24 Ibid., 134, 143; Barrow, *Anglo-Norman Era*, 84–6.

25 Barrow, *Feudal Britain*, 224.

26 *RRS*, i, 27–56.

27 M. O. Anderson, *Kings and Kingship in Early Scotland* (Edinburgh, 1973); J. Bannerman, *Studies in the History of Dalriada* (Edinburgh, 1974).

28 Duncan, *Kingdom*, chs. 3–6.

29 Ibid., 132.

30 E.g. G. W. S. Barrow, *David I of Scotland (1124–53): The Balance of New and Old* (Reading, 1985)

31 G. W. S. Barrow, 'The pattern of lordship and feudal settlement in Cumbria', *Journal of Medieval History*, i (1975), 117–38.

32 G. W. S. Barrow, 'Badenoch and Strathspey, 1130–1312, 1: secular and political'. *Northern Scotland*, viii (1988), 1–15.

33 Ibid., 9–10.

34 G. W. S. Barrow, 'The lost Gaidhealtachd of medieval Scotland', in W. Gillies, ed., *Gaelic and Scotland: Alba agus a' Ghaidlig* (Edinburgh, 1989), 67–88.

35 C. J. Neville, 'The Earls of Strathearn from the Twelfth to the Mid-Fourteenth Century' (University of Aberdeen, unpublished PhD thesis, 1983), 30, 63; A. Grant, 'The Higher Nobility and their Estates in Scotland, *c.*1371–1424' (University of Oxford, unpublished DPhil thesis, 1975), 232–9. See also chapter 6, below, by Cynthia Neville.

36 E.g. *RRS*, ii, nos. 206, 474; Barrow, 'Badenoch and Strathspey', 5.

37 R. D. Oram, 'A family business? Colonisation and settlement in twelfth- and thirteenth-century Galloway', *SHR*, lxxii (1993), 111–45.

38 See esp. K. J. Stringer, 'Periphery and core in thirteenth-century Scotland: Alan son of Roland, Lord of Galloway and Constable of Scotland', in Grant and Stringer, *Medieval Scotland*, 82–113; Oram, 'Family business', 134.

39 Oram, 'Family business', 134–45.

40 Grant and Stringer, *Medieval Scotland*.

41 Ibid., p. xvi.

42 J. Bannerman, 'MacDuff of Fife', in Grant and Stringer, *Medieval Scotland,* 20–38; and see also the earlier parts of A. Grant, 'Thanes and thanages, from the eleventh to the fourteenth centuries', in the same volume.

43 Barrow, 'Earls of Fife', 54–5.

44 Bannerman, 'MacDuff of Fife', 38.

45 R. R. Davies, *Domination and Conquest: The Experience of Ireland, Scotland and Wales 1100–1300* (Cambridge, 1990); Frame, *Political Development*.

46 Frame, *Political Development*, 3–4.

47 K. J. Stringer, *Earl David of Huntingdon 1152–1219: A Study in Anglo-Scottish History* (Edinburgh, 1985). Many of these themes are explored as 'case studies' in Stringer, *Nobility*. For works by Barrow, see 'Northern English society in the twelfth and thirteenth centuries', *Northern History*, vi (1969), 1–28; 'The pattern of lordship and feudal settlement in Cumbria', *Journal of Medieval History*, i (1975), 117–38; or 'Das mittelalterliche englische und schottische Königtum: ein Vergleich', *Historisches Jahrbuch*, cii (1982), 362–89, translated and expanded to take account of Davies and Frame as 'Kingship in medieval England and Scotland', in *Scotland and Its Neighbours in the Middle Ages* (London, 1992).

48 N. H. Reid, ed., *Scotland in the Reign of Alexander III, 1249–1286* (Edinburgh, 1990).

49 N. Mayhew, 'Alexander III – A Silver Age? An essay in Scottish medieval economic history', in Reid, *Alexander III*, 53–73.

50 D. D. R. Owen, *William the Lion, 1143–1214: Kingship and Culture* (East Linton, 1997).

51 M. Lynch, *Scotland: A New History* (2nd edn, London, 1992), pp. xv, 83.

52 W. E. Kapelle, *The Norman Conquest of the North: The Region and its Transformation, 1000–1135* (London, 1979); Lynch, *Scotland*, 74–6, 79.

53 Kapelle, *Norman Conquest*, 202–13.

54 J. Green, 'Anglo-Scottish Relations, 1066–1174', in M. Jones and M. Vale, eds., *England and her Neighbours, 1066–1453: Essays in Honour of Pierre Chaplais* (London, 1989), 59–65; idem, 'David I and Henry I', *SHR*, lxxv (1996), 1–19; cf. Duncan, *Kingdom*, 134–7, 217–19.

55 K. J. Stringer, *The Reign of Stephen: Kingship, Warfare and Government in Twelfth-Century England* (London, 1993), 28–37; also idem, 'State-building in twelfth-century Britain: David I, king of Scots, and northern England', in J. C. Appleby and P. Dalton, eds., *Government, Religion and Society in Northern England, 1000–1700* (Stroud, 1997), 40–62.

56 Duncan, *Kingdom*, 222–4; Stringer, *Reign of Stephen*, 35.

57 B. E. Crawford, *Scandinavian Scotland* (Leicester, 1987); idem, ed., *Scotland in Dark Age Europe* (St Andrews, 1994); idem, ed., *Scotland in Dark Age Britain* (St Andrews, 1996); idem, ed., *Conversion and Christianity in the North Sea World* (St Andrews, 1998).

58 R. Bartlett, *The Making of Europe: Conquest, Colonisation and Cultural Change, 950–1350* (London, 1993).

Robert Bruce:
The Turn of the Tide

Extracted from GWS Barrow 1988 'The Turn of the Tide', Chapter 11 of his *Robert Bruce and the Community of the Realm of Scotland*, Edinburgh (Edinburgh University Press; 3rd edn), 187–202, 364–366.

It is easy to regard the period from 1309 to 1314 as a mere prelude to Bannockburn, as though the Scots spent these years preparing themselves for an inevitable and decisive trial of strength with the English Crown. In truth, Bruce's famous battle was the least inevitable event in the whole war of independence. Bruce himself never seems to have been certain in his own mind that his crown and the independence of the Scottish kingdom would ultimately have to be vindicated in a single great trial by combat. An English observer in 1311 wrote that Bruce 'did not believe he was able to meet the [English] king's forces in a plain field',[1] an estimate which surely holds good for the whole period from Methven to the dramatic council of war held on the night of June 23rd–24th, 1314, between the first and second days of the battle of Bannockburn. Bruce's thinking was dominated by the principles summarized and made famous in later years in *Good King Robert's Testament*: dependence on infantry, scorched earth, guerrilla raids and sorties, and the systematic demolition of castles and fortifications; in short, caution in strategy, boldness in tactics. The English, in his view, must be so harassed and exhausted that they would come to feel that Scotland was not worth the effort and expense of conquest.

We must not exaggerate the success which Bruce had achieved by 1309, even while admitting that this success was extraordinary when we consider the almost ludicrous weakness of his position only two years before. The subjugation of Buchan, Ross and Argyll (a list soon to be augmented by Galloway), the resumption of communications with France, the winning over of many prominent nobles and lairds, the holding of a parliament at St Andrews – these were notable achievements, which bade fair to make 'King Hob' (as the English called him in ridicule)[2] a much more serious exponent of kingship than any but his most devoted followers of 1306–7 would have believed. But in 1309 he had still not won over the whole of Scotland. It is true that as a result of brilliant campaigns, his Scottish enemies no longer had any base for concerted action outside Lothian, and even Lothian had come under heavy attack as early as December 1308.[3] If Scotsmen still wanted to fight against Bruce, they must now do so simply as individual members of the English forces, and they were, indeed, described as 'English' by the later Scottish chroniclers. But Bruce had to recognise – as we also must recognise if we wish to grasp the significance of the years before Bannockburn – that an unmistakable change had come over the struggle with England since 1304. On the one hand there was defeatism, bred of the memory of actual defeat in the field and of material destruction and misery, and leading to a breakdown of order and to opportunist shifts of allegiance. On the other, there were the doubts entertained by many men of power and influence as to the lawfulness of Bruce's claim to the throne, the open belief or less articulate suspicion that he was a private man furthering a private ambition.

For many years King Robert's strength lay in the country north of Forth and in the 'middle west' – Lanarkshire, Ayrshire, Lennox and the Firth of Clyde. In 1311, for example, we are told on good authority that Piers Gaveston was sent to occupy Perth by Edward II 'so that Bruce who at the time was on an expedition towards Galloway *should not return north of Forth to recruit an army*'.[4] It was precisely in these regions that the English hold was weakest, not because of the exceptional hostility of the inhabitants but rather because of their remoteness from English bases and their excessively poor internal communications. Anyone attempting the recovery of Scottish independence in 1306 would have been obliged, if only for strategic and geographical reasons, to begin with the north and the west.

Looking at the struggle for Scottish independence as a whole, from 1286 to 1328, the balance of military and especially political importance was weighted much more towards Lothian and the south east. Before 1304, as we have already seen, not only was the south east – Lothian, Tweeddale, Teviotdale and the Forest – repeatedly the scene of major campaigns, but many south-eastern landowners were prominent on the Scottish side. But even after Bruce's revolutionary *coup de force*, it is not true to say that the south east was unimportant or that all Lothian men remained hostile or apathetic until Bannockburn inspired or terrified them into patriotism. Between 1307 and February 1312 the following Lothian landowners had joined Bruce: William de Vieuxpoint (Vipont) of Langton in Berwickshire; Sir Thomas Hay, Sir Robert Keith the marischal and (in Keith's following) Godfrey Broun of Colston (December 1308); Geoffrey Farsley (1308); Edmund Ramsay of Dalhousie (1309 or 1310); Peter Pinkie and Aymer of Hadden (November 1310).[5] A series of fascinating documents from November 1312[6] throws a flood of light on the situation in Lothian a year and a half before Bannockburn, revealing it to be one of much complexity. These documents show us the plight of the communities of 'King Edward's men' – presumably including both the genuinely English and the Scots loyal to Edward II – in the sheriffdoms of Edinburgh, Roxburgh and Berwick. On one side the Scottish king was treating them exactly as he was treating the indisputably English communities of Cumberland, Northumberland and County Durham, forcing them to pay him swingeing sums of blackmail for immunity from burning, devastation and worse. On the other side, the English garrisons, especially at Edinburgh, Roxburgh, Jedburgh and Berwick, were brutally ignoring these dearly bought truces or *souffrances de guerre*. They refused to contribute their own share of the cost of a truce, and when local landowners took refuge inside these castles in order to evade their responsibilities, they refused to allow these evaders to pay the proper share due from their estates. Finally, they seized the goods and cattle of Bruce's own supporters in their sheriffdoms, when these were being brought to market peaceably under the terms of the truce. In consequence, not surprisingly, the 'civilian population' (if they may be so called) feared reprisals by Bruce because the truce had been violated. Nothing in the record of this time is more ironical than to see King Edward II sternly rebuking his own sheriffs and garrison commanders for attacking the enemy and for making life harder for Edward's own supporters. Nothing is more illuminating than to read in these official records of 1312 explicit reference to the men in Lothian 'who adhere to the side of the aforesaid Robert [Bruce]'.[7]

A passage in the Lanercost chronicle describing the situation at the turn of the years 1311 and 1312 strikingly reinforces the impression given by these official records.[8] The writer states that the men of the earldom of Dunbar, who had hitherto been in the English king's peace, were forced to pay very heavily for immunity from Bruce's attacks. We have already seen that the earl of Dunbar had been consistently pro-English throughout the Anglo-Scottish war. His attitude will easily account for the fact that his earldom was loyal to Edward II, but though it consisted of a large group of estates in East Lothian and Berwickshire the earldom of Dunbar was not Lothian. It may be relevant to add that the two magnates who were prominent in these years as leaders and spokesmen of the English party in Lothian were the earl of Dunbar himself and Sir Adam Gordon, who was a kinsman of the earls of Dunbar and held his principal estate, the village of Gordon in Berwickshire, as a member of the earldom. The Lanercost writer continues with these remarkable words:

> In all this fighting the Scots were so divided that often a father was with the Scots and his son with the English, or one brother was with the Scots and another with the English, or even one individual was first on one side and then on the other. But all or most of the Scots who were with the English were with them insincerely or to save their lands in England; for their hearts if not their bodies were always with their own people.[9]

The men and women of south-eastern Scotland were, indeed, in an unenviable plight. If many of them remained in the increasingly ineffective 'peace' of King Edward, it would be unrealistic to attribute this to a lack of patriotic feeling. A few years later, when the triumphant Scots were raiding the English northern counties at will, many of the local inhabitants went over to the Scots. It does not occur to English historians (any more than it occurred to Edward II) to put this down to traitorous motives or lack of patriotism. They were prompted by stark necessity. No such necessity burdened the people north of Forth, where the majority were free to give effect to a patriotism which was neither more nor less pronounced than that which might be found in any feudal kingdom of comparable development.[10]

Fourteenth-century patriotism was not a total, all-embracing patriotism, any more than fourteenth-century warfare was total warfare, but both, for all that, were real enough. We must not be too surprised, therefore, if we find hard-pressed Lothian gentry supporting the English, or impoverished young men from the surrounding countryside serving in the enemy garrisons of Linlithgow or Bothwell,

Perth or Dundee. Nor must we be too surprised if we find that a number of prominent men from districts well to the north or west of Lothian were conspicuously loyal to the English king and inveterate enemies of King Robert. It is a striking fact that the hard core of Scots who fought consistently against Bruce, who either never submitted, not even after the tide of victory had turned decisively in his favour, or submitted at the eleventh hour, was composed of men from regions at a considerable distance from the English border or with little or no experience of anglicization: Sir Dungal Macdouall of Galloway, Sir Alexander Abernethy of Abernethy (Perthshire) and Inverarity (Angus), Duncan of Frendraught (on the borders of Aberdeenshire and Banffshire), his father-in-law and brother-in-law, the elder and the younger Gilbert of Glencarnie, from the highland parish of Duthil in Inverness-shire,[11] and John Bacach Macdougall, lord of Lorn.

The years from 1309 to 1314 were years not of orderly preparation but of dour and confused struggle. The elimination of concerted Scottish resistance to Bruce meant that the king's main efforts could be directed towards clearing his kingdom of English garrisons and re-establishing its independent position within the community of North Sea countries. Save for the summer and autumn of 1309, which he evidently spent traversing the west from Loch Broom in the north to Dunstaffnage in Argyll,[12] and the autumn of 1312, when he stayed for some weeks in Moray to witness the conclusion of the treaty with Norway, King Robert's time was chiefly spent in the centre and south of Scotland, or else beyond the border, raiding Cumberland and Northumberland. One further exception may be seen in the autumn of 1310 and earlier part of 1311, when he let an English army under Edward II, and latterly under Piers Gaveston, penetrate deep into Scotland to little purpose, since they found no Scots troops to defeat in open battle and not enough food to sustain either themselves or their horses.[13]

The chief castles still in enemy hands after the end of 1309 were concentrated in the south. On the line of the Tay the English retained Perth and Dundee. North of this line they held only Banff, which may have fallen to the Scots during 1310. Between Tay and Forth the English position was surprisingly weak: Cupar, which they still held in the spring of 1308, was lost not long afterwards, and only the small fortalice of Muckhart, belonging to the bishop of St Andrews, remained in enemy hands, apparently as late as 1311.[14] On the crucially important line of the Forth, or immediately south of it, the first-class castles of Stirling and Edinburgh were English-held, and precariously linked by the minor strongpoints of Linlithgow and Livingston. Already in 1309 the supply of these garrisons was proving difficult and dangerous. Food, stores and weapons were obtained from Berwick. Oddly enough, remote Banff and Dundee, because they could be supplied by sea, were easier to replenish than Stirling or Edinburgh. West of Stirling, 'English troops' (many of whom were actually Scotsmen) still controlled Kirkintilloch and Bothwell.[15] They must have felt increasingly isolated, though Bothwell, perhaps because of its exceptional size and strength, actually held out until the morrow of Bannockburn, when its Scottish commander, Walter, Gilbert's son, saw the light in time, handed Bothwell over to Edward Bruce, and survived to become the ancestor of the powerful Hamilton family. The still great isolation of Ayr by December 1309 is shown by the fact that Edward II classed it along with Perth, Dundee and Banff as a castle whose commander was instructed to 'take what truce he could until Whitsun next (June 7th, 1310)'.[16] Rutherglen, which was being besieged in December 1308, was apparently taken by Edward Bruce.[17] Dumbarton may have been handed over to Bruce when its keeper Sir John Menteith joined him, before the spring of 1309.

The castles of the extreme south west could be expected to hold out longer, at least until the English lost their command of the Solway Firth. In these regions, moreover, a higher proportion of the local people were Bruce's enemies. It was thus some years before the Scots regained Lochmaben, Caerlaverock, Dumfries, Dalswinton, Tibbers and Buittle. As late as the autumn of 1311 an enemy garrison held Bruce's own island fortress of Loch Doon in Carrick. Although they were besieged, an 'English' force under David of Strathbogie, earl of Atholl, was making a strenuous effort to relieve them.[18] Dumfries and Caerlaverock were probably the strongest of these castles. Dumfries was at last surrendered, to King Robert in person, on February 7th, 1313, by his old enemy Dungal Macdouall.[19] With a clemency and respect for military honour conspicuously absent in Edward I's behaviour towards defeated garrisons, Macdouall was allowed to go free. He crossed to the Isle of Man and prepared to hold it against the king of Scotland, its lawful lord.

It was, of course, in the south east that the English position seemed, if not impregnable, at least formidably entrenched. It was not merely that they held, in addition to Edinburgh, three other first-class castles – Jedburgh, Roxburgh and Berwick – as well as numerous second- or third-rate strongpoints (Haddington, Luffness, Dirleton, Yester, Dunbar, Selkirk and Cavers).[20] Even more useful was the fact that the close, 'four-square' grouping of these castles, the relatively good communications between them, and the proximity of most of them to a North Sea coastline still dominated by English maritime power, combined to make the whole English position much less vulnerable in this area than anywhere else in Scotland. Bruce knew that there was no easy short-cut to victory here. Every single one of the major fortresses must be patiently invested, starved, and, when the right moment came, seized by a mixture of stratagem and daring. The methods of castle warfare used by the English were simply not available to Bruce, for he was woefully short of heavy siege engines and the skilled men to work them, and also of the food-supplies needed to sustain prolonged sieges.

If the south east seemed to present obstacles which would not be easy to surmount, the south west offered a brighter prospect and was no less important. By the summer of 1310, if not earlier, the Scots had been peaceably received in Ireland and allowed to buy not only corn, meat and other foodstuffs but also sorely-needed iron and steel weapons and armour.[21] Since these can hardly have been Irish-made they were presumably re-exports from England or the continent. Scottish access to Ireland was made possible by the superiority which Bruce now enjoyed in Argyll, the isles and the seas between Galloway and Ulster. A persistent line of English strategy at this time was to encourage John Macdougall, the ousted lord of Lorn, to lead a naval expedition against the Hebrideans and Argyllsmen and try to win them over. For this Macdougall was appointed 'admiral and captain' of a special fleet in 1311, and given a base in one of the east-coast Irish ports, perhaps Dublin or Drogheda.[22] Here he could count on the support of dissident west highlanders such as John Macsween of Knapdale and his brothers Toirdelbach and Murdoch.[23]

As long as the English controlled the Isle of Man the south-western approaches of Scotland were vulnerable to attack on or from the sea. For their part the Scots had much to gain from pursuing an aggressive policy by preying on the English shipping routes to Ireland. Recovery of Man would be essential if this strategy was to succeed. Towards the end of 1310, Robert I was reported to be planning an assault upon Man with a fleet from the Outer Isles, and it was said that many Manxmen were already adhering to him.[24] For the English, the defence of Man had been complicated by the fact that Edward II had given the island to Piers Gaveston a few weeks after his accession.[25] The English baronage might well have preferred Man to be in Scots hands than see it serve as a possible bolt-hole for their king's hated lover. But by 1310 the island seems to have been once again under at least the nominal control of Anthony Bek, bishop of Durham, and administered by Bek's steward Gilbert Macaskill.[26]

Nothing came of King Robert's threat, Bek died in March 1311, and by May Edward II had transferred the island to Sir Henry Beaumont,[27] but since he too incurred the suspicion of the king's opponents, the Lords Ordainers, Beaumont's custody must have been brief. At some date before April 1313 Man was evidently seized in a baronial *coup* involving Simon Montagu,[28] and it was evidently at this time that Dungal Macdouall was made commander of Rushen. These English vacillations were Bruce's opportunity. Gathering a large fleet, the king of Scots landed at Ramsey on May 18th, 1313, crossed the hills to Douglas two days later, and laid siege to the castle of Rushen (Castletown), nine miles to the south, on the 21st. On June 12th Bruce had the satisfaction of accepting Macdouall's second surrender of a castle in four months.[29] Once more set free, Macdouall became a veteran in the English king's service, dying about the end of 1327 and leaving a large family to become pensioners of the Westminster exchequer.[30]

Although Beaumont seems to have been restored in 1314 as custodian of the island, he cannot have made this good by physical possession, and it was not until early in 1315 that John Macdougall apparently wrested Man from the Scots.[31] Robert I then made a prospective grant of the lordship of Man to Thomas Randolph, whose reported efforts in July 1317 to recover the island for Scotland must have been successful, for it was evidently under Scottish rule from c 1317 till 1333 and formally acknowledged to be so in 1328 by the English king and parliament.[32]

In the first half of Edward II's reign the English lost control of the western approaches. By the autumn of 1315 Scots ships, mostly under the command of Thomas Dun, had grown bold enough to raid English shipping at Holyhead.[33] Dun helped Edward Bruce while he was campaigning in Ireland, and in 1317 two new vessels, built and equipped in Devon or Cornish ports, were ordered to be used against him. This move was evidently successful, for Dun's capture was reported on

July 13th, at the same time as Randolph was menacing the two islands of Man and Anglesey.[34]

The tactics of Bruce and the bold young men – Douglas, Randolph, Boyd and Edward Bruce – who under him were already forming a band of famous captains, would have astonished and amused Edward I. Castles must be surprised during the hours of darkness, and an entry must be forced at the most suitable point on the walls by means of rope ladders fitted with iron grappling-hooks. These simple but ingenious scaling ladders, evidently light enough to be carried by one or two men, may well have been used at Forfar and elsewhere in the north. The first occasion on which they are recorded was the attempt on Berwick, on the night of December 6th, 1312.[35] It is characteristic of the audacity of Bruce and his captains that the first big south-country stronghold to be attacked in earnest was the town nearest to the English border. The attempt was frustrated by the barking of a dog inside the walls, but in little more than a month Bruce was investing the town of Perth. Because of its strategic position, Perth (like Stirling) was of crucial importance to the English. Gaveston had been sent to hold and strengthen the town in February, 1311,[36] during the campaign which Edward II conducted in southern Scotland between September 1310 and August 1311. The Perth garrison was large, with a high proportion of Scotsmen.[37] Since October 1311 at latest, they had been commanded by the Perthshire knight Sir William Oliphant. As the brave young commander of Stirling castle on behalf of King John and the Guardians, Oliphant had won great renown. He had been in an English prison from July 1304 until December 1308, when he was released on condition of fighting against Bruce.[38] He had already given a gloomy report of the situation at Perth as early as autumn 1311,[39] and by January 1313 things must have seemed wellnigh hopeless. The town was surrounded by a stone wall with turrets, and by a water-filled ditch (except on the east where the River Tay gave protection). On the night of January 7th–8th, 1313 – 'a myrk nycht' says Barbour[40] – the garrison failed to keep a good watch, believing from Bruce's movements that the Scots had lifted the siege. Carrying their ladders and light weapons, the Scots waded through the moat in the darkness. To the astonishment of a French knight in his entourage, their king himself led the way through the black, icy water, which at one point came up to his throat, and with the help of his own rope ladder was the second man to scale the town wall. The men of Perth surrendered almost without a fight.

For some moments Bruce had clearly been in great danger; but it was during such moments as these that he won not merely the castles but also the hearts of Scotland. In most ages of history, the Scottish soldier (unless extremely well-trained) has not possessed the gift which has been the conspicuous mark of his English counterpart: the capacity to hold on coolly and philosophically, through thick and thin, regardless of either leadership or conditions. On the other hand, no one has responded more heroically to the inspiration of an outstanding leader, a Murray of Bothwell, a James IV, a Montrose, a Moore. And it seems undeniable that a successful leader of Scotsmen must have above all the power to kindle both affection and imagination. It is not normally the mark of a good general that he fights alongside his men. But Bruce had to be more than a good general; he had to be a Joshua, a captain of his people, one who could not only draw on existing loyalty but awaken dormant loyalty and win over to himself the loyalty previously given to his enemies.

The English in Perth were allowed to go free. The leading Scots burgesses were slain, though if we may believe Barbour the number of those killed was small.[41] The example – if such it was – proved effective, for we hear of no more cold-blooded killings. Slaughter of this kind, though common enough in the period, was highly uncharacteristic of Robert Bruce. As we have seen, only a month after the fall of Perth (February 7th, 1313) Dumfries Castle was starved into surrender. The king had taken personal command of the attack upon Dumfries, Caerlaverock and Buittle during the previous July, perhaps because he felt that his brother had not done well enough in this task. It seems likely that after the surrender of Dumfries the other two castles also fell into Scottish hands, and the West March with them. There was no mistaking it now: the tide had turned.

Stirling, commanded by Sir Philip Moubray, a Scot, was the next big castle to be attempted. Edward Bruce laid siege to it from Lent nearly to midsummer 1313, without success.[42] Then, by an act of characteristic chivalry and folly, he committed his brother to a pact which threatened to ruin all Bruce's cautious strategy and to change the very nature of the war Bruce had chosen to fight. The hard-pressed Moubray asked for a year's respite in which help was to arrive or else his position be proved untenable. This extremely generous term was conceded by Edward Bruce. If no English army came within three miles of Stirling to do battle for the castle before Midsummer 1314, Moubray would surrender. Possibly, in view of Edward II's struggle with his own great lords, embittered as it was by their judicial murder of Gaveston in 1312, Edward Bruce may have thought that Stirling would be cheaply bought. Yet faced by so public a challenge neither the king nor the barons of England could ignore the threat to their honour and the opportunity of ending the Scottish war once for all. King Robert was virtually compelled to meet the enemy in a pitched battle, the one thing he had striven to avoid since June 1306.

The affair earned Edward Bruce a sharp rebuke from the king,[43] but was not allowed to interfere with his plans to reduce the remaining enemy-held strongpoints. In the following winter Bruce turned to the two formidable strengths of Roxburgh – 'le March Mont (Marchmont)' in popular usage – and Edinburgh, 'le chateau des pucelles' or maidens' castle, clinging as stubbornly as lichen to its knob of volcanic rock. Well-guarded, these castles should have proved more than a match for ill-equipped besiegers. In fact, they fell within the space of a single Lent. On the night of February 19th–20th, 1314 (this was Shrove Tuesday and Ash Wednesday),[44] the Scots under James Douglas broke into Roxburgh castle and overwhelmed the garrison. Douglas and his men approached the walls at dead of night, crawling on their hands and knees, their body armour invisible under black surcoats. They carried the usual ingenious rope ladders, on this occasion apparently made by a man called Sim of the 'Ledows'.[45] Sim was the first man up. He made the way safe for the rest when he 'stekit upward with ane knyff' a sentry roused by the clatter as the grappling-hook of his ladder was lodged on the wall-head. Because it was Shrove Tuesday (Fastern's Eve) the garrison were relaxed, drinking and dancing. Taken utterly by surprise, many were killed or captured. Only their commander, a knight named Guillemin de Fenes from Bouglon in Gascony,[46] made any real resistance, shutting himself into a small turret. He surrendered the next day, however, and with his men was allowed to go freely to England.

Edinburgh castle was taken three weeks later by Thomas Randolph, obviously determined not to be outdone by Douglas.[47] The folk-hero in this case was William Francis, a local man whose father had served in the castle and whom the king afterwards rewarded with forfeited lands in Sprouston, Roxburghshire.[48] As a youth, Francis had had experience of climbing out of Edinburgh castle after dark when, without his father's knowledge, he was paying visits to his sweetheart in the town. On the night of March 14th, 1314 – once again, mercifully dark – a diversion was carried out at the East Port – 'the only place', says a contemporary, 'where an assault could be made'.[49] This sent the garrison rushing to the spot. Meanwhile, Francis and the other nimble leaders of the genuine assault party, rock-climbers before the art had been invented, inched their way in darkness up the steep and slippery north precipice, and swung their light siege ladders on to the masonry parapet. Up the ladders swarmed their followers, in numbers sufficient to over-whelm the astonished guards. The East Port was opened to admit the still larger force outside, and all was over. Most of the defenders fell in the fighting, but the commander, Sir Pierre Libaud (another Gascon), entered Bruce's service, only to be executed for treason soon afterwards. In accordance with his consistent policy, Bruce caused both Edinburgh and Roxburgh ('that fine castle', the Lanercost writer called it)[50] to be razed to the ground.

By their respective exploits at Roxburgh and Edinburgh, Douglas and Randolph set the seal on their already notable reputations. Already, in 1312, Bruce had demonstrated his confidence in Randolph and shown the value he set upon his support by making him earl of Moray and granting him, with wide powers, the lands of an earldom which had been in the possession of the Crown since 1130. Bruce, of course, was a man of his time. The greatest prizes in his gift went to men who were his own kin, like his nephew Randolph, or belonged to the circle of friends and allies of the Bruce family, like James Douglas and Walter Stewart, who had the greatest prize of all, the marriage of Bruce's daughter (and ultimate heir) Marjorie. His own brother Edward could hardly fail to be ennobled and honoured by Robert, but he and all the men to whom Bruce granted high office, noble title and rich estates proved their worth during the reign.

It is impossible to calculate the total of castles captured by Bruce between the autumn of 1307, when he took Inverlochy, and the fall of Edinburgh six years later. On any showing, this must be reckoned one of the great military enterprises of British history. But the achievement appears even more remarkable when we set it in its context of activity in three other spheres. The first, keeping open the Irish supply line and recovering the Isle of Man, we have noted already. The two other spheres consisted of profitable raids south of the Border and the resumption of commercial and diplomatic links with towns and countries of the continent.

From 1311 onward, the English in England itself came to learn what Bruce meant by 'defending himself with the longest stick that he had'. His idea of defence was attack, again and again at the same place or at many different places in rapid succession. He gave the enemy no rest. As early as 1307 Gallovidians and the cattle inseparably associated with them were sheltering from Bruce in Inglewood Forest, along with men from Liddesdale. Very soon there was no safety to be found in Cumberland, or indeed in any of the northern counties of England. It is true that between February 1309 and March 1310 (mainly owing to French exertions) some pretence of peace was maintained along the Border by a series of precarious truces. But after the collapse of Edward II's expedition of 1310–11 and his withdrawal from Scotland (August 1311) Bruce became far more aggressive.

Two students of this period, the late James Willard and Jean Scammell, have examined the effect of the Scottish raids upon the north of England.[51] Willard's starting-point was the records of the central government, especially the exchequer. He showed that in 1307, for example, Northumberland paid its normal share of a national property tax: £916 18s 11d. Two years later the county paid nothing, and in 1313 it was exempt. Much the same holds true for Cumberland and Westmorland. Working from the local north-country records as well as those of the central government, Mrs Scammell was able to fill in the grim details behind these bare fiscal facts. The 'community' of Northumberland, like the 'community' of Lothian, was forced to buy a truce from King Robert in 1311 and again from 1312 to 1313, each time for the colossal sum of £2,000. No one knew where the Scots would strike next – one month they poured across the fords of Solway to pillage and burn in Gilsland and the valley of the South Tyne; the next month they broke into Coquetdale and Redesdale, burning as far as Corbridge. There was no organized resistance. The English either tried to buy Bruce off or themselves resorted to burning to prevent the Scots getting supplies. What the Scots wanted more than anything was money, cattle and corn, the first two capable of being moved across difficult country with relative ease. Where possible they obtained what they wanted in the form of blackmail: for example, the mean of the earldom of Dunbar won temporary respite in 1313 for 1,000 quarters of corn.[52] If blackmail was not paid they overran the country with fire and sword, though the killing of human beings was relatively uncommon and was not Bruce's object. In August, 1311, for example, the Scots in upper Tynedale slew only those men who offered resistance.[53] But in the following summer they penetrated south of the Tyne, surprising a great throng of folk at Durham on market day. Here they inflicted great destruction, burning the town and killing many of the local people.[54] A few leading gentry of the Bishopric at once acted on their own initiative, for the bishop, Richard Kellaw, was away in the south attending parliament. They met Bruce in person at Hexham (August 16th, 1312) and bought a truce till midsummer 1313 for two thousand marks, 450 to be paid at Holm Cultram abbey by September 29th, 1312.[55] Cumberland, Coupland and Westmorland also bought a truce for the same period, and since they could not raise the whole sum were forced to yield hostages. On the approach of midsummer 1313, the Scottish king notified the northern counties that if they did not buy a fresh truce they would be raided. The mere threat was enough to bring promises of payment from the county communities. But when Cumberland had failed to pay by April 1314, instead of injuring the hostages, the Scots under Edward Bruce established themselves at Rose Castle and ravaged the surrounding countryside for some days.[56]

These raids and truce-bargains were extremely well organized and far more profitable and effective than the wild ravaging of Wallace's incursion in 1297. The Scottish staff-work was excellent, and discipline, now under royal authority, was strictly maintained. Estates which had obtained no immunity were systematically plundered. Estates which had paid for a truce were left in peace. Only in one case, the town of Hartlepool (where the Bruces had held lordship for over a century),[57] did the king appear to show vindictiveness. In 1315, the men of Hartlepool could not buy any truce from the Scottish king, and were forced to take refuge out at sea while their town was sacked (though not burned) by James Douglas.[58] In general, however, the English could have peace if they paid heavily for it. The effort proved too much for Northumberland, an ill-organized county which in any case was too vulnerable once the national defence system had broken down. After 1314 it 'ceased to negotiate as an entity',[59] The palatinate bishopric of Durham was much tougher, but the price which it paid for immunity (some £5,000 between 1311 and 1329) was at least twice what it would normally have paid in taxes; and even then it was forced to allow the Scots free passage across the county to raid south of the Tees. By the time Edward II had gathered his large army in the summer of 1314 to meet the challenge of Stirling, the four northern counties of England were close to exhaustion, either devastated or impoverished or both. The money which they should have paid to the exchequer at Westminster had gone, with two- or three-fold increase, to fill Bruce's empty war chest. The men who should have joined Edward's army resented the appeals of a king who could not defend his realm. Some had no money left, some had been slain or put to flight, some had even gone over to the Scots. For some years the northern counties contributed little to the English war-effort and actually contributed more to that of Bruce, but we are not entitled to conclude that their patriotism was lukewarm. Given strong leadership and an adequate defence system the English borderers would once more give a good account of themselves, as they had done in the twelfth and thirteenth centuries.

The vigour and high morale infused into the Scots by their king were not enough. Scotland needed arms and armour from abroad, and allies in every quarter where English interests were vulnerable or where English influence might be damaging. It is doubtful if, during the whole course of the Anglo-Scottish war, there was ever any prolonged blockage of the lines of communication between Scotland and the continent. The chief single reason for this lay in the fact that Scotland's attraction for foreign merchants consisted in her wool, an annual crop which it was best to dispose of without delay. It was always in demand in the Low Countries because of its fine quality. It did not occur to Edward I or his son to stop the trade in Scottish wool altogether, but naturally in the districts they controlled such profit as it made for the Crown went to the English, not Scottish coffers. Of course they did try to place an embargo on trade with Scots 'rebels'. But the Flemings, and perhaps still more the German or 'Eastland' merchants, with their ancient, well-established contacts with Scottish ports, showed no reluctance to trade with independent Scotland whether it was under the Guardians or under Robert Bruce. In December 1302, for example, a ship freighted with clothing, armour and other goods for independent Scotland, probably bound for Aberdeen and almost certainly coming from the Low Countries or a Hanseatic port, was captured off Filey in Yorkshire.[60] Merchants of St Omer were buying wool, hides and deerskins in Moray in 1303 or 1304.[61] In October 1309, Edward II complained bitterly to the count of Flanders that the Scots and their 'accomplices' the German merchants had been getting great help in succour from the Flemish towns.[62] Men of Hainault were involved in the Scottish trade in 1312.[63] We hear of a ship from the Baltic port of Stralsund being in alliance with the Scots some time before 1312, and of German merchants who before January 1313 had seized an English ship bound for occupied Scotland, sold the cargo at Aberdeen and taken the hull itself to Stralsund.[64]

It is true that our earliest record of formal relations between King Robert and continental powers, especially the Hanseatic, Flemish and other Low Country cities and principalities, comes from comparatively late in the reign. From 1321, for example, we have a royal letter to Lübeck and privileges issued in favour of Bruges;[65] from 1323 a letter to the count of Holland and Hainault.[66] It is not until 1316 that we have positive documentary evidence of the king negotiating with Genoese firms (then the best shipbuilders in Europe) for the supply of weapons and ships.[67] All this was after Bannockburn, and admittedly nothing succeeds like success. But it would be a mistake to think that foreign merchant communities waited for results before investing in the Scottish enterprise. Moreover, surprising as it may seem, the Scots found some of their best friends among English merchants of North Sea ports such as Harwich, Norwich, King's Lynn, Hull and English-held Berwick. The temptation to smuggle contraband to Scotland overcame both patriotism and fear of the harsh penalties threatened against those who trafficked with the 'rebels'.[68]

The evidence, though patchy and slight, is conclusive. During the early part of Bruce's reign the Scots and their North Sea associates were able to keep trade routes open, and supplies of foodstuffs, weapons and armour, iron and steel, all absolutely essential to the war effort, were reaching Scottish ports. Presumably these imports were being paid for by exports of wool, hides and timber in sufficient quantities to imply a recovery of the fairly simple Scottish economy from the dislocation and destruction of the years before 1304 and of the period from 1306 to 1309. Of course, in these years Scotland must have been even shorter of luxuries than usual, and prior to Bannockburn Bruce certainly never had enough weapons and ships to equip his forces as he would no doubt have liked. But, so far as these matters are ever determined by purely technological considerations, the thin yet steady trickle of vital imports seems to have made the difference between success and failure.

The importance which Bruce attached to the resumption of continental alliances is shown by his readiness to receive envoys from the French kings, although the truces with England which were several times arranged through their influence were not much to his liking. There is record of truce negotiations of this kind, some of which may have been meant seriously to lead to a peace treaty, in 1308–9, in 1309–10, and in January 1312.[69] In January 1313, Abbot Maurice of Inchaffray, one of King Robert's most loyal and trusted supporters, was given an English safe-conduct to visit Edward II,[70] presumably to discuss a truce or a peace, and later in the same year representatives of King Robert (including Bishop Lamberton) and of King Edward appear to have been appointed to negotiate truce or peace in conjunction with the agents of the king of France and at his request.[71] We shall see that six years after Bannockburn the French king was deeply involved again in efforts to secure peace between Scots and English. There is no reason to believe that Bruce's attitude towards these negotiations was frivolous or cynical. But it is clear that he never allowed them to affect his military and strategic dispositions, and also that any serious peace talks would have to start from a recognition of his title to the Scottish Crown on the part of Edward II.

Long before there was anything which could be called a revived Franco-Scottish alliance (as distinct from friendly intercourse) Bruce had taken measures to preserve the good relations with Norway which had existed more or less continuously since 1295.[72] Scoto-Norwegian friendship had been threatened by a number of incidents. It seems that pirates from Scotland had kidnapped the seneschal of Orkney, a Norwegian knight, after he had collected the royal revenues and while the money was still in his possession. He had been held to ransom both for himself and for his money. In addition, there had been Scottish raids on Shetland. For their part, the Scots complained that an esquire named Patrick Mowat had been arrested in Orkney by a royal bailiff, beaten, chained, robbed of his goods and forced to ransom himself for forty merks. Still more serious was the affair of some Scots merchants, burgesses of St Andrews, who on arrival in Norway for the purpose of trading seem to have been treated as hostages. Their goods, worth £600, were seized, and they themselves suffered a lengthy imprisonment before they were allowed to sail home empty-handed. These incidents may have an ugly look, but by the standards of international behaviour prevailing at the time none of them was atrocious. They can hardly have put Scoto-Norwegian relations in serious jeopardy, and for sheer horror cannot compare with an incident of 1316 which must have imposed a much greater strain upon relations between Norway and England.[73] Some English merchants from Berwick, having put in at a Norwegian port, invited aboard the provincial governor and ten other noblemen, who to save their hosts expense went unarmed and without servants. Instead of a second course, the merchants showered their guests with boiling water and hot cinders and then killed them with daggers and swords. Norwegian grievances against Scotland were probably less concerned with incidents, major or minor, than with the Scottish failure to maintain the terms of the treaty of Perth in 1266, by which the Scots kings were bound to pay a perpetual annuity to Norway of 100 merks. The agreement sealed at Inverness on October 29th, 1312, between King Robert in person and the envoys of King Hakon V, shows that both sides were anxious for a settlement and prepared to be sensible and statesmanlike. The Perth treaty was renewed without any alteration, and though nothing was said about past failures to pay the annuity its regular payment was promised in the future. The Scots agreed to pay 600 merks in final compensation for the kidnapping of the seneschal of Orkney; the Norwegians restored the goods taken from the merchants of St Andrews. The plundering of Shetland and the affair of Patrick Mowat were to be investigated by faithful inquest.

Among the few persons whom we know to have been involved in making the treaty of Inverness there are two clergymen, Farquhar Bellejambe bishop of Caithness and Bernard the chancellor, whose participation is worth noting. From the date of his appointment to the archdeaconry of Caithness in 1297[74] by King Edward I we have no evidence that Farquhar Bellejambe, who rose to be dean and then (1306) bishop of Caithness, played any positive part in political affairs or that he had supported the Guardians before the collapse of 1304. Nor does he seem to have come out in support of Robert Bruce in his early years, as the bishops of Moray and Ross had done. In 1312, however, Bishop Farquhar was one of the two Scots churchmen who took oath on behalf of King Robert for the security of the Inverness treaty, and it is clear that by this time, if not indeed earlier, the king had gained the allegiance of one more Scottish bishop. As for Chancellor Bernard, his importance to the king has already been emphasized. Between March 1310 and June 1311 there is no evidence that King Robert made use of his great seal to authenticate his written instruments.[75] Instead, he seems to have used the privy seal only. The great seal was, of course, kept by the chancellor, and used only on his own authorization. Now it was about this time that Bernard was made abbot of Arbroath,[76] and it can hardly be a coincidence that an abbot of Arbroath was absent in Norway on the king's business (and his own) at some unknown date within this general period.[77] It is more than probable that Bernard was sent to Norway to conduct the negotiations which led to the treaty of Inverness. If so it would be a clear indication of the great store which King Robert set by the continuance of Norwegian friendship.

If, in the spring of 1314, Robert Bruce, now in his fortieth year, had taken stock of the situation in which Scotland found itself, his feelings could surely have been summed up as a sort of anxious satisfaction. Much, incredibly much, had been achieved in the vindication of Scottish independence. Scarcely one castle was left with a foreign garrison which could inflict serious harm on the surrounding inhabitants. Within the Scottish kingdom itself every province from Galloway to Caithness, from the Outer Isles to Buchan acknowledged Bruce as king. Beyond the Border, from Tweed and Solway southward as far as Stainmore and the Tees, the English had been made to feel the menace of a Scotland awakened and revivified under a new ruler. Armies had been raised under a new generation of young captains who were accustomed to victory instead of defeat, and who showed a flexibility in tactics and a readiness to depend upon properly trained infantry which was in the sharpest contrast with the kind of warfare waged by the Guardians. Something like the accustomed machinery of government was once again in operation, and it is fair to infer that judicial activity and the collection of royal revenue had been resumed on a national scale. Three parliaments had been held, at St Andrews in 1309 and at Inchture[78] and Ayr in 1312, and probably there were others of which we have no record. King Robert and his subjects were now taken seriously by foreign kingdoms such as France and Norway, and by foreign trading cities and industrial princi-palities, such as the Hanse and Flanders. If, at this point, the king of England and his barons had been capable of far-sighted statesmanship, there was surely nothing to prevent a resumption of the happier relationship which prevailed between England and Scotland during the reign of Alexander III. Alas, in Edward of Caernarvon England possessed one of the stupidest kings who have ever sat upon her throne, and among the ranks of his baronage and higher clergy (with the possible exception of Aymer de Valence, earl of Pembroke) one may search in vain for anything resembling statesmanship. Perhaps the nearest approach to peace had come in 1312 or 1313, after the collapse of King Edward's second Scottish expedition. The negotiations, though encouraged by Philip the Fair, had failed, and there seemed no possibility of the English king recognizing Robert Bruce's title to the throne of Scotland. The challenge of Stirling Castle was thus the occasion rather than the cause of a head-on clash between the forces of the two countries. Reluctantly perhaps, but methodically and with determination, Bruce began to prepare his troops for the greatest trial of strength they had yet faced.

NOTES

1 *Calendar of Documents Relating to Scotland*, ed. J. Bain (Edinburgh, 1881–88), iii, no. 202.

2 T. Wright, *Political Songs of England* (Camden Soc., 1839), 216: 'Now Kyng Hobbe in the mures gongeth/For te come to toune nout him ne longeth.' The news of Bruce's rising and of his flight in the heather quickly reached Italy, for Villani refers to Edward I's failure to subdue 'Ruberto di Busoo' who with his followers had fled to the bogs and wild mountains of Scotland; G. Villani, *Historiae universali de suoi tempi* (Florence, 1570), 340–1.

3 *Rotuli Scotiae in Turri Londinensi et in Domo Capitulari Westmonasteriensi Asservati* . . . eds. D. Macpherson and others (1814–19) [*Rotuli Scotiae*], i, 61 (for 'Landyan' read 'Laudyan', Lothian).

4 *Chronicon de Lanercost* (Maitland Club, 1839) [*Chron. Lanercost*], 214.

5 *Rotuli Scotiae*, I, 61b; *Cal. Docs. Scot.*, iii, no. 245.

6 *Ibid.*, no. 186 (= PRO, Ancient Petitions 7743). It is clear from the original that Bain's dating is wrong, and that this belongs to 1312, and refers to the truce mentioned in *Rotuli Scotiae*, i, III. Bain's summary is misleading and inadequate.

7 *Rotuli Scotiae*, i, III; *illorum qui ex parte predicti Roberti se tenent*; PRO, Ancient Petitions 7743, para 2: *les gentz del enemiste*.

8 *Chron. Lanercost*, 217.

9 *Ibid.*, 217. This is borne out by surviving letters of Sir John Graham referring to Eskdale in 1309 (*Melrose Liber*, nos. 378–80).

10 For an assessment of the position of the inhabitants of south-eastern Scotland in this period, cf. G. W. S. Barrow, 'Lothian in the first War of Independence', *Scottish Historical Review*, lv, 151–71; *idem.*, 'The aftermath of war: Scotland and England

in the late thirteenth and early fourteenth centuries', *Transactions of the Royal Historical Society*, 5th Ser., xxvii (1978), 103–25.

11 W. Fraser, *The Chiefs of Grant* (Edinburgh, 1883), iii, no 11. For a tradition concerning the lordship and name Glencarnie (Glenchernich), whose seat was where Boat of Garten now is, see L. Shaw, *History of the Province of Moray* (1775), 39n. The lands of Glencarnie were held of the earls of Strathearn.

12 A charter of August 8th, 1309, preserved at Cawdor Castle, is dated 'Loch Bren', ie Loch a 'Bhraoin, now in Scots Loch Broom; another, of October 20th, 1309, is dated at Dunstaffnage: *Register Regum Scottorum*, eds. G. W. S. Barrow and others [*RRS*], v, nos. 9, 10.

13 *The Chronicle of Walter of Guisborough*, ed. H. Rothwell (Camden, 3rd ser., lxxix, 1957) [*Chron. Guish.*], 385–6: the English burned and laid waste, and the Scots lurked in hills and boggy places. *Rotuli Scotiae*, i, 80 and *Cal. Docs. Scot.*, iii, no. 218 are the chief authorities here.

14 *Cal. Docs. Scot.*, iii, no. 221.

15 *Rotuli Scotiae*, i, 80.

16 *Ibid.*

17 *Ibid.*, 60a; J. Barbour, *The Bruce*, ed. W. M. Mackenzie (London, 1909), 190

18 *Rotuli Scotiae*, i, 106.

19 *Cal. Docs. Scot.*, iii, no. 304; cf. no. 279.

20 *Ibid.*, no. 218.

21 *Rotuli Scotiae*, i, 86.

22 *Ibid.*, 99b; cf. 90a, 93b.

23 *Ibid.*, 90b.

24 *Ibid.*, 96.

25 *Chron. Lanercost*, 210.

26 *The Chronicle of Man and the Sudreys*, eds. P. A. Munch and Rev Dr Goss (Manx Society, Douglas, 1874) [*Chron. Man*], 233–4; *Rotuli Scotiae*, i, 96, 107a; *Cal. Docs. Scot.*, iii, no 481.

27 *Ibid.*; cf. nos. 277, 391.

28 *Ibid.*, nos. 307, 391. Simon Montague's involvement in Man seems to have gone back as early as 1305 (*Chron. Man*, 233).

29 *Chron. Man*, ed. P. A. Munch (Christiania, 1860), 27–8.

30 *Cal. Docs. Scot.*, iii, *passim*, references in index. In 1317 Dungal supervised the funeral in London of John Macdougall of Lorn who died at Ospringe in Kent while on pilgrimage to Canterbury; Dungal may have regarded the lord of Argyll as his kinsman: *Cal. Docs. Scot.*, v, pp 230-1.

31 *Ibid.*, iii, no. 420; J. R. S. Phillips, 'The mission of John de Hothum to Ireland, 1315–1316' in *England and Ireland in the Later Middle Ages*, ed. J. F. Lydon, 62.

32 *Cal. Docs. Scot.*, no. 562.

33 *Ibid.*, no. 451.

34 Barbour, *Bruce*, 257; *Cal. Docs. Scot.*, iii, no. 562.

35 *Chron. Lanercost*, 220.

36 *Ibid.*, 214; *Chron. Guish.*, 386.

37 *Cal. Docs. Scot.*, iii, 425–7.

38 *Ibid.*, no. 45; *Rotuli Scotiae*, i, 61b.

39 *Ibid.*, 105b.

40 Barbour, *Bruce*, 158.

41 *Ibid.*, 160; but cf. *Johannis de Fordun, Chronica Gentis Scotorum*, ed. W. F. Skene (Edinburgh, 1871–2) [*Chron. Fordun*], I, 346; *Chron. Lanercost*, 221-2.

42 Barbour, *Bruce*, 191.

43 *Ibid.*, 192.

44 *A Scottish Chronicle known as the Chronicle of Holyrood*, ed. M. O. Anderson (Scottish History Society, 1938) [*Chron. Holyrood*], 180; Barbour, *Bruce*, 178–82.

45 *Ibid.*, 179, Sym of the Ledows. Ledhous (Leidhous, etc) was the name of some lands beside Crossford in Lesmahagow parish, the next parish north of Douglas.

46 *Ibid.*, 181; *Chron. Lanercost*, 223; *Cal. Docs. Scot.*, iii, 406 and elsewhere *passim*; *Scalacronica by Sir Thomas Gray of Heton Knight* (Maitland Club, 1836), 140, reading *de* for *et* before Burglioun. Bouglon is in dep Lot-et-Garonne, arr. Marmande.

47 Barbour, *Bruce*, 182–90; *Chron. Holyrood*, 180.

48 *Registrum Magni Sigilii Regum Scotorum*, eds., J. M. Thomson and others (Edinburgh, 1877–), i, Appendix II, nos. 285, 373.

49 *Chron. Lanercost*, 223, perhaps meaning 'east' port, not 'south'.

50 *Ibid.*

51 J. F. Willard, 'The Scotch raids and the fourteenth-century taxation of northern England', *University of Colorado Studies*, v (1907–8), no. 4, 237–42; Jean Scammell, 'Robert I and the north of England', *English Historical Review.*, lxxiii, 385–403.

52 *Cal. Docs. Scot.*, iii, no. 337.

53 *Chron. Lanercost*, 216.

54 *Ibid.*, 220; *Historia Dunelmensis Ecclesiae Scriptores Tres* (ed. J. Raine, Surtees Soc.), 94.

55 *Ibid.*; E. C. G. Stones, *Anglo-Scottish Relations 1171–1328: Some Selected Documents* (2nd edn., 1970), no. 37; *RRS*, v, no. 21.

56 *Chron. Lanercost*, 224.

57 PRO, D. L. 36, iii, fo. 12, 3rd doc; *Cal. Docs. Scot.*, i, no. 321; iii, no. 413.

58 *Chron. Lanercost*, 230; cf. also *Cal. Docs. Scot.*, iii, nos. 602, 631, 648, the last two referring to the capture of a Scottish ship at or off Hartlepool early in 1319.

59 J. Scammell, *art. cit.*, 386.

60 *Cal. Docs. Scot.*, ii, no. 1479.

61 *Ibid.*, no. 1639 and 443.

62 *Rotuli Scotiae*, i, 78b.

63 W. Stanford Reid, 'Trade, traders and Scottish independence', *Speculum*, xxix, 217, citing H. J. Smit, *Bronnen tot Geschiedenis van den Handel med Engelond etc.* (The Hague, 1928), i, 214. The whole of Reid's article, and also that by Jas. W. Dilley, 'German merchants in Scotland, 1297–1327' *Scottish Historical Review*, xxvii, 142–55, should be read for a survey of the evidence on trade between Scotland and the continent in this period.

64 *Cal. Docs. Scot.*, iii, nos. 252, 679.

65 Jas. W. Dilley, 'Scottish–German Diplomacy', *Scottish Historical Review*, xxxvi, 83.

66 *Ibid.*, 85.

67 W. Stanford Reid, *art. cit.*, 422.

68 Reid, *art. cit.*, stresses the importance of smuggling for the Scots in this period.

69 *Rotuli Scotiae*, i, 59–60; 107–8.

70 *Cal. Docs. Scot.*, iii, no. 300; cf. *Rotuli Scotiae*, i, 112.

71 *Ibid.*; *Cal. Docs. Scot.*, iii, no. 346.

72 *The Acts of the Parliament of Scotland*, eds. T. Thomson and C. Innes (12 vols., Edinburgh, 1814–75), i, 461–4.

73 *Cal. Docs. Scot.*, iii, no. 346.

74 *Ibid.*, ii, no. 927. Farquhar Bellejambe had been a canon of Aberdeen.

75 *RRS*, v, Introduction.

76 *Liber S. Thome de Aberbrothoc* (Bannatyne Club, 1848–56), i, no. 332.

77 *Ibid.*, no. 360.

78 *RRS*, v, nos. 17, 18.

The Exercise of Power: The King

Extracted from JM Brown 1977 (ed), *Scottish Society in the Fifteenth Century*, London (Edward Arnold), 33–51.

Government in fifteenth-century Scotland was monarchical government, the most familiar form of medieval government and having much in common with other western European monarchies. Scottish kings, like their contemporaries, worked through formal institutions, their chancery and exchequer, council and parliament. These institutions were less sophisticated and complex than their English or French counterparts. At the most formal and technical level, Scottish royal clerks were perfectly competent in producing official documents, as comparison between English and Scottish privy-seal and signet letters illustrates.[1] But there was no equivalent in Scotland of, for example, the vigorous English house of commons, highly self-conscious about its rights and privileges. Nor did there exist established central courts of justice or a secular legal profession: it was only in this century that there came into existence a central court at all – the session, brought into being by James I to relieve the council of some of the burden of judicial cases. Moreover the Scottish crown was not wealthy by any standards and certainly not in comparison with the English; the incomplete financial records make it impossible to be certain about the king's revenue, but it would appear that it was at best one tenth of that of the English monarch, and very probably less.[2]

The Scottish crown was, therefore, comparatively impoverished, both in real terms and in the sense that its central institutions were relatively undeveloped. In addition there was the appalling problem of successive royal minorities, amounting overall between 1406 and 1488 to thirty-eight years, compared to the forty-four when an adult king was on the throne. Yet from another point of view, the Scottish monarchy of the fifteenth century enjoyed a position of greater strength than that of England. It was unchallenged. Only once was there anything which can be accurately described as a usurpation attempt, and that was the unsupported claim to the throne by James III's brother in 1482. Nor was it endangered from without, for the last serious threat of English overlordship came from Edward III. Indeed, far from being defensive, the Stewart kings showed a new, outward-looking self-confidence. For the first time since 1286, they looked further afield than their own country or England for brides; a daughter of James I was married to the dauphin, and James II regarded himself as of sufficient European importance to offer to arbitrate in a dispute between the French king and his heir. If there were weaknesses, there was also certainly strength. The problem is the source of that strength.

The question of what monarchy meant in Scotland would be difficult to answer even with a great deal more information than exists. Commentary on an accepted form of government was rare in the middle ages, and virtually non-existent in Scotland, while what there was tended to be very general, going no further than the dictum of the English lawyer, Sir John Fortescue: 'Regis namque officium pugnare est bella populi sui, et eos rectissime iudicare'.[3] General as they were, however, these two principles were fundamental, and they provide some kind of yardstick in assessing what was expected of a Scottish king, as is indicated by the known reactions to the actions of the kings themselves.

The first principle was taken literally. The idea of the king taking the field in battle died out in Britain in the mid-eighteenth century, earlier than in Europe. But until then, in spite of occasional disasters, such as Neville's Cross in 1346, when David II was captured by the English, saddling his country with the problems of an absentee king and a large ransom, and Roxburgh and Flodden, when James II and James IV were killed, both leaving a child to succeed them, it was never seriously questioned that kings should lead their army in person. Thus in March 1482, faced with the threat of an English invasion, it was resolved in parliament that if the English wardens led the invading force it should be met by the Scottish wardens and lieutenants given sufficient power for the time; but if the 'saide Revare Edward [Edward IV] happinis to cum in proper persoun, to be resistit be oure soverane lord in proper persoun'.[4] A century later, while there was no occasion for the principle to be called into operation, its continued acceptability is attested by the growing legend of James III, which depicted him as a man who had no ability in warlike pursuits and failed as a military leader, ultimately dying a coward's death in flight from battle.[5] Even shortly after Flodden, a disaster on an unparalleled scale in a country where battle with the English normally meant defeat, John Major could write an account of that earlier disaster, the death of James II at Roxburgh in 1460, which showed no sign of any feeling that the price might be too high: 'for vigorous kingship, most writers give the first place to this monarch, seeing that he gave himself with all zeal to things of war and naught else; and in time of war he was fellow to every private soldier. I, however, prefer before him his father, the first James, alike for his natural endowment and his fortitude in field.'[6]

The first of Fortescue's principles is straightforward enough. The second is more complicated, for it meant far more than is immediately implied by the word 'iudicare', and indeed, it is curious that it is expressed in terms of justice rather than of good government. Two long-accepted and standard comments on medieval kingship were that government was the king's government, personally controlled and inspired by him, and that the king was the fountain of justice; but in the fifteenth century, reference was normally made only to the second of these.[7] In fact the idea that a king should provide justice for his subjects was very comprehensive. It did not simply mean that he had a duty to make available justice in his courts, although that was part of it, and in the fifteenth century there was increased demand for royal justice. It included also the obligation to deal justly with his subjects, to cope adequately with rebellion and disorder, to create conditions in which people could obtain justice, with all the benefits of peace and security for person and possessions which would follow from that; in other words, to provide strong government as well as effective courts.

But to defend one's country and to govern it, kings required money, or, at any rate, so the kings of England and France thought. So also, to an extent, did the kings of Scotland, the problem being that they had much less of it. Their lack of money had a profound effect on how they exercised royal power. They could not, even if they wanted, aim at anything like the degree of centralization of the governments of England and France, nor begin to build up power at the centre at the expense of power in the localities: for they could not pay officials in the way that the English crown could pay, for example, its wardens of the marches, nor could they pay the judges and lawyers. And at no time did they have the money to raise a contract army.[8]

Yet the problem is not simply that the Scottish crown was too impoverished to emulate its European contemporaries. Poverty can be a relative thing. By comparison with the revenues of the kings of England and France, that of the kings of Scotland was so small as to appear derisory. But their expenditure as rulers of a smaller country with a much smaller population was also very much less. Moreover, it is difficult to say with certainty that the Scottish monarchy was particularly poor, in the sense that it did not have money for the things that it wanted. The evidence is so far from complete that only once is it possible to estimate the king's revenue – £16,380 Scots for the year 1486 – and even that is probably too generous. The evidence is also conflicting, for it suggests grave financial problems, sometimes crises.[9] But it also shows, for at least parts of the period, a surprising degree of spending power, and on one occasion the possession by the crown of a very considerable amount of money. All the Stewart kings were conspicuous spenders, interested in building, in presiding over a court which, though smaller than those of fellow monarchs, was by no means one of which they need feel ashamed, in being patrons of the arts, if again on a comparatively limited scale, in spending great sums on artillery, on the navy, on dress, on making a show which befitted a king. James I was apparently in debt at his death in 1437, though that was a situation far from unique to Scottish kings. James III was in financial straits in 1482 yet, after his death at Sauchieburn in 1488, boxes were found, including one picked up on the battlefield, containing sums of money amounting to £24,517 10s, an amount perhaps equal to two years' revenue. It has been rightly pointed out that this 'serves as a warning to those who try to write the financial history of his reign from the exchequer rolls alone'; but it is simply not known how he managed to acquire this money.[10]

What this seems to suggest is a curious hand-to-mouth quality about the attitude of the fifteenth-century kings to their cash revenue, a desire to have money for specific purposes, but a lack of long-term economic thought and an indifference to capitalizing on such opportunities as they had. A striking feature of this century is the great increase in the amount of land possessed by the crown. Both James I and James II were in marked degree acquisitive, indeed avaricious. Both added considerably to the royal demesne, principally through the forfeiture of a few great families; the extensive lands of the Douglases, which came to the crown after their forfeiture in 1455 as a single windfall, were a dramatic addition. Yet these lands were not used, to anything like the extent they could have been, to build up cash revenue. This was not simply because of lack of currency; it has been argued, in a discussion of crown lands in the late fifteenth and early sixteenth centuries, that 'the continued appearance of rents [of crown lands] in kind in the rentals and exchequer rolls should be ascribed to the conservatism of the financial system, not to the poverty of the country or the shortage of coin.'[11] In 1455 and again in 1458, suggestions for change actually came not from the crown but from parliament.

The first move was the act of annexation of 1455, the attempt to make the crown husband its resources. This began with the statement that 'the poverte of the crowne is oftymis the caus of the poverte of the Realme' – admittedly hardly profound economic comment – and went on to insist that certain lands, lordships and castles, which were listed, should be annexed to the crown and inalienable by it without consent of parliament. The act went on to make the amazing provision that if the king did grant any of these lands without consent, they were recoverable by the crown, and the recipient would be obliged to pay back any profits he had made. It stated that James was sworn to observe this, and that his successors would be likewise bound in their coronation oaths. This was followed up in 1458 by a suggestion which, if adopted, would have increased the crown's money revenue: parliament thought it 'speidfull that the king begyne and gif exempill to the laif' by feuing his lands.[12] But the crown did not adopt the idea, to any significant extent, until the reign of James IV, when its cash income was indeed increased by this method.

What parliament wanted was, presumably, a situation similar to that demanded much more frequently in England, that the king should live of his own.[13] There is no evidence in Scotland of a tradition of conflict between king and parliament about this principle. But if it was not a matter for regular discussion, the point made in 1455 was the same, that the king had sufficient lands to do two things, both admirable – one, to give grants to those who served him well and merited them; the other, to support his household and government without recourse to other means, provided that he acted on the first point with moderation. But there was one element lacking on the Scottish side, taxation; only in a negative sense can it be regarded as an issue, to the extent that, if the act was observed, regular taxation would not be necessary. This, even more than the failure to take up the idea of feuing, is the remarkable and crucial difference between the kings of Scotland and their northern European contemporaries. They did not tax regularly. David II had done so, in the last decade of his reign, but that was exceptional, and can be explained largely in terms of the ransom he was obliged to pay.[14] Yet James I was also saddled with a ransom, and he did not manage to impose regular taxation. It is not enough to explain this on the grounds that there was resentment against taxation itself, and against James's use of his ransom as an excuse while pocketing the money for other purposes. Probably there was resentment, but the question is the wider one of why the Scottish kings did not make use of a practice which was long established in England and becoming so in France.

No doubt part of the explanation of the contrast between Scotland and France in this period lies in the fact that the French kings could do what the Scottish kings could not, namely use war as a legitimate reason for taxing regularly, and having begun, simply continue.[15] Lack of taxation in itself helps to explain why Scottish government was much less complex than that of England or France; without it, there was less money to pay royal officials, but also less need for them, for the administrative sophistication of these other countries. It helps, moreover, to explain the failure of James I's attempt to involve the lairds, the equivalent of the English knights of the shire, in parliament; there was less incentive for them to turn up, to assert their rights, when their pockets were touched very much less. The argument at this stage becomes circular. But there is a central point at the heart of it. It is not just that Scottish subjects consistently managed to put up successful resistance to attempts by the crown to levy taxation regularly. The kings themselves did not think as their contemporaries thought in England and France. They did not try to tax regularly. Even when they did require to raise an army, or needed money for embassies or a royal marriage, they did not necessarily demand taxation and, on the occasions when they did, their demands were limited. This suggests a different approach to the business of governing their country on the part of the kings of Scotland, and makes the yardstick which could be used in England and France – the degree of success which kings had in building up government at the centre – much less applicable.

There were positive reasons why Scottish kings should not have tried to tax. Given the much smaller population, they would, for example, have had to tax infinitely more heavily than the kings of England or France to pay for an army of comparable size. It is not surprising that they did not try to do so; it was a matter of common sense. But there is a danger here of imposing too great a degree of rationalization. There remains the question of whether they began with the assumption that it was unrealistic to try to impose regular taxation and that therefore they had to accept a different style of government, even if it was second best, or whether they simply assumed that their style of government was suited to the country they ruled and that as a result they did not consider substantially different possibilities.

In fact, they relied heavily on the personal cooperation of their most powerful subjects, more heavily than other fifteenth-century monarchs, although this was a matter of degree not of kind. Thus when they were involved in war, they depended on the landowners using their personal power to turn out their men. This did mean that they had problems not faced by kings who could pay their troops. There is a certain irony, for example, in the later legend of James III, in that on four occasions James proposed military campaigns which foundered on the refusal of the magnates to fight. Any war must have a measure of popular support. But James III's experience demonstrates the peculiar relevance of this in Scotland, to an extent not found, for example, in England, where kings could pay for their armies. In 1400, Henry IV, the usurper, attempting to increase his prestige, sought to do so by mounting an expensive and, as it proved, humiliating campaign against Scotland. It was made clear in parliament that it was the king's decision, but the fact that the enthusiasm of both Lords and Commons was less than the king's did not prevent the campaign from taking place. Henry raised an army, not by indenture, but by summons to those who had personal bonds with him. It cost over £10,000; the money came mainly from loans, which the king repaid by the third year of his reign.[16] This is something which could not have been undertaken by the Scottish crown.

Even when the Scottish kings did raise money, the contrast with England was dramatic. In 1482, £13,000 was allocated from the English exchequer to finance an army of 20,000 men under Richard, duke of Gloucester, to take Berwick and return home in twenty-eight days; a further £595 was paid out for a force of 1,700 men to remain in the north with Gloucester for fourteen days thereafter.[17] In Scotland, in April 1481, under threat of an English invasion, parliament agreed to raise a 'contribucioun' of 7,000 merks Scots each from the clergy and barons, and 1,400 from the burghs, with exemption for those landed men who went in person to Berwick. In March 1482, with invasion certain, the estates agreed that, as the king had already financed the strengthening of the fortifications of Berwick and would pay for a garrison of 500 men for three months, they would provide and pay for 600 soldiers, to be stationed along the borders. The detailed attention given to this makes curiously pathetic reading when set against the machine-like efficiency of the English plan of campaign. All that was done to ensure that, when these small garrisons of sixty or more frequently twenty men were mown down by the English, there would be a Scottish army to meet them, was to direct the sheriffs to hold weapon-showings every fifteen days, and to be ready to call out the lieges, well armed and with provisions, and turn up as quickly as possible when summoned.[18] The obligation of able-bodied men to fight for their country was a common one; in Scotland it did not necessarily involve payment from the crown.

The king was therefore particularly dependent on the cooperation of men of influence in the localities, and this gave heightened importance to the popularity of the campaign. Neither James I nor James II had any difficulty in raising armies to besiege Roxburgh, the English-held town which was a thorn in the side of the Scots, because it was an English enclave within Scotland. James I's campaign in 1436 failed. But this did not lessen the enthusiasm to try again, as is reflected in the contemporary chronicler's account of the great host which accompanied James II in 1460. No estimate can be made of what was meant by 'ane gret ost', but the army's own enthusiasm is indicated by the fact that even when the king had been killed when watching a gun which exploded, it remained to capture Roxburgh.[19] These campaigns and occasional forays into northern England, popular with the border lords, attracted support; they had the double advantage of offering the chance of fighting the traditional enemy, England, while not involving the Scots in a pitched battle where the odds were weighted against them. Indeed, the desire to avoid engaging the English in battle was a marked feature of military policy since the reign of Robert II, arousing the contempt of the French troops who came to Scotland in 1385, but remarkably successful in its effect of leaving invading English armies with no one to fight and nothing to do but create a certain amount of havoc in the lowlands, and retreat.[20]

The other important element which had a bearing on men's willingness to fight was the personal prestige of the king. Both James I and James II commanded respect, and proposed popular campaigns. The other military enterprise which roused tremendous and remarkable enthusiasm was the Flodden campaign in 1513. This was a distinct break in the pattern of not fighting the English, and it was a battle fought as a result of James IV's ambitious foreign policy, in French interests. What the overwhelming support for it reflects is the extent of the popularity which the king enjoyed. In sharp contrast are the reactions to the military proposals of James III.

Early in his reign, James sought to raise armies for campaigns which were both over-ambitious and frivolous. In 1471 he proposed to take over part of the duchy of Brittany, and in 1473 to acquire Saintonge and annex the duchy of Gueldres. In no way could this be regarded as defence of the kingdom and indeed, one of the main points of the clergy's opposition in 1471 was the danger of leaving Scotland vulnerable to English attack.[21] In 1473, parliament again objected strongly to James's plans, this time telling him bluntly 'to tak part of labour apon his persone & travel throw his Realme & put sic Justice & policy in his awne realme that the brute & the fame of him mycht pas in utheris contreis'.[22] This stricture gives one contemporary evaluation of what was wanted of the king – to get on with the business of governing his country, and not to seek renown in risky and grandiose schemes for foreign adventuring.

A decade later, lack of enthusiasm for a particular campaign and hostility to the king came together to create a situation which ended with the brutal humiliation of James III. A number of the magnates, summoned to the muster of the army at Lauder in July 1482, chose to ignore the threat from the invading English army, which included Alexander, duke of Albany, making a bid to seize his brother's throne; instead, they forced a showdown with James, who was brought back to Edinburgh and temporarily incarcerated in the castle by his half-uncles, the earls of Buchan and Atholl, and the bishop-elect of Moray. Defence of Berwick, the main target of the English attack, was much more justifiable than James's earlier schemes. But there is room for doubt about the extent of Scottish commitment to retaining Berwick. For the English, in spite of the criticisms of one contemporary, on the grounds of the expense and difficulty of holding the town, it was a matter of prestige; they had held it from 1356 until 1461, when it was handed over to the Scots by Henry VI and Margaret of Anjou, desperate for support after the Lancastrian defeat at Towton.[23] To James III also, Berwick was important; after its loss, he made it an issue in negotiations with England during the last six years of his reign. But his concern does not seem to have been shared by others. An offer to consider handing over Berwick and Roxburgh made in 1433 by the English, anxious to weaken the Franco-Scottish alliance, was rejected, and the Scots concentrated their military efforts only on Roxburgh, lying within Scotland. Nor was there any military attempt to retrieve the loss of 1482. The refusal to defend Berwick suggests that they did not regard it as a matter of top priority at a time of internal crisis, when grievances against the king's government had come to a head.

What this episode demonstrates is that this king did not command the respect and support of his greatest subjects. Thus his chances of persuading them to support him were reduced and, lacking the resources to pay for an army, James's intention to fight could be checkmated. But the refusal to support the king was a symptom and not the cause of the trouble. In 1473, James was told by parliament what was the business of a king; indeed, successive parliaments, in the 1470s and 1480s, criticized him for his laziness, his interest only in the profits of justice. That he failed to raise an army in 1482, and was faced instead with an opposition which this time resorted to violent means, is a measure of the extent to which his authority had broken down.[24] The feature common to both parliamentary criticism and violent opposition was that the way in which James had acted as king was regarded as unacceptable. Parliament in 1473 had indicated where he had gone wrong when it begged the king to 'put sic Justice & policy in his awne realme'. It was talking about the other great principle that the king should follow, the principle that he should do justice. In fifteenth-century Scotland, the general lack of enthusiasm for warfare and the particular reaction to James III suggest that here, as elsewhere, this was by far the more important principle.

Reliance on personal cooperation, not paid service, is as evident in the way in which the fifteenth-century kings governed their country as it is in the way they defended it. This is in no way lessened by the fact that there were, not surprisingly, developments and improvements in administration; the business of government tends at any time to produce increasing quantities of red tape. For example, greater attention was paid to the keeping of records, and to making them easier to use and refer to by having them in book form rather than rolls. There was an increasingly bureaucratized attitude to authentication, and the order of chancery – signature, signet, privy seal and great seal – was established certainly by the reign of James IV, and probably earlier. The number of royal officials in financial administration grew; in the reign of James I, the treasurer and comptroller replaced the chamberlain as the crown's chief financial official, and *ballivi ad extra* appeared on the royal demesne.[25]

But administrative developments do not necessarily mean increased centralization. How remote was the desire to increase central power at the expense of local power is nowhere more clearly seen than in the attitudes of both king and subjects to the way in which the king should fulfil his second obligation, to provide justice. Both law and the lawyers were becoming more professionalized, and there was set up, by James I, a royal court intended to remove pressure of business from council and parliament.[26] But the original idea of how this court should function was not that it should be a central court; rather, it was peripatetic, meeting three times a year in different part of the country. There was no encouragement for people to come to the capital when they sought royal justice. Indeed, it is not altogether clear where the capital was in the early fifteenth century, for it was not until the reign of James III that Edinburgh shook off rivalry from Perth and Stirling as the place where the king's business was done, where council and parliament met.[27] James III, the one king who did try to bring people to the centre, rather than making royal justice available to them in the localities, by letting the sessions fall into abeyance and replacing them by lords of council hearing cases almost exclusively in Edinburgh, and by refusing to go on justice ayres, thereby earned for himself the reputation of being lazy and indifferent. His successor found a much better balance. Criminal justice was pursued by the king in the localities and, while the lords of session now met in Edinburgh, they administered justice at fixed terms, and shires were grouped into areas for summons. This made it infinitely easier for those who wanted to bring their case before the king's court; it is an indication of how little men in the fifteenth century had equated royal justice with a central court that such apparently obvious provisions were not made until the end of the century.

Moreover, giving time to judicial business was something which was expected of men of political power, the men involved in the king's government. They were not paid to do so. Parliament in 1458 gave them short shrift for suggesting that their expenses might be met and, having considered 'the gret gude of the Realme', it decided that the lords of session 'of thir awne benevolence sulde beir thir awne costis'.[28] In the end, successful and permanent central courts for civil and criminal justice did need more than reliance on people to do the work 'of thir awne benevolence', but the payment of judges and the development of a lay legal profession centred in Edinburgh belonged to the sixteenth century. Professional knowledge of the law was still the preserve of churchmen, who might hope for advancement through royal service. With them sat lay lords, amateurs who dispensed justice in local courts, in private settlements (about which more will be said in the second part of this chapter) and as members of the king's council. Their right to do so was not challenged by the crown and their duty to do so was expected by it.

In practice, of course, only a small proportion of the landowners sat as judges in the king's court. It was certainly the intention to share out the work, and this may have happened before the court came to be held in Edinburgh. The sederunts, however, which survive from the reign of James III onwards, show the same people turning up again and again.[29] Most lords, apart from a few of the greatest magnates and some others, were reluctant to take the time and trouble to come to the king's council, court or parliament; the king's natural counsellors were by no means endlessly eager to give him their advice. The Scottish parliament, by comparison with that of England, was more restricted and less sophisticated in its view of its place in government and, as late as the end of the sixteenth century, it was still possible to debate the superiority of parliamentary statute over council ordinance, an issue settled in England in the mid-fourteenth century.[30] The problem was rather to persuade people to turn up than to persuade them to modify their demands. A crucial factor, again, is taxation. The fact that English kings regularly taxed their subjects has much to do with the development of the lower house in the English parliament. Although it is impossible to be certain, because the loss of the official record of proceedings before 1466 means that it is not known who came to parliament until after that date, it is probably that there was a connection between the lack of taxation and the comparative lack of interest of the lairds and burgesses; the only obvious explanation for an unusually large attendance of lairds and burgh commissioners at the parliament of March 1479 is that this was one of the rare occasions when taxation was levied.[31]

Yet limited though it was, the Scottish parliament should not be written off as weak and ineffective, the rubber stamp for the crown.[32] The introduction of the lords of the articles, the people who did the work of drafting and agreeing on legislation to be presented to the full parliament, may have something to do with the difficulty of securing attendance, although the practice of giving people leave to go home was stopped after 1425. It is more likely that it reflects the strength of parliament and the desire of the crown to control it, and certainly with the much fuller evidence available in the reign of James VI, it is clear that this was the case. The initiative taken by parliament over James II's finances, the repeated criticisms of James III, show that it did not regard itself as existing simply to represent the royal will. Indeed, it may have developed in the course of this century an increased degree of self-awareness, though lack of evidence makes it possible to trace this only in the most general terms. James I used parliaments extensively. His parliaments produced a flood of legislation on all manner of things, from the important to the trivial. To have a parliament regarded as a body of importance and authority was much more use to him than to have a rubber-stamp. By the reign of James II, there is some suggestion that there had been a change of emphasis; legislation tended to begin with a statement not of what the king, or king and parliament, thought, but what the lords of the three estates thought, and this may be more than a verbal detail. In any event, it is extremely unlikely that parliament was a subservient body. The degree of dependence on the cooperation of the landowners did not stop at the business of raising an army and, when the landowners were summoned, not to fight, but to attend parliament, they did not come simply to acquiesce.

Lack of money, comparatively undeveloped government institutions, royal justice still a matter for the council, with the new court set up in this period surviving sometimes with difficulty, sometimes, probably, not at all, the necessity of relying on personal cooperation and therefore ultimately on personalities – all these may seem to give grounds for the long-held concept that the Scottish monarchy of the fifteenth century was itself weak. But when fifteenth-century Scotsmen talked about the strength or weakness of the crown, its success or failure in governing, they did not think primarily about the efficiency or degree of sophistication of the king's formal administration. They thought in much more personal terms. There are two comments on the effectiveness, or lack of it, of the crown which are worth considering in this context; both are linked to particularly dramatic and ruthless actions, the first by a magnate, the second by a king. In 1398, the chronicle of Moray, written in an area of the country which had suffered, during the 1390s, from the rampant disorder created by Robert III's brother, Alexander, earl of Buchan, the 'Wolf of Badenoch', lamented that:

In diebus illis non erat lex in Scocia sec quilibet potencior minorem oppressit et totum regnum fuit unum latrocinium. Homicidia depredaciones et incendia et cetera maleficia remanserunt inpunita et justicia utlegata extra regni terminos exulavit.

By contrast, parliament in 1458 took the almost unique step of praising a king, James II, acknowledging that

> God of his grace has send our soverane lorde sik progress and prosperite that all his rebyllys and brekaris of his Justice ar removit out of his Realme and na maisterfull party remanande that may caus only breking in his Realme so that his hienes be inclynit in himself and his ministeris to the quiet & commoune profett of the Realm and Justice to be kepit amangis his lieges

and expressed the hope that James would continue to deserve praise by putting into effect the acts of this parliament.[33]

Both these comments refer to justice and neither is concerned only with justice in the courts. The Moray chronicler can hardly have believed that to bring the king's brother before the courts was a practical solution. He painted his picture of unpunished crime and violence against the backcloth of the breakdown of political power; Robert II and Robert III, both well-intentioned but pathetically weak personalities, had lost political control, to the extent of failing to hold their family in check. The effect of this, as experienced in Moray, was not the only possible one. Although there was faction fighting, there were repeated attempts in this period to stop the rot, to give impetus to government and to provide effective justice by transferring authority to other members of the royal family. This suggests that not all who held political power thought only of the chance offered by the absence of a strong monarchy to further their own interests by means more violent than usual. The situation in Moray was particularly bad because the extension of royal power to the locality through the local magnate had become uncontrolled power exercised by an individual magnate, without fear of reprisal. The significance of the most dramatic of the many acts of violence committed by the Wolf of Badenoch, the burning of Elgin Cathedral in 1390, is that it demonstrates in extreme form what could happen when the monarchy was weak. It is a comment on the importance of individual ambition and personality in the case of the magnates. But it was not usual, even in a Scotland traditionally regarded as lawless, for a powerful lord to burn a cathedral because the bishop had stopped paying for his protection. This event, and the whole of Buchan's career, have been rightly linked with the weakness of the crown. What is not so readily explained is why this was so, why it mattered that the king should be personally effective, and what effect he was supposed to have. Whatever royal authority meant, it did not mean tight control from the centre. What then would make it possible for a stronger personality on the throne to do better for those of his subjects remote in Moray?

This is not a problem which can be discussed in absolute terms and at best it is a matter of relative success or failure. But the compliment paid to James II reveals something of what men at the time thought was the answer. The rebels and breakers of justice whom James had removed from the realm, the masterful party which no long existed, almost certainly refer to the Black Douglases, finally defeated after several years of conflict with the king, and driven out of the kingdom in 1455. If so, parliament in 1458 was congratulating a king for actions which were as extreme as the actions of a magnate deplored in the 1390s. The Douglases cannot simply be explained away as rebels or overmighty subjects. Certainly by the mid-fifteenth century they had reached a position of exceptional power, based on their three earldoms, that of Douglas, with its extensive lands in the southwest, and Moray and Ormond, acquired in the minority of James II, and giving them influence in the north; and a fourth Douglas brother was lord of Balveny. Yet however potentially dangerous this was, one has to turn to writers of the following century, notably Lindsay of Pitscottie, to find detailed accounts of their misuse of power and open defiance of the king. These accounts may have been based on stories handed down. But they are still open to doubt, for they are hardly likely to have been inspired by the losing and exiled side, the Douglases, and much more likely to derive from the propaganda of the winning side; and it is hard to give any credence at all to one of the best of the stories of Douglas outrage, the account of their execution of the tutor of Bombie, who has left not a trace of his existence in any contemporary record. Nor does the idea that the king's onslaught on the Douglases can be explained on the grounds of their treasonable dealings with England carry weight until after James's murder of Earl William in February 1452.[34] The apparent reason for the murder, Douglas's refusal to break his bond with Alexander, earl of Crawford and John, Lord of the Isles, cannot be regarded as the valid reaction of a king who rightly wanted to stamp out the pernicious practice of the magnates of making bonds with one another, thus building up alliances which threatened the crown. No late medieval king thought in this way, and indeed James himself made bonds, being the only king who made use of this normally non-royal practice.[35] What is left is the scanty contemporary evidence which, small though it is, points to the fact that initially James was the aggressor, taking the provocative action of seizing the Douglas lands of the earldom of Wigtown in 1450–51, during the earl's absence abroad, not as a measure against an overmighty family, but because he wanted them for his wife.[36]

In any event, a king who murders is hardly showing concern for royal justice. The murder of an earl by a king was as unique as the burning of a cathedral by an earl. It happened not because James regarded it as justifiable treatment of an overmighty subject, but because he lost his temper, as indeed his lords had feared he would do.[37] Yet he was saved from the consequences of his own action because the magnates were prepared to support him. Not only was the new earl of Douglas, brother of the murdered earl, forced to come to terms with the king to whom, in the immediate aftermath of the killing, he had publicly renounced allegiance, but when the final crisis took place in 1455, the Douglases were left to fight alone, deserted by their former allies. The reference in 1458 to 'rebellys and brekaris of his Justice' was not as inaccurate a description of the Douglases after 1452 as before. Even so, the whole episode, the reaction of the magnates who backed the king, and the tribute paid to James, who had acted in this affair not only strongly but outrageously, suggest a new dimension in the problem of understanding what people meant when they admired a Scottish king for providing 'quiet & commoune profett' and 'Justice' in his realm.

Why did James get away with murder? There is little doubt that those who feared what might happen felt misgivings, embarrassment, even perhaps horror when it did happen. The exoneration of the king produced by the parliament which met in June 1452 illustrates the dilemma. It is quite remarkably vague; it seems that those asked to inquire into the circumstances of Douglas's death took the easy way out, and gave the king an answer which was no answer, saying that he had acted defensibly in doing something for which there was no real defence.[38] How much easier it was in 1458, when the Douglases, now a real rather than a potential threat, had been crushed by the king, for then uncertainty and embarrassment could give way to admiration which was genuine enough.

Yet even in 1452 there was no alternative. James had not provided justice, had stepped outside the law, had acted with a violence and barbarity condemned in lesser mortals. But he had all the prestige and power of monarchy on his side. He was, admittedly, helped by being able to use patronage, though even this shows how confident he was. It was hardly lavish, there was no question of it being liberally distributed by a terrified king and, indeed, within a few years, some of it had been withdrawn.[39] Part of the explanation of why the king's position was so strong is to be found in the attitudes and position of the magnates, which form the theme of the second part of this chapter. But in terms of royal power, James was right to be confident. The Scottish monarchy was strong because of what it had to offer – political and social stability. It alone could keep a balance of power in the state, could bring to an end too great a concentration of power in the hands of one family, Stewarts or Douglases. Far from not being given support by their greatest subjects, the evidence suggests that kings received a considerable amount, even in outrageous circumstances. The emphasis on the risk to a king who was not backed up by a strong centralized administration, and therefore relied on personal cooperation, has been overstated. The greater risk was to the subjects, dependent not on state control, but on the personality of an individual monarch. There was no way of doing without the king; he was utterly necessary, the lynchpin of society. If he was weak, like Robert III, then individuals, though not the nobility as a whole, might cause havoc, while others made an attempt to stagger on, keeping some measure of control, until death removed him. If he combined laziness and indifference with a high degree of whimsical arbitrariness, as James III did, then he might build up sufficient resentment to provoke the political solution of rebellion, although only a handful were prepared to take this course. But the idea that there was conflict between the crown and nobility is two-dimensional. It does not allow for the interplay of individual personalities, nor does it give sufficient weight to the fact that, in a situation where personality was of supreme importance, the fifteenth-century kings, including James III, had the inestimable advantage of being exceedingly tough and powerful men. It made them extraordinarily difficult to deal with, and certainly to oppose, without recourse to extreme action. It gave them the ability to rule with considerable power.

NOTES

1 I am indebted for this point to Professor A. L. Brown of the University of Glasgow.
2 A. L. Murray, 'The Comptroller, 1425–1488', *Scottish Historical Review* Lii (1973), p. 13; Ranald Nicholson, *Scotland: the Later Middle Ages* (Edinburgh, 1974), pp. 453–4. It is suggested that the estimate for *c*1486, £16,380 Scots, is too high. This indicates that James III was doing well if he got an income of about £5,000 sterling. An English king would have at least £50,000 and often considerably more.
3 Sir John Fortescue, *De Laudibus Legum Anglie*, ed. S. B. Chrimes (Cambridge, 1949), p.2.
4 Thomas Thomson and Cosmo Innes, eds., *Acts of the Parliament of Scotland* (12 vols., Edinburgh, 1814–75) (hereafter APS), ii, p. 139.
5 See above, chapter 2, p. 17.
6 John Major, *A History of Greater Britain* (Scottish History Society, 1892), p. 386.
7 S. B. Chrimes, *English Constitutional Ideas in the Fifteenth Century* (Cambridge, 1936), p.15, cites Fortescue on one occasion writing about the king's duty as administrator as well as judge; this is an unusually wide view, even for Fortescue himself.
8 They did, of course, give wages and pensions to their household servants and other servants outside the household, but these were not large; A. L. Murray, *Exchequer and Crown Revenue, 1437–1542* (unpublished PhD thesis, Edinburgh, 1961), pp. 222–5.
9 The introduction, for example, of a drastically debased coinage by James III, the 'black money', was one of the causes of resentment in the period immediately preceding the Lauder crisis of 1482. Nicholson, *The Later Middle Ages*, pp. 499–500.
10 Murray, 'The Comptroller', p.29. In an interesting article on the use of feudal practices of little social relevance, R. G. Nicholson points to the success of James IV in making money by adapting these practices to a money economy, in the development of feuing, sales of land and apprisings, but, as he says, although this did not begin only in James IV's reign, it was of far less financial significance before then: 'Feudal Developments in Late Medieval Scotland', *Juridical Review* 18 (1973), pp. 1–2.
11 Murray, *Exchequer and Crown Revenue*, p. 198.
12 *APS*, ii, pp. 42, 49.
13 B. P. Wolffe, *The Crown Lands, 1461–1535* (London, 1970), pp. 1–28. No Scottish king used as propaganda, as Edward IV did, the promise that he would relieve his subjects of financial burden by living of his own, although no Scottish king had quite the need to advertise the advantages of his kingship that Edward IV had.
14 Nicholson, *The Later Middle Ages*, p. 454, points out that James III's revenue cannot have been greater than David II's, in the last year of his reign, a century earlier. Most of James's income came from crown lands, most of David's from taxation and the great customs.
15 P. S. Lewis, *Later Medieval France: the Polity* (London, 1968), pp. 104–7. G. L. Harriss, *King, Parliament and Public Finance in Medieval England to 1369* (Oxford, 1975), pp. 509–17, shows the effect of war on English public finance and on the role of Lords and Commons in parliament in financial matters. These developments in England and France

are not paralleled in Scotland, although Scotland had had its time of war also, from the late thirteenth to the mid-fourteenth century.

16 A. L. Brown, 'The English Campaign in Scotland, 1400' in *British Government and Administration: Studies presented to S. B. Chrimes*, eds. H. Hearder and H. R. Loyn (Cardiff, 1974), pp. 40–54. Another example is the Agincourt campaign where the enthusiasm felt for Henry V should not obscure the earlier doubts about the proposal to fight; E. F. Jacob, *The Fifteenth Century* (Oxford, 1961), pp. 138 and 141. While not so heavily dependent as a Scottish king on the reaction to his proposed campaigns, an English king could not, of course, be indifferent to it, as is shown by J. R. Lander, *Crown and Nobility, 1450–1509* (London, 1976), pp. 220–41.

17 N. A. T. Macdougall, *James III: a Political Study, 1466–1488* (unpublished PhD thesis, Glasgow, 1968), pp. 138–9.

18 *APS*, ii, pp. 134 and 139–40.

19 *Asloan Manuscript 1*, pp. 229–30.

20 Nicholson, *The Later Middle Ages*, pp. 196–8; Brown, 'The English Campaign in Scotland, 1400', pp. 43–4.

21 *APS*, ii, p. 102.

22 *Ibid.*, ii, p. 104.

23 The Second Croyland Continuator, in *Rerum Anglicarum Scriptorum Veterum*, ed. W. Fulman (Oxford, 1684), p. 563. It was certainly Berwick that the English were after. The presence of Albany was no doubt useful as a threat – as Edward IV had used the earl of Douglas and the Lord of the Isles in 1462, when the Scottish government was still supporting the Lancastrians – but there was no intention of mounting an expensive campaign on Albany's behalf, and no attempt to force the Scots to accept him as king when there was obviously no support for him in Scotland.

24 Even if the ringleaders in the Lauder crisis were motivated by personal reasons, James had, apparently, remarkably little support, except temporarily from the archbishop of St Andrews, Scheves, and Andrew, Lord Avandale, chancellor until June 1482. Macdougall, *James III*, chapter 4, 'The Crisis of 1482–3 and its Aftermath'.

25 J. Maitland Thomson, *The Public Records of Scotland* (Glasgow, 1922), pp. 29, 58 and 64–6, Murray, 'The Comptroller', pp. 1–29.

26 See below, chapter 7; A. A. M. Duncan, 'The Central Courts before 1532' in *An Introduction to Scottish Legal History* (Stair Society, 20, Edinburgh, 1958), pp. 330–39.

27 All but two of James I's parliaments and general councils were held in Perth; one was in Stirling, one in Edinburgh. In James II's reign, the figures are Edinburgh 13, Stirling 9, Perth 6. Every one of James III's parliaments and general councils were held in Edinburgh, except for one, held during his minority at Stirling. It is not impossible that a reason for Perth's loss of popularity as the centre of government, and the move south, was the murder of James I at Perth in 1437.

28 *APS*, ii, p. 48.

29 This was demonstrated by Professor A. L. Brown who has made a statistical analysis of the sederunts of James III's reign and the early part of James IV's. I am indebted to him for the information.

30 Councils could deal with matters of considerable importance. It is rather surprising to find, for example, that James I's 'parliamentary' act of 1428, attempting to introduce shire commissioners and a speaker, was passed not by a parliament, but by a general council; the act was to apply to both councils and parliaments. *APS*, ii, p.15.

31 *APS*, ii, 120–21. One hundred and four people turned up, the largest number to attend

any of James III's parliaments and they included forty-one lords of parliament and lairds, and commissioners from twenty-eight burghs. In March 1482, when the cost of the war was part of parliamentary business, there was again a large attendance, including thirty barons and lairds, and commissioners from twenty burghs; *ibid.*, ii, pp. 136–7. There is not always a correlation; the last two parliaments held by James III, in October 1487 and January 1488, were also unusually well attended by barons and lairds, forty-three and forty, although less so by the burgh commissioners, eleven and fourteen. It would be stretching the argument beyond conviction to regard as the explanation for the numbers in 1488 the £250 to be raised for an embassy, £100 each from prelates and barons, and £50 from the burghs. A more possible explanation is that justice, both royal and local, was very much a matter of concern in both; *ibid.*, ii, pp 175 and 180–82. But the figures do suggest that money was one of the reasons, while not the only one, why more people than usual made the effort to come.

32 R. S. Rait, *The Parliaments of Scotland* (Glasgow, 1924) regarded parliament as the mouthpiece for the crown, or for the ruling clique in the minorities; in the section 'From James I to the Reformation', pp. 30–47, parliament is described as 'thoroughly obedient' and reference is made to its 'accustomed role of registration'.

33 *Moray Registrum*, p. 382; *APS*, ii, p. 51. It should be stressed that the Moray chronicler, though writing what purported to be a general comment on the state of the kingdom, was in fact describing the situation in the north.

34 For the tutor of Bombie, see Robert Lindsay of Pitscottie, *The Historie and Cronicles of Scotland* (STS, 1899–1911), I, pp. 89–92; J. M. Brown, 'Taming the Magnates?' in *The Scottish Nation*, edited by G. Menzies (London, 1972), p. 47. *Asloan Manuscript*, I, p. 237 describes the Douglases fighting successfully in the north of England in 1449 in what seems to have more than a border raid. In a tantalizing fragment of a story in the same chronicle, Sir James of Douglas is described as being 'with the king of yngland land tyme and was mekle maid of', why, as the chronicler says, 'men wist nocht redelye'; but this was involved with an embassy negotiating for truce, and it is difficult to know what weight to give to the sinister element – or, indeed, whether that was simply hindsight: *ibid.* I, p. 239.

35 Two bonds exist, one certainly and the other probably connected with the Douglas crisis. James, earl of Douglas, came to terms with the king in August 1452. In January 1453, there was a second agreement, more favourable to the earl and it included a bond by the earl to James II, promising manrent. It is known only from a copy, wrongly ascribed to the year 1402, which is impossible, there being no Earl James at that time, and the terms of the bond exactly fit the agreement of 1453. It is unfortunate that the original does not survive, for it refers to 'thir my letters written with my hand' and to the king's 'lettres written with his hand', which would be interesting evidence of literacy. It is printed in *The Additional Case of Elisabeth, claiming the title and Dignity of the Countess of Sutherland* (Sutherland Case, 1771), Appendix X. The other bond is a bond of maintenance given to James Tweedie of Drumelzier on 8 March 1455, in return for Tweedie's manrent and service. This bond, made to a laird whose lands lay in southern Scotland, suggests a connection with the build-up to the final onslaught on the Douglases, ending with their defeat at Arkinholm on 1 May 1455, and although Tweedie was a reasonably important laird, it is unlikely that he was singled out as the only one to whom James made such a bond. *HMC, Various Collections*, v, p. 11.

36 *Asloan Manuscript*, I, p. 239, describes William, earl of Douglas, coming to the parliament of June 1451, and putting himself in the king's grace; and 'at the Request

of the qwene and the thre estatis' James received him into his grace, and gave him back the lands he had taken, with the exception of Wigtown. 'And all gud scottismen war rycht blyth o that accordance.' This suggests that James's actions had caused unease and that there was sympathy with Douglas.

37 *Ibid.*, I, p 240, refers to the agreement made by all the lords who were with the king in Stirling before the murder that 'supposs the king wald brek the band forsaid [his safeconduct to the earl] that they suld let it at thair powere'; this certainly suggests fear of what the king might do.

38 *APS*, ii, p. 73.

39 *Asloan Manuscript*, I, pp. 242–3 gives a list of creations made in the parliament of June 1452; two Crichtons received the earldoms of Moray and Caithness, and Lord Hay the earldom of Erroll, and a number of people including former Douglas adherents like Fleming of Cumbernauld, were made lords of parliament. But neither Crichton had his earldom for long. Both were in the king's hands by 1454, and there is some doubt whether the Crichtons ever actually held them. A. I. Dunlop, *The Life and Times of James Kennedy, Bishop of St Andrews* (Edinburgh, 1950), pp. 148–50.

Crown and Nobility in Late Medieval Britain

Extracted from A Grant 1987 in RA Mason (ed), *Scotland and England, 1286–1815*, Edinburgh (John Donald), 38–42.

If the comparatively low-key nature of late medieval Scottish politics cannot adequately be explained by personal factors, it is obviously necessary to turn to impersonal ones. Can differences in the political structures of the two countries be used to explain the contrast in their political histories? Although medieval Scotland's political society had close ties with England's – most of Scotland's central and local institutions and a large number of its noble families derived from twelfth-century England – over the centuries many differences developed between them, and it does seem that several of these had a direct bearing on the raising and lowering of political tension. This will be argued by considering first the crowns and governments of the two countries, and then their nobilities and localities.

The immediate reaction to any comparison of the Scottish and English crowns in the late middle ages is that the English was infinitely stronger. So far as the machinery and institutions at the crown's disposal are concerned, that is true enough. In the late middle ages, Scotland still had a simple household administration, which did not even have a fixed central location like Westminster. The chamberlain was until 1428 the crown's chief financial officer, and there was no full-time Exchequer, audits simply being held on an *ad hoc* basis at irregular, roughly annual intervals by boards of specially appointed auditors. Financial turnover was very low, hardly ever above £10–£12,000 sterling a year, and more usually less than half of that; the money came from customs on exports (especially wool) and from crown lands, but not from direct taxation, which was relatively rare in Scotland. Scottish military institutions were equally simple. There were none of the great English military developments: Scottish armies, throughout the later middle ages, continued to be raised through the age-old obligation of defensive military service on all able-bodied men, and they were always unpaid (which explains the rarity of direct taxation, the low financial turnover, and indeed the apparent lack of development of the Scottish parliament). The same applies to judicial institutions. The only central courts were those of parliament, the royal council, its fifteenth-century offshoot the sessions, and the peripatetic courts of the two justiciars; local courts were held by the sheriffs and the more important landowners. Scotland had no *corpus* of professional judges like England's; the justiciars and the sheriffs all belonged to the nobility, and the main lay and ecclesiastical landowners were not only in charge of seigniorial justice but were also the leading members of the parliamentary and conciliar courts.[1]

Yet although late medieval Scottish royal government seems rudimentary by English standards, it was not necessarily ineffective. Medieval governments should be judged by their results, not by their machinery.[2] The hub of all medieval government was the royal council, and there are striking similarities both in personnel and in function between the late medieval Scottish and English councils.[3] Scotland also had an adequate system of communications between the council and the localities through brieves (the Scottish equivalent of writs) and precepts.[4] In finance, it was the English system which suffered from bad tallies, perennial arrears and long delays, not the Scottish; and the Yorkist and early Tudor methods of chamber finance, which simplified the fiscal system and greatly increased the yield from the crown lands, were little different from those used in Scotland from James I's reign on.[5] As for military matters, Scotland won its wars in the later middle ages (in other words its war aims, the maintenance of national independence and integrity, were achieved); England did not. Admittedly the Scots suffered several military disasters, but these tended to come at the beginning of periods of hostility, so that much of Scotland's warfare consisted of gradual recovery from initial setbacks. For England the pattern was the opposite: initial success followed by gradual failure. Judged by eventual results, then, the vast differences in the two military machines are deceptive. Much more relevant is the fact that the English pattern of increasingly unsuccessful warfare, and the constant requirement of heavy taxation to pay for it, were both considerable sources of political tension which Scotland was spared. And (as will be argued more fully) the complexity of the English judicial system was by the late middle ages more of a hindrance than a help to the administration of justice. In Scotland, on the other hand, the machinery for settling disputes, although largely run by amateurs and extremely simple by English standards, appears in practice to have operated no worse than in England, and perhaps indeed rather more successfully, as the statistics for acts of political violence given in the first part of this essay indicate.

Furthermore, it is possible to argue that the very 'sophistication' of the English system of government could lead to political problems. The more complex a medieval government was, the more there would be to go wrong; the more centralised it was, the more it would depend on efficiency at the centre. To work to its full potential, English medieval government seems to have required full-time, competent direction from the centre – which it normally did not receive. It has been shown that the English system of criminal law was likely to work at all satisfactorily only when it received the personal attention of a vigorous monarch,[6] and this conclusion can probably be applied to the administration as a whole. Yet not until the reign of Henry VII did England have a king who was prepared to be a full-time professional ruler.[7] The argument, however, does not apply to the far less sophisticated, less centralised Scottish system of government – which because of its simplicity was much more likely to 'muddle along', even if there was less than first-class direction at the centre.

More specifically, in late medieval England both the theoretical and the actual strength of the crown can be shown to have been sources of political tension. Because of the exalted nature of English kingship, one of the major themes of late medieval English history is a politically dangerous intransigence and an excessive regard for the royal prerogative on the part of several kings. Another is the concept of accroachment, in which the exercise of royal power by someone who was not the king was regarded as treason, and which could be used against both the king's ministers and his opponents (one obvious reason for the dangers of English political life). A third is the difficulty of distinguishing between the crown's public powers of administering the royal household, which were not so limited and at times could be applied very extensively.[8]

None of these themes seems to have been very important in late medieval Scotland. An episode like Richard II's 'questions to the judges' in 1387, in which all three issues featured prominently,[9] would have been inconceivable north of the Border. There the religious mystique of kingship was less developed: although Scottish kings had long styled themselves 'rex Dei gratia', they did not enjoy ecclesiastical coronation and unction until 1331, and by then the popular theory of kingship had been affirmed in the Declaration of Arbroath of 1320.[10] David II perhaps had a more exalted view of kingship than his predecessors,[11] but after him Scottish kings appear to have been much more pragmatic about it, at least until the reign of James III. Late medieval Scotland did have treason trials, but not very many, and mostly on the basic charges of armed rebellion and alliance with England. Scotland's treason law seems even more limited than Edward III's English statute (which was often exceeded in practice), and no equivalent to the concept of accroachment can be found until 1469, at the end of James III's minority.[12] As for the royal household, this never appears as an important political issue – no doubt largely because in Scotland's much less formal system of government the distinction between the public and private powers of the crown was never so significant as in England, and also perhaps because the Scottish royal household, unlike the English, did not have the bureaucratic stimulation of running a great war machine. Only the faintest echoes of contemporary English disputes over the household can be found in Scotland, such as the statements in parliament under Robert I and David II that requisitions or 'prises' for the household would be limited according to ancient custom, or the drawing up of an ordinance for the king's and queen's households by Robert II's council in 1371.[13]

In late medieval England, the issue of the royal household was closely connected with the subject of crown patronage. The dispensation of patronage – grants of land, leases, wardships, annuities, cash, licences, privileges, perquisites, favours, and appointments in administrative and judicial areas – made a vital contribution to the strength of the English crown. Operating within a highly centralised system of government, it meant (as Sir Richard Southern has stressed) that the crown was normally able 'to reward those who mattered, and to ensure that those who were not rewarded continued not to matter'.[14] From as far back as Henry I's reign (and no doubt earlier), this use of patronage for political ends was a fundamental feature of

English kingship. The system of patronage, however, was open to abuse by members of the royal household and court, as often happened during the late middle ages. Having easy and sometimes exclusive access to the king and the central administration, they were able to manipulate patronage for their own benefit, monopolising favour for themselves and their followers and denying it to those beyond the immediate court circle, especially to their political opponents, whose affairs they could frequently disrupt. Thus among the most serious political grievances of late medieval England were the waste of royal resources on favourites, and the disruption of the proper course of justice by delaying or expediting proceedings and employing biased judges and officials. Also, because the tentacles of late medieval English government reached so far, the partisan operation of the patronage system often had damaging effects on the local communities. Most positions of local power, for example the shrievalties, custodianships of castles, and even commissions of the peace, were central appointments, and were thus vulnerable to political factions – especially the shrievalties, which (by an act of 1340[15]) had to change annually. At times of partisan government, attempts were naturally made to maintain a grip on the country through local appointments: household domination of the shrievalties is very marked in Henry VI's reign, for instance, while under Richard III the king's northern followers flooded into offices in the south of England.[16] One consequence was that corrupt practices by court-backed officials were likely to go unchecked.[17] Another was that changes in central power tended to affect local government and local power structures; thus at the height of the Wars of the Roses alternating Lancastrian and Yorkist governments carried out purges of each other's local administrations.[18] Both consequences tied local and central politics closely together, often forcing many gentry to take sides in central power struggles in order to look after their own local interests. Abuse of royal patronage, therefore, was a major cause of political tension in late medieval England. But because royal patronage was mostly a private matter – the king exercising the royal prerogative as he and those closest to him wished – it sometimes became impossible to rectify the abuses satisfactorily without removing the king himself.

Again, late medieval Scotland seems not to have suffered so badly from these problems – royal favourites never caused political trouble, except perhaps under David II and James III.[19] Admittedly crown patronage took much the same form as it did in England, and attitudes to it were similar. Its distribution was generally politically motivated and often unbalanced, it could operate negatively as well as positively, and it was a factor in at least four rebellions.[20] The general dangers from the abuse of patronage, however, appear much less in Scotland – not because the patronage was distributed more wisely, but because its scope and extent were much more limited. The crown lands had been exhausted by the share-out of territories to Bruce supporters in the Wars of Independence, and when they were rebuilt, the crown had to use them as the main basis of its revenue. Grants of land were therefore fairly uncommon. Cash grants and annuities were much more usual, especially between 1371 and 1424, but the paucity of the crown's revenue meant that relatively little was available; rarely more than £1,000 sterling a year went on patronage, and much less after 1424. (In contrast, Edward III spent at least £13,000 a year in the 1360s, while Henry IV at the beginning of his reign was spending over £30,000[21]). And because Scottish government was less centralised, the manipulation of administrative and judicial affairs, although it did take place, was never so important as in England. Apart from the wardenship of some great castles (to which appointments were made centrally, sometimes with serious political consequences), local offices were mostly dominated by local magnate families. Shrievalties changed hands much less frequently, and indeed during the late middle ages most of them became hereditary possessions.[22] This of course would not have prevented corrupt practices by the sheriffs, and indeed quarrels over appointments can be connected with at least two violent deaths;[23] but it did remove them from the sphere of everyday political patronage. Thus the shrievalties (and indeed most other local offices) were relatively unaffected by changes in power at the centre – something which probably contributed greatly to the stability of late medieval Scottish politics.

A further point about crown patronage in late medieval Scotland is that its most characteristic form was the granting of privileges: the erection of baronies and regalities (which gave lords judicial powers over their estates), the waiving of feudal incidents through concessions of tenure 'in blench ferme' (for an honorific *reddendo* like a penny or a glove), the bestowal of permission to arrange the descent of estates in a particular way, the grant of peerage titles, and the remission of customs dues on exported goods.[24] Most significantly, all this kind of patronage was self-contained, simply affecting the recipient's own lands or goods without disappointing or damaging the interests of anyone else. Such patronage might have caused individual jealousies; it probably did not generate widespread tension within the political community as a whole.

The impressive nature of the medieval English crown and its governmental system – especially in theory – seems therefore to have been at best a mixed blessing. The opportunities it gave for predatory,[25] partisan rule were often difficult to resist. Thus it has been stated that 'the two depositions of the fourteenth century suggest not the weakness but the strength of the English medieval monarchy',[26] and the same point seems to apply also to the five occasions when a king lost his throne in the fifteenth century. In late medieval Scotland, on the other hand, there was much less chance that central power struggles, incompetent monarchs, or selfish courtiers would have wide-ranging and damaging effects on the country as a whole. Instead, the apparent weakness of the monarchy – or perhaps, to put it in more neutral terms, the relative simplicity of the system of government – appears to be one of the main factors in explaining why Scotland was spared the repetitive English sequence of upheavals, political violence, and regicides.

NOTES

1 A. Grant, *Independence and Nationhood: Scotland 1306–1469* (Edinburgh, 1991), ch. 6. For a much fuller and rather different discussion of fifteenth-century Scottish government, see L. J. Macfarlane, *William Elphinstone and the Kingdom of Scotland*

(Aberdeen, 1985), 1–15 and chs. 3, 5, 8; Dr Macfarlane has a gloomier view of Scotland's governance than I do, but his account of the machinery and institutions is admirable.

2 'English writers often assume that copious records are a sign of good government, and clear evidence of the superiority of medieval English administration over that of almost all other medieval systems of government except perhaps that of the papacy. Yet records do not necessarily mean efficiency. The fullest of medieval English records belong to the fifteenth century, a period which is not often regarded as one of the great administrative achievement. Records reflect bureaucratic departmentalisation . . .': B. Webster, *Scotland from the Eleventh Century to 1603* (Cambridge, 1975), 149.

3 A. L. Brown, 'The King's Councillors in the Fifteenth Century', *Transactions of the Royal Historical Society*, 5th ser, xix (1969); A. L. Brown, 'The Scottish "Establishment" in the Later fifteenth Century', *Juridical Review*, new ser, xxiii (1978); J. F. Baldwin, *The King's Council in England during the Middle Ages* (reprinted Oxford, 1969); A. A. M. Duncan, 'The Central Courts before 1532', in *Introduction to Scottish Legal History* (Stair Society, 1958), 324–36.

4 T. M. Cooper (ed.), *The Register of Brieves* (Stair Society, 1946); H. McKechnie, *Judicial Process upon Brieves* (Glasgow, 1956).

5 A. Steel, *The Receipt of the Exchequer, 1377–1485* (Cambridge, 1954); B. P. Wolffe, *The Royal Demesne in English History* (London, 1971), chs. VI, VII; A. L. Murray, 'The Comptroller, 1425–1388', *Scottish Historical Review*, lii (1973), esp. 1–3, 13–22; C. Madden, 'The Finances of the Scottish Crown in the late Middle Ages' (Glasgow University PhD Thesis, 1975).

6 J. G. Bellamy, *Crime and Public Order in England in the Later Middle Ages* (London, 1973), 4–12. Cf. Michael Clanchy's comment, in his review of Bellamy's and other books, that 'It might even be argued that royal power contributed to disorder and that the judicial authority of the crown was a public nuisance'; 'Law, Government, and Society in Medieval England', *History*, lix (1974), 78.

7 This emerges clearly from M. M. Condon, 'Ruling Elites in the Reign of Henry VII', in C. Ross (ed.), *Patronage, Pedigree and Power in Late Medieval England* (Gloucester, 1979), and from Wolffe, *Royal Demesne*, ch. VII; cf. A. Grant, *Henry VII* (London, 1985).

8 J. G. Bellamy, *The Law of Treason in England in the later Middle Ages* (Cambridge, 1970), ch. 5; S. B. Chrimes, *English Constitutional Ideas in the Fifteenth Century* (Cambridge, 1936), ch. 1; C. Given-Wilson, *The Royal Household and the King's Affinity: Service, Politics and Finance in England, 1360–1413* (New Haven, 1986), esp. ch. III; T. F. Tout, *Chapters in the Administrative History of Medieval England* (Manchester, 1923–35), vols. II, IV, *passim*; Tuck, *Richard II*, ch. 3; Wolffe, *Henry VI*, chs. 6, 7; Ross, *Edward IV*, chs. 13,14.

9 S. B. Chrimes, 'Richard II's Questions to the Judges, 1387', *Law Quarterly Review*, lxii (1956).

10 Thomas Thomson and Cosmo Innes (eds.) *Acts of the Parliament of Scotland* (12 vols., Edinburgh, 1814–75) (hereafter *APS*), i, 474–5.

11 Presumably provoking the enactment of 1370, that royal officers must not carry out mandates under the great, privy and signet seals contrary to the statute or common law: *APS*, I, 509. Cf. David's employment of Roman law authorities against the earl of Ross, mentioned in the earl's *Quaerimonia* of 1371: C. Innes (ed.), *Ane Account of the Family of Innes* (Spalding Club, 1864), 71.

12 T. M. Cooper (ed.), *Regiam Majestatem* (Stair Society, 1947), 249–50; *APS*, I, 632; ii,

186. Compare the charges against the lord of the Isles in 1475 with those against the ninth earl of Douglas and his family in 1455: *ibid*, ii, 108–9 and 75–7.

13 *Ibid.*, 476, 508, 547.

14 R. W. Southern, 'King Henry I', in his *Medieval Humanism and Other Studies* (Oxford, 1970), 231. Cf. Given-Wilson, *Royal Household*, chs. III, IV; A. Tuck, 'Richard II's System of Patronage', in F. R. H. Du Boulay and C. M. Barron (eds.), *The Reign of Richard II* (London, 1971); Wolffe, *Royal Demesne*, 60–5, 76–112; Ross, *Edward IV*, 312–8; and, for the contemporary record of Richard III's patronage, R. E. Horrox and P. W. Hammond (eds.), *British Library Harleian Manuscript 433* (Gloucester, 1979–83).

15 *Statutes of the Realm*, I (Record Commission, 1810), 283.

16 R. M. Jeffs, 'The Later Mediaeval Sheriff and the Royal Household' (Oxford University DPhil Thesis, 1960), ch. v; followed by Griffiths, *Reign of Henry VI*, 333–41; A. J. Pollard, 'The Tyranny of Richard III', *Journal of Medieval History*, iii (1977), 157–62; Ross, *Richard III*, 118–24.

17 Most notoriously, because of the *Paston Letters* (ed. J Gairdner [reprinted Gloucester, 1983]), in East Anglia during the 1440s and '50s; see e.g. Griffiths, *Reign of Henry VI*, 584–92. But, as Griffiths points out (p. 584), East Anglia 'was in no fundamental sense peculiar in fifteenth-century England'. For the fourteenth century, see e.g. J. R. Maddicott, *Law and Lordship: Royal Justices as Retainers in Thirteenth- and Fourteenth-Century England* (Past and Present Supplements, 1978).

18 Jeffs, 'Later Mediaeval Sheriff', 173–6, 195–7, 212, 214–18, 226; Griffiths, *Reign of Henry VI*, 784–5, 801–2, 823; Ross, *Edward IV*, ch. 4; C. A. Robertson, 'Local Government and the King's "Affinity" in 15th-Century Leicestershire and Warwickshire', *Transactions of the Leicestershire Archaeological and Historical Society*, lii (1976–7).

19 In general, Scottish crown patronage is a seriously neglected subject; but it can now be studied for David II in B. Webster (ed.), *Regesta Regum Scottorum*, vi: *The Acts of David II* (Edinburgh, 1982), and for James III in Macdougall, *James III* (which explodes the old myth about James's 'low-born favourites', but suggests that the influence of men like Archbishop Scheves may have been resented), while some details about it in the period 1371–1424 are to be found in A. Grant, 'The Higher Nobility in Scotland and their Estates, c 1371–1424 (Oxford University DPhil Thesis, 1975), chs. III, IV. A vast amount of relevant material is also contained in *Registrum Magni Sigilli Regum Scottorum [RMS]*, vols. i (ed. J. M. Thomson, Edinburgh, 1912) and ii (ed. J. B. Paul, Edinburgh, 1882) and in G. Burnett and others (eds.), *The Exchequer Rolls of Scotland* (Edinburgh, 1878–1908).

20 (1) 1363: the earl of Douglas rebelled partly because 'the said king had not shown him such fair lordship as he would have liked', *Chron. Scalacronica* (Maxwell), 173; (2) 1411: part at least of the lord of the Isles' motive for the Harlaw rebellion seems to have been that his niece, the unmarried heiress to the earldom of Ross, was being made to direct its descent away from him and towards the family of the governor, the duke of Albany; (3) 1451: the lord of the Isles (now earl of Ross) revolted because he had been disappointed over a promise of 'gud lordschippe' from the crown: *Asloan MS*, I, 224; cf. A. Grant, 'The Revolt of the Lord of the Isles and the Death of the Earl of Douglas, 1451–2', *SHR*, lx (1981), 169–71.

21 Grant, *Independence and Nationhood*, 165; cf. Grant, 'Higher Nobility', 267–70; G. L. Harriss, *King, Parliament and Public Finance in Medieval England to 1369* (Oxford, 1975), 486–7, 497–8; A. L. Brown, 'The Reign of Henry IV' in Chrimes (ed), *Fifteenth-Century England*, 19–20.

22 W. C. Dickinson (ed.), *The Sheriff Court Book of Fife* (Scottish History Society, 1928), xxxiii–xxxvi.
23 Both times the office of sheriff of Roxburgh was involved. In 1342 Sir Alexander Ramsay's appointment was followed by his seizure and murder by Sir William Douglas of Liddesdale, who wanted, and eventually gained, the office. In 1406 Robert III appointed his courtier Sir David Fleming of Biggar to it (it had been held by Douglases since 1342), and shortly afterwards Fleming was killed by Sir James Douglas of Balvenie; there were other motives, but the shrievalty may have been one factor. See Nicholson, *Later Middle Ages*, 144, 291; *RMS*, I, app. I, no. 156.
24 See the sources cited in note 19, above.
25 The adjective is Sir Richard Southern's; see his 'Henry I', *Medieval Humanism*, 231.
26 Tuck, *Richard II*, 225.

Scotland's 'Celtic Fringe' in the Late Middle Ages: The Macdonald Lords of the Isles and the Kingdom of Scotland

A Grant 1998 in RR Davies (ed), *The British Isles 1100–1500. Comparisons, Contrasts and Connections*, Edinburgh (John Donald), 118–141.

The most obvious common factor in the relationships of the three 'Celtic' countries of the British Isles to their 'non-Celtic' neighbour during the middle ages is that all three suffered more or less successful English attempts at conquest. This common factor, however, should not be over-emphasised, for Wales, Ireland and Scotland had very different experiences at England's hands. It can be argued, indeed, that the best parallel for the English conquests in Wales and Ireland is not the attempts by Edward I and his successors to conquer Scotland, but the process whereby the Scottish crown extended its own authority northwards and westwards.[1] Throughout 'Celtic' Britain the imposition and extension of royal authority – the English crown's in Wales and Ireland, the Scottish crown's in Scotland – depended largely on the activities of Anglo-Norman barons and knights in the centuries after Hastings. In all three countries Anglo-Norman incomers and their descendants were primarily responsible for overawing and, when necessary, defeating native Celtic opposition, and also for consolidating submissions and victories by establishing powerful, efficient, local lordships defended with castles. They did so to benefit themselves; but, because they recognised the suzerainty of the English crown in Wales and Ireland (albeit reluctantly at times) and (more positively) that of the Scottish crown in Scotland, they also brought royal authority to the areas under their control. Thus what Edward I did in Wales – complete the final stage of Anglo-Norman penetration – had already been achieved in the Scotland of Alexander III (1249–86) with 'the Winning of the West',[2] when royal authority was imposed on the West Highland lords, and the Western Isles were annexed from Norway in 1266.[3] But what happened after the West was won? How did the kingdom of Scotland get on with the geographically fringe and culturally Celtic region of the Western Highlands and Isles during the fourteenth and fifteenth centuries? These are the questions for the present essay.

Let us start by returning to the Anglo-Norman penetration of Scotland, Wales and Ireland. Despite the similarities, there is one crucial difference between the Normanisation of twelfth- and thirteenth-century Scotland and that of Wales and Ireland. Scotland already had a relatively unitary kingship,[4] and the Anglo-Norman penetration of it took place on behalf of, not in opposition to, the Scottish crown. So Scotland's Anglo-Norman were not *conquistadores* destroying indigenous political structures, as in Wales and Ireland.[5] Instead they upheld the power of the native Scottish kings, against the latter's Celtic opponents. But the Scottish kings' Celtic opponents were a minority; most Celtic landowners supported the crown – alongside, and in conjunction with, the Anglo-Norman incomers. Moreover, while the Scottish crown became increasingly Anglicised and Normanised, the kings themselves were of Celtic descent, and so Scotland, in theory, remained a Celtic kingdom. As that assertion of Scottish independence, the Declaration of Arbroath (1320), put it, 'in their kingdom [that of the Scottish nation] one hundred and thirteen kings of their own royal stock have reigned, the line unbroken by a single foreigner'.[6] It was, of course, a Celtic royal stock.

In such circumstances a formal, collective, sense of Celtic inferiority could hardly develop. So although medieval Scotland had much the same ethnic and linguistic divisions as Wales and Ireland, Scottish Celts did not suffer from the institutionalised racialism found in Wales and Ireland;[7] in Scotland there was no legal gulf between Celt and non-Celt, no exclusion of Celts from the political processes, no treatment of them as second-class citizens or hostile enemies, no sense that the normal state of affairs in the country was one of internal warfare.[8] Instead of the divisions within Wales and Ireland – which became stronger during the thirteenth century – in Scotland there is a growing sense of Scottishness. It is symbolised in the 1180s, when in royal charters the racial form of address (in which French, English, Scots and occasionally Gallovidians were specified) was finally replaced by the phrase, 'to all the good men of [the king's] whole land'.[9] And it was consolidated, particularly at the elite level, by constant intermarriage between Celtic and non-Celtic families.[10] The result was that Alexander III's Scotland, instead of being split between Celt and Norman, or Gael and Gall,[11] was a hybrid country – with hybrid kingship,[12] hybrid institutions, hybrid law, a hybrid Church, and an increasingly hybrid landowning class.

But while this absence of divisions based on race is clear for the thirteenth century, is it also the case for the fourteenth and fifteenth? It is, after all, the fourteenth century that produces the first evidence for that Highland–Lowland divide which was to be such a feature of subsequent Scottish history. During that century the Gaelic language retreated to roughly the geographical Highland line, and from then on the Highlands were virtually synonymous with the Gaelic-speaking area, the Lowlands with the English- or Scots-speaking area.[13] At the same time an awareness of cultural and social divisions developed. An English poet wrote of 'wild' and 'tame' Scots – Highlanders and Lowlanders – in the middle of the century,[14] and the distinction is spelled out forcefully in a much-quoted passage from Fordun's *Chronica Gentis Scotorum*, written in the 1380s:

> The manner and customs of the Scots vary with the diversity of their speech. For two languages are spoken amongst them, the Scottish [ie Gaelic] and the Teutonic [ie English]; the latter of which is the language of those who occupy the seaboard and plains, while the race of Scottish speech inhabits the highlands and outlying islands. The people of the coast [ie the Lowlanders] are of domestic and civilized habits . . . The Highlanders and people of the islands, on the other hand, are a savage and untamed race, rude and independent . . .[15]

Similar comments can be found in many later writings, both Lowland and Highland, though the Highlanders expressed the contrast somewhat differently: as one authority on Celtic Scotland put it, 'What we have in Gaelic traditions is a vision of Alba (Scotland) in which the Galldachd (Lowlands) is the country of an alien dress – black coats and hats; or they are mere tillers of the soil; or they are gloomy whisky-drinkers instead of high-born topers of red wine'.[16] Moreover, the sense of a Highland–Lowland division is borne out by political history, for late-medieval Scotland's worst internal battles and conflicts mostly occurred in the Highlands, and many statements in the parliamentary records indicate that the problems of law and order were considered particularly bad there.

Nevertheless, there was nothing like the collective divisions into 'us and them', so to speak, still evident in Wales and Ireland (especially Ireland).[17] In fourteenth-century government documents 'there is no absolutely no suggestion that king, council of *capella Regis* ('chancery') was conscious that grants and infeftments of landed estates in the Highlands or in the Isles differed in any fundamental respect from those made by the Crown elsewhere in the realm. This impression is confirmed by the treatment of the Highlands in the *Exchequer Rolls* and other records of central government.'[18] Highland lords were not at any time excluded from national politics, and they still commonly intermarried with Lowlanders. And, for all the trouble that the crown experienced in the Highlands, there was no blanket condemnation of Highland, Celtic, society. Troublemakers were condemned, to be sure, but not the Highlanders, not the Gaels, as a whole. There is no sense that the Highlanders were outside the national community.

Fordun's terminology makes this point well. For the linguistic races within Scotland he used *gens*; Lowlanders were *gens maritima*, Highlanders *gens Montana*. But he then stated that the Highlanders were very cruel 'to the people and language of the English' [populo quidem Anglorum et linguae], 'but also, because of the diversity of speech, to their own nation' [sed et propriae nationi]. Thus, to Fordun, there was the Highland *gens* and the Lowland *gens*, who spoke respectively the Scots (by which he meant Gaelic) and the Teutonic languages, but who together made up the *Scottish* nation, which he distinguished carefully from the inhabitants of England – 'the people and language of the English'.[19] Fordun's most significant point, moreover, is that 'the Highlanders are, however, faithful and obedient to their king and country, and easily made to submit to law, if properly governed'. The same point, if slanted differently, comes from Highland sources. 'There is never', it has been stressed, 'any suggestion in poetry or elsewhere that the Gaels do not owe allegiance to the true line of Malcolm III no matter how much their loyalty might become obscured in the turbulence of history or how much hostility the policies of an individual monarch and the attitudes of the central authorities might provoke.'[20]

Despite the growing awareness of Highland–Lowland divisions, it is therefore clear that in the later, just as in the earlier, middle ages, the Highlanders were considered an integral part of the Scottish nation. The implication, moreover, is that the problems of the late-medieval Highlands were really those of governance and lordship. But that is a conclusion for the Highlands as a whole.[21] How well does it apply to the 'fringe' region of the western seaboard and islands?

Throughout Scotland's history, the relationships between centre and localities always depended essentially upon the crown's relations with the local magnates, and so it is in these relationships that the answer will be sought. The ideal was to have loyal, responsible magnates controlling outlying areas on behalf of the king; that was the foundation of the crown's success in the twelfth and thirteenth centuries. Now west-coast, Celtic, magnates who filled exactly that role can readily be found. For instance, in the forty years between the final 'Winning of the West' in 1266 and the outbreak of civil war caused by Robert Bruce's seizure of the throne in 1306, the MacDougall lords of Lorn fitted without difficulty into the aristocratic community of the Scottish realm and acted as the main royal agents in the task of governing the West. Unfortunately for the MacDougalls, the ties they formed with the Comyns of Badenoch meant they took what turned out to be the losing side in the civil war.[22] But after their eclipse, their place in Argyll and their role as crown agents in the West were ultimately taken over by their Campbell neighbours. In the late thirteenth century the Campbells were at feud with the MacDougalls, which no doubt helps explain why they supported Robert Bruce. Neil Campbell took the king's sister Mary as his second wife, and their son was made earl of Atholl, only to die childless at the battle of Halidon Hill in 1333. The descendants of Neil and his first wife flourished, however, and except for an estrangement in the 1360s continued to be staunch crown supporters. Royal patronage and judicious marriage brought them extensive lands; they were sheriffs of the new sheriffdom of Argyll; and from 1383 they were also royal lieutenants in part, and eventually in all, of it. By the early fifteenth century they were in the top flight of Scottish nobles, with one of the highest magnate incomes. Duncan Campbell married a daughter of the Regent Albany, and early in the 1440s became one of the first lords of parliament (equivalent to English peers). His grandson and heir Colin rose further: earl of Argyll in 1457, Master of the Royal Household in 1464, and Chancellor of Scotland in 1483. Colin's son, the second earl, continued as Master of the Household, and along with his brother-in-law the earl of Lennox, commanded the Scottish right wing at Flodden, where both died beside their king.[23]

In the fifteenth century the Campbells thus developed from local magnates into national ones, prominent at the centre of affairs. They held that position for centuries – but also kept their grip on their local power base, and indeed strengthened it as much as possible. They knew that local and national power went together, and in that they are typical of successful Scottish noble families of the fifteenth century. Yet, although in the 1470s the first earl apparently added the 'P' in the surname 'Campbell' to make it look Norman,[24] they never lost their place in the Gaelic world. A Gaelic poem in the *Book of the Dean of Lismore* states, 'Write expertly, learnedly, . . . Bring unto MacCaléin no poem lacking artistry to be read'. MacCaléin, the judge of Gaelic poetry, was the Campbell chief, probably the second earl of Argyll.[25]

The title earl of Argyll itself is important: unlike the other new and honorific peerage titles of the fifteenth century, it was a territorial designation like those of the old provincial earldoms.[26] It probably reflected the Gaelic '*Ri Airir Goidel*' ('king' of Argyll), one of the titles of Somerled, 'King of the Isles and Argyll', in the twelfth century, and used until the early fourteenth by his MacDougall, MacRuari and MacDonald descendants.[27] When the Campbells became earls of Argyll, were they not claiming a place in the Gaelic world roughly equivalent to that of Somerled's main descendants, the MacDonald Lords of the Isles? The Campbells could not claim descent from Somerled, and were probably known to have originated in British Strathclyde; so what they did, apparently, was to acquire a superior pedigree back to King Arthur and to Merlin, the prophet of a united Celtic Britain. Sixteenth-century Campbell poetry calls them 'head of the Gael', thereby challenging the MacDonald position.[28] More prosaically, after the final forfeiture of the Lordship of the Isles in the early sixteenth century, half a dozen mainland chiefs of the Lordship can be found associated with the earls of Argyll, while in 1519 the third earl received bonds of manrent from seven island chiefs and from the captain of Clanranald, the main MacDonald cadet branch.[29] By then the Campbells were clearly out to replace the MacDonalds altogether within the west-coast Gaelic world, and even in the fifteenth century they were probably setting themselves up as rivals; they were prominent in many of the crown's moves against the MacDonalds.[30]

In this context, the sole occasion when a Campbell witnessed a Lord of the Isles charter is significant. It was at Edinburgh on 22 December 1478, shortly after John MacDonald the fourth Lord had lost his earldom of Ross and had been declared a lord of parliament, the junior rank in the peerage. The charter's witnesses were headed by 'Colin, Earl of Argyll, Lord Lorn and Campbell, Master of the Household of our Supreme Lord the King'.[31] That looks like self-satisfied one-upmanship on Argyll's part, reflecting not only his superior status, but his closeness to the crown. The message appears to be, 'Work with the king, for your mutual advantage; that is how to get on in the world' – a world which to the Campbells, despite their west-coast origins, ties, and power base, was the same hybrid Scottish world inhabited by Alexander III. The examples of the Campbells and MacDougalls demonstrate that there was no automatic west-coast Gaelic antipathy to the kingdom of Scotland.

The MacDougalls and Campbells, however, were not the greatest magnate houses of the medieval Scottish West; that position belonged to the MacDonald Lords of the Isles.[32] The MacDonalds' dealings with the crown were very different from those of the MacDougalls and Campbells: they included a sequence of confrontations and crises, several pitched battles, and eventually the long-drawn-out process of forfeiture. And, unfortunately, these unhappy crown–MacDonald relations, rather than the happier crown–Macdougall and crown–Campbell ones, coloured perceptions of the relationships between the Celtic fringe and the kingdom as a whole in the late middle ages.

To examine what went wrong between the Lords of the Isles and the crown, let us first look back to the thirteenth century, when rivalries and feuds among the descendants of Somerled were one of the main themes of west-coast history. These rivalries helped ensure that while the MacDougalls co-operated with the Scots crown in the 1260s, the MacDonalds did not. If anything, they seemed closer to their Norwegian overlords, and joined King Haakon's 1263 expedition against Scotland (albeit reluctantly).[33] Thereafter Alexander III relied on and favoured the MacDougalls, and in the settlement of the West – as formalised in King John Balliol's ordinance of 1293 – the MacDonalds were frozen out. The region's northern part was placed under William earl of Ross, the central part under Alexander MacDougall, and the southern part under James the Steward, while the Great Glen was dominated by John Comyn of Badenoch, head of Scotland's most powerful kindred. Since John Comyn was a kinsman through marriage of both Alexander MacDougall and the earl of Ross (and King John's brother-in-law), this in effect created a vast Comyn hegemony in the West, in which there was no room for the MacDonalds. [34] The initial 'Winning of the West', therefore, did nothing to foster MacDonald commitment to the kingdom of Scotland.

That, no doubt, determined MacDonald attitudes in the 1290s and 1300s, leading Alexander MacDonald of Islay to appeal in 1292–3 beyond King John to Edward I of England (then Scotland's overlord) for justice against Alexander MacDougall, and to serve Edward after 1296, whereas the Comyns and MacDougalls (then) upheld the Scottish cause.[35] Angus Óg MacDonald also served Edward I, in 1301[36] – but in 1306, when the Comyns and MacDougalls sided with the English in implacable opposition to Robert Bruce, he chose to help King Robert.[37] It was a fortunate decision, for Robert I destroyed the MacDougalls, and granted much of their territory to the MacDonalds.[38] Too much, however, can be made of the grants. The MacDougall lands had probably already been overrun by the MacDonalds during the war. Elsewhere, Kintyre, which Angus Óg might have hoped for, went to Robert, son of Walter the Steward; Lewis, similarly, probably went to Hugh earl of Ross; and while Angus was given the Comyn lordship of Lochaber, that was incorporated into Thomas Randolph's earldom of Moray.[39] Moreover, under Robert I as under John Balliol, the earl of Ross dominated the northern part of the region and the Stewarts dominated the south. In the centre the MacDougalls were replaced by the Campbells, and to the east the place of the Comyns was filled by Thomas Randolph earl of Moray. Each of these received far more territory than the MacDonalds did from Robert I. Also, Walter the Stewart married the king's daughter, Hugh Ross and Neil Campbell married the king's sisters, and Thomas Randolph was the king's nephew.[40] Robert I, in fact, created a Bruce family hegemony throughout the West, and once again there was little room for the MacDonalds.

Why this was so in unclear. Perhaps Robert was less sure of them than of

Randolph, Stewart, Ross and Campbell. More probably, however, the reason is that Angus Óg died shortly after Bannockburn (1314), and his successor as MacDonald chief was killed at Dundalk (or Faughart) in 1318. The MacDonald pedigree is obscure at this point; the kindred may have been indulging in infighting, and probably would not have been in a position to compete for patronage.[41] At any rate, when Angus Óg's son John emerged as chief of the MacDonalds in the 1330s, hostility towards Robert I's west-coast policy and its beneficiaries seems largely to have determined his attitude. In 1335 he rejected overtures made on behalf of David II (1329–71) by John Randolph, earl of Moray (the overlord of Lochaber), and instead the following year made an agreement with Edward Balliol. Balliol guaranteed him much of his former MacDougall land, and promised new grants of the isles of Skye and Lewis, one certainly and the other probably at the expense of the earl of Ross, and Kintyre at the expense of Robert the Steward.[42] John, in the 1330s, was clearly hoping to benefit from the collapse of the Bruce regime.

In the event, however, it was the Balliol cause which collapsed, and by 1343 John had made his peace with David II. The settlement was generous, giving him the rest of the islands once held by the MacDougalls plus Lewis, and freeing Lochaber from Randolph superiority, but it was only made 'after diligent discussion and bearing the common utility and peace of our realm in mind' – a grudging tone which suggests David II was less than enthusiastic.[43] John never, in fact, developed good relations with David II, and in 1369 was forced to submit to the king's mercy; he was allowed to keep his lands only by promising to obey royal officials, pay taxes, expel enemies and rebels from his lordship, and deliver hostages.[44] Such terms suggest that the MacDonald commitment to the kingdom of Scotland had hardly strengthened since the 1330s.

Yet once the Balliol cause had collapsed, John did apparently make a conscious decision to move closer into the aristocratic community of the kingdom, if not the king's good graces. This is demonstrated by a number of marriages. In 1337, shortly after his agreement with Balliol, he had married Amy MacRuari, sister of the MacRuari chief, Ranald. That marriage, to a fellow descendant of Somerled, had a purely west-coast relevance – and was the most advantageous for John, for when Ranald MacRuari died childless in 1346 he was able, in his wife's right, to take over the MacRuari share of Somerled's territory, the lordship of Garmoran.[45] Some four years later, however, he remarried – Amy either had been divorced or, more probably, had simply died – and his second wife was the eldest daughter of Robert the Steward.[46] Also, in about 1342, one of his sisters married the earl of Ross, while his eldest son married a daughter of the chief of the Campbells some time in the 1350s.[47] These marriages indicate that in the 1340s and '50s John was establishing links with magnates who had previously seemed his rivals; in that respect he was coming in from the fringe. Moreover, in the 1360s John's bad relations with David II probably strengthened his ties with Robert the Steward and the earl of Ross, both of whom also clashed with King David.[48]

One reason for John MacDonald's marriage to the Steward's daughter was probably to gain Kintyre. That duly happened – but the formal grant of it did not come until 1376, when Robert was king (Robert II, 1371–90). [49] Waiting so long for the charter may not have mattered to John; but it is significant that in 1376 Kintyre and other MacDonald lands were made into a jointure for John and his wife. The impetus for this arrangement may have come from Robert II rather than John, for jointures were alien to Gaelic society; at any rate after John's death in 1388 his widow's claims to her jointure probably caused a serious breach between the crown and the MacDonalds. [50] Furthermore, although John was not cold-shouldered by Robert II, he might have expected grants of public office. Robert made his own son Alexander royal lieutenant for the Highlands north of the Moray Firth, and made Gillespie Campbell royal lieutenant in Argyll, [51] but John MacDonald did not become, for example, royal lieutenant for the Isles – a position which would not have given him much more actual power, but which would have increased his prestige and tied him closer to the crown. It is arguable, therefore, that after Robert the Steward became king MacDonald–Stewart ties weakened.

MacDonald–Ross ties, on the other hand, became stronger. In 1366 Earl William of Ross, his brother Hugh of Balnagown and his brother-in-law John MacDonald were all condemned for contumacious absence from parliament, and Hugh Ross in particular may have gravitated towards the MacDonald orbit. [52] Then, after Earl William had died in 1372 and his daughter Euphemia had inherited Ross (in place of William's preferred heir, Hugh), an attempt was made to bring the earldom into the hands of the royal family by marrying Countess Euphemia to Robert II's son Alexander Stewart (the 'Wolf of Badenoch'). [53] The marriage was disastrous, and – probably as a reaction against it – Euphemia's daughter by her first husband was married to her cousin Donald, the second MacDonald Lord of the Isles. [54] This second MacDonald–Ross marriage was particularly momentous, for in 1437 the son of it, Alexander the third Lord, eventually inherited the earldom of Ross.

The inheritance, however, was far from straightforward. After the death of Countess Euphemia, her son by her first marriage succeeded, only to die in 1402 leaving a young daughter. Two men seem to have claimed her wardship: her maternal grandfather the Duke of Albany (brother of King Robert III and of the 'Wolf of Badenoch'), who was then running Scotland, and her paternal uncle, Donald MacDonald, Lord of the Isles. [55] In 1411 Donald launched a campaign into Ross, where the Rosses of Balnagown and other leading families (presumably objecting to the Stewart's designs on the earldom) apparently welcomed him. [56] He then attacked the earl of Mar (son of the 'Wolf of Badenoch', and main crown agent in the north at that time), but was checked at Harlaw in Aberdeenshire, and was forced to submit. In 1415 the heiress to Ross transferred it to Albany's second son, and then entered a nunnery. [57] But the new earl died in 1424, and Alexander MacDonald, Lord of the Isles, was left as the legitimate heir. For most of James I's personal rule (1424–37), Alexander's claims were resisted; the years 1428–31 saw James's arrest of numerous Highland chiefs at Inverness, Alexander's rebellion, defeat and imprisonment, and the reversal of Harlaw when the forces of the Lordship defeated a crown army led by Mar at Inverlochy. [58] Eventually, however – perhaps after Mar's death in 1435 removed a major stumbling-block – Alexander was finally recognised as earl of Ross, either just before or just after James I's own death in 1437.[59]

Alexander's acquisition of Ross brought the MacDonalds' possessions right across to the Moray Firth. They had come in from the 'fringe' with a vengeance, being now by far the dominant power in the whole Highlands, and indeed, in terms of area, the greatest landowners in the kingdom. Unlike his predecessors, moreover, Alexander held public office: the minority government of James II (1437–60) actually made him justiciar (chief justice) north of the Forth.[60] And the MacDonalds' new place at the very top of Scottish magnate society is reflected in the famous tripartite bond which was made with the kingdom's two other greatest lords, the earls of Douglas and Crawford.[61]

In the east-coast traditions recounted in the seventeenth-century *Brieve Cronicle of the Earlis of Ross*, 'Alexander Ila was erll of Ross and Justice for the North; he was valzeant in all his acts, and lovinglie governit the erldome in tranquilite and peace, and deyit at Dingwall and was buryit at the channerie of Ross, 8th May 1449'.[62] His burial was at Rosemarkie, not with his ancestors in Iona; as has aptly been said, 'he seems to have died as he had lived, as Earl of Ross rather than as Lord of the Isles'.[63] The MacDonald muniments also indicate a clear eastward shift in emphasis.[64] Sixty-seven charters, precepts and other similar documents survive from the period of the MacDonald tenure of Ross, from 1437 to 1475. Of these, fifty – almost exactly three-quarters – concern lands in the east of the earldom of Ross or the east-coast lands associated with it; sixteen – less than a quarter – concern lands in the Lordship of the Isles or in wester Ross; and one concerns land in Ayrshire. The documents' place-dates show the same pattern. Fifty-six of them have place-dates, and of these forty-two – again three-quarters – are at Inverness, Dingwall, or nearby, whereas only fourteen – a quarter – are in the west-coast region. In this period the MacDonald muniments appear to be more those of the earldom of Ross than those of the Lordship of the Isles – except that in the surviving witness-lists the names of west-coast chiefs predominate, even in the charters issued in the east. What that shows is that when Alexander MacDonald and his son John moved east, they brought their leading west-Highland followers with them.

Under John MacDonald, the fourth Lord, the east-coast emphasis also appears in his confrontations with the crown. When John revolted in 1451, it was largely because of a broken crown promise to give him custody of the castles of Urquhart, on Loch Ness, and Ruthven in Badenoch, which controlled the two major routes through the Highlands, and which he duly seized.[65] At that time King James II's main preoccupation was his power-struggle with the earl of Douglas – with whom the MacDonald earls of Ross were joined in the tripartite bond. It was because Douglas would not break this bond that James killed him in 1452. In the ensuing civil war, MacDonald forces raided Bute and Arran,[66] but, particularly in the final conflict of 1455, they made little effort on behalf of the Douglases. John MacDonald was probably looking to be bought off, or rewarded, by the king. But that did not happen. So, instead, during the next few years, John and his half-brother Celestine of Lochalsh, acting sheriff of Inverness, simply moved in on forfeited Douglas lands on the shores of the Moray Firth, helping themselves to nearly £1,500 or rents which should have gone to the crown.[67] Not surprisingly, there was another confrontation; and one consequence of this piece of MacDonald disenchantment with the crown was that John listened to overtures from Edward IV of England and from the exiled earl of Douglas – making a treaty with them in 1462. It was a secret treaty, but in 1475 Edward IV deliberately leaked it; John was condemned for treason, and the earldom of Ross, together with Kintyre and Knapdale, was forfeited.[68]

John did not, however, forfeit the Lordship of the Isles in 1475; what the crown did was push him back to the 'fringe'. But the next – penultimate – chapter in MacDonald history repeated the pattern of the fifteenth century, for one of its main themes was the effort to regain Ross. Whether or not that should be attempted seems to have been a fundamental cause of disputes between John MacDonald and Angus, his illegitimate son and heir. Angus, in particular, tried to regain Ross. He attacked Inverness and demolished the castle, and then defeated a government army at 'Lagebraad', somewhere in the earldom, in c1480. Subsequently, he may have made Inverness his base, and was murdered there by his mad Irish harper in 1490.[69] His successor as the young, aggressive MacDonald heir, Alexander MacDonald of Lochalsh, then raided easter Ross in 1491. This sequence of raids seems finally to have provoked the crown; in 1493 James IV directly attacked the Lordship of the Isles and imposed forfeiture on the Lord.[70] Even after 1475, therefore, the east-coast territories were fundamentally important in the Lordship's history.

The idea of the MacDonalds moving in from the 'fringe' can also be developed in another way. When the fourth Lord revolted in 1451, he did so, according to the *Auchinleck Chronicle*, partly because 'the kingis awne persoun . . . hecht [promised] him gud lordschipe, the quhilk he had nocht gottin bot ewynn the contrary in all thingis'.[71] His predecessors would no doubt have sympathised. Now 'good lordship' is, of course, one of the most common general themes in late-medieval crown–noble relations. Another major theme of late-medieval noble history is evident in the way MacDonald territory was amassed. Royal grants were involved (albeit insufficiently for the MacDonalds), but acquisitions *via* heiresses were even more important, and so was the fortuitous exploitation of other magnates' political and genetic mis-fortunes (most of the MacDonalds' rivals eventually died out without male heirs). Thus the growth of MacDonald power provides an excellent example of the familiar 'snowball'[72] process within the late-medieval nobility: more and more land coming into the hands of fewer and fewer magnates.

Moreover, the most influential modern analysis of the Lordship of the Isles, although approaching it chiefly in terms of Gaelic kin-based society, states that in the later middle ages, 'their cultural and social system did begin to exhibit certain features which derived from a closer contact with East Scotland'.[73] One of these features was the recognition that heiresses could transmit territory, which was involved in the acquisition of both Garmoran (1346) and Ross (1436/7). Another was the application of primogeniture: in contrast to what happened after Somerled's death and possibly within the MacDonald lands until the early fourteenth century, the late-medieval MacDonald Lordship was not partitioned on the death of any of the Lords, and succession went to the eldest sons (except that the first Lord's successor was his eldest son by his second wife, the king's daughter). A third feature of this assimilation of 'Lowland' practices was what may be called 'feudal' charters: these were issued to cadets when, instead of partitioning the Lordship, they were endowed with land to be held subordinately of the Lord; and were also issued to other heads of kindreds in the region, establishing that their lands were likewise held of the Lords of the Isles.[74]

In these ways the Lords of the Isles can be said to be becoming more and more like typical late-medieval magnates in Scotland, and indeed in England and France. In particular, there are close similarities with the histories of Scotland's old Celtic earldoms,[75] and with the MacDougall and Campbell lordships in Argyll, the implication is that despite the intense Celtic ethos of the Lordship of the Isles,[76] the MacDonald Lords were moving in much the same way as the twelfth-century Celtic earls, the MacDougalls in the later thirteenth century, and the Campbells in the fourteenth and fifteenth. In that case the conflicts with the crown could be attributed to the accidents of politics – much as the destruction of the MacDougalls can. And a MacDonald apologist – a MacMhuirich shennachie, perhaps – could readily blame the crown for what went wrong. It is not difficult to portray the Lords of the Isles as wanting to come in from the 'fringe' to the centre of the kingdom, and the kings as consistently trying to block their efforts to do so.

Yet, while that conclusion neatly fits the general thrust of this essay, it is too superficial. If the MacDonald Lords of the Isles were very similar to other Scottish magnates from both the east and the west of the kingdom, they also stood apart from them in several important ways. One is in their relations with England. Up to the 1330s, these were perhaps not much out of the ordinary. But although John MacDonald came back into David II's allegiance in 1343, he and his successors did not give up their dealings with the English crown, and indeed they seem to have been regarded south of the border as the king of England's allies.[77] Admittedly nothing came of this, at least not until the 1462 treaty. But it must surely have irritated the Scottish kings, and have sown serious doubts about the MacDonalds' commitment and even their loyalty to the kingdom of Scotland.

Secondly, the MacDonalds were unconventional and provocative in the way they took the law into their own hands when pursuing territorial claims. Admittedly all Scottish nobles were perfectly ready to employ extra-legal means in disputes when necessary. The scale of the MacDonalds' activities, however, sets them apart. No doubt they had good reason to feel disgruntled about royal patronage, and especially about their claim to Ross. But capturing Urquhart and Ruthven castles in 1451, seizing crown rents in the Inverness area after the forfeiture of the Douglases, and marching with an army into and beyond Ross in 1411, are all spectacular actions. Other magnates may have done similar things, but against rivals, not against the crown, and not on the MacDonalds' grand scale; no other territorial dispute ever led to a full-scale pitched battle like Harlaw.

The Lords of the Isles' pretensions are illustrated in more peaceful terms by some administrative documents relating to inheritances within Ross. Normally, when a landowner died, the heir obtained a brieve from the royal chapel (equivalent to the English chancery) requiring an inquest to be held; its findings would be returned, or 'retoured' to the royal chapel, which would then instruct the overlord to give the heir sasine; and the lord would duly issue a precept. In 1464, after John the fourth Lord had submitted to crown authority, this procedure was carried out properly.[78] Four earlier precepts of sasine, however, show that before that date John and his father were administering inheritances in Ross themselves, just as they no doubt did in the isles, following retours to their own chapel.[79] That procedure was only permissible within regalities, which Ross was not. Here, therefore, Alexander and John MacDonald were in effect acting as lords of regality – without a royal grant.

Some of the Lords' charters are also illuminating. While many are conventional conveyances, a number, to members of the Lords' own family and to other highland chiefs, have unconventional wording which suggests that a meaningful lord–man relationship was intended.[80] Four are particularly significant: Donald in 1415 to Angus MacKay, 'for homage and service . . . against all mortals of this life';[81] Alexander in 1427 to Gilleownan MacNeill, 'for homage and service . . . against all men and women of whatever status . . . in peace and war on land and sea';[82] John in 1456 to Somerled son of John 'for homage and service . . . against any mortal whatsoever';[83] and John in 1469 to Hugh his son, 'for homage and service . . . in war and peace on sea and land as is required . . . against . . . any mortal male or female whatsoever'.[84] Such phraseology, specifying service to the lord against everyone else, is unique among late-medieval Scottish charters. But it closely echoes the specification of service in fifteenth-century bonds of manrent – with one vital difference, for bonds of manrent almost always excepted the king from those against whom the service was due.[85] That exception did not guarantee that a man would put the king before his lord; but leaving it out, as it is left out of these charters, shows the Lords of the Isles not even bothering with the conventional recognition of obligations towards the crown. And if that clause was omitted from these charters, might it also have been omitted from the Lords' most famous, lost, document: the bond with Douglas and Crawford?[86] That might explain James II's violent reaction.

Finally, the aftermath of James's reaction against the Douglas–Crawford–MacDonald bond highlights the greatest contrast between the Lords of the Isles and the rest of the Scottish nobility. When the earl of Douglas was killed in 1452, his brothers rebelled; but when they burned Stirling, they had only 600 men with them, and when their ally the earl of Crawford confronted a crown army at Brechin his men deserted rather than oppose the royal banner.[87] The Douglases' rebellion quickly subsided, and when James II finally attacked them in 1455, their resistance was no more effective.[88] When the Lords of the Isles were confronted by the crown, they too generally submitted – but then carried on as before. The scale of their confrontations was also very different. Harlaw was a major battle, with many thousands engaged on each side;[89] the government classed it with battles against the English;[90] and it was a draw. In two other pitched battles, at Inverlochy in 1431 and at 'Lagebraad' in Ross in c1480, the Lordship's armies inflicted the only defeats suffered by royal forces at the hands of rebels between 1100 and 1500, apart from

Sauchieburn (1488). Moreover, after the Lordship's final forfeiture in 1493, the next fifty years witnessed no fewer than seven serious rebellions, all well supported by west-coast chiefs, aimed at restoring John's heirs.[91] The scale and duration of the resistance which the MacDonalds were able to mount against the crown are unparalleled in late-medieval Scottish history.

That was partly a matter of manpower. The statement of an eighteenth-century clan chief that his lands were worth 'five hundred men' illustrates the importance in the highlands of lordship over men.[92] It emerges clearly from the chronicler Bower's account of the arrest of highland chiefs in 1429, for each name is followed by the number of their men: Angus Dubh (Mackay), 'dux quator millium'; Kenneth Mor (MacKenzie); dux duorum millium'; John Ross, William Lesley, Angus Murray and 'Macmaken' (? Matheson), 'duces duorum millium'; Alexander MacRuari, 'dux mille hominum'; and John MacArthur, 'dux mille hominum'.[93] Bower was probably fairly accurate with figures,[94] and the manpower levels he gave tally reasonably with those which Duncan Forbes of Culloden recorded for Highland clans in 1745.[95] As for the Lords of the Isles, Bower stated that Donald had ten thousand men with him at Harlaw.[96] Even allowing for exaggeration, the contrast with what the Douglases put in the field in 1452 is dramatic.

There is, of course, a difference between the number of men theoretically at a lord's disposal and those who actually turned out when summoned – as medieval nobles often found to their cost. But the Lordship of the Isles not only provided the Lords with large numbers of fighting men, but with followers who were generally reliable and loyal – much more so than the followings of other Scottish rebel magnates. This was no doubt due partly to the strong warrior ethos of the Celtic world, and partly, too, to the MacDonalds' success in pursuing the expansionist dynamic of Celtic kin-based society during most of the late middle ages,[97] thereby providing not only prestige and glory but also booty and ready patronage for their followers. Yet most medieval societies had their warrior ethos and their expansionist dynamic. More specifically, whereas the Rosses and other east-coast families probably welcomed the MacDonald acquisition of Ross, the Gaelic MacKenzies strongly opposed it.[98] And in 1429, when James I himself defeated Alexander, the third Lord, 'in a bog in Lochaber', two mainland clans, the Mackintoshes and Camerons, fled rather than fight against the royal banner[99] – just as Crawford's men did at the battle of Brechin in 1452. Thus the scale and loyalty of MacDonald support cannot simply be explained in terms of a Gaelic/non-Gaelic dichotomy.

Instead, the implication is that the actual exercise of MacDonald lordship within the Lordship of the Isles was peculiarly effective by the normal standards of late-medieval Scotland – both in the Highlands and the Lowlands. Some likely reasons for that have already been indicated: the cohesiveness and continuity of the Lords' power, following their adoption of the principle of primogeniture; and their formal assertion of superiority over cadets and dependent kindreds in their charters. Both of these are ways in which the MacDonalds can be said to have been institutionalising their lordship. The early fifteenth-century document recording the genealogies of all the kindreds in the area of MacDonald dominance is perhaps another instance of this.[100] So too may be the existence of formal administrative offices: secretary, chancellor, chamberlain, steward, and chief judge (*archiiudex*).[101] But probably the most significant institution was the 'Council of the Isles'. Noble councils were not uncommon in late-medieval Scotland, but that of the isles seems unusually regularised, for it apparently consisted of the heads of the major kindreds in the Lordship, rather than of men arbitrarily chosen by the Lords. It was associated with all the important matters of the Lords' rule, including their succession and inauguration, their marriages, their dealings with the crown, with the English, and with the earldom of Ross, their finances, their patronage, and their justice as the Lordship's supreme court of appeal.[102] Through the Council (and to a lesser extent through some of the administrative offices), the dependent chiefs were tied closely into the MacDonalds' lordship – to such an extent that they accompanied the third and fourth Lords to Dingwall, to Inverness, and to Edinburgh.[103]

As well as institutionalising the MacDonald's power, the Council's workings also no doubt helped ensure that their lordship, so far as the dependent chiefs were concerned, was particularly 'good'. Moreover, MacDonald 'good lordship' was unchallenged for most of the period. After the mid-fourteenth century they had no effective rivals within their west-coast region (admittedly the Campbells were their rivals, but from outside, from another part of the west; they do not seem to have attracted support from within the Lordship of the Isles until the sixteenth century, and even then ineffectively). More significantly, the Lords of the Isles were not threatened within the Lordship by the crown. There is no evidence of any royal patronage being bestowed there independently of the Lords. Nor could royal justice be put into effect there independently, which meant there was little point in the crown's encouraging appeals against the decisions of the Lords and their Council. Thus the crown was unable to poach MacDonald dependants and undermine the MacDonalds' regional power – as James II, for instance, seems to have done with the Douglases in the 1450s.[104]

What the analysis amounts to, in the last resort, is to suggest that the MacDonalds were exercising something closely approaching sovereignty. Were not the Lords of the Isles, in practice, behaving much as sovereign rulers? And was that perhaps implied in their style? *Dominus* is a notoriously difficult word to translate. When, in parliament in 1476, the last Lord of the Isles (having renounced all claims to Ross and Kintyre) was created and named by the heralds 'baron banrent and lord of [the king's] parliament',[105] the intention must have been to assert that it meant the lowest rank in the Scottish peerage. Before then, however, it was not a specific peerage rank, but a translation of the Gaelic *Rí* – which can be translated king.[106] It is hard to believe that MacDonald Lords of the Isles were not conscious of this, and of the semi-sovereign status which that implied. Moreover, the earliest known use of 'Dominus Insularum' by John MacDonald the first Lord was in a letter to Edward III of England, dated 21 September 1336.[107] This was the third of three contemporary documents. In the others, the indenture with and a letter to Edward Balliol, John was simply 'of Islay'.[108] That suggests that 'Dominus Insularum' was added for Edward III's benefit – in a letter in which John requested confirmation of the grants which Balliol had promised him, otherwise John would not *ally* with Balliol. The tone of the letter indicates that while John recognised Edward Balliol as king of Scots, he was dealing with him on equal terms. In that case, might the use of *Dominus* have been intended to carry much the same status as the king of England's 'Dominus Hibernie'?

Judging by their actions, that is probably how the Lords of the Isles saw themselves, and that is where they differed from all the other lords and magnates of late-medieval Scotland. This claim was based on a Celtic concept of lordship rather than a feudal one, and it was bolstered by many of the characteristics of Celtic kin-based society. On the other hand many of the factors – such as primogeniture – which lay behind MacDonald power were alien to traditional Celtic society. Thus the Lordship of the Isles must be considered a hybrid, like most of the other lordships and earldoms of medieval Scotland. Its hybridity, however, was rather different; the Lords of the Isles seem to have adopted those features of both Celtic and feudal lordship which suited their own interests best.

However we view the Lordship of the Isles, the MacDonalds' power was such that, had they wanted to, they probably would have been able to integrate the west-coast region fully into the kingdom of Scotland. That, unfortunately, was prevented by their bad relations with the crown. But the crown's policy of keeping the Lords of the Isles at arm's length, out on the 'fringe', can now be seen to be understandable and even justifiable. The MacDonalds' history shows them as wanting to take far more from the kingdom of Scotland than they were prepared to give to it, and that is something of which all the kings from Robert I to James IV were probably well aware. But by trying to keep the MacDonalds out on the 'fringe', the crown did not give them a vested interest in the kingdom; it was a vicious circle, which eventually brought the Lordship's collapse.

Nevertheless the Lordship of the Isles must be regarded as one of the greatest success stories of the medieval 'Celtic' world. Indeed in terms of size, manpower, durability and prestige within its own cultural milieu, it can stand comparison with any late-medieval lordship in Scotland, Ireland, Wales, England, and even, perhaps, in Europe. In some ways comparisons with the duchies of Brittany and even, perhaps, Burgundy, are not out of place. But the most appropriate comparison for the Lordship of the Isles is with that other hybrid lordship which emerged from Scottish Gaeldom: the kingdom of Scotland itself. In the fourteenth and fifteenth centuries, were not the Lords of the Isles doing very much what the kings of Scots had done three or four centuries earlier – with almost as much success? That brings this essay full circle. It started with the vital significance of the early evolution of the unitary kingdom of Scotland. It finished with the evolution of what came very close to being a unitary 'state' of the Isles – and the decisive, if much less happy, importance of that for the relations between the 'Celtic fringe' and the kingdom of Scotland as a whole.

NOTES

Abbreviations used in the notes
APS   *Acts of Parliaments of Scotland*
CDS   *Calendar of Documents Relating to Scotland*
RMS   *Registram Magni Sigilii Regum Scotorum*, eds JM Thomson and
        others (Edinburgh, 1882–1914)
RRS   *Regesta Regum Scottorum*
SHR   *Scottish Historical Review*

1 For the process in Scotland, see G. W. S. Barrow, *Kingship and Unity* (1981), chapters 2, 3, 6; A. A. M. Duncan, *Scotland: The Making of the Kingdom* (Edinburgh, 1975), chapters 7, 8, 19, 20; G. W. S. Barrow, *The Anglo-Norman Era in Scottish History* (Oxford, 1980). I am greatly indebted to my colleague Dr Keith Stringer for his kind but rigorous comments on a draft of this essay.

2 The phrase is G. W. S. Barrow's; see his *Kingship and Unity*, chapter 6.

3 One answer to the hackneyed question, 'Why did Edward I fail in Scotland, having succeeded in Wales?' would therefore be that in Scotland he was attempting something new, the conquest of an already 'Normanised' kingdom. Cf. A. Grant, 'The Triumph of Scotland', in *The Making of Britain: The Middle Ages*, ed. L. M. Smith (1985), 71–86, at 71–9.

4 When, for example, Macbeth, ruler of the northern province of Moray, killed King Duncan I in 1040, he did not take Moray out of the kingdom but, instead, became king himself. See, in general, A. P. Smyth, *Warlords and Holy Men: Scotland AD 80–1000* (1984), chapters 6, 7; Barrow, *Kingship and Unity*, 24–32; Duncan, *Scotland: The Making of the Kingdom*, chapters 4, 5, esp. 111–6.

5 D. Walker, *The Norman Conquerors* (Swansea, 1977), chapters 2–5; R. Frame, *Colonial Ireland* (Dublin, 1981), chapters 1, 2.

6 *APS* I, 475; I have used A. A. M. Duncan's translation, in *The Nation of the Scots and the Declaration of Arbroath* (Historical Association, 1970), 34–7.

7 Walker, *The Norman Conquerors*, chapter 5; R. R. Davies, *Lordship and Society in the March of Wales* (Oxford, 1978), chapter 14; Frame, *Colonial Ireland*, chapter 5; A. Cosgrove, *Late Medieval Ireland, 1370–1541* (Dublin, 1981), chapter 5; R. R. Davies, 'Lordship or Colony', in *The English in Medieval Ireland*, ed. J. F. Lydon (Dublin, 1984), 142–60. In practice, as opposed to theory, the division were never absolute; but, as other essays in this volume show, they became more acute during the thirteenth century.

8 Davies, *Lordship and Society*, chapter 3; R. Frame, 'War and Peace in the Medieval Lordship of Ireland', in *The English in Medieval Ireland*, 118–41.

9 *RRS* II, 76–7; cf. E. J. Cowan, 'Myth and Identity in Early Medieval Scotland', *SHR* 63 (1984), 111–35, at 130–1

10 See the accounts of Scotland's leading families in *The Scots Peerage*, ed. J. B. Paul (Edinburgh, 1904–14); cf. G. W. S. Barrow, *The Kingdom of the Scots* (1973), 373–83.

11 As in Ireland, *Gall*, which originally meant foreigner, was the Gaelic term for the non-Celtic people of Scotland; but those to whom it applied counted as Scots (Albannach*)*, in contrast to the English, or *Sasunnach*. 'It would be a contradiction in terms to speak of an Albannach Sasunnach.' See J. MacInnes, 'Gaelic Poetry and Historical Tradition', in *The Middle Ages in the Highlands*, ed. L. Maclean (Inverness, 1981), 142–63, at 144.

12 A theme examined in depth in N. Reid, 'The Political role of the monarchy in Scotland, 1249–1329' (Edinburgh University PhD thesis, 1985).

13 Barrow, *Kingdom of the Scots*, 362–4; except that Gaelic did remain the ordinary language of Galloway until much later (cf. A. I. Dunlop, *The Life and Times of James Kennedy, Bishop of St Andrews* [Edinburgh, 1950], 372).

14 R. Nicholson, 'The Highlands in the Fourteenth and Fifteenth Centuries', in *An Historical Atlas of Scotland*, ed. P. McNeill and R. Nicholson (Conference of Scottish Medievalists, 1975), 67–8, at 68.

15 John of Fordun, *Chronica Gentis Scotorum*, ed. W. F. Skene (Edinburgh, 1871–2), I, 24.

16 MacInnes, 'Gaelic Poetry and Historical Tradition', (as cited in n. 11), 160.

17 Davies, *Lordship and Society in the March of Wales*, chapter 13; Cosgrove, *Late Medieval Ireland*, chapter 5.

18 G. W. S. Barrow, 'The Sources for the History of the Highlands in the Middle Ages', in *The Middle Ages in the Highlands*, ed. Maclean, 11–22, at 19.

19 The point is lost in F. J. H. Skene's version, in which both *gens* and *natio* are translated as 'nation' – a mistake followed in A. Grant, *Independence and Nationhood: Scotland 1306–1469* (1984), 201. Fordun, of course, was trying to reconcile Scotland's hybridity with the common medieval concept of one nation, one language; cf. E. J. Cowan, 'Myth and Identity', *SHR* 63, 113–4.

20 MacInnes, 'Gaelic Poetry and Historical Tradition', 147.

21 Discussed for the Highlands in general in Grant, *Independence and Nationhood*, chapter 8.

22 A. A. M. Duncan and A. L. Brown, 'Argyll and the Isles in the Earlier Middle Ages', *Proceedings of the Society of Antiquaries of Scotland* 90 (1956–7), 192–220, at 216–8'; G. W. S. Barrow, *Robert Bruce and the Community of the Realm of Scotland* (2nd edn, Edinburgh, 1976), 76–9, 219, 227, 254–8, 406–9.

23 See, in general, *Scots Peerage*, I, 319–34; also *Historical Manuscripts Commission*, 4th report, 473–83 (for royal grants); A. Grant, 'The Development of the Scottish Peerage', *SHR* 57 (1978), 1–27, at 12–15 (for their income and their lordship of parliament); and N. Macdougall, *James III* (Edinburgh, 1982), 54, 124 (for their 1st earl of Argyll).

24 J. W. M. Bannerman, 'The Lordship of the Isles: Historical Background', in K. A. Steer and J. W. M. Bannerman, *Late Medieval Monumental Sculpture in the West Highlands* (Edinburgh, 1977), 201–13, at 211.

25 *Ibid.*, 211; MacInnes, 'Gaelic Poetry and Historical Tradition', 148.

26 Cf. Grant, 'Scottish Peerage', 307.

27 J. W. M. Bannerman, 'The Lordship of the Isles', in *Scottish Society in the Fifteenth Century*, ed. J. M. Brown (1977), 209–40, at 211–2.

28 Cf. Grant, 'Scottish Peerage', 3–7.

29 Bannerman, 'Lordship of the Isles', *West Highland Sculpture*, 212; J. Wormald, *Lords and Men in Scotland: Bonds of Manrent, 1442–1603* (Edinburgh, 1985), 178.

30 Macdougall, *James III*, 64, 121–4; Bannerman, 'Lordship of the Isles', *West Highland Sculpture*, 211–2.

31 *Acts of the Lords of the Isles, 1336–1493*, ed. J. Munro and R. W. Munro (Scottish History Society, 1986), no 113. I am extremely grateful to Jean and Billy Munro for kindly letting me use a typescript of the texts in advance of their publication.

32 This use of the family name 'MacDonald' hardly ever appears in official documents before about the middle of the sixteenth century (*ibid*, lxxxi); in their acts, the Lords of the Isles' normal surname is 'de Yle', ie 'of Islay'. But in the unique Gaelic charter the

Lord is simply called *Macdomhnaill*, ie, 'The MacDonald' (*ibid*, no 16) and that perhaps gives some sanction to the convenient but, strictly speaking, anachronistic practice of using 'MacDonald' for members of the 'de Yle' kindred in the middle ages.

33 Duncan and Brown, 'Argyll and the Isles', 213–5.

34 *APS* I, 447; Duncan and Brown, 'Argyll and the Isles', 216–7; Barrow, *Kingdom of the Scots*, 377–80; *Scots Peerage*, I, 506–9; VII, 233.

35 Barrow, *Robert Bruce*, 79–80, 153, 231.

36 *Ibid.*, 231, n.

37 Cf. A. A. M. Duncan's essay in this volume, above, Chapter 6.

38 Barrow, *Robert Bruce*, 254–8, 406–9; *RMS* I, app. II, nos. 56 (Morvern and Ardnamurchan), 57 (Lochaber), 58 (Duror and Glencoe – all to Angus Óg), and 653 (Tiree, Mull and other lands, to 'Alexander younger lord of the Isles'). Although it is possible that Ardnamurchan and Morvern were in MacDonald hands in the thirteenth century (Duncan and Brown, 'Argyll and the Isles', 204), I think it is more likely that they were then MacDougall territories.

39 Kintyre was held by Somerled, and was traditionally part of the MacDonald heartland, but only part of it was held by them in 1296, and Robert I granted it to his young grandson, Robert Stewart (Bannerman, 'Lordship of the Isles', *West Highland Sculpture*, 202–3; J. G. Dunbar and A. A. M. Duncan, 'Tarbert Castle', *SHR* 50 [1971], 1–17, at pp 16–17; *RMS* I, app. II, no. 661). The evidence that Lewis was held by the earls of Ross is its inclusion in a charter of 1382 listing all their hereditary possessions (though by then it had actually been transferred to the MacDonalds; see below, at note 43); it might have been gained under Alexander III, along with Skye (*ibid.*, I, no. 742; cf app. II, no. 61; Duncan, *Scotland: The Making of the Kingdom*, 582; *Acts of the Lords of the Isles*, xxix–xxx). The western bounds of Moray included Lochaber and the territory northwards to Glenelg, which is on the western seaboard (*RMS*, app. I, no. 31).

40 For grants to the Stewarts and Randolph, see Barrow, *Robert Bruce*, 397–8, and to the Campbells, *ibid.*, I, app. I, nos. 5, 8; app. II, nos. 55, 61, 63, 64, 65, 383. For the family relationships, see *Scots Peerage*, I, 8; II, 434–5; VI, 290–1.

41 Cf. the different versions in Bannerman, 'Lordship of the Isles', *West Highland Sculpture*, 202–3, *Acts of the Lords of the Isles*, 279–83, and W. D. Lamont, 'Alexander of Islay', *SHR* 60 (1981), 160–8. It seems to me that Bannerman's arguments about the deaths of Angus Óg and his successor present the fewest difficulties, and I have followed them in my text; but it is impossible to be certain.

42 Andrew of Wyntoun, *The Orygynale Cronykil of Scotland*, ed. D. Laing (Edinburgh, 1872–9), II, 419; *Acts of the Lords of the Isles*, no 1. The territories listed are the isles of Islay, Gigha, Jura, Colonsay, Mull, Skye, and Lewis, the lands of Kintyre, Knapdale, Morvern, and Ardnamurchan, and the wardship of Lochaber until the son of David of Strathbogie (the Comyn heir) came of age.

43 *RRS* VI, no 72. The territories listed are the isles of Islay, Gigha, Jura, Colonsay, Mull, Tiree, Coll, Lewis, and the lands of Morvern, Lochaber, Duror, and Glencoe, together with what was called 'custody of the *royal* castles of Cairn na Brugh More, Cairn na Burgh Beg, and Dun Chonnuill'.

44 *Acts of the Lords of the Isles*, no. 6 and lxiv–lxv; cf., *APS* I, 503, 507, 508.

45 *Acts of the Lords of the Isles*, 242, 286. Ranald MacRuari was in fact killed at the instigation of William earl of Ross (*Chron Wyntoun* (as cited in n. 42), II, 472), who was married to John's sister; was that more than a coincidence?

46 *Acts of the Lords of the Isles*, 242, 286. Historians have generally stated that John

divorced Amy (but kept hold of Garmoran), but J. and R. W. Munro point out, 'as no document is known proving divorce or annulment of the marriage with Amy MacRuari, the possibility that she died before her husband's remarriage cannot be ruled out' (*ibid.*, 286).

47 *Ibid.*, 242, 282, 287.

48 R. Nicholson, *Scotland: The Later Middle Ages* (Edinburgh, 1974), 169, 178–9; Grant, *Independence and Nationhood*, 175–6.

49 *RMS* I, nos 569. John is recorded as being in possession of Kintyre in 1367 (*APS* I, 528); but see the following note.

50 *RMS* I, nos. 567, 568, 569 (their terms show that in nos. 567 and 568 John's own lands were being made into a jointure, whereas no. 569, the charter of Kintyre [and half Knapdale to the north] states that it was Robert II's lands which were being transferred); *APS* I, 556–7; Grant, *Independence and Nationhood*, 214.

51 *RMS* I, no. 556; *Historical Manuscripts Commission*, iv, 485, no. 235.

52 *APS* I, 498; Scottish Record Office, GD 297 (MSS J. and F. Anderson)/194, by which Hugh Ross exchanged all his lands in Aberdeenshire for those of his brother, the earl of Wester Ross. I hope to examine the relationship between the Lords of the Isles and the earls and earldom of Ross in more depth at a later date. See also *Acts of the Lords of the Isles*, xxxi–xxxiv, and J. Munro, 'The Earldom of Ross and the Lordship of the Isles', in *Firthlands of Ross and Sutherland*, ed. J. R. Baldwin (Edinburgh, 1986), 59–67.

53 *Scots Peerage*, VII, 238–41. The marriage took place in 1382, some five months after the death of Euphemia's first husband, Walter Leslie (he was a courtier of David II, and had been married to Euphemia against her father's wishes).

54 *Ibid.*, VII, 241; *Registrum Episcopatus Moraviensis*, ed. C. Innes (Bannatyne Club, 1837), no. 271. We do not know when Donald married Euphemia's daughter, but it was probably in the 1380s (cf. Steer and Bannerman, *West Highland Sculpture*, 149); was Euphemia looking to her west-coast kinsmen for help?

55 *Ibid.*, 149; *The Book of the Thanes of Cawdor*, ed. C. Innes (Spalding Club, 1859), 5, where Albany is styled 'Dominus warde de Ross' in 1405.

56 Nicholson, *Scotland: The Later Middle Ages*, 233–4. Cf. Scottish Record Office, GD 297/195, which narrates how in 1412 Albany declared that Walter Ross of Balnagown had offended against him and the state; the offence must surely have been siding with Donald of the Isles in 1411.

57 Scottish Record Office, RH6, (MSS Register House Charters)/243; *Scots Peerage*, VII, 242–3.

58 Nicholson, *Scotland: The Later Middle Ages*, 315–7.

59 *Acts of the Lords of the Isles*, xxxiv, n. 54, and nos. 23–5.

60 *Ibid.*, 302.

61 We do not know when this bond was made. The only contemporary reference to it is in the Auchinleck Chronicle (*The Asloan Manuscript*, ed. W. A. Craigie [Scottish Text Society, 1923–5], I, 240) under the year 1452, by which time Alexander's son John was Lord of the Isles. In the early seventeenth century, however, Sir James Balfour's *Annales* stated that the bond was dated 7 March 1445 (ie 1445/6, in Alexander's lifetime (though Balfour attributed it to 'Donald Lord of the Iles')). The date 1445/6 would fit the political circumstances fairly well. See *Acts of the Lords of the Isles*, no. 45; A Grant, 'The Revolt of the Lord of the Isles and the Death of the Earl of Douglas, 1451–1452', *SHR* 60 (1981), 169–74, at 172; and below, note 86.

62 *Ane Brieve Cronicle of the Earlis of Ross*, ed. W. R. Baillie (Edinburgh, 1850), 10.

63 J. Munro, 'The Lordship of the Isles', in *The Middle Ages in the Highlands*, ed. Maclean, 23–37, at 29.

64 This analysis is based on the documents issued in the names of Alexander and John as earls of Ross, 1436–1475, excluding duplicates, published in *Acts of the Lords of the Isles*.

65 Grant, 'Revolt of the Lord of the Isles', 169–71.

66 *Ibid.*, 173; *Asloan Manuscript*, I, 221–2.

67 *The Exchequer Rolls of Scotland*, ed. G. Burnett *et. al.* (Edinburgh, 1878–1908), VII, 20, 128–9, 235, 356–7.

68 *Acts of the Lords of the Isles*, no. 75, and lxx–lxxi; *APS* II, 108–9, 111, 113.

69 H. Macdonald, 'History of the Macdonalds', in *Highland Papers*, ed. J. R. N. Macphail (Scottish History Society, 1914–34), I, 49; Bannerman, 'Lordship of the Isles', 216; Steer and Bannerman, *West Highland Sculpture*, 110–1; *Acts of the Lords of the Isles*, lxxi–lxxii, 313.

70 Nicholson, *Scotland: The Later Middle Ages*, 541.

71 *Asloan Manuscript*, (as cited in n. 61), I, 224–5.

72 The description is K. B. McFarlane's; see his *The Nobility of Later Medieval England* (Oxford, 1973), 152–3.

73 Bannerman, 'Lordship of the Isles', *West Highland Sculpture*, 201–13, at 202; cf. Bannerman, 'Lordship of the Isles', 209–40.

74 *Acts of the Lords of the Isles*, nos. 4, 7, 11–13, 17, 21, 22, 33, 42, 60, 61, 73, 76, 80, 88, 96.

75 Which gradually became 'feudalised' during the twelfth and thirteenth centuries; cf. Duncan, *Scotland: The Making of the Kingdom*, 164–8, 178–9, 187–8, 199–200, 368–70; C. J. Neville, 'The Earls of Strathearn from the 12th to the mid 14th century' (Aberdeen University PhD thesis, 1983).

76 For which see Bannerman, 'Lordship of the Isles', 209–40, and Bannerman, 'Lordship of the Isles', *West Highland Sculpture*, 201–13.

77 See, e.g., R. Frame, *English Lordship in Ireland* (Oxford, 1982), 151, for John and the English in the 1350s; *Rotuli Scotiae in Turri Londiniensi . . . asservati*, ed. D. Macpherson *et. al.* (1814–19), II, 94–5, for a mission to John's sons in 1389, to renew certain 'ligis confederationibus et amicitiis' between the king of England and his subjects on the one hand, and John's sons, 'subditos suos terras et dominia sua quecumque'; *CDS*, IV, no 876, for Donald's appearance as an ally of both the English and Scottish kings in an Anglo-French truce of 1416; and, in general, *Acts of the Lords of the Isles*, lxxiv–lxxviii.

78 *Ibid.*, no. 84; cf. no. 83, and *Introduction to Scottish Legal History*, ed. G. C. H. Paton (Stair Society, 1958), 171–3, for the procedure.

79 *Acts of the Lords of the Isles*, nos. 31, 28, 56, 67; cf. nos. 55, 71 and *The Court Book of the Barony of Carnwath*, ed. W. C. Dickinson (Scottish History Society, 1937), xli–xlii, for regalities.

80 In addition to the four cited below, see *Acts of the Lords of the Isles*, nos. 11–13, 17, 73, 80, 88.

81 *Ibid.*, no. 19.

82 *Ibid.*, no. 21.

83 *Ibid.*, no. 61.

84 *Ibid.*, no. 96.

85 Wormald, *Lords and Men*, 66–70.

86 That, in fact, is what Sir James Balfour stated; according to his *annals*, the tripartite bond

was 'ane offensive and defensiue Leauge & Combinatione against all none excepted (not the king him selue)'; *Acts of the Lords of the Isles*, no. 45. It seems unlikely that Balfour made that up, especially since his *annals* were intended to be an 'annalistic summary of such facts as he could ascertain'. As a leading herald, Balfour did extensive archival research, and 'his documents and notes . . . are still of use to scholars, for many of the documents which he copied are now lost'; B. Webster, *Scotland from the Eleventh Century to 1603* (Sources of History, 1975), 22–3. Where might Balfour have seen the bond? One possibility would be in the crown archives, for it is highly likely that James II would have had a copy kept in or after 1452. And this could well have been lost along with so many other Scottish crown records when they were sent back from England in 1660; cf. *ibid.*, 125–6.

87 *Asloan Manuscript*, I, 237–8, 241.

88 *Ibid.*, I, 243–4

89 Nicholson, *Scotland: The Later Middle Ages*, 234; W. Bower, *Scotichronicon*, ed. D. E. R. Watt (Aberdeen, 1987) (hereafter *Chron. Bower*), VIII, 74–7.

90 By a statute of council-general, the heirs of those killed at Harlaw 'pro defensione patrie' were to be treated as being of full age, even if they were minors: *Registrum Episcopatus Aberdonensis*, ed. C. Innes (Maitland and Spalding Clubs, 1845), I, 215. This privilege was otherwise only granted to the heirs of those killed in battle with the English.

91 Bannerman, 'Lordship of the Isles', *West Highland Sculpture*, 209–10; Dr Bannerman makes an apt comparison with the sequence of Jacobite risings in the seventeenth and eighteenth centuries.

92 I. F. Grant, *Everyday Life on an Old Highland Farm* (1924), 98.

93 *Chron. Bower*, VIII, 260–1.

94 He stated, for example, that the Scottish army sent to France in 1419 numbered 7,000 (*ibid.*, VIII, 112–13), and French sources suggest that it was in fact some 6,000 strong; G. du Fresne de Beaucourt, *Histoire de Charles VII* (Paris, 1881–91), I, 320–1. It is perhaps significant that Bower was one of two men put in charge of tax collection by James I (*Chron. Bower*, VIII, 240–1).

95 I. F. Grant, *The Social and Economic Development of Scotland before 1603* (Edinburgh, 1930), 493–5.

96 *Chron. Bower*, VIII, 74–5.

97 Cf. Bannerman, 'Lordship of the Isles', 211–3.

98 *Ibid.*, 212; cf. *Exchequer Rolls of Scotland*, IV, lxxxvi, 211.

99 *Chron. Bower*, VIII, 262–3.

100 I.e. 'MS 1467', see Bannerman, 'Lordship of the Isles', *West Highland Sculpture*, 205.

101 Bannerman, 'Lordship of the Isles', 226–7

102 *Ibid.*, 221–6; *Acts of the Lords of the Isles*, xlvi–xlix.

103 See the witness lists in *ibid.*, *passim*.

104 Cf. Macdougall, *James III*, 22–31, 84. David II does seem to have tried to do that in *c*1341 with his charter granting Angus son of John (of Ardnamurchan) much of the original MacDonald territory, but nothing came of this (*RMS* I, app. I, no. 114 and above, note 41). The MacIans of Ardnamurchan (so called from their descent from Angus's father John, or Ian in Gaelic) seem to have been loyal followers of the Lords of the Isles during the latters' heyday, but after the Lordship's forfeiture in 1493 the crown found a vigorous supporter in John MacIan of Ardnamurchan, who played a major role in crushing several MacDonald risings. John MacIan was no doubt largely motivated by personal rivalries, but was there also a sense that his kindred had as much right as Angus

Óg's to power in the West Highlands and Isles? See Bannerman, 'Lordship of the Isles', *West Highland Sculpture*, 210 (and the notes at *ibid.*, 113); *Acts of the Lords of the Isles*, 225, 230, 233, 259–60, 282, 284.

105 *APS*, II, 113.

106 Bannerman, 'Lordship of the Isles', *West Highland Sculpture*, 201–2.

107 *Acts of the Lords of the Isles*, no. 3; first pointed out in Frame, *English Lordship in Ireland*, 152, n. It is a nice coincidence that the paper from which this essay derives was delivered on 21 September 1986 – exactly 600 years later.

108 *Acts of the Lords of the Isles*, nos. 1, 2.

The Papacy and Scotland in the Fifteenth Century

DER Watt 1984 in RB Dobson (ed), *Church, Politics and Patronage in the Fifteenth Century*, Gloucester (Alan Sutton), 115–129.

The opening of the fifteenth century came in the middle of the Great Schism, and it should be noted immediately that it was the pope at Avignon (not yet, of course, styled an anti-pope) who enjoyed recognition in Scotland. It is true that in the year 1400 itself Pope Benedict XIII was not very accessible, for he was then a virtual prisoner in the papal palace, and for the time being he was recognized just by Aragon and Scotland. This was the stage in the forty years of schism when France had led the way in trying to force both popes to resign by withdrawing obedience in 1398 from the line of popes whom she had recognized since 1378. But Scotland had not followed suit, even if individual Scots then at the University of Paris had been in favour of the French royal policy.[1] Scotland in 1400 therefore was behaving independently, almost idiosyncratically, in remaining loyal to the pope at Avignon. This is the starting point for the fifteenth-century story.

It is generally assumed that Scotland had chosen in 1378–80 to recognize Pope Clement VII because her ally France invited her to do so. Certainly in 1379 we know of envoys from King Charles V as well as from Clement coming to Scotland in search of support,[2] and we do not know of any envoys from Pope Urban VI. It is curious, however, that there is no evidence of King Robert II calling a parliament or an ecclesiastical provincial council to advise him on this matter; and in fact we do not know when or why he decided to adhere to Clement. It may well be that a political or diplomatic motive was not uppermost. As early as February 1379 while Clement was still in Italy, the Scottish chancellor (Bishop John de Peblis of Dunkeld) was negotiating with him for a second consecration as bishop, on the grounds that his earlier consecration by authority of Urban VI before the schism was now questionable; and by July 1379 in his other capacity as papal collector in Scotland some funds which Peblis had collected were being paid into the papal treasury at Avignon rather than at Rome.[3] It is probable that the moving spirit was his colleague Bishop Walter de Wardlaw of Glasgow, who had been employed at the curia in the early 1370s before the schism and had certainly known Clement as Cardinal Robert of Geneva there. Wardlaw in his turn was to be made the first ever Scottish cardinal by this pope in December 1383.[4] It is likely therefore that it was the preference of such leading clergy in favour of Clement rather than Urban that decided the issue in Scotland. It was not long before the whole Scottish episcopate was populated by bishops who owed their promotion to Clement or from 1394 his successor Benedict XIII.[5] Only in Galloway and the Isles were there some complications raised by the presence of alternative bishops loyal to the Roman pope: these problems were solved by the expulsion to England of the Romanist claimant to Galloway, and by the effective splitting of the Isles diocese into Romanist and Avignonese halves. Otherwise there was for forty years a steady supply of bishops loyal only to Avignon in the kingdom of Scotland. Besides Cardinal Wardlaw two successive bishops of St Andrews were particularly concerned over a long period to keep the Avignonese connection going – Walter Trayl, who came back to Scotland in 1386 after employment in Pope Clement's chancery and served until 1401;[6] and Henry de Wardlaw (the cardinal's nephew) who, on returning to the country as bishop in 1403 after long years of study at Avignon, held office until 1440.[7] Bishop Gilbert de Grenlaw of Aberdeen (1390–1421), who was chancellor of Scotland for more than twenty-four years from 1397, seems to have been another steadying influence for a long time.[8] With such committed Episcopal leaders, the Scottish government remained unwaveringly loyal to Benedict XIII right through the years of withdrawal of obedience and the councils of Pisa and Constance until at last it grudgingly offered recognition to Martin V in July–August 1419.[9]

This independent line contrasts with that taken in most other countries. While political considerations everywhere had some part in shaping attitudes to the schism, in Scotland they did not have much influence. It was much more a matter of clerical preference and convenience. This stage in Scoto-papal relations has to be set in the context of the previous 200 years, during which the *ecclesia Scoticana* had been officially and uniquely regarded collectively as a 'special daughter' of the pope, with ten equal bishops and no archbishop.[10] This could have the comparatively simple implication that the pope regarded himself as metropolitan for Scotland.[11] But obviously he was no ordinary metropolitan. From one point of view his authority was weak, for the Scottish bishops and other prelates from 1225 met periodically in provincial council, and delegated authority between meetings to one of their number as conservator,[12] so that a degree of uniformity in practice and of discipline was achieved by self-help within the kingdom without reference to or interference from the Roman court. But from another point of view papal power in Scotland was unusually effective, for when the pope was brought into things he was no mere metropolitan: indeed the Universal Ordinary and Vicar of Christ was one stage in the hierarchy more accessible to Scottish clergy and laity than in most other countries. Recourse to Avignon in person or through an agent had become familiar to most leading Scots during the fourteenth century, with no impediments such as the politics of the Hundred Years' War or statutes of provisors to get in the way. Every advantage was taken of the complex procedures which led to the issue of papal letters of grace on a wide range of business concerning benefices, dispensations, privileges, and justice.[13] Certainly on the benefice front there were by the end of the fourteenth century few of the cathedral or the more substantial parochial benefices in ecclesiastical patronage where it was not customary for would-be incumbents to seek a papal title by way of a bull of provision. And there was frequently keen rivalry and litigation up to the level of the Roman court between claimants with papal titles of a contradictory character. In such circumstances there was a need to keep in with the pope who was generally recognized in Scotland; and two printed volumes of papal letters issued by Clement VII and Benedict XIII in favour of Scots have recently been published, which give a vivid (if incomplete) picture of the regularity and complexity of papal business concerning Scotland right through the schism. It is no wonder that the Scots did not want to abandon the popes who were so accessible and so useful to them. Indeed they could not face switching to Alexander V or John XXIII after the council of Pisa, and had very little to do with the council of Constance – occasional envoys travelled between the council and Scotland, but no official participants were sent.[14] This had the effect of making the final desertion of Benedict XIII in favour of Martin V all the more traumatic. In the end it was the masters of the university of St Andrews who took a lead in pushing the country in the direction of submitting to the pope who was now universally acknowledged; and typically they made it their business to ensure that Scotland's final act of adherence was accompanied by Martin's confirmation of the status of their university along the lines of the privilege granted by Benedict in 1413.[15]

The transition from one pope to the other was not an easy one. Martin was elected at Constance in November 1417; but until as late as January 1419 some Scots were still obtaining letters of grace from Benedict at Peñiscola in Aragon, often with the backing of the Duke of Albany who was then governor of Scotland.[16] In parallel with this, however, there were others who from as early as January 1418 onwards were anticipating the government's change of allegiance by frequenting the curia of Martin at Constance, Geneva, Mantua or Florence.[17] Some of these had the backing of the Earl of Douglas, who was a political opponent of the Duke of Albany at home: others were sponsored by the young King James I, then a prisoner in England, who chose to adhere formally to Martin in July 1418, a whole year before the official adherence of the Albany government.[18] A consequence was that candidates were provided by both popes for some important benefices such as the bishopric of Ross, the priorship of St Andrews, or the archdeaconry of Teviotdale in Glasgow.[19] It was an unsettling and disputacious period, as the different political factions in Scotland sought to help their followers by latching on to different popes. This unprecedented period of confusion lasted well into the 1420s, and was still raising tricky problems after King James returned from captivity in 1424. So far as Scotland is concerned, it can be argued that the greatest evils arising from the Great Schism came after it had in the eyes of most of Europe been ended.

Another period of unfortunate confusion came in the early 1440s as a result of the 'Little Schism'[20] created in 1439 by the council of Basel. Scotland had changed her attitude to general councils after adhering to Martin V. A large official delegation was sent to the council which met at Pavia and Siena, though only three members in fact reached it in time to join in some anti-English deliberations for about ten days just before the council was dissolved in March 1424.[21] They were said to have been briefed on the various ways in which the church in Scotland was suffering inter- ference from temporal lords in its rights and jurisdiction; but presumably it was

Murdoch Duke of Albany, the governor, and his advisers who thought it worthwhile to send such official representatives. King James I took the same view of the council of Basel in its turn, and from mid-1433 onwards maintained an official delegation there, which for some considerable time included his chancellor, Bishop John Cameron of Glasgow.[22] Some twenty-eight other Scottish clergy also took part in this council's affairs during its most active period, February 1434–February 1437. It is no wonder that in 1436 Pope Eugenius IV was willing to send the first papal legate that Scotland had seen for nearly 200 years to try to establish a concordat with even so distant and comparatively petty a king.[23] The assassination of the king in February 1437, however, introduced a period of faction politics in Scotland during the long minority of James II, and this was matched in time by the split between the council and the pope. Though at least Bishop James Kennedy of Dunkeld did attend the pope at the council of Florence in July 1439 when the famous union of the eastern and western churches was proclaimed,[24] and though the majority of lay and clerical leaders in Scotland continued to support Eugenius after the remaining councillors at Basel had indulged in the Little Schism by electing Pope Felix V in November 1439, the Livingston–Douglas faction who dominated the Scottish government in the 1440s took the chance of adhering to the alternative pope for internal political reasons, and so caused even more disruption in the Scottish church than had ever been experienced during the Great Schism or its aftermath.[25] Thomas Livingston, Abbot of Dundrennan, was now a leading member of the rump council at Basel,[26] and Scots supporting his family's faction appeared there and at the curia of Felix to obtain alternative papal titles to many bishoprics and lesser benefices in Scotland.[27] This had the dire effect of attaching new vested interests to the factions in Scotland, which survived the death of the Earl of Douglas in March 1443 and held out in many cases until after 1449, when on the one hand the Livingstons were ousted from power, and on the other western Christendom as a whole accepted one pope again in the person of Nicholas V. At the same time King James II was old enough to take a grip of things in Scotland. But the unfortunate coincidence of the papal schism and a royal minority had for about a decade a critically divisive and harmful effect on Scottish affairs. Conciliarist ideas must clearly have been much bandied about in Scotland in the 1430s and 1440s, and not merely in academic circles;[28] and for her own internal reasons the country was taken into the European swim in a way that Governor Albany had not permitted at the time of Pisa and Constance. But since it was the pro-papal rather than the pro-conciliar faction which won locally in the end, it turned out that it was respect for co-operation with the papacy rather than hostility to it which in Scotland as elsewhere was to govern later fifteenth-century attitudes.

Co-operation between pope and king had, of course, long been the normal situation. This was common enough elsewhere, but was particularly evident in a country whose church came directly under Rome and which produced no Anselm, Becket, Langton or Winchelsey. Nowadays we are escaping from the historical tradition of taking papal propagandists at face value and realize that church liberties in any era exist only insofar as the state is prepared to allow them. The organized church in later medieval Scotland is therefore best approached as the greatest of the jurisdictional franchises in the country. The king normally sent his representatives to sit with the prelates when they met in provincial council;[29] and he could be quite direct in giving them instructions about a piece of local legislation which he wanted them to accept. This was exemplified in July 1427 when an act was passed in parliament on a matter of procedure in the church courts, the intention being to make things quicker and less expensive for lay plaintiffs against clerical defendants: the provincial council, which was also meeting at Perth at the same time, was simply expected to put this royal act into effect by adding its own authority to it.[30] It is true that this example comes from a time when the young James I, just back from eighteen years of captivity in England, was particularly active in a review of many interlocking aspects of the administration of Scotland; but the main point is that the prelates co-operated with him and were prepared to work with him as a reformer.

This king took a personal interest also in institutions purely ecclesiastical. In 1425 he urged in parliament that the abbots and priors of the Benedictine and Augustinian orders in Scotland should hold general chapters to achieve a revival of the religious life to its pristine state:

'He appeared to cherish and favour equally all churches and religious orders for the quality of their life, praising highly men of religion and their way of life as he heard of it. And if he found anything less than praiseworthy among them (during his frequent visits to monasteries), he discussed it charitably without pretending to be embarrassed, quietly persisting until by some convenient way they might be turned back to the normal way of life.'[31]

This is the man who founded a monastery for Carthusians at his capital at Perth in 1429.[32] King James also took a close interest in the new university at St Andrews which was developing very slowly and contentiously. After threatening to move it to Perth, he stirred up sufficient constructive response for him to feel able to agree in 1432 to confirming the privileges which he had originally given to the university community – but only at the cost of their accepting his interference in their internal affairs thereafter. He seems to have imposed his own man (Laurence de Lindores) as perpetual dean of arts, and laid down the law on such matters as how the dean was to conduct himself, how the students were to be disciplined, and how the masters were to develop a healthy corporate life.[33] Whether therefore it was church justice, the monastic life, or university organization, it was the king who set the standards. He thought it his responsibility to supervise positively the franchise jurisdictions within his kingdom. In all these examples there is no mention of the pope. It was just royal authority which was being accepted in matters internal to the *ecclesia Scoticana*, and no one seems to have wanted to bring in the pope.

Royal authority could, however, be exercised more debatably in the traditional delicate borderline territory between church and state, as happened in 1450 when the young James II was in his turn being assertive in the royal interest. He then made a solemn parliamentary definition on a series of matters related to the property and rights of bishoprics in the interval between the decease or demission of one bishop and the admission of his successor.[34] Such matters had been in contention between conflicting interests in most countries for centuries, and now in Scotland we find emerging from discussions between the king and his prelates the kind of balanced definition that was meant to be lasting. On the one hand bishops were to be allowed to dispose of their movable goods by testament (a practice which both kings and popes had from time to time sought to prevent). Then the general point was made that during the vacancy spiritualities were to be administered by a vicar-general accountable to the next bishop, while temporalities were to be at the king's disposal. Lastly the patronage of benefices in the bishop's gift was to be exercised by the crown. It is quite likely that at this date the main weight was put on the last of these four definitions.[35] It was not in itself new, but a series of explanatory acts of provincial council and of parliament over the rest of the century makes it clear that the main intention was to assert royal right not against local ecclesiastical patrons, but against competing papal claims to provide to the benefices in question under general or special reservations.[36] We can see therefore that in just this one category of church patronage king and clergy in Scotland were combining to exclude the papal interest in favour of regalian right. In practice this was a major interference with the usual flow from Rome of confident letters of provision; and since it was governed by unforeseeable circumstances, it must have been a vexatious complication for clerical benefice-hunters who throughout the century were still eagerly 'playing the system' of papal provisions.

But the act of 1450 was not a statute of provisors. And this brings us to the papal reaction to these Scottish kings who were so confidently setting their own limits to the liberty of the Scottish church. The story has sometimes been told in terms of a 'prolonged trial of strength';[37] but there are dangers in adopting a framework for discussion in terms of 'struggle' and ultimate 'victory' for the crown. Since both sides had as usual much to gain from co-operation, any periods of dispute should be examined in terms of the special circumstances which brought them about, rather than used as the basis of generalizations about overall trends. If we first consider Pope Martin V, we find that as part of his commitment to re-establishing papal authority after the Great Schism he ran a curia that was most attentive to providing many services to Scottish laymen and clerics; but he was hardly in a position to seek a showdown with the Scottish government. He was remarkably helpful in the early 1420s to ambitious and litigious clerics, who seem to have been all too willing to commit themselves to paying substantial fees by way of annates to the papal treasure in return for papal provisions of various complicated kinds.[38] Not only were dispensations for pluralism freely granted, but the convenient device of allowing one claimant to a benefice to buy off the claims of another by settling a pension on him from the revenues of the benefice was sometimes approved.[39] When James I came on the scene, he reacted to this situation by a series of acts of parliament in 1424, 1427 and 1428 that was aimed at stopping this practice of 'purchasing pensions' and more generally at controlling the flow of clerics or their agents to the Roman court.[40] There is interesting mention of a nefarious practice to which the word 'barratry' was attached. This expression was derived from a root meaning 'to deceive', and a 'barrator' was a cleric who was considered to have used underhand means to obtain a benefice which properly belonged to another.[41] The introduction of such a pejorative term into royal legislation at this time is an instructive indication of the way in which the pope's easy generosity was being regarded by those who felt responsible for the health of the Scottish church. In practice this legislation was unworkable and not generally enforced; but Martin did for a time in 1429–30 take seriously certain accusations made by the Scottish cleric William Croyser (who was an active barrator by any standards) against Bishop John Cameron of Glasgow, the king's chancellor, who was said to have been chiefly responsible for these parliamentary statutes, which were in papal eyes 'against ecclesiastical liberty and the rights of the Roman church'.[42] The bishop was cited to Rome under threat of deprivation; but no great crisis followed; the king just sent his envoys to arrange for the exoneration of Cameron, on the vague understanding that he might sometime try to arrange for the offending statues to be repealed. It was in effect an agreement not to define the rights of pope and king too clearly. Perhaps the affair is more noteworthy for the king's patience with some of the inconvenience which arose from papal openness towards barrators than for any serious interest in principles on the pope's part. Certainly James for his part did pursue Croyser for a time, not just for barratry, but for treason;[43] and this ever-resourceful cleric was to take another chance which came his way in June 1434 at the council of Basel to retaliate by accusing the king of anti-papal acts:

> 'The king himself disposes of ecclesiastical benefices as he likes against the pope's decisions; many clerics and priests with papal letters have been killed in the kingdom; and those coming to the Roman court are being deprived of their goods, etc.'[44]

But this was very much an *ex parte* statement: the council did not take the matter up. It is true that as part of continuing protection for Croyser Pope Eugenius IV in 1436 raised again the matter of the Scottish legislation which was designed to restrict the free access of Scottish clerics to the curia;[45] but the legislation remained on the books and, so far as most people were concerned, unenforced. Perhaps the issue might have been pressed further from the papal side if the visit of the legate to Scotland in 1437 had not been made abortive by the murder of the king. It may be argued that neither Martin nor Eugenius had been much worried by the Scottish apparently hostile legislation. Their protests seem to have been forced out of them mainly by the litigious William Croyser, whose benefice-hunting activities at the curia both king and bishops at home wanted to curtail. From his self-seeking point of view he wanted Scottish clerics to be free to benefit from the facilities offered at the papal curia; but the occasional declarations of principle which two popes were prepared to make on his behalf were just so many words on parchment. Croyser was no Becket.

It can accordingly be argued that Scoto-papal relations in this period were dominated by the personal rivalries of individual clerics playing politics as they tried their best to use the system to their own advantage, and that no one was much interested in principles. Yet some financial aspects of these relations did have an important general influence. The pope needed all the fees which he could extract from the beneficiaries of papal graces; ambitious clerics in Scotland thought it worth their while to pay these fees; but the government took the view that the cost of these papal services to the Scottish church was unsuitably high, and made efforts to control the flow of money from the country in this connection. Ranald Nicholson puts it rather well: 'James I, who fully shared the mercantilist outlook looked askance at any flow of bullion from his kingdom, particularly one that brought in return not an import of goods but merely a reallocation of Scottish benefices, sometimes to the disadvantage of the crown.'[46]

It was a similar sense of duty about the need to protect the rights of the crown which lay behind the legislation of James II in 1450 with respect to the exercise of ecclesiastical patronage at times of Episcopal vacancies. For the rest of the century the crown was quite firm in continuing to assert its rights in the face of papal counter-claims. The need for repeated legislation on this matter, however, shows that the pope kept interfering in particular cases. This was traditional enough, and suggests simply that the complexity of the system for papal control of church patronage was too great for the curia to be willing to incorporate eccentric local variations into its procedures. The distance and time factors were always a major problem for the papacy in trying to deal with matters of detail pertaining to a country so far away as Scotland. Financial pressures and bureaucratic inertia therefore both had a part to play in keeping a certain tension going throughout the century between Rome and Scotland. These provide a background against which should be set the actions of individual clerics such as Croyser and his kind.

This background has to be borne in mind too when we examine the fundamental change in the constitutional position of the Scottish church which was approved by the papacy in 1472, namely the erection of the bishopric of St Andrews into a metropolitan see.[47] This act makes general sense within the political trend of the time, when there was a need to adjust the definition of *ecclesia Scoticana* to fit better with current political theory that young King James III had 'full jurisdiction and free empire within his realm'.[48] By this date the country had its own two universities at St Andrews (from 1410) and Glasgow (from 1451). The religious orders such as the Franciscans (both Observant and Conventual) and the Dominicans were being organized for the first time into separate Scottish provinces.[49] It was therefore logical for the pope to take account of political reality and detach the diocese of Galloway from the province of York and the dioceses of the Isles and Orkney from the province of Trondheim. In the first two of these cases the change was long overdue: so far as Orkney was concerned this was papal acknowledgement of a royal ambition to hold on to the Northern Isles, which had only very recently been transferred to Scotland from the kingdom of Denmark and Norway as a pledge for an unpaid dowry for the queen.[50] But why in 1472 did the pope add to this territorial adjustment a rejection of the 'special daughter' arrangements which were of nearly 300 years' standing, and of the unifying provincial council of prelates (which seems to have been in good running order)? We may take Ranald Nicholson, as a recent exponent of a long historical tradition about this remarkable change of papal policy.[51] He presents us with a picture in 1471 of the ambitious James III emerging from his minority and using parliament as James I and James II had done to pass acts warning the pope against unwelcome interference in Scotland, discouraging traffic with the curia, and once again emphasizing the financial loss involved in the papal connection. It is then suggested that the new pope, Sixtus IV, reacted to this situation by taking up the ambitious personal plans of a favoured Scottish cleric at the Roman court, namely Bishop Patrick Graham of St Andrews, that his see should become a metropolitan one. The pope is seen as taking the initiative quite suddenly and without consulting the king or the other Scottish bishops. If this is the true explanation for what happened, it was surely an astonishing break with the normal conventions of papal diplomacy over the centuries, and certainly Sixtus would have been doing something much more drastic for Patrick Graham than either Martin V or Eugenius IV ever did for William Croyser. But even Nicholson has to admit that nothing in the bull of erection alluded to what he argues was the leading cause of controversy – the disputed control of ecclesiastical patronage. Indeed this traditional explanation does not hold water in my view; and here I am in the good company of the late David McRoberts, who observed that the circumstances whereby the change of 1472 came about form 'one of the more intractable problems of Scottish history'.[52]

It is possible to suggest a novel solution to this problem. The bull of erection itself[53] emphasizes the inconvenience and expense to which inhabitants of Scotland are put in having to come to the Roman court when appealing against actions of their bishops; it claims that as a consequence some cases have been taken instead to a 'forbidden forum' (perhaps parliament is meant); and it asserts that some bishops have been taking advantage of their distance from Rome to exceed their proper powers, so that it will be advantageous for them to be subjected to a metropolitan for their transgressions to be punished. This language hardly suggests that the Scottish provincial council of prelates as a body had helped to draft the petition to the pope which (though now lost) must have provided at least some basic material for the subsequent bull. But this language could well have emanated from the king and his advisers as, following the troubles of his minority, they sought to arrange with the pope for a more tightly organized *ecclesia Scoticana* and sent Bishop Graham to Rome to negotiate a revised settlement. It would be attractive to the government to have co-extensive boundaries for church and state, to lessen the traffic in appeals to Rome, to have church cases properly adjudged in church courts, and to have one trusted leading prelate in Scotland to discipline the others. This all makes more sense than the theory of a sudden papal initiative to impose a new organization on an unwilling king.

This new interpretation is offered in full awareness that the hopes which lay behind the bull of erection were not to be realized in their entirety. In the long run, however, it did bring some advantages to Scotland. The setting up of a metropolitan court under the official of St Andrews did help with all of the objectives set out in the bull. We know from the recent work of Simon Ollivant on such records as survive from the mid-sixteenth century that this court became a very busy one, which probably did attract business away from civil courts because of the better standard of justice it offered, and which certainly helped to control the activities of the suffragan bishops by reviewing cases from their courts which were brought to it on appeal.[54] But the pull of the Roman Court for litigation over ecclesiastical benefices remained until the Reformation. Though it is only recently that James Robertson has started work on the records left in Rome by this litigation, it already seems clear that benefice cases continued to be rare in the local ecclesiastical courts in Scotland and were still normally taken to Rome by those who could afford it.[55] The setting up of a metropolitan court therefore did not end the most complex category of traffic to the curia, even if it offered local remedies for other categories of business. It must surely, however, have done something to keep the circulation of money for legal costs within the country.

In the years immediately following 1472 there was some delay in putting the new arrangements into effect as a consequence of what I take to be the wholly unexpected mental deterioration of Patrick Graham.[56] He was of royal blood and a nephew of James Kennedy, his predecessor as bishop of St Andrews and a dominant political figure in Scotland for a time during the minority of James III. Graham was made bishop of Brechin in 1463 and translated to St Andrews in 1465 on his uncle's death, when still aged about thirty. His ambition to hold a monastic abbacy or priorship *in commendam* along with his see soon aroused opposition of a general kind in parliament as well as from his rivals,[57] though this may well have been politically motivated while the Boyd faction was in power during the later sixties. We should reserve judgement on whether his motives were pastoral with an eye to monastic reform or merely financial with an eye an increased income, though at this date the latter motive is quite likely.[58] There seems to be no good reason to deny the possibility that the young James III, once he had rid himself of the Boyd faction in November 1469, saw in Graham a suitable ally to help in putting the Scottish church under firmer control. It is more likely than not that it was with the king's backing that he went off to Rome to negotiate the bull of erection which was eventually granted on 17 August 1472.[59] It was more than a year after that before he returned to Scotland, and this delay has traditionally been explained by the suggestion that there was already an outcry there, with both king and clergy up in arms against the whole plan for a metropolitan see.[60] But this interpretation of events rests mainly on the assertions of historians writing a hundred years after these events, whose views are not supported by contemporary evidence. We should do better to note the fact that Graham in February 1473 was appointed by the pope to the office of legate *a latere* in Scotland with duties which included raising support for a crusade against the Turks and reforming all the monasteries in the country.[61] Such unpopular responsibilities may well have been imposed on him by the pope as a quid pro quo for agreeing to the bull of erection, and it is possible that by now Graham was beginning to feel the pressure of his double duty to king and pope (though of course mental illness need not have any external cause at all). At any rate by August 1473 (while he was still no nearer home than Bruges) we get the first hints that the king had learned something of the confusion which was overtaking the poor man, presumably progressively.[62] Here was a problem that was unexpected and embarrassing. The general council of the kingdom was consulted at about the end of the year over what was to be done about the archbishop,[63] who seems to have returned to Scotland about then. We know of no solemn celebrations at St Andrews to mark his new status: instead we can trace a series of measures designed to protect the rights of king and pope until the situation could be clarified.[64] An old acquaintance (or possibly a friend) from his student days at St Andrews University in the 1450s (when the two of them were members of an Arts class of about a dozen) was now brought into the picture, apparently with the king's support, in these frustrating circumstances while the future of Graham's mental conditions was unknowable. This was William Scheves.[65] It seems to have been with Graham's help that he became archdeacon of St Andrews by early 1474,[66] then vicar-general for the presumably incapacitated archbishop by June 1475,[67] and then with the blessing of both king and pope coadjutor in the metropolitan office in September 1476.[68] A papal enquiry established formally the delusions of poor Graham, and in January 1478 he was eased out of office into suitable confinement and Scheves was confirmed by the pope as archbishop in his stead.[69] Only now was it possible to put the policy of the bull of erection of 1472 into effect. There was general agreement that this should be done, and it is surely a mistake to describe this in terms of a victory for any of the parties concerned, as is sometimes done.[70] It had indeed been a sad imbroglio, from which probably most people emerged with relief.

The policy of 1472 (however motivated) was deprived of its logical simplicity twenty years later when in January 1492 Pope Innocent VIII yielded to a campaign from Scotland conducted in the name of the young James IV, and by another constitutional re-arrangement divided the Scottish church into two ecclesiastical provinces instead of one. Glasgow was erected into a second metropolitan see with four suffragan sees all withdrawn from the province of St Andrews.[71] There seems to be no justification for tracing this development back to the 1470s, with the implication that the overweening authority of St Andrews was resented from the beginning. It is true that in February 1473 both king and pope agreed that Bishop Thomas Spens of Aberdeen might have personal exemption from the authority of the new archbishop for his lifetime;[72] but it should be noticed that this was justified on the two grounds that he was a senior figure in the Scottish church (he had been a bishop since 1459) and that he should not be subjected to someone with whom he was currently conducting a lawsuit. He may well have been the one crusty bishop in the country whom it was worthwhile to conciliate in order to establish the new metropolitan regime. Once Scheves became archbishop, Spens seems to have been formally subjected to St Andrews again for the last year or so of his life.[73] But during the 1480s Scheves came to suffer for his personal loyalty to James III. As some of the younger generation of bishops began to push from below, the pope acceded in March 1487 to the king's request that the archbishopric of St Andrews be raised to the level of primate and legate *natus* on the model of Canterbury.[74] But Pope Innocent did not stick by his man at St Andrews: when first Bishop Andrew Stewart of Moray and then Bishop Robert Blackadder of Glasgow sought personal exemption from the authority of St Andrews, this was granted in April–May 1488.[75] Before these privileges can have been known in Scotland, the political revolution which caused the death of James III had taken place. Archbishop Scheves was now on the losing side, and Blackadder received official backing from the new king and parliament for his own elevation to metropolitan (though more on the York than the Canterbury model). The aim of both pope and king in 1472 that they should deal with the Scottish church through one leader was now frustrated under a different pope and a different king: as a result the country was to see much bickering between the two archbishops. An over-flexible papacy had allowed the personal rivalries of some of the local bishops to override the ideal of a well-disciplined branch of the church.

It seems right to emphasize yet again the note of co-operation between king and pope when we consider the broad picture of Episcopal appointments over the century.[76] In the absence of a local metropolitan it had been the custom at least from the thirteenth century for Scottish bishops to seek confirmation of their election from the pope. The fourteenth century brought the papal practice of cancelling these elections as a matter of routine and substituting the formality of a papal bull of provision, with the concomitant charging of the fees known as the services in accordance with the supposed resources of the see. There was no challenge to this general system in the fifteenth century, when (as before) the form of election by the local chapter was usually in all likelihood a blind for the reality of royal nomination. In Archie Duncan's phrase, the fifteenth-century popes were 'able to resume broadly the comfortable working relationship with the monarchy which obtained before the Great Schism'.[77] Popes knew well that the king held the whip hand with his power to refuse to release the temporalities, and they must have been wary of trying to impose unwelcome candidates on him. It is interesting that the only appointment of an Italian papal familiar to a Scottish see in the whole of the Middle Ages (Prospero Camogli de'Medici of Genoa to the poor see of Caithness in 1478) is found in this period;[78] but it happened when pope and king (as it seems) had been working particularly closely over the problem of the lunatic Archbishop Graham, and appears to have been accepted obligingly by James III. There is on the other hand a long stream of royal familiars whom the pope accepted as bishops without apparent demur. The number of contested appointments outside the periods of schism was remarkably small: there are less than half-a-dozen affecting thirteen dioceses. Three of these attract attention because it would appear that the candidate supported by the crown was passed over by the pope in favour of someone else. In 1466 the pope's rejection of a royal nominee for Dunblane comes just after the taking of power by the Boyd faction, and may well reflect a change in the way patronage was exercised in the name of the young James III. Much more seriously the pope rejected two crown-supported candidates separately in 1483 – for Glasgow in March (when Robert Blackadder was provided) and for Dunkeld in October (when George Brown was provided). But this was another exceptional period of political strife, when the crown's authority was in contention between King James and his brother the Duke of Albany; and it has been plausibly argued recently by Norman Macdougall that in fact James supported Blackadder's mission to Rome to displace a bishop-elect who was Albany's candidate rather than his own.[79] This makes it all the more remarkable that in October Pope Sixtus hastened to appoint Brown to Dunkeld without waiting to learn the king's wishes for this see (which as it turned out were strongly in favour of someone else). It was an exceptionally rash move, which was probably engineered by Cardinal Rodrigo Borgia,[80] and which was quite uncharacteristic of papal practice throughout most of the century. It is even more surprising that Sixtus and his successor Innocent VIII stuck to this choice despite fierce opposition from James and his parliament; but a direct consequence (following two visits to Scotland of an Italian papal legate and the sending of a Scottish embassy to Rome)[81] was the famous bull of 20 April 1487, which in fact served as a concordat for years to come.[82] The pope agreed to take no action to fill vacancies in bishoprics and abbacies above a certain value for at least eight months, to allow time for the king to nominate candidates of his choice. This procedure had been requested by the king because of the importance of such appointees in his parliament and council.[83] Thus the furore aroused by papal flouting of the usual conventions produced a lasting written definition of the joint responsibilities of king and pope (but not of local electors) in arranging the most important church appointments in Scotland. Rather later in the century than some other countries, Scotland in this way obtained its concordat, and the uniformity of the papal procedures was eroded yet again in order to encompass national aspirations.

We may note briefly how the headships of the larger Scottish monasteries progressively became more and more subject to papal provision following royal nomination in the course of the later fourteenth and fifteenth centuries, though some important houses such as Melrose, Jedburgh, Dryburgh and Cambuskenneth escaped until quite late.[84] As with the bishoprics, less and less attention was paid to the wishes of the community who were technically entitled to choose their own head. Also more use was being made latterly of the device of entrusting monastic headships to secular clerics *in commendam*. It is no doubt correct to suggest that the papal attitude was becoming more concerned with achieving a regular income from appointment fees and less with taking trouble over the suitability of the appointees. Where the popes led, kings were in their company. It is all too well known how in 1497 King James IV had no difficulty in obtaining papal approval for his teenage brother James, Duke of Ross to hold the archbishopric of St Andrews *in commendam* along with the abbacies of Holyrood, Dunfermline and Arbroath.[85] For royal cadets to be endowed with so lavish an income from ecclesiastical benefices was a new trend: but it was just the logical extension of what was common form in fifteenth-century attitudes to the making of higher church appointments. There had been changes of emphasis, for James IV was no church reformer like James I, and Alexander VI was no Martin V. Yet it is fair to sum up papal attitudes to major church appointments in

Scotland throughout the century as displaying a casual lack of concern for suitability, and an acceptance in most circumstances of the over-riding utility of co-operating with royal wishes. From the Scottish evidence at least the popes of the fifteenth century emerge more as followers than as leaders.

NOTES

1 E.g. Walter Forrester (D. E. R. Watt, *A Biographical Dictionary of Scottish Graduates to AD 1419* [Oxford, 1977], 197–9).

2 N. Valois, *La France et le Grand Schisme d'Occident*, I (Paris, 1896); Watt, *Dictionary*, 141, 472; *Copiale Prioratus Sanctiandree*, ed. J. H. Baxter (Oxford, 1930), xxxvii.

3 Watt, *Dictionary*, 442–3.

4 *Ibid.*, 570, 671, 574.

5 *Fasti Ecclesiae Scoticanae Medii Aevi ad annum 1638*, second draft, ed. D. E. R. Watt (Scottish Record Society, 1969), under each diocese. At this time Orkney diocese still lay in the kingdom of Norway.

6 Watt, *Dictionary*, 539–42.

7 *Ibid.*, 564–9.

8 *Ibid.*, 237–9.

9 *Joannis de Fordun Scotichronicon cum Supplementis et Continuatione Walteri Boweri (Chron. Bower)*, ed. W. Goodall (Edinburgh, 1759), I, 374–5; *St Andrews Copiale*, 23–9; Watt, *Dictionary*, 250, 482, 508.

10 This arrangement was confirmed by Pope Celestine III on 13 March 1192 (R. Somerville, *Scotia Pontificia* [Oxford, 1982], 142–4, no. 156). To the nine dioceses mentioned then Argyll came to be added (cf. A. A. M. Duncan, *Scotland: The Making of the Kingdom* [Edinburgh, 1975], 275–6).

11 Eugenius IV in 1436, when appointing a legate to visit Scotland (*Concilia Scotiae*, ed. J. Robertson [Bannatyne Club, 1886], i, lxxxvi, n. 3).

12 *Ibid.*, ii, 3, 9–10.

13 *Calendar of . . . Petitions to the Pope*, ed. W. H. Bliss (London, 1896); *Calendar of . . . Papal Letters (CPL)*, ed. W. H. Bliss and others (London, 1893); *Calendar of Papal Letters to Scotland of Clement VII of Avignon, 1378–1394*, ed. C. Burns (Scottish History Society, 1977); *Calendar of Papal Letters to Scotland of Benedict XIII of Avignon, 1394–1418*, ed. F. McGurk (Scottish History Society, 1977).

14 See *St Andrews Copiale*, 9 for a list of these embassies.

15 *Chron. Bower*, ii, 449–51; *Acta Facultatis Artium Universitatis Sanctiandree 1413–1588* (Edinburgh and London, 1964), 12–13; cf. R. Swanson, 'The University of St Andrews and the Great Schism, 1410–1419', *Journal of Ecclesiastical History*, xxxvi (1975), 223–45.

16 *Cal. Benedict XIII*, 362–86, for graces issued Nov 1417–Jan 1419.

17 *Calendar of Scottish Supplications to Rome* (Scottish History Society, 1934–70), i, 1–231 for petitions granted Jan 1418–Aug 1420.

18 *Ibid.*, 3, 8–9, 13–16; cf *St Andrews Copiale*, 18–20, 27–8.

19 Watt, *Fasti*, 268 (Ross), 175–6 (Teviotdale); Watt, *Dictionary*, 249, 357 (St Andrews).

20 This useful phrase was coined by Ranald Nicholson in his *Scotland: The Later Middle Ages* (Edinburgh, 1974), chapter 12.

21 W. Brandmüller, *Das Konzil von Pavia-Siena*, ii (Münster, 1974), 356–9, 392, 394–5, 397–400, 430–3.

22 Full details in J. H. Burns, *Scottish Churchmen and the Council of Basel* (Glasgow, 1962); see index for Cameron.
23 Robertson, *Concilia*, i, lxxxvi, n. 3; *CPL*, viii, 229, 288–90; cf. *St Andrews Copiale*, 461.
24 A. I. Dunlop, *The Life and Times of James Kennedy Bishop of St Andrews* (Edinburgh and London, 1950), 27, 37.
25 See discussion in Nicholson, *Later Middle Ages*, 334–8.
26 Burns, *Scottish Churchmen*, index.
27 *Ibid.*, 65–81.
28 Cf. J. H. Burns, 'The conciliarist tradition in Scotland', *Scottish Historical Review*, xlii (1963), 89–104.
29 *Formulary E: Scottish Letters and Brieves 1286–1424*, ed. A. A. M. Duncan (Glasgow, 1976), 31, no. 65; *The Register of Brieves*, ed. Lord Cooper (Stair Society, 1946), 47, no. 67.
30 *The Acts of the Parliaments of Scotland (APS)*, ed. T. Thomson and C. Innes (Edinburgh, 1814–75), ii, 14, c. 5.
31 *Chron. Bower*, ii, 508–9.
32 *Medieval Religious Houses: Scotland*, 2nd edition, ed. I. B. Cowan and D. E. Easson (London and New York, 1976), 86–7.
33 *St Andrews Acta*, 34–5, 37–9; cf. xviii–xx.
34 *APS*, ii, 37–8, 61–2; *Registrum Magni Sigilli Regum Scottorum*, ed. J. M. Thomson and others (Edinburgh, 1882–1914), ii, No. 307; see discussion in G Donaldson, 'The rights of the Scottish crown in Episcopal vacancies', *Scot. Hist. Rev.*, xlv (1966), 27–35.
35 Cf. *ibid.*, 34–5.
36 Robertson, *Concilia*, ii, 78–80, 282–3.
37 L. Macfarlane, 'The primacy of the Scottish church', *Innes Review*, xx (1969), 111.
38 *Cal. Scot. Supp.*, i and ii, passim' *CPL*, vii, passim; *The Apostolic Camera and Scottish Benefices 1418–88*, ed. A. I. Cameron (Oxford, 1934), passim.
39 E.g. *Cal. Scot. Supp.*, ii, 3, 32, 40; *CPL*, vii, 262.
40 *APS*, ii, 5, cc. 14–16; 14, c. 2; 16, c. 9.
41 *A Dictionary of the Older Scottish Tongue*, ed. W. A. Craigie (Oxford, 1937–00), *s. v.* 'barate', 'barratour', 'barratry'.
42 *CPL*, vii, 18–19; see generally Watt, *Dictionary*, 133–4; E. W. M. Balfour-Melville, *James I, King of Scots* (London, 1936), 177–9.
43 *CPL*, viii, 286–7, 344–5.
44 *St Andrews Copiale*, 433.
45 *Ibid.*, 369–72; Watt, *Dictionary*, 134; cf. Balfour-Melville, *James I*, 237–8.
46 Nicholson, *Later Middle Ages*, 293–4.
47 *Vetera Monumenta Hibernorum et Scotorum Historiam Illustrantia*, ed. A. Theiner (Rome, 1864), 465–8, no. 852.
48 *APS*, ii, 95, c. 6.
49 D. McRoberts, 'The Scottish church and nationalism in the fifteenth century', *Innes Review*, xix (1968), 3–14, especially 12.
50 Nicholson, *Later Middle Ages*, 414–18. This ecclesiastical change must have been particularly welcome to King James II, who from 1470 onwards is thought to have shown some ingenuity in consolidating his newly acquired rights in the Northern Isles (*ibid.*, 417).
51 *Ibid.*, 460–2. See also Macfarlane, 'Primacy', 112; N Macdougall, *James III* (Edinburgh, 1982), 105

52 McRoberts, 'Scottish church', 12.

53 See above, note 47. Dr I. B. Cowan tells me that the related petition to the pope (which might have provided some background information) has not survived in the papal archives.

54 S. Ollivant, *The Court of the Official in Pre-Reformation Scotland* (Stair Society, 1982), 119, cf. 129–38, 159.

55 *Ibid.*, 126; J. J. Robertson, 'The development of the law', in *Scottish Society in the Fifteenth Century*, ed. Jennifer M. Brown (London, 1977), 151

56 For his biography see J. Herkless and R. K. Hannay, *The Archbishops of St Andrews*, I (Edinburgh and London, 1907), chapter 1.

57 *APS*, ii, 85, c. 4.

58 Herkless and Hannay, *Archbishops*, i, 74; cf. 31–2.

59 He may well have been assisted in his mission by Henry, Abbot of Cambuskenneth, who was commissioned as royal envoy to the curia on 25 June 1471 (*Reg. Mag. Sig.*, ii, no. 1034); cf. Nicholson, *Later Middle Ages*, 461.

60 *Ibid.*, 62–3; Macdougall, *James III*, 106.

61 *CPL*, xiii, 202–6; cf. J. A. F. Thomson, 'Some new light on the elevation of Patrick Graham', *Scot. Hist. Rev.*, xl (1961), 82–8 for the argument that some influential vested interests in Scotland may have been aroused against Graham as a consequence of some of the powers and favours granted to him by the pope at this stage.

62 *Accounts of the Lord High Treasurer of Scotland*, ed. T. Dickson and Sir J. Balfour Paul (Edinburgh, 1877–1916), I, 67 (the king has been inquiring of a chaplain of St Andrews 'anent certain matters anent the Bishop of St Andrews'); cf. *ibid.*, 44. It was only in Sept 1476 that he is said specifically to have lost his reason (*CPL*, xiii, 555–6). His delusions are well vouched for in the bull ordering his deposition in 1478 (see below, note 67).

63 *Treasurer Accts*, I, 46.

64 *Ibid.*, 47: *The Exchequer Rolls of Scotland*, ed. J. Stuart and others (Edinburgh, 1878–1908), viii, 318–19; *CPL*, xiii, 38–9, 555–6; cf. Thomson, 'Some new light', 87–8.

65 Biography in Herkless and Hannay, *Archbishops*, i, chapter 2; *St Andrews Acta*, 103, 111.

66 *CPL*, xiii, 33–4. He had made use of a dispensation granted by Archbishop Graham on papal authority. Thus was Graham's new status being recognized in royal circles in Scotland.

67 *Ibid.*, 41.

68 *Ibid.*, 555–6; cf. Cameron, *Apostolic Camera*, 252.

69 'Instructions for the trial of Patrick Graham', ed. R. K. Hannay, *Miscellany of the Scottish History Society*, iii (1919), 171–8; Theiner, *Monumenta*, 478–81, nos. 862–3; *CPL*, xiii, 277. It was intended that Scheves should not claim unauthorized papal privileges as Graham had sometimes done.

70 Cf. Macfarlane, 'Primacy', 115; Macdougall, *James III*, 107.

71 *Registrum Episcopatus Glasguensis* (Bannatyne and Maitland Clubs, 1843), ii, 470–3; cf. *CPL*, xv, 564, no. 1448 for evidence that no copy of this bull has survived in the papal archives. See discussion in J. A. F. Thomson, 'Innocent VIII and the Scottish church', *Innes Review*, xix (1968), 29–30.

72 Theiner, *Monumenta*, 473–4, no. 858.

73 *CPL*, xiii, 68–9.

74 *CPL*, xiv, 152; Robertson, *Concilia*, i, cxix.

75 Cameron, *Apostolic Camera*, 223; CPL, xiv, 220–1; Theiner, *Monumenta*, 502–3, no. 885.
76 See Watt, *Fasti* for details.
77 W. Croft Dickinson, *Scotland from the Earliest times to 1603*, 3rd edition, ed. A. A. M. Duncan (Oxford, 1977), 273.
78 Cameron, *Apostolic Camera*, xlvii–viii.
79 Macdougall, *James III*, 222–3.
80 *Ibid.*, 224–5.
81 *Ibid.*, 227–9.
82 Herkless and Hannay, *Archbishops*, i, 157–8; CPL, xiv, 4.
83 APS, ii, 171, c. 9.
84 Cameron, *Apostolic Camera*, xxxix; cf. Nicholson, *Later Middle Ages*, 459.
85 Herkless and Hannay, *Archbishops*, i, 184, 191–3, 197–8.

The Flemish Dimension of The Auld Alliance

A Stevenson 1996 in GG Simpson (ed), *Scotland and the Low Countries, 1124–1994*, East Linton (Tuckwell Press), 28–42

Despite the hallowed place of the Auld Alliance with France in Scottish popular tradition, its origins and early history have remained remarkably obscure. That it was cemented by a common enmity towards England is generally agreed, but as a defence against English hostilities its recorded achievements are surprisingly slight. Narrowly defined, early Franco-Scottish contacts were few. Two vital components seem to be missing: how physical contact was maintained and what ties there were in the long intervals between embassies, treaties and military expeditions.

Much as foreigners generally ignore the fact that Scotland is historically distinct from England, so too there is a tendency to forget that Flanders was for centuries part of the kingdom of France. Belgian historians have been reluctant to dwell on the former dependence of any of their territories upon France; and, on the only border area where French sovereignty has been rolled back, the French themselves are reticent. Add to that English historians' tendency to exaggerate the independence of Flanders, by over-emphasising its ties with England, and it is not surprising that the Scots have customarily drawn a mental line approximating to the modern frontier between France and Belgium.

Actually, Flanders was part of the Frankish heartland, from which the Germanic Franks expanded to conquer what became France. The county of Flanders developed between the ninth and twelfth centuries as a northern march of the French kingdom.[1] Its counts were among the most powerful of the peers of France and several were notably active in French affairs. Thus Count Baldwin V was guardian of Philip I of France in the only royal minority of the eleventh century; and Count Philip d'Alsace was the power behind the throne in the only royal minority of the twelfth century, that of his godson Philip Augustus in 1180. Seven years earlier it was this position of influence, as the French king's foremost adviser,[2] which brought about the first Franco-Scottish alliance. Perhaps because of a wish to find earlier origins,[3] it is an event that has received surprisingly little attention – notwithstanding William the Lion's humiliating recognition of English suzerainty to which it led (with all the bitter consequences that entailed) and the exceptionally detailed contemporary chronicle which describes the entire episode.[4]

The chronicler Jordan Fantosme implies that it was Philip d'Alsace, count of Flanders, who first persuaded Louis VII of the value of an alliance with the king of Scots against Henry II of England. The Scots were to be brought into a grand alliance, with Henry's rebellious sons, and proposals were apparently sent to Scotland by Philip in the younger Henry's name. The proposed bait was the return of Cumbria to the Scottish crown, but this proved insufficiently attractive to William and his council. Rather than fight against Henry II, Fantosme states that William first sought Northumberland from the English king in return for Scottish support. Only when that was refused did he put the same proposal to the French court, accompanied by a request for Flemish reinforcements. And, Fantosme continues, it was Philip who championed the Scots' terms, persuaded Louis to accede to them, and promised forthwith to send aid from Flanders.

Badly co-ordinated plans were made for Franco-Flemish assaults on Henry II's French territories, a Scoto-Flemish invasion of northern England, and Flemish landings in Suffolk which, it was hoped, would lead to general rebellion in England. But the war was lost on all fronts, with the rout of the Scoto-Flemish army at Alnwick and the capture of King William, in July 1174, its greatest disaster.[5]

There were widespread reports in England that the Flemings who landed in Suffolk were weavers, attracted by the lure of English wool.[6] Not only do commercial ties provide a key to Flemish interest in England, they are also the probable reason for the count of Flanders' knowledge about Scottish affairs and his interest in establishing closer relations with the Scots.[7]

By the 1170s there was a large Flemish community in Scotland and commercial ties must have been close. Flemings played a vital part in the transformation of the Scottish economy during the twelfth century and in the foundation and early development of the Scottish burghs. There was extensive feudal settlement of Flemings throughout southern Scotland and along the Moray Firth;[8] and most of the earliest recorded residents of Scottish burghs, merchants and craftsmen, have Flemish names.[9]

Principal and earliest of these is Mainard the Fleming, whose departure from Berwick and consequent transfer of allegiance from David I to the bishop of St Andrews is recorded in a unique charter of about 1144. It describes how Mainard had come to St Andrews, with the active encouragement of David I, to build and establish the new burgh. Like the chief executive of a new town today, his tasks must have been to organise the construction of the burgh, to find craftsmen and merchants to settle there, to persuade other merchants to come there to do business, to advise the bishop and his tenants how to develop the commercial potential of their estates, and thus to promote the burgh's trade.

Apart from the opportunities afforded by a backward country, whose monarchy was actively seeking to promote economic development – the property, the trading privileges common to burgh settlers, the lack of competition – what attracted the Flemings to Scotland were its pastoral products and fisheries. Belgic and Frankish fishermen were reported to be active in the Firth of Forth during the reign of David I.[10] But the earliest direct reference to Scottish trade with Flanders is an undated charter of Philip d'Alsace, endorsed by Pope Lucius III in the early 1180s, which exempted the monks of Melrose from all tolls in Flanders, and guaranteed them protection in any dispute between English and Flemish merchants.[11] The implication is that by the 1180s trade links were well-established and that both Flemish and Anglo-Scottish merchants were involved (in twelfth-century charters the native inhabitants of south-east Scotland are invariably referred to as *Angli*). The early importance of Flemish trade with Scotland is clarified in a list, drawn up about 1200, of goods from most parts of the known world then traded in Flanders: in which Scotland is listed second, after England, supplying wool, hides, cheese and tallow.[12]

The Flemish woollen cloth industry developed rapidly during the twelfth century, to become the largest commercial enterprise in medieval Europe, transforming Flanders into the richest and most urbanised territory north of the Alps. Scattered references to wool imports from England suggest that Flemish wool supplies were insufficient to meet local demand by the early twelfth century;[13] and cloth regulations and tariffs of the thirteenth century indicate that British wool was found to be superior to that of Flanders. Thus, at Bruges, cloth regulations of 1282 decreed that cloth made from English wool was to be marked with three crosses, from Scottish wool with two crosses, from Irish wool with one cross, and from Flemish wool with a half cross; and at St Omer, in the mid-thirteenth century, duty was levied at 3s per sack on wool from England and Scotland, but only at 2s 6d per sack on wool from Wales and Ireland (the wool of no other country is mentioned).[14]

In the twelfth century most of Scotland's trade was probably with southern Flanders. St Omer was Flanders' principal early entrepôt, and Arras was Flanders' principal city and financial centre.[15] Significantly, the battle-cry of William the Lion's Flemish levies was 'Arras'.[16] Only after Philip Augustus's seizure of southern Flanders did the centre of the cloth trade shift decisively northwards, although Scotland continued to trade extensively with St Omer until the fourteenth century.

Until the thirteenth century Scottish connections with France must have been much less important than with Flanders. But from the late twelfth century onwards the French crown pursued a consistent policy of reducing the power and independence of the French magnates, and the counts of Flanders were among the first to be brought to heel. What became the county of Artois was unwisely offered by the childless Philip d'Alsace as a dowry on the marriage of his niece to Philip Augustus, albeit he carefully retained a life-interest. His death in 1191 gave Philip Augustus the opportunity to occupy most of Artois, including Arras, in the name of his son Louis; and Louis seized the rest for himself, including St Omer, in 1212. Following the defeat and capture of Count Ferrand of Flanders, at the battle of Bouvines in 1214, the subjugation of Flanders was completed. Thereafter the French crown secured personal oaths of allegiance from the Flemish barons and urban patriciate, heard Flemish cases on appeal, and increasingly intervened in Flemish affairs.[17]

Despite the disruption of the early thirteenth century, the cloth industry expanded rapidly within the reduced county of Flanders and became central to the economy of much of northern France; from Picardy, where many of the dyestuffs were produced, to the Champagne fairs, where much of the cloth was sold. And it was this growth in demand (not just for wool, but also for cowhides, sheepskins and fish), combining with the long period of peace with England, which brought about Scotland's so-called 'golden age'.[18] The importance of these links is attested by the series of marriage alliances made between the Scottish royal house and the northern French nobility during the thirteenth century: Alexander II's marriage to Marie de Coucy in 1239, the marriage of Alexander III's eldest son to Margaret of Flanders in 1282, and Alexander III's marriage to Yolande de Dreux in 1285. French influence must have been strong in thirteenth century Scotland but, as in the twelfth century, it would have been filtered mainly through Flanders.

Ironically, far from strengthening ties, the Flemish marriage alliance seriously damaged Scoto-Flemish relations because of the Scots' failure to maintain payments on a pension of £1,000 *per annum* (perhaps £1 million in modern money), settled on prince Alexander's widow under the terms of the marriage treaty. In April 1292, while the Scots were distracted by the Great Cause, the count of Flanders ordered the seizure of all Scottish-owned goods and money in Flanders, in an attempt to recover the arrears.

Peace overtures were made by the Bruges authorities in June 1292. But it was not until July 1293, after the dispute had been submitted to the bishop of Durham for arbitration, that a provisional settlement was reached with the count of Flanders, guaranteeing reciprocal protection and freedom of trade to Scottish and Flemish merchants, except for debts relating to Margaret's pension. In November 1293 John Balliol agreed to pay the arrears in full by the following Easter and on 16 May 1294 he ordered resumption of the annuity with effect from 1 August.[19]

It is against this background that the much better known affairs concerning England need to be viewed. In parallel with these developments, the count of Flanders was secretly negotiating with Edward I of England for the marriage of his daughter Philippine to Edward of Caernarvon, later Edward II. As Anglo-French relations deteriorated Count Guy de Dampierre's urgent desire to maintain a foot in both camps is readily explicable. An unofficial naval war – between Normans and Flemings on one side, and English and Gascons on the other – gave Philip IV of France an excuse, in the view of his most recent French biographer, to contrive the imposition of royal control over Gascony.[20]

Relentless pressure was applied by Philip over a period of about a year, culminating in Edward I's forfeiture of the duchy of Aquitaine on 19 May 1294 (just three days after Balliol's final settlement with the count of Flanders). In retaliation, Edward introduced an embargo on trade with all parts of the French kingdom at the end of May and began preparations for war. Although the trade ban was rigorously enforced against Flanders, Edward simultaneously pressed ahead with the previously desultory Flemish marriage negotiations, as part of a general network of alliances, and reached an agreement with Guy de Dampierre at the end of August.

Intelligence of the secret marriage treaty rapidly reached the French king. On a visit to Paris, Guy was arrested and released only after Philippine had been surrendered into her godfather Philip's custody and a string of other measures had been introduced to strengthen Franco-Flemish ties.[21] Flanders' loyalty was thereby secured in the ensuing war with England, with the consequence that Edward I continued to embargo English wool supplies.

Since Flemish and Artesian cloth was made almost exclusively of English, Scottish and native wool (probably in that order), this was indeed a punitive measure. But, to be fully effective, it was necessary to ensure that the Scots complied with the English trade ban. This they refused to do. Scottish trade with Flanders and other parts of the French kingdom probably continued as before, despite English harassment.[22]

Thus matters continued until 3 March 1295 when, following Edward's example, Philip IV of France introduced a blanket ban on trade with the British Isles.[23] The timing of the French ban is significant because it was issued during a slack season in the wool trade. It must therefore have been intended primarily as a warning, aimed particularly at the Scots, who had no alternative outlets for most of their exports: since English wool, hides and sheepskins had, of necessity, swamped all other markets. Two years later the English barons claimed that nearly half of England's wealth was derived from wool;[24] with its limited arable lands, Scotland's reliance upon the wool trade must have been significantly greater. By 10 May the Scots had secured a six-month truce.[25]

Discussion of the Scottish embassy to France in July 1295 has always focussed upon Edward I's attempted coercion of Scotland. Philip's far more successful coercion has never been noted – in keeping though it is with his extraordinarily ruthless and unscrupulous conduct towards Gascony, Flanders, the Jews, the Papacy and the Knights Templar. Yet it is surely much more likely that the parliament held at Stirling early in July 1295 was convened primarily because of the need to send an embassy to France, in order to prevent reimposition of the French trade embargo on 1 November and the slump which would inevitably have followed. Given the period of notice required to summon a parliament, and the travelling time between France and Scotland, the timescale is exactly right.

That Edward I's assertion of overlordship must have bulked large in the proceedings, along with John Balliol's incompetence in defending Scottish interests, is inescapable. Doubtless these were reasons for the appointment of a governing council; but that the deciding factor was a decision to send an embassy to France, to *propose* an anti-English alliance, is convincing only if the threatened trade embargo is overlooked. The record of English chronicles, written after Edward's occupation of Scotland and concerned to emphasise Scottish perfidy, can hardly be regarded as impartial evidence.[26]

The letters of credence for the Scottish embassy to Philip IV refer to the strengthening of relations with France through a marriage alliance between Edward Balliol and a French princess, not to a treaty against England.[27] It is far from clear that a full offensive alliance was in Scotland's interest, particularly one which required the Scots both to mount an attack on England without first receiving reinforcements (unlike earlier or later campaigns) and to maintain hostilities for the duration of the Anglo-French war. But such terms were much to the advantage of Philip IV.

In this context, it is interesting to note that Guy de Dampierre was again seizing Scottish goods by July 1295, a month before the annuity fell due, and that Philip then ostentatiously took all Scottish merchants under his protection for the duration of the truce.[28] It looks very like a heavy-handed reminder to the Scots that their well-being depended upon the French king's goodwill. It is also significant that the Scottish embassy remained at the French court for nearly three months and agreed to the terms of a full offensive and defensive alliance against England only a week before the expiry of the trade truce.[29] Far from being the driving force behind the alliance, the Scottish government may thus be seen as a hapless pawn in the struggle between Edward I and Philip IV. Neutrality had ceased to be an option. A French alliance preserved Scottish trade and could be further justified as possibly the only means of forcing the English king to renounce his suzerainty.

From Philip's viewpoint the initial outcome of the alliance was eminently satisfactory. In the next campaign season Edward I felt obliged to turn his attention from Gascony to Scotland.[30] But the English occupation of Scotland was disastrous for the Flemings. Although it was not the spark which ignited the Flemish revolt, the loss of all wool from Scotland (as well as from England) must have been a major factor in bringing Flanders to the brink of rebellion; albeit the full impact would not have been felt until the peak wool exporting season during the summer and autumn.[31]

Scotland had fallen by the summer of 1296 and Flanders rebelled in the autumn. An Anglo-Flemish truce was concluded on 2 November, which included provision for the reopening of trade links with both England and Scotland (and made specific reference to the release of wool), and a full alliance was agreed on 7 January 1297.[32] Flanders' fate mirrored that of Scotland. It was largely occupied by the French in the summer of 1297, before the arrival of Edward I at the end of August with an English army.

After the annihilation of the English army in Scotland at Stirling Bridge, on 11 September 1297, Edward was obliged to abandon his Flemish confederate in order to concentrate his forces upon the reconquest of Scotland. On 9 October he agreed a humiliating truce with Philip IV, which left Philip in possession of Gascony and enabled him to complete the reoccupation of Flanders after Edward returned to England the following March. Edward insisted upon the inclusion of the count of Flanders in the original truce, but not in its successors. When the Franco-Flemish truce expired in 1300 Guy de Dampierre and his most prominent supporters were imprisoned. Flanders was then added to the French royal domain.[33]

In the days of relatively primitive sailing ships the English Channel acted as a natural barrier between northern and southern Europe. Whilst access from the south presented few problems, prevailing winds and currents made access from the north slow and difficult. Navigation around western Britain was also hazardous. Flanders and Artois therefore occupied a pivotal position between north and south.

As the only French territories adjoining the North Sea, Flanders and Artois provided Philip IV with much the most reliable means of furnishing the Scots with the money and supplies they needed to repel the English invaders. Such action may have been contrary to the Anglo-French truces,[34] but it was probably the only way Philip could ensure that the English were too preoccupied to interfere in continental affairs.

Is it coincidental that much of Scotland escaped the shackles of English occupation from 1297 to 1302, at the same time that Philip possessed Flanders? Or that Scotland was reoccupied between 1303 and 1304, after the stunning success of the next Flemish revolt, in which a seemingly invincible French army was overwhelmed and most of its cavalry massacred at the battle of Courtrai? Or that the revolt of Robert Bruce took place only after it became apparent that the Franco-Flemish peace settlement of 1305, with its reinstatement of the count of Flanders, had secured the prospect of further support?

The Flemings seized Scottish goods in Flanders at the outset of their revolt,[35] presumably as a sop to win English support in their struggle against the French king. To prevent English aid to the Flemings, Philip IV was obliged to conclude a full peace treaty with England, restoring Gascony to Edward I, in May 1303.[36] Not until Flanders had been pacified could the Scots hope for significant French aid. But, by the same token, any Flemish support for the Scots was likely to be viewed by the French king as a gesture of loyalty to himself.

As early as 10 April 1305 the magistrates of Bruges wrote to the English government insisting that Flanders was open to all nations, the Scots included, and six days later the count of Flanders did likewise.[37] The following year, when an English commission tried to claim massive damages from the French government for losses attributed to French support for the Scots from 1297 onwards,[38] an advocate for the count of Flanders insisted that the Anglo-French truces and treaty did not affect France's obligations to the Scots, under the treaty of 1295, and testified to the importance (to Flanders) of relations with Scotland. Given the concurrence of Philip IV with this view, it seems probable that Flanders continued to provide a haven for the Scots thereafter. At least, that is the implication of a memorandum concerning the English claims and the countervailing French arguments, submitted to Edward II about 1309.[39]

Dutchmen, Flemings and Germans appear repeatedly in English records as suppliers and supporters of the 'Scottish rebels', and Flanders was the base from which they mainly operated.[40] As Franco-Flemish relations deteriorated once more, the English government mistakenly hoped it could at last bring pressure to bear upon the Flemings and began a stream of protests to the count of Flanders about the trade and military aid that his territories, and Bruges in particular, were providing to the Scots.[41] Bruges had latterly been the principal centre of Scoto-Flemish trade before the Wars of Independence,[42] and it consolidated that position by becoming a focal point for Scottish relief activities.

It was perhaps during this period that a Scottish staple was first established at Bruges, in imitation of the English staple at St Omer; the institution of which, in 1313,[43] must have forced the Scots finally to abandon their trade with Artois. The same year, incidentally, that English agents reported the departure from the Zwyn (the long, silted-up harbour of Bruges between Damme and Sluys) of a convoy of 13 ships, laden with arms and supplies for the Scots.[44] Although the first allusion to a Scottish staple does not occur until 1347, its context implies that the staple was by then well established.[45] And the copy of a letter of 1321, from Robert Bruce to the magistrates of Bruges, in the Dunfermline Abbey cartulary – informing them that he had granted Dunfermline Abbey its own cocket seal (entitling the abbey to collect customs duty on goods exported from its estates) and requesting the Bruges authorities to accept it as they would his own – suggests that by then Bruges was already the officially recognised centre of the Scottish export trade.[46]

Despite increasing hostility towards Flemish merchants in England and disruption of their trade, and the renewed friction between Flanders and the French crown from 1310 to 1320, the Flemings continued to maintain friendly relations with the Scots. All attempts by the English government to persuade the Flemish authorities to obstruct Scottish trade were rebuffed. The intensity of Flemish feelings in this regard is emphasised in a letter, written in 1317 by an English ambassador to Flanders, which noted that '[the Flemings] would never consent to refuse the Scots entry to their lands, or to prevent their merchants from trading in Scotland'. It therefore counselled that ships and goods seized from Flemings who were suspected of trading with the Scots should be restored, lest action be taken against English merchants in Flanders.[47]

Although it has never been remarked, Robert de Béthune, count of Flanders from 1305 to 1322, must have been Scotland's most resolute foreign supporter during the Wars of Independence. That is confirmed by the rapidity with which his grandson, Count Louis de Nevers, bowed to English demands and expelled the Scots from Flanders in April 1323, seven months after Robert's death, in an effort to improve Anglo-Flemish relations.[48]

Since Louis had been brought up at the French court and remained under French tutelage, this implies that by then the French government was itself indifferent to the Scottish cause.[49] As Professor Nicholson has suggested, the loss of Flemish support and the Scots' exclusion from Flanders may well have been the catalyst which forced the Scots to accede to a thirteen-year truce with England at the end of the following month.[50] Measures to protect Scotland's overseas trade are a major feature of the truce because, as John Barbour (Robert Bruce's fourteenth-century biographer) noted, attacks on Scottish trade with Flanders were the one way in which the English could still seriously damage Scottish interests.[51]

The Flemings rebelled against their young count in the winter of 1323. Flanders was convulsed by civil war until King Charles IV gathered an army to occupy the county and thus imposed a peace settlement in April 1326.[52] It is therefore highly significant that the Franco-Scottish alliance was renewed the following week (for the first time since 1295) and in terms geared to securing the Scots' position in France, as well as to ensuring that Scotland and France would support each other in any conflict with England.[53] Once again it is Flanders that was central to Scottish concerns. Scottish interests were most threatened by the English through Flanders; only French influence could then provide an adequate counterbalance, and only through Flanders could French military aid readily reach Scotland.

When the English again attacked Scotland, Flanders once more became a major supplier of military aid to the Scots. In April 1333 Edward III protested to Louis de Nevers and the major Flemish towns about the arms, supplies and men being sent to

Scotland from Flanders.[54] Two years later a large force was apparently fitted out by order of the French king and sent to Scotland under Flemish command;[55] and in March 1337 English agents reported that five ships were preparing to sail to Aberdeen from the Zwyn with arms and munitions for the Scots. This was followed in both May and September 1337 by royal writs to the English sheriffs warning them of the scale and frequency of aid being sent to the Scots 'from Flanders and elsewhere'.[56] Thereafter there is a gap until 1355, when both Fordun and the *Scalacronica* record the despatch of a small French expedition from Sluys to Scotland.[57]

In the interim a further Flemish revolt, in 1338, had seriously damaged Scoto-Flemish relations. England initially strongly supported the Flemish rebellion. Like most fourteenth-century Flemish uprisings, the rebellion was centred upon Ghent, mainly situated as it was in imperial Flanders and thus lacking ties of loyalty to the French crown. By contrast, Bruges, Flanders' most Francophile city, was an un-willing participant.[58] At what point the Scots were forced out of Bruges is unclear. The only evidence for the Scots' departure is two surprisingly late decrees of the Scottish council, on 12 November 1347; one authorising the establishment of the Scottish staple at Middelburg (25 miles to the north, on the island of Walcheren, in Zeeland); the other ordering the exclusion of Flemings from Scotland, in retaliation for the expulsion of the Scots from Flanders.[59]

In 1348, with Flemish opposition to the English alliance rapidly escalating, particularly in Bruges, the English abandoned the Flemish rebels. The Scots seem to have returned to Bruges gradually in the course of 1348,[60] although Ghent held out against Count Louis de Male until January 1349. The Franco-Scottish alliance was renewed in 1352, on the initiative of King John of France, and again in June 1359,[61] the latter renewal while negotiations were in progress for an Anglo-Flemish staple treaty.[62] This was followed in November by the first surviving Scottish staple treaty with the count of Flanders,[63] possibly the result of French pressure to ensure that Scottish interests were protected after the brief return of the English staple to Bruges in July. Like the arrangements proposed for the Middelburg staple, the comital treaty was presumably complementary to staple agreements, now lost, already made with the Bruges authorities.

Although Bruges played a vital role between 1357 and 1373, as the financial centre through which instalments of David II's English ransom were raised and channelled, there was a lull in diplomatic activity thereafter until the accession of Robert II in 1371. He promptly renewed the Franco-Scottish alliance (the first king to do so upon his succession). The treaty was couched in similar terms to its predecessors; but new guarantees were given to protect the rights, honour, profit, privileges and franchises of the subjects of both countries, and to do all in the kings' power to prevent harm from befalling them.[64]

The reasons for these new guarantees are unclear, but were probably related to a serious piratical incident at Sluys late in 1370; when French warships seized Scottish, German and other vessels, killing some of their crews, capturing others and pillaging their cargoes, on the pretext that they were enemies of France. This caused consternation in Flanders. Intense lobbying by the count of Flanders and the major Flemish towns persuaded King Charles V to release the ships, goods and men taken in the attack.[65] But the lack of French recognition which these seizures imply must have left the Scots feeling exceptionally insecure, both economically and politically. They were powerful arguments for a formal renewal and clarification of the alliance at the outset of the reign.

The next test of the alliance was also focussed upon Flanders. After thirty years of relative peace, Flanders was rent by civil war between 1379 and 1385. Once more based in Ghent, the rebels rapidly overran the county, but most of it was won back for Louis de Male by a French army in 1382. As in previous revolts the rebels secured English support. An English force devastated much of western Flanders in the summer of 1383 and another was sent the following year to swell the Ghent garrison.

In January 1384 Count Louis de Male died and was succeeded by his son-in-law, Philip the Bold, duke of Burgundy.[66] Having bottled up the rebels in Ghent, Philip and the French government turned their attention to a highly ambitions plan for a two-pronged invasion of England. Preparations for this had begun as early as 1383, when Robert II had agreed to accept 1,000 French troops, arms and money, in the event of war with England.[67]

Military stores were prepared throughout northern France and a fleet was assembled in the Zwyn. The main army was to have landed in Kent, to move up through southern England, while a combined Franco-Scottish army invaded England from the north – much as Philip d'Alsace had planned two centuries before. In the event only the northern force was despatched. Jean de Vienne sailed from Sluys with an army of 1,500 men and extensive money and supplies for the Scots on 20 May 1385. The southern army was to have assembled and embarked two months later. But on the night of 14 July a large force from Ghent seized Damme, the town at the mouth of the Bruges canal, thus stopping all seaborne traffic with Bruges and rendering the Zwyn anchorages unsafe.

The planned invasion of Kent had to be abandoned and the army diverted to the siege of Damme. Consequently the Vienne expedition lost its purpose and the Scots found themselves facing England alone. Much of Berwickshire, Roxburghshire and Lothian was devastated and Edinburgh was sacked by an English army that would otherwise have been required to defend southern England. In such circumstances, it is hardly surprising that the Scots soon turned hostile towards Vienne and his men, and that they concluded a truce with England as quickly as possible (almost at the moment that the Ghent rebels agreed to an armistice).[68] Set in context, the Scots' notorious behaviour in the campaign of 1385 appears much less rash and mean-spirited than is generally supposed.

After these unhappy events the Scottish government refused to be drawn into the next four years of ineffectual Anglo-French hostilities. A series of truces followed, which lasted until the early 1400s and included Scotland as a French ally, enabling Philip the Bold to consolidate his position in both Flanders and France.[69]

Since Philip intended to spend most of his time in Paris, as his nephew King

Charles VI's principal adviser, he established a council to govern Flanders in his absence. One of the main responsibilities listed in its constitution was 'the protection of the privileges granted to foreign merchants like the Scots, the Italians and the Hansards'.[70] The order is illuminating because the value of trade with both Italy and the German Hanse must have been considerably greater than with Scotland. The precedence accorded to the Scots can only be explained in terms of the Franco-Scottish alliance, since by then the Scottish wool trade was in marked decline.

Space precludes any discussion of the complex issues surrounding this decline, or the upsurge in piracy which followed the renewal of Anglo-Scottish hostilities at the end of the fourteenth century.[71] Suffice it to note that they led to a breakdown in Scoto-Flemish commercial relations in 1406, which was remedied by a further renewal of the Franco-Scottish alliance in 1407. In the process of this the magistrates of Bruges were dismissed by the duke of Burgundy; and the Flemish towns were forced to rescind all judicial measures taken against the Scots, to provide compensation for Scottish losses in Flanders, and to extend Scottish commercial privileges. Similar pressure prevented a further breakdown of relations in 1416.[72]

That was almost the last occasion when the Auld Alliance could be invoked to protect Scottish interests in Flanders. The assassination of John the Fearless, duke of Burgundy, in 1419 – by supporters of the Dauphin, later Charles VII, and in the Dauphin's presence – must have been considered in Scotland to be as great a disaster as it was in France. Many Scots, including the earls of Douglas and Mar, had served the duke of Burgundy; and, before news of the assassination reached Scotland, a Scottish army of 6,000 men had set sail, under the misapprehension that it would be joining a combined Dauphinist and Burgundian campaign to expel the English from northern France. Indeed, much of the army may have been sent to France in fulfilment of a treaty, made by the earl of Douglas in 1413, to supply the duke of Burgundy with a force of 4,000 men, if required (the earl's eldest son was one of the leaders of the Scottish expedition).[73]

After the death of John the Fearless, French interests collapsed in Flanders. His son Philip the good created, for the first time, an essentially Netherlandish state by expanding Burgundian power into the patchwork of imperial counties and duchies to the north and east of Flanders.[74] The Flemish dimension of the Auld Alliance underwent a half-life thereafter, until a separate Scoto-Burgundian alliance was sealed in 1449. French sovereignty continued to be recognised in Flanders until after the accession of Charles the Bold.[75] But, in practice, the Scottish crown treated the Burgundian Netherlands as an independent power from the 1420s onwards and its dealings with the French government were correspondingly circumscribed. Only in the sixteenth century did the Franco-Scottish alliance regain its previous importance, by which time major direct trade links had been established between Scotland and France, following a further sharp decline in Scottish trade with Flanders.[76]

Unfashionable though it may be to stress the importance of economic affairs in the formulation of medieval foreign policy, that has to be the conclusion of this survey. Most of Scotland's export trade was geared to the Flemish market from the twelfth to the fifteenth century and the security of that trade was essential to the well-being of the Scottish economy. When subversion of Flanders became a key objective of English foreign policy, it posed a serious threat to both France and Scotland. Their interests merged: an anti-English alliance was a natural outcome.

English domination of Scotland also posed a serious threat to Flanders because the Flemish cloth industry would then have been dependent upon a monopolistic supplier (until Scottish wool was increasingly displaced by Spanish from the late fourteenth century onwards). Aid to Scotland was supplied by both the Flemings and the French government and was channelled through Flanders. Since Flanders provided the mainspring of the Auld Alliance, it should not be surprising that the main events in the alliance's early history can be linked so closely with Flemish affairs, or that periods of instability in Flanders were so damaging to the Scots.

NOTES

1 Henri Pirenne, *Histoire de Belgique* (hereafter Pirenne, *Histoire*), i (5th edn., Brussels, 1929), 56–60, 103–18, 203–7, 217–19; Jean Dunbabin, *France in the Making, 843–1180* (Oxford, 1985), *passim*. The counts also secure territory along the east bank of the river Scheldt and reclaimed lands in the delta, which were known collectively as imperial Flanders because they lay within the borders of the Holy Roman Empire.

2 Marcel Pacaut, *Louis VII et son royaume* (Paris, 1964), 38, 176.

3 A late medieval legend that the Franco-Scottish alliance originated in the reign of Charlemagne probably derives from reports of Frankish contacts with the Irish (*Scotti*); and the suggestion of an earlier alliance with Louis VII is derived merely from English rumours of a Scottish embassy to France in 1168: Alan O. Anderson, *Early Sources of Scottish History* (2 vols., Edinburgh, 1925), i, 251; Sir Archibald C. Lawrie, *Annals of the Reigns of Malcolm and William, Kings of Scotland* (Glasgow, 1910), 116–17.

4 Jordan Fantosme, 'Chronique de la guerre entre les Anglois et les Ecossois', in *Chronicles of Stephen, Henry II, and Richard I*, ed. Richard Howlett (Rolls Series, no. 82), iii (hereafter Fantosme, 'Chronique'), 222–377.

5 Fantosme, 'Chronique', 243–377; Austin L. Poole, *From Domesday Book to Magna Carta, 1087–1216* (2nd edn., Oxford, 1955), 276–7, 333–7; Archibald A. M. Duncan, *Scotland, the Making of the Kingdom* (Edinburgh, 1975) (hereafter Duncan, *Kingdom*), 228–30.

6 Fantosme, 'Chronique', 287–9; Gervase of Canterbury, *Historical Works*, ed. William Stubbs (Rolls Series, no. 73), I, 246.

7 For an outline of Philip d'Alsace's exceptionally active commercial policies, see H. van Werveke, 'The Low Countries' in *The Cambridge Economic History of Europe*, ed. Sir Michael M. Postan, E. Rich and Edward Miller, iii (Cambridge, 1963), 342–50.

8 Geoffrey W. S. Barrow, *The Anglo-Norman Era in Scottish History* (Oxford, 1980), 35–60; Duncan, *Kingdom*, 137–9. Estimating the extent of Flemish settlement is complicated by the fact that Flemings were almost invariably included within the term *Franci* in twelfth-century Scottish charters: Sir Archibald C. Lawrie, *Early Scottish Charters* (Glasgow, 1905), (hereafter *ESC*), *passim*; Geoffrey W. S. Barrow and others, eds. *Regesta Regum Scottorum* (Edinburgh, 1960) (hereafter *RRS*), i–ii, *passim*. See also above, p.3.

9 Four of the seven burgh residents named in charters of the reign of David I have names that are certainly Flemish, one has an Anglo-Saxon name, and two have Franco-Norman names that were also common on southern Flanders: *ESC*, nos. 169, 193, 238, 248, 268.

10 Alexander P. Forbes, ed. 'Fragment of the life of St Kentigern', in *The Historian of Scotland*, v (Edinburgh, 1874), 131.

11 Cosmo Innes, ed. *Liber Sancte Marie de Melros* (2 vols., Bannatyne Club, 1837), i, nos. 14 and 15.

12 L. Gilliodts van Severen, ed., *Cartulaire de l'ancienne estaple de Bruges* (2 vols., Bruges, 1904–6) (hereafter Gilliodts, *Cartulaire*), i, no. 14. The only fish listed were herring from Denmark, as a minor Danish export.

13 Terence H. Lloyd, *The English Wool Trade in the Middle Ages* (Cambridge, 1977) (hereafter Lloyd, *Wool Trade*), 1–6.

14 Georges Espinas and Henri Pirenne, eds., *Receuil de documents relatifs à l'industrie drapière en Flandre* (3 vols., Brussels, 1906–20), i, 396; iii, 367.

15 Jan A. van Houtte, *Bruges: essai d'histoire urbaine* (Brussels, 1967), 18; Pirenne, *Histoire*, i, 207–8.

16 Fantosme, 'Chronique', 305, 353.

17 Robert Fawtier, *The Capetian Kings of France*, trans. Lionel Butler and R. J. Adam (London, 1960), 111–17; Pirenne, *Histoire*, I, 219–41, 253–61, 335–43.

18 Alexander Stevenson, 'Trade with the south' (hereafter Stevenson, 'Trade'), in *The Scottish Medieval Town*, ed. Michael Lynch, Michael Spearman and Geoffrey Stell (Edinburgh, 1988), 184–7; Nicholas Mayhew, 'Alexander III – a silver age?' in *Scotland in the Reign of Alexander III*, ed. Norman H. Reid (Edinburgh, 1990), 53–73.

19 Joseph Stevenson, ed., *Documents illustrative of the History of Scotland, 1286–1306* (2 vols., Edinburgh, 1870) (hereafter Stevenson, *Documents*), i, nos. 24, 233, 234, 246, 248, 311, 315, 323; Gilliodts, *Cartulaire*, i, no. 102.

20 Jean Favier, *Philippe le Bel* (Paris, 1978), 206–12; Sir Maurice Powicke, *The Thirteenth Century, 1216–1307* (2nd edn., Oxford, 1962), 644–9; Frantz Funck-Brentano, *Philippe le Bel en Flandre* (Paris, 1896) (hereafter Funck-Brentano, *Flandre*), 23–6.

21 Pirenne, *Histoire*, I, 398–400; Favier, *Philippe le Bel*, 216–17; Funck-Brentano, *Flandre*, 139–51.

22 Thomas Rymer, ed., *Foedera* (3rd edn., 10 vols., The Hague, 1739–45), Iiii, 129; Joseph Bain and others, eds., *Calendar of Documents Relating to Scotland* (5 vols., Edinburgh, 1881–1986) (hereafter *CDS*), ii, 162.

23 Stevenson, *Documents*, ii, no. 334.

24 Lloyd, *Wool Trade*, 1.

25 Stevenson, *Documents*, ii, no. 335.

26 Joseph Stevenson, ed., *Chronicon de Lanercost* (Maitland Club, 1839), 161–2; Harry Rothwell, ed., *The Chronicle of Walter of Guisborough* (Royal Historical Society, 1957), 264.

27 Rymer, *Foedera*, Iiii, 146–7.

28 Stevenson, *Documents*, ii, nos. 337–8.

29 Rymer, *Foedera*, Iiii, 152. Translated in: Walter Bower, *Scotichronicon*, ed. Donald E. R. Watt and others (Aberdeen, 1987–), 6, 45–51.

30 Michael Prestwich, *Edward I* (London, 1988) (hereafter Prestwich, *Edward I*), 381–5.

31 For Philip's threatened dispossession of Guy de Dampierre, which finally triggered the revolt, see Pirenne, *Histoire*, I, 401–8.

32 Gilliodts, *Cartulaire*, i, nos. 119, 122; Rymer, *Foedera*, Iiii, 168–70.

33 Funck-Brentano, *Flandre*, 198–349; Pirenne, *Histoire*, I, 409–12; Prestwich, *Edward I*, 392–6.

34 Rymer, *Foedera*, Iiii, 191–5; Iiv, 4, 24–6.

35 Gilliodts, *Cartulaire*, i, no. 136.

36 Favier, *Philippe le Bel*, 242, 314–15; Funck-Brentano, *Flandre*, 426, 465–6; Prestwich, *Edward I*, 397; Rymer, *Foedera*, Iiv, 24–6.

37 Gillodts, *Cartulaire*, i, no. 153; *Foedera*, Iiv, 39–40.

38 *CDS*, v, no. 428.

39 *Ibid.*, no. 528.

40 William S. Reid, 'Trade, traders and Scottish independence', *Speculum*, 29 (1954), 210–22; *idem.*, 'The Scots and the staple ordinance of 1313', *Speculum*, 34 (1959), 598–610; *idem.*, 'Sea-power in the Anglo-Scottish war, 1296–1328', *Mariner's Mirror*, 46 (1960), 7–23; James W. Dilley, 'German merchants in Scotland, 1297–1327', *Scottish Historical Review*, 27 (1948), 142–55; Lloyd, *Wool Trade*, 102–14.

41 David Macpherson and others, eds., *Rotuli Scotiae* (2 vols., London, 1814–19) (hereafter Macpherson, *Rotuli Scotiae*), I, 78, 136, 193–4; Rymer, *Foedera*, Iiv, 177; Iii, 35–6, 170–1.

42 Stevenson, 'Trade', 187.

43 Lloyd, *Wool Trade*, 106.

44 *Calendar of Close Rolls, 1307–13* (London, 1892), 570–1.

45 See below, p. 39.

46 *RRS*, v, 458.

47 *CDS*, v, no. 634.

48 Terence H. Lloyd, *Alien Merchants in England in the High Middle Ages* (Brighton, 1982), 103–4; *Calendar of Patent Rolls, 1321–4* (London, 1924), 269, 276.

49 Pirenne, *Histoire*, ii (3rd edn., Brussels, 1922), 7–9.

50 Ranald Nicholson, *Scotland, the Later Middle Ages* (Edinburgh, 1974) (hereafter Nicholson, *Scotland*), 105–6.

51 Rymer, *Foedera*, IIii, 73–4; John Barbour, *The Bruce*, book xix, lines 193–204.

52 But after the French army dispersed the revolt flared up again. It was finally suppressed by another French army in 1328; Pirenne, *Histoire*, ii, 88–98.

53 Thomas Thomson and Cosmo Innes, eds., *Acts of Parliaments of Scotland* (12 vols., Edinburgh, 1814–75), (hereafter *APS*), xii, 5–6.

54 Macpherson, *Rotuli Scotiae*, i, 233–4.

55 Jean Froissart, *Chroniques*, ed. S. Luce and others (13 vols., Société d'histoire de France, 1869–1957) (hereafter Froissart, *Chroniques*), i, ccxxi.

56 Macpherson, *Rotuli Scotiae*, i, 485, 490, 498.

57 William F. Skene, ed. *Johannis de Fordun, Chronica Gentis Scotorum* (2 vols., Edinburgh, 1871–2), ii, 360–1; Joseph Stevenson, ed. *Scalacronica, by Sir Thomas Gray of Heton, Knight* (Maitland Club, 1836), 302.

58 Pirenne, *Histoire*, ii, 105–35.

59 *RRS*, vi, 140–1.

60 Gilliodts, *Cartulaire*, i, nos. 272–4.

61 *APS*, xii, 8; Paris, Archives Nationales, Trésor des chartes, J 677, no. 7.

62 Lloyd, *Wool Trade*, 209–10.

63 Matthijs P. Rooseboom, *The Scottish Staple in the Netherlands* (The Hague, 1910), appendix 10.

64 Quoted *verbatim* in the 1391 renewal, after the accession of Robert III: John Stuart and others, eds., *The Exchequer Rolls of Scotland* (23 vols., Edinburgh, 1878–1908), iii, xcvii–civ.

65 Gilliodts, *Cartulaire*, i, no. 344.

66 Richard Vaughan, *Philip the Bold* (London, 1962) (hereafter Vaughan, *Philip the Bold*), 19–31, 34–5.

67 *APS*, xii, 19.

68 Vaughan, *Philip the Bold*, 35–6; Froissart, *Chroniques*, 11, xlv–lxxi; Nicholson, *Scotland*, 196–8; Alexander Grant, *Independence and Nationhood: Scotland 1306–1469* (London, 1984) (hereafter Grant, *Independence*), 41.

69 Froissart, *Chroniques*, 11, lvii–lxii; 13, i–xxx; Vaughan, *Philip the Bold*, 37, 48–50.

70 Richard Vaughan, *John the Fearless*, (London, 1966), 19.

71 The reasons are discussed in: Stevenson, 'Trade', 191–2; *idem.*, 'Trade between Scotland and the Low Countries in the later Middle Ages' (PhD, University of Aberdeen, 1982) (hereafter Stevenson, 'Thesis'), 21–6; David Ditchburn, 'Piracy and war at sea in late medieval Scotland', in *Scotland and the Sea*, ed. T. C. Smout (Edinburgh, 1992), 48–9.

72 Stevenson, 'Thesis', 27–31, 42, 68–9.

73 Vaughan, *John the Fearless*, 55, 259–61, 267–86; Grant, *Independence*, 47; Nicholson, *Scotland*, 249–50; Rymer, *Foedera*, IViii, 131–2.

74 Richard Vaughan, *Philip the Good* (London, 1970), *passim*.

75 *Ibid.*, 19–20, 350–3; Richard Vaughan, *Charles the Bold* (London 1973), 57–8, 73.

76 Stevenson, 'Thesis', 74–85, 102–20, 262–3, 317–25, 330; Grant, *Independence*, 48–53; Jenny Wormald, *Court, Kirk, and Community: Scotland 1470–1625* (London, 1981), 6–7.

New Solutions to Old Problems: The Stewarts and the Alliance

Extracted from N Macdougall 2001 *An Antidote to the English: The Auld Alliance, 1295–1560*, East Linton (Tuckwell Press), 41–51.

David II had received his early schooling in chivalry in France. Now, following his capture at Neville's Cross in 1346, he would find a new chivalric mentor in Edward III of England, sharing his enthusiasm for Arthurian legends of the Round Table and the new Order of the Garter, and attending at least two St George's Day tournaments, at Windsor in 1349 and Smithfield in 1357. Though he was nominally King of Scots for twenty-five years after his capture in 1346, David spent eleven of these as a prisoner in England, lending himself to the chivalric ethos of his captor, and most of them concocting abortive plans for his release, and subsequently for the remission of his huge ransom and an English succession in Scotland if he should die without a legitimate heir. Thus the 'second reign' of David II (1357–71) stood in stark contrast to the first; and the Franco-Scottish alliance hardly figured in it at all.

To a large extent, the alliance was kept alive by the man who had deserted King David at Neville's Cross (though he was hardly alone in this), Robert the Steward. The heir presumptive's military experience – the sieges, raids, and scorched earth of the 1330s – was very different from that of his royal uncle. Warfare was no chivalric game in Scotland, more a grim struggle for survival. In this sense at least, the Steward was an appropriate replacement for David II; he had already been royal lieutenant in 1335 and 1338–41, and was to occupy the office again from 1347 to 1350, and from around 1354 to 1357. A far more astute diplomat than David, the Steward espoused a different, and more cautious, view of the Auld Alliance: it would continue to serve as a guarantee of the integrity of the independent Scottish kingdom, and the two allies would co-operate, as far as possible, in winning back territory lost to the common English enemy – in the case of the Scots the southern sheriffdoms overrun by the English and Edward Balliol a few months after Neville's Cross.

King David's position, whether as Edward III's prisoner or during his short periods on parole, did not improve. It may have been a demand by the English king in 1349 for David's recognition of Edward as lord superior of Scotland as a condition of his release which drove David to propose, as early as 1350, that a younger son of Edward III should be recognised as heir presumptive in Scotland. With such a proposal, of course, went the necessity of making concessions to the disinherited and the removal of Robert the Steward from the succession. When David was eventually released by the Treaty of Berwick of 1357, he was saddled with an enormous ransom of 100,000 marks (£66,666 sterling), to be paid in instalments over ten years; much of the remainder of his life was taken up with plans to have the ransom annulled in return for some form of English succession in Scotland. Apologists for David II have claimed that the king's policy was a wise one, achieving the double objective of undermining the Steward and cancelling the ransom. When this had been achieved, the argument runs, David would confound the English by producing a son and heir.

Perhaps; but there is no way of knowing that this is what was in David's mind, and in the event the king's second marriage, to Margaret Logie in 1362, ended not with an heir but with a divorce. It may be that David, a prisoner who had to watch the Steward's power in Scotland become more and more entrenched during his enforced absence, made a complete *volte-face* in diplomatic policy with no clear idea where it would lead, but in order to frustrate his rival and experiment with alternative settlements. He had, after all, inherited the French alliance from his father Robert I; he had done his best for it, and failed; and he never formally renewed it.

By contrast, Robert the Steward was a committed supporter of the alliance. His motives may have been cynical; obviously after 1346, and especially after King David's first proposals of an English succession, the Steward could further his own cause by wrapping himself in the national flag and adhering to the Auld Alliance. Scots were, and remained, divided over David's 'English' proposals and the political alternatives to these; but it seems that a majority – perhaps a large majority – would have no truck with David's various diplomatic schemes, especially as the 1360s advanced. The Steward, in pointing up the differences between himself and the king and taking advantage of David's temporary weakness, may be regarded as an unscrupulous opportunist; but he was also heir presumptive, a great magnate with a large family and huge affinity, and a man who had experienced the hard times – and French assistance – of the 1330s at first hand.

As lieutenant, the Steward wasted little time in showing his French sympathies. In November 1347, he issued acts under the captive David II's great seal banning all Flemings from Scotland and transferring the Scottish staple from Bruges in Flanders to Middelburg in Zeeland. The aim was probably political rather than commercial, as the Flemings had sided with Edward III against Philip VI of France. Less than a fortnight later, on 22 November 1347, the Steward requested – by way of the kings of France and Scotland – a papal dispensation for his marriage to the late Elizabeth Mure (the couple had been within the forbidden degrees of consanguinity) and the right to legitimise the sizeable offspring – by this stage four sons and two daughters – of the match. The dispensation, promptly granted by the French Avignonese pope Clement VI, former archbishop of Rouen and supporter of Philip VI of France, brought the Stewart dynasty a step closer; and the captive David II was apparently powerless to prevent what he must have regarded as the misuse of his seal in enhancing the status of his rival.

In August 1350 Philip VI died and was succeeded by his son John II, a man of similar chivalric ideals and impulses. In 1351, when a David II release deal seemed to be in the offing, and possibly on the prompting of the Steward, the French king wrote to the Scots warning that King David might be restored by force by the English; to avert this he offered the services of 500 men-at-arms and 500 archers. In subsequent letters, he offered to restore the French lands of Edward Balliol, who by this stage was clinging on to Buittle castle in Galloway and not much else. Balliol, John claimed, was in any case considering making peace with France and the Scots. Finally, in the summer of 1352, the French king offered the services of his fleet to protect Scottish merchant shipping, and promised to maintain the Franco-Scottish alliance.

David was not released at this time, so that John II's letters to the Scots were no more than diplomatic straws in the wind. In the spring of 1355, however, the French king sent Eugene de Garancières – a soldier already familiar with Scotland – with fifty men-at-arms, later reinforced with a gift of 40,000 gold *écus* (around 15,000 marks) to be distributed amongst the Scottish magnates on condition that they broke the English truce. The earls of Angus and March did so, joining with the French in a surprise assault on Berwick in November 1355. Edward III, just returned from France, was forced to intervene, coming north to relieve Berwick and to conduct the devastating raid on south-east Scotland which was later dubbed 'The Burnt Candlemas' (Feburary 1356). It was certainly bad enough: the Franciscan friary in Haddington was burned, the pilgrimage church of Whitekirk was pillaged, and Edward III's armies laid waste the countryside in what was to prove his last Scottish campaign. Yet signs of a Scottish recovery were already underway; for at Roxburgh in January, Edward Balliol had at last given up the unequal struggle. He formally resigned his kingdom – now virtually lost – to Edward III in return for a fat English pension and an initial gift of 5,000 marks. Rivals for the Scottish throne had been reduced from three to two.

This see-saw of international diplomacy and war lurched violently in one direction in the autumn of 1356. On 19 September, at Maupertuis near Poitiers, a huge French host led by King John himself encountered an English force under the command of Edward, the 'Black Prince', Edward III's son. At the French council of war before the battle, the king knighted William, lord of Douglas (the future first earl), who had joined the army with his kinsman Archibald Douglas and a retinue estimated at 200–300 men, many of them archers. The French were confident of victory, and refused attempts to negotiate; but they were concerned not to charge headlong at the strong defensive English position and be mown down by archers in the attempt. According to the chronicler Froissart, it was the lord of Douglas who gave King John the advice that the French cavalry should dismount and advance on foot. The result, after trudging uphill *en masse* in full armour, was a hard-fought struggle in which the French were totally defeated; worse, King John was captured. To all appearances the Franco-Scottish alliance was in ruins: Edward III now had the kings of Scotland and France as his prisoners.

However, at this point the English king overplayed his hand in France. In a misjudged expedition which was intended to place him on the French throne, Edward III laid siege to Rheims, where French kings were traditionally crowned. Stout resistance, followed by appalling weather, forced Edward to move on, and his encirclement of Paris produced no results. This was largely because the French had at last learned the lessons of Crécy and Poitiers; the young dauphin Charles (the future Charles V), proclaimed Regent for the captive John II and struggling to contain internal insurrection in France (the *Jacquerie* of 1358) and the indiscriminate pillaging of mercenary Free Companies, had the good sense not to engage the English king in a pitched battle. Edward III ran short of supplies, his campaign fizzled out, and the Treaty of Brétigny (1360) was the eventual result. This 'dishonourable peace' left Edward III with an enlarged Gascony, and in the north, Ponthieu, Calais, and Guines, all to be held in full sovereignty; but the English king had to give up using the title of King of France. Neither side had satisfactorily resolved the issues which had been at stake at the outset of the war, so Brétigny amounted to no more than an extended truce. Edward III's sizeable consolation was the agreed ransoms – £66,000 sterling already agreed for David II at Berwick in 1357, and ten times that figure for Jean II of France in 1360.

The Treaty of Brétigny had also stipulated the breaking of the Franco-Scottish alliance. However, the continuing popularity of that alliance had been demonstrated as recently as 1359. Michael Penman has argued convincingly that David II's efforts to impose an English succession deal in return for an annulment of his ransom came to a head in a general council at Dundee in April of that year; in spite of growing Anglo-Scottish trade, pilgrimage, and an English commitment to the establishment of a system of border tribunals to preserve the truce, King David had seriously underestimated the anti-English sentiment of the Scottish estates. This is strikingly revealed in the commission granted on 10 May 1359 to the Scottish ambassadors who were to proceed to France to secure a 'firmer alliance and confederation' between the two kingdoms. For the alliance, if renewed, was to be binding upon 'the king of Scots, *of his lieutenant, or others of sufficient power*' [my italics]. Previous, and indeed later, Franco-Scottish treaties were all made on behalf of the king of Scots and his heirs. Clearly David II faced strong Scottish opposition to his English schemes in the spring of 1359; thus in June, though the Scottish ambassadors in Paris spoke in the name of their king, they were in fact seeking to further the pro-French policy of Robert the Steward.

Franco-Scottish negotiations led to an agreement ratified by the Regent Charles on 29 June 1359. If it had been taken further, this new Treaty of Paris would have committed the Regent to paying the Scots 50,000 marks by the following Easter; in return the Scots would renew the alliance and – at some unspecified time – make war on the English.

This treaty of 1359, though ratified by the Regent Charles, was overtaken by the events of the following years. But it stands as an example of the growing strength of the alliance, for it was made, not by two kings, but by a tenacious lieutenant and a hard-headed dauphin, acting on behalf of, but probably not with the consent of, their chivalric master. Certainly on the Scottish side, the French alliance had become closely associated with the wishes of a majority amongst politically active Scots.

Thus the 1360s proved to be no more than a temporary setback for the alliance. Within Scotland, there was undoubtedly 'intensive government', as Dr Nicholson calls it, on the part of David II, but no acceptable solution to the problems posed by the succession and the ransom was found. David's aggressive advancement of his friends and obvious hostility to the large and powerful Stewart affinity would probably have led, sooner rather than later, to civil war; but on 22 February 1371, King David suddenly died in Edinburgh at the age of forty-seven. The Bruce dynasty died with him. His nephew Robert the Steward, eight years David's senior, the man against whom the late king had struggled for a generation, became the first ruler of the Stewart dynasty as Robert II. Not surprisingly, the new king, who had fought with the French in the late 1330s and who was mainly responsible for the 1351–2 and 1359 negotiations, ordered an embassy to France within three days of his coronation. Its leader was Archibald Douglas, lord of Galloway (the future 3rd earl), who had fought at Poitiers; and the result was the Treaty of Vincennes of 28 October 1371, the first formal renewal of the alliance since Corbeil in 1326. For almost two centuries after 1371, every Stewart ruler would renew the Auld Alliance and, unsurprisingly, most English rulers would seek to bring it to an end, by negotiation or, more frequently, by war.

Growing English concern over the Franco-Scottish alliance is understandable; for the high-water mark of Edward III's success in the Hundred Years' War was the late 1350s, after the battle of Poitiers. But from the late 1360s, a decline in English fortunes began to set in. Partly this was a result of Edward III's failure to evolve a coherent strategy when the war was renewed in 1369; but there was also the matter of vastly improved leadership on the French side. In April 1364, John II of France, having chivalrously re-entered English captivity after his hostage second son Louis, duke of Anjou, had escaped, died in London; he was succeeded by Charles V, who as dauphin had already acted as Regent and was an opponent of a much more formidable stamp. In 1369 Charles, by consenting to hear judicial appeals from lords within the duchy of Gascony, whose duke was Edward, the Black Prince, effectively renewed the war with England. The French king had the advantage of the support of Henry of Trastamara, King of Castile; for the Black Prince had backed the wrong horse in the recent Castilian civil war, with the result that the French now had an ally with a powerful fleet. In 1372 an English fleet bringing reinforcements to Gascony was defeated in a sea battle off La Rochelle by the Castilian navy, and the English position in the duchy became increasingly precarious. Highly expensive English expeditions in 1369, 1373 and 1375 achieved little in any of the main areas of conflict, Gascony, Brittany, and the north; and the French refusal to be drawn into battle – a tactic of Charles V and (when the king could restrain him) his great Breton lieutenant, Bertrand du Guesclin – frustrated the English commanders and led to vociferous complaints at home, where the war was increasingly regarded as a costly failure.

The Franco-Scottish Treaty of Vincennes of October 1371 should therefore be seen in this European context of French revival and English decline. Some elements of the treaty were traditional: French aid and counsel to the Scots against England, Scots assistance to the French in the Anglo-French war once the short truce between the two enemies had expired or been annulled, and a Scottish requirement that the French would not conclude a truce or peace with the English without the kingdom of Scotland being included in its provisions. It is clear, however, that the French wished to go further than this; Charles V offered to pay off the substantial remainder of David II's ransom and to send a French expedition to Scotland to re-open the second front against England. Robert II, as the founder of a new dynasty less than a year old, rejected this French offer and chose to continue the payments of the late king's ransom to Edward III. Robert's caution is understandable; from his predecessor he had inherited not only a substantial debt but also a fourteen-year truce with English; and indeed there had been no fighting with the English since 1356. As king – rather than as a great magnate opposing the king – Robert was treading warily in his relationships with the warlike border magnates, the earls of Douglas and March and Archibald Douglas, lord of Galloway, for he was not in a position to dictate to them. Robert II, unlike the deceased David II, was a consensual rather than a confrontational ruler; he had to be.

So the official line in 1371 was to renew the Auld Alliance in the same terms as its earlier incarnations of 1295 and 1326; and twenty years later Robert II's son and successor, Robert III, would follow the same path in the Franco-Scottish treaty of 1391. This essentially defensive view of the alliance reflected the Scottish crown's initial weakness; but in the summer of 1377 Edward III, the Scottish kingdom's opponent over half-a-century, died, leaving Richard II, a boy of ten, as king. The Scots promptly ceased their annual payments of David II's ransom. As Ranald Nicholson succinctly puts it: 'The wars of independence were over. A war of chivalry on the borders was about to begin'.

That war would be conducted by the great border magnates, whose motives certainly included the recovery of territory lost to the Scottish kingdom during the Wars of Independence, but who were also moved by the prospect of extending their march lordships. Robert II did not attempt to stop, for example, the sacking and burning of Roxburgh by George, earl of March, in 1377, or William earl of Douglas's great raid through the west march as far as Penrith in 1380. The king may have approved; by August of 1383 he had gone back on his earlier refusal to receive French expeditionary forces in Scotland; but late in the following year he was removed from government by his son and heir John, earl of Carrick (the future Robert III), who publicly espoused a more aggressive approach to Anglo-Scottish relations.

Such was the context of one of the most famous of all the border raids of the 1380s, the Franco-Scottish expedition of the summer of 1385. Although this foray was later described by the Scottish chroniclers Wyntoun and Bower, the account of it most often cited is the highly coloured version of Jean Froissart. From this we have the enduring view of Robert II as a weak and ineffective ruler, arriving in Edinburgh late and reluctant to fight. Froissart, however, is a heavily biased source; he had visited Scotland in 1365, admired the chivalric approach to war of David II and the Douglases, and was not only anti-Stewart but anti-Scots in his outlook. 'In Scotland', he remarks, 'you will never find a man of worth: they are like savages, who wish not to be acquainted with any one.'

Froissart makes much of the unsurprising fact that when the French expedition of 1385, led by the Admiral of France, Jean de Vienne, had arrived and billeted itself in the Lothians, servants of the French knights were beaten up by the locals when they went out foraging for their masters. He also comments unfavourably on the Scots nobles' refusal to give battle to a superior English army, adopting instead the tactics of scorched earth, harrying and burning which should surely have been familiar to the chronicler from the strategy employed by Charles V of France in the 1360s and 1370s.

The raid of 1385 was in any case intended only as part of a grand design, a dual invasion of England with one French army joining with the Scots and invading from the north, while a larger French force would make the sea crossing from Sluys in Flanders and attack southern England. An advance party – around thirty French knights and squires – jumped the gun and landed at Montrose in 1384, subsequently conducting a raid on northern England. But the main event was the landing, at Leith and Dunbar in May 1385, of Jean de Vienne and his army. This was apparently of a decent size, perhaps around fifteen hundred men; and they brought some fifty thousand gold francs as a further incentive to their allies.

The grand design, however, fell apart because no French fleet was sent with troops to invade southern England, from Sluys or anywhere else. Its failure to materialise freed the young Richard II of England and his uncle John of Gaunt to intervene personally in Scotland with a huge army. Robert II's arrival in Edinburgh to summon the Scottish host provided a further opportunity for Froissart to castigate the king as 'no valiant man', and as having 'red bleared eyes, of the colour of sandalwood'. No reference is made to the fact that the king was sixty-nine, that the Scots were facing almost certain defeat in battle, or even that Robert had been removed from power in a *coup d'état* the previous November.

Apart from the presence in the Scottish army of an unprecedentedly large number of French troops, the campaign which followed was depressingly familiar. The Scots could not risk encountering the host of Richard II in a pitched battle, and contented themselves with savage raids on the west march of England; the east border and the Lothians, virtually undefended, were plundered by the English. The great abbeys of Melrose, Dryburgh and Newbattle were burned, as was the burgh of Edinburgh and the church of St Giles; and Holyrood abbey would have suffered the same fate if John of Gaunt had not interceded on its behalf with Richard II. The English king was able to give monasteries to the flames with impunity, for in the Great Schism of the papacy in 1378, England had backed Pope Urban VI, while the French and Scots supported his rival Robert of Geneva, elected by eleven French cardinals and taking the name of Clement VII. Thus, very conveniently for the English invading army, the Scots clergy were in league with the anti-pope and could be regarded as schismatics who ought to be rooted out. The dismal summer war came to an end when the

English, desperately short of provisions, withdrew and left the Scots to count the cost. Understandably the French were not popular in Lothian, and damages were laid against them; if Froissart is to be believed, Jean de Vienne was left as a hostage in Scotland until the money for his release was raised at Bruges. The departing French expedition, as Froissart has it, cursed the Scots, 'and wished the King of France would make a truce with the English for two or three years, and then march to Scotland and utterly destroy it'. One modern writer puts it more kindly when he suggests that 'the auld alliance was always more cordial when French and Scots were at a distance'.

Perhaps: but the alliance had survived throughout the fourteenth century because both kingdoms, to a greater or lesser degree, needed each other. Neither side could live up to Étienne de Conty's impossibly optimistic claim, made in 1400, that the Scots had always loved the French, and the French the Scots; but it would be difficult to deny that the Auld Alliance, in its first century of existence, had achieved much more than could reasonably have been expected of it, or that the French had helped to preserve the independence of the Scottish kingdom in the 1330s. The fifteenth century would see a reversal of roles, with the Scots being called upon to save the kingdom of France.

The Myth of the Medieval Burgh Community

Extracted from EP Dennison 1998 'Power to the People? The Myth of the Medieval Burgh Community', in S Foster *et al* (eds), *Scottish Power Centres*, Glasgow (Cruithne Press), 112–117.

What precisely did this 'burgh community' mean to Scottish townsmen and women? '*Communitas*' was a word in regular use from the thirteenth century in central government records and burghal documentation,[1] and the terms 'community of the realm' and 'community of the burgh' held a recognised place in legal parlance, although the terms were never conceptualised by definition in the records. Historians have inferred that such vocabulary expresses a strong sense of oneness, whether applied to the kingdom or to the burgh. Yet the notion of 'community' is open to various interpretations. Precisely how 'community', as applied to the realm, should be understood has already led to some disagreement.[2] There is also a divergence of opinion in how embracing was the scope of the term 'community of the burgh'. Few twentieth-century historians would now follow the somewhat dated view of the burgh epitomising true democracy. A narrower interpretation of the burgh community as merely the community of burgesses is, arguably, more acceptable. There is, however, a viewpoint that has a certain sympathy with the older notion and envisages a more all-embracing community that could include, through common interests, the greater grouping of the townspeople, whether free or unfree.[3]

There is on the surface much in medieval burgh life that might appear to favour this latter view. Pont's manuscript maps illustrate graphically the 'apartness' of towns: townspeople, both free and unfree, were psychologically distanced from their rural neighbours by physical demarcations – ports, ditches, and pallisading – and also by rights, rules, and regulations. This separateness was reinforced by close proximity to other townspeople within an urban space that was small enough to be walked easily and covered a sufficiently slight area that the church bells and cries of promulgation from the town cross were never far removed, even in the burgh rigs and crofts outwith the town precincts. The closeness of this urban space was at times pushed to extremes, even as increasing trade and wealth brought demand for prime land within the larger towns.[4] Repletion in backlands and congestion at the market centre was the natural response rather than significant expansion beyone the traditional medieval confines into suburbs.[5] Close proximity engendered a sense of oneness, to the exclusion of outsiders.[6]

This sense of oneness was reinforced by the notion of a single parish. Scottish towns, unlike their English and most continental counterparts, did not house multiple parishes.[7] Worshipping as a single spiritual community, the town became synonymous with a *corpus christianum*. This identity of parish and burgh, even though it might include a rural landward area, and although it would become strained within larger towns experiencing population expansion in the sixteenth century, was to survive until the Reformation and remain till then one of the basic foundations of medieval urban society.[8]

The dual wholeness of the spiritual and secular urban community reached perhaps its apotheosis in the annual *Corpus Christi* procession.[9] There is firm evidence of the celebration of the feast in Edinburgh by 1498 and Aberdeen by 1512.[10] The records of Lanark, Perth, Haddington, and Dundee all refer to this annual event and suggest that the *Corpus Christi* procession was not confined solely to the greater burghs.[11] Underlying this urban spectacular was a pervading theme: the image of the body, oneness, and wholeness. The significant element of the procession was the body of Christ in the form of the host, supported by clerics, accompanied by the magistracy, the guild merchant, and the crafts of the burgh in order of precedence,[12] all of which was witnessed by the passive participants, the townspeople. The body politic was thus portrayed as a structured and stratified whole community.

It is this very display of the element of structured stratification that epitomises the true nature of medieval urban society: inequality. Just as the *Corpus Christi* procession may be viewed as the expression of urban unity and wholeness,[13] it is equally valid to see in it a vivid enactment not of oneness but of exclusion: non-burgesses and frailer members of society were not genuinely involved. It may be suspected, however, that there was little point in such public drama if there was no audience,[14] but it is perhaps asking a little much of human nature to posit that participation by spectating the urban hierarchy parading and by the communal pleasure in the accompanying pageants should spill over into everyday life. It should also be doubted whether all lesser members of society accepted their subordinate role without resentment: lack of popular riots, or at least lack of evidence of them, within the Scottish towns does not necessarily imply contentment with their lot by all strata of society.[15]

Perhaps one of the exclusions from this medieval procession that would be most striking to modern observers was that this was an all-male performance: women had no place in the urban hierarchy. Although they might at times hold the position of burgess,[16] play a significant role within the urban economy,[17] on occasion appearing in the records as ship owners and custumars,[18] and by the fifteenth century be witnessed in the burgh courts turning a technically disadvantageous legal system to their own advantage,[19] the male domination of the burghal administration was not broken.[20]

Exclusive tendencies in burgh society may have started early. A number of burghs had guilds merchant by the thirteenth century, most of them, as far as can be seen from extant evidence, drawing 'craftsmen' into their circle as well as 'merchants', there being little distinction made between the two at this time.[21] This group of influential men formed a community within the burgh community. A study of Aberdeen, however, suggests that the craftsmen there might even be viewed as a community in their own right, albeit within the all-embracing burgh community, as early as the thirteenth century.[22] Certainly, once craft guilds began to adopt a formalised existence in the larger burghs in the last quarter of the fifteenth century, and in the smaller a little later, they, too, through collective interest, mutual aid, and fraternity polarised into exclusive sects within the larger burgh community. Their support of patron saints and altars within the parish church was manifested by parading on holy days, carrying aloft the banners of their saints. Precedence in such parades was of utmost importance, giving rise to complaints from certain crafts if it was felt that their due status was slighted.[23] Such public display, yet again, served not only to highlight the differences between certain economic groups, but also to undermine the theory of 'oneness'. This intrinsic feature of urban society survived the Reformation. The reaction of the fleshers to the baxters of Dundee, for example, when decorating their lofts in the new South Church of the town, is a significant comment on the divisiveness latent within medieval and early modern urban communities. The baxters had painted above their pews 'Bread is the Staff of Life'. Their neighbours, the fleshers, countered with the embellishment 'Man Shall Not Live by Bread Alone'.[24]

Certain secular festivities, most notably the May revels, are seen to have served as a counterbalance to the overt display of the burgh hierarchy. Traditionally the 'abbot of unreason' presided at the May revels, when the conventional order and rule of burgh society was upturned. These celebrations are to be witnessed in many towns: an 'abbot or prior of Bonacord' in Aberdeen; 'abbot of unrest' in Peebles; 'abbot of narent' and 'lord of inobedience' in Edinburgh.[25] The cult of Robin Hood was also well known in Scotland from at least the early fifteenth century and traces of Robin Hood can be found in the May games of several towns.[26] Although the documentary sources are somewhat reticent with details of how precisely the lower elements of society celebrated on this one annual occasion when their word was supposedly law, there are telling clues that perhaps belie the traditional view of the May revels as a time of 'upturned order'. Perhaps most significantly, the occasion had the official blessing of the authorities: in both Aberdeen and Haddington the town paid the abbot to fulfil his role and the Edinburgh guild merchant gave financial support to Robin Hood from 1492, as did the guild in Dunfermline.[27] The choice of man to lead the common people in their day of dominance is also interesting. It was decided in Aberdeen, in 1445, that, due to 'diverssin enormities in tyme bigane be the Abbits of this burgh callit Bone Acorde', there should be 'nae sic Abbotis'. This position was in future to be held only by the alderman or a worthy bailie.[28] In Ayr, it became the practice for the burgh treasurers to adopt the role of Robin Hood and Little John.[29] At Dunfermline, the position was at times filled by a member of the prominent local Halkett of Pitfirrane family, which held municipal office in the town on a number of occasions.[30] It is clear, then, that although the May revels may have served to release tensions within burgh society, they were monitored by the ruling group to the extent that the abbot and Robin Hood may have been direct appointments by the alderman, bailies, and council, as in Aberdeen.[31] Indeed, the parliamentary ruling of 1555 that there should be no impersonations of Robin

Hood, Little John, the abbot or unreason, and the queen of May may be precisely proof of such. As so often in legislation dealing with social matters in the fifteenth and sixteenth centuries, this was probably a response to a particular problem in a particular town rather than a matter of general national concern: in one of the major four towns the annual ritual of supposed disorder had perhaps begun to display precisely this character and it had to be stopped.[32] In Edinburgh, the association of Robin Hood and the lord of inobedience with civil disorder climaxed in 1561 when, it was claimed by John Knox, 'the reachall multitude war stirred up to mak a Robene Hude' by 'papistis and bischoppis',[33] a number of townspeople were brought to trial for appointing a Robin Hood and the lord of inobedience.[34] Even in this most seemingly egalitarian of festivities there was no question that participation implied truly co-operative involvement on the part of the ordinary people.[35]

Little real effort was made to support these weaker elements of society. It is perhaps unrealistic in a late twentieth-century democracy, which does not itself adequately cater for the genuinely poor and homeless, to look back to the Middle Ages and expect otherwise. References to the support of orphans, widows, or 'decayed' persons often conceal an assistance to families of members of the guild merchant or craft guilds, not the lower echelons of society. Some burghs introduced support for the poor by a cheap food policy, by gifts in money or kind, by the reduction of burial fees for 'pur creaturis', or by the free education of a pauper boy, but such measures did not genuinely alleviate the lot of the under-privileged.[36] Laudable as it might be to want to believe in a strong, supportive community spirit, there is no evidence that the majority of the sick, infirm, and very old were cared for in almshouses or hospitals[37] – their main hope was self-help, often in squalid backlands.

There was a subtle marginalisation of several sections of the community prevalent in Scottish towns, possibly in the name of good order or health, but exclusion none the less. For example, prostitutes were distanced to the edges of towns;[38] those suffering merely from disfiguring skin diseases were banished;[39] the island of Inchkeith housed all those expelled from Edinburgh after contracting syphilis, according to a 1497 decision of James IV;[40] and banishment or drowning was considered worthy punishment for concealing evidence of the plague in Edinburgh.[41] To modern eyes many of these measures may appear entirely prudent. Whether so or not, they serve as indications that within the medieval burgh community there were those who were acceptable and those who were not.

By the sixteenth century there appears an increasing desire to deal with the problem of the poor in urban society by stronger measures. Some of the concern arose as a result of an influx of beggars from rural hinterlands.[42] To this end, Edinburgh town council enacted in 1536 that 'na beggares be fund in this towne bot thaie that ar borne within the same, and thai to be impotent febill or auld and waik persouns that thai may nocht labour for thair leving, under the payne of byrning of thair cheiks and banesing the towne'.[43] In Dundee, the council records of 1521 indicate that the burgh serjeands were to keep 'the pur fowk out of the kirk' on holy days.[44] Two years later the rule was extended to Sundays and festival days.[45] Such rulings are found in other burghs.[46] Doubtless the common rabble could cause undue disturbance, but there is little here to encourage a view of a medieval town in-dweller with 'a sense of oneness and community both with his God and his neighbour'.[47]

Whether there was a truer sense of community throughout all inhabitants in earlier and smaller burghs is unclear through lack of evidence. Certainly, smaller groupings of people might have a greater chance of cohesion, but whether it is valid to trace this sense of community back to the 'very beginnings' of burghal history is dubious.[48] Even in burghs supposedly established totally anew, some form of settlement very often preceded them. There is little likelihood that all these local dwellers were granted burgess status.[49] Some were, undoubtedly, a few being recognisable by their locality names. Those who did not were probably assimilated as the unfree, in-dwelling work-force. Other burgesses might come from further afield, drawn by the incentive of 'kirseth'. This was normally a period of a year and a day, although it might be longer in less desirable areas such as Dingwall (ten years) and Dumbarton (five years),[50] when an immigrant was granted a period of grace to build or 'big' his burgage plot without payment of burgh dues. Significant also in the early burghal populations were incomers from Flanders, the Rhineland, England, and France,[51] encouraged by the crown for the skills they could offer. How far such a disparate group of people could function as a 'community', at least in the first generation of burgh life, must be questioned. 'Stadtluft macht frei', a notion of the nineteenth century, was an anachronism in the twelfth.

The evidence suggests that the 'community of the burgh' probably never embraced this wider grouping of all residents in the burgh. This was certainly the case in many early towns in Europe, such as Lübeck with its *hereditates*, Novgorod with the Boyars, and Ghent with its dominant Scabini group, indicating that the 'community' encompassed only the privileged few.[52] It was most certainly not in the town dwellers as a body that power was vested. [53] The *Leges Burgorum* specified that the burgh magistrates, the alderman, bailies, and lesser officials, taking up office after the Michaelmas head court, should be appointed 'thruch the consaile of the gud men of the toune, the quhilk aw to be lele and of gud fame'.[54] The 'gud men of the toune' were the burgesses. These were the people who had power. This was reinforced in most burghs by the use of seals, first evidenced in the early thirteenth century, which added authority to specific transactions when appended to charters. Significantly, it was felt essential to have not only seals for the bailies and alderman but also a 'common seal' or 'seal of the community'. This latter was at times kept for safety, and to prevent misuse, in two halves by two separate individuals, not office holders, and represented the power of the burgesses, not merely the magistrates.[55] However, the use of the bailies' seal when the common seal was not available would suggest caution in a too literal acceptance of precise distinction between the authority of the community and that of its representatives.[56]

NOTES

1 G. W. S. Barrow, *Kingship and Unity: Scotland 1000–1306* (London, 1981), 124; E. Ewan, *Townlife in Fourteenth Century Scotland* (Edinburgh, 1988), 140.

2 G. G. Simpson, 'The Declaration of Arbroath revitalised', *Scottish Historical Review*, lvi (1977), 29, 32–33; and R. Nicholson, *Scotland: The Later Middle Ages* (Edinburgh, 1974), 101. Compare with Barrow, *Kingship and Unity*, 125–129.

3 See, for example, Ewan, *Townlife*, 136–160. R. L. K. Hunter, 'Corporate personality and the Scottish burgh', in G. W. S. Barrow (ed.), *The Scottish Tradition* (Edinburgh, 1974), 223–236, assesses the influences on the development of a notion of corporation in the medieval burgh.

4 For example in Glasgow, S. Stevenson and E. P. D. Torrie, *Historic Glasgow, the Archaeological Implications of Development* (Scottish Burgh Survey, 1990), 51.

5 Scottish burghs did not often have suburbs. Perth is a rare exception. See M. Spearman's series of plans in 'The medieval townscape of Perth', in M. Lynch, M. Spearman, and M. Stell (eds.), *The Scottish Medieval Town* (Edinburgh, 1988), 46–54.

6 For example, *Leges Burgorum*, c. 85; *Acts of the Parliament of Scotland* (*APS*), ii, 14; E. P. Torrie, *The Gild Court Book of Dunfermline, 1483–1597* (Scottish Record Society, 1986), fo. 31.

7 The establishment of St Maria ad Nives resulted from a supplication in 1498 to the pope, authorised by James IV, requesting the restructuring of the parish boundaries of Kirkton of Seaton, the St Machar Cathedral parish, and also the erection of a new parish of Old Aberdeen which would exclude the cathedral and chanonry, but include the market region, the area where William Elphinstone was to establish a university, and the nearby Spital region, L. J. MacFarlane, *William Elphinstone and the Kingdom of Scotland, 1431–1514* (Aberdeen, 1985), 134 and 315; E. P. Dennison and J. Stones, *Aberdeen. The Archaeological Implications of Development* (Edinburgh, 1997), 101.

8 Neighbourliness did not extend to parishioners from outwith the burgh precincts during the time of plague, although limited access was granted to stranger parishioners in Kirkcaldy in 1585 to attend the parish church, L. MacBean (ed.), *The Kirkcaldy Burgh Records* (Kirkcaldy, 1908), 11.

9 The feast of Corpus Christi, authorised by papal bull in 1264 and published in 1317, is known to have been first celebrated in Britain at Ipswich in 1325, M. James, 'Ritual, drama and social body in the late medieval English town', *Past and Present*, xcviii (1983), 11.

10 A. J. Mill, *Mediaeval Plays in Scotland* (Edinburgh, 1927), 72 and 62; E. Bain, *Merchant and Craft Guilds. A History of Aberdeen Incorporated Trades* (Aberdeen, 1887), 52.

11 Mill, *Mediaeval Plays*, 68–71.

12 Bain, *Merchant and Craft Guilds*, 56.

13 C. Phythian-Adams, 'Ceremony and the citizen: the communal year at Coventry, 1450–1550', in R. Holt and G. Rosser (eds.), *The Medieval Town, 1200–1450* (London, 1990), 240.

14 R. Holt and G. Rosser, 'The English town in the Middle Ages', in Holt and Rosser, *Medieval Town*, 14.

15 Cf. C. Dyer, 'Small-town conflict in the later Middle Ages: events at Shipston-on-Stour', *Urban History Review*, xix, pt 2 (1992), 183–210; R. A. Rotz 'Urban uprisings in Germany: revolutionary or reformist? The case of Brunswick, 1374', *Viator*, iv (1973), 207–223.

16 For example, *The Burgh Records of* Dunfermline, ed. E. Beveridge (Edinburgh, 1917) (hereafter *Dunf. Recs.*) 70, 87, 89; R. Renwick (ed.), *Extracts from the Records of the Burgh of Peebles* (*Scottish Burgh Record Society*, 1910), 97.

17 M. Lynch, 'The social and economic structure of the larger towns, 1450–1600', in Lynch, Spearman and Stell, *Scottish Medieval Town*, 277; Ewan, *Townlife*, 32, 81; G. Rosser, 'La rinascita della città medievale in Inghilterra: ricerche recenti e prospettive per il futuro', *Storia Urbana*, 67–68 (1994), 77–94.

18 MS Dundee Burgh and Head Court Book, 6 October (1486? – insert in 1523 records); *ER*, I, pp. xcv, 76, 95, 170–172, 275, 316–317, 368.

19 E. Ewan, 'Scottish Portias: women in the courts in mediaeval Scottish towns', *Journal of the Canadian Historical Association* (1992), 27–43.

20 This compares perhaps unfavourably with the role of women in rural society where there is evidence of women sharing in the election of the clerk of the parish church of Killern, GD 86/97, Fraser charters, 29 August 1531. I am indebted to Dr E. Ewan for drawing this to my attention.

21 For example, Torrie, *Gild Court Book of Dunfermline, passim*; M. Stewart (ed.), *Guild Court Book of Perth* (Scottish Record Society, 1993), *passim*.

22 E. Ewan, 'An urban community: the crafts in thirteenth-century Aberdeen', in A. Grant and K. Stringer (eds.), *Medieval Scotland: Crown, Lordship and community* (Edinburgh, 1993), 156–173.

23 Bain, *Merchant and Craft Guilds*, 56.

24 J. Maclaren, *The History of Dundee* (Dundee, 1874), [an enlarged edition of a work produced by James Thomson, 1847], 210–211.

25 Mill, *Mediaeval Plays*, 21.

26 Haddington, Peebles, Dumfries, Edinburgh, Dundee, and Dunfermline, for example. In some towns the abbot and Robin Hood became intermingled: both were lords of the May games; and where there is no mention of the former, Robin Hood may have developed out of the abbot, Bain, *Merchant and Craft Guilds*, 58.

27 Mill, *Mediaeval Plays*, 24–25; Torrie, *Gild Court Book of Dunfermline*, fo. 49.

28 Bain, *Merchant and Craft Guilds*, 51.

29 Mill, *Mediaeval Plays*, 29.

30 *Dunf. Recs*, 152, 224. In 1552 Master George Halkett was admitted into the guild because he held the position of Robin Hood, Torrie, *Gild Court Book of Dunfermline*, fo. 49. In Dundee in 1521 Robin Hood, in honour of the status, was granted burgess-ship free, as happened on occasion in Edinburgh, MS Dundee Burgh and Head Court Book, 4 April, 1521; C. B. B. Watson (ed.), *The Roll of Edinburgh Burgesses and Guild Brethren, 1406–1700* (SRS, 1929), 16. Fifteen years later in Ayr, three people were fined by the burgh authorities for their refusal to undertake the role of abbot of unreason, Mill, *Mediaeval Plays*, 29.

31 Bain, *Merchant and Craft Guilds*, 51.

32 *APS*, ii, 500.

33 D. Laing (ed.), *The Works of John Knox* (Bannatyne Club, 1846), ii, 157.

34 R. Pitcairn (ed.), *Criminal Trials in Scotland from 1488 to 1624* (Bannatyne Club, 1833), i, 409.

35 For a more general discussion of the legend of Robin Hood and his role in the May Games see J. C. Holt, *Robin Hood* (London, 1982), 159–162.

36 Torrie, *Medieval Dundee*, 93.

37 Barrow, *Kingship and Unity*, 94. See also J. Durkan, 'Care of the poor: pre-reformation hospitals', *Innes Review*, x (1959), 269–280.

38 Ewan, *Townlife*, 26. See also J. A. Brundage, *Law, Sex and Christian Society in Medieval Europe* (London, 1987), 463–472.

39 I. B. Cowan and D. E. Easson (eds.), *Medieval Religious Houses: Scotland* (London, 1976), 162.

40 *Ed. Recs*, I, 71–72.

41 Ibid, ii, 37 and 42.

42 Lynch, 'Social and economic structure', 263 and 275, discusses the urban poor. See also M. Lynch, 'Whatever happened to the medieval burgh? Some guidelines for sixteenth- and seventeenth-century historians', *Scottish Economic and Social History*, iv (1984), 16.

43 *Ed. Recs*, ii, 80.

44 MS Dundee Burgh and Head Court Book, 30 September, 1521.

45 Ibid, 30 March, 1523.

46 *Ed. Recs*, iii, 194.

47 Torrie, *Medieval Dundee*, 81.

48 Early charters are in favour of 'the burgesses' or 'the burgesses and their heirs', not 'the burgh'. Some would argue that there is in consequence no corporate right or succession, H. A. Merewether and A. J. Stephen, *The History of the Boroughs and Municipal Corporations* (London, 1835), 364. Cf. E. Ewan, 'The community of the burgh in the fourteenth century', in Lynch, Spearman and Stell, *Scottish Medieval Town*, 228.

49 Cf. Ewan, *Townlife*, 137.

50 W. M. Mackenzie, *The Scottish Burgh* (Edinburgh, 1949), 35.

51 Barrow, *Kingship and Unity*, 92.

52 R. Hammel-Kiesow, 'Property patterns, buildings and the social structure of urban society: some reflections on Ghent, Lübeck and Novgorod', in F. E. Eliassen and G. A. Ersland (eds.), *Power, Profit and Urban Land* (Aldershot, 1996), 39–60.

53 There are, however, occasional references in local records that suggest a wider participating in decision making. In 1372 an indenture between Forfar and Montrose was made by 'the burgesses, guild brethren and inhabitants' of the two burghs, Montrose Archives, M/W1/1.

54 *Leges Burgorum*, c. 70.

55 *Dunf. Recs*, 41.

56 MS. Aberdeen University Library, M390, Mass 8/3, 10/11, for example.

Aberdeen before 1800: The Medieval Market, c.1400–1550

Extracted from IB Blanchard, E Gemmill, N Mayhew and ID Whyte 2002 'The Economy: Town and Country', in EP Dennison *et al* (eds), *Aberdeen Before 1800: A New History*, East Linton (Tuckwell Press), 137–147.[1]

The records that tell us most about the domestic economy of medieval Aberdeen are the registers containing the proceedings of its council and of its head, bailie and guild courts. These are, essentially, the records of the burgh's judiciary and government, and they are a jewel in the crown of Aberdeen's, and indeed, Scotland's medieval archives. They survive in an almost uninterrupted series beginning in 1398, and they contain a wealth of information about the economic life of the town, as well as about its social and political circumstances and developments. It seems that the main elements of the trading framework that can be observed in such a detailed way from the fifteenth century onwards were well established by that time. In particular, the town had enjoyed a weekly market and an annual fair since the thirteenth century.[2] The economic evidence contained in the registers is mostly in the form of burghal ordinances governing trade and commerce, of proceedings against those who infringed the rules which had been made, and of civil lawsuits which sometimes resulted when buying and selling – especially the trade between merchants – went wrong. Because the records are those of the local government and courts of law, they can give the impression that things were always going wrong – that the craftsman constantly needed to be instructed and reprimanded because he was, by his very nature, greedy and delinquent; that the merchant was always at law because he was by nature greedy and quarrelsome. Of course, things were not always so; trade and commerce were supposed to be peaceable and co-operative activities. Nevertheless, they were controlled and regulated in a much more direct and intricate way than would be expected today, and we need to understand the nature of the supervision in order to see how the market itself worked.

As the opening lines of extracts from the guild court of October 1507 demonstrate, the town certainly sought to exercise a thorough control over the work of its craftsmen and women. The basis of many of the regulations published by the provost, bailies and council were the rules and conventions set out in earlier collections of laws relating to burgh government.[3] The town authorities periodically (typically in the guild court following the Michaelmas head court, which marked the beginning of the new burghal year) issued series of ordinances such as this, which were addressed to a range of craftsmen and others and were intended to ratify and to strengthen the established customs. In addition, particular circumstances would prompt the authorities to issue special reminders of their duties to craftsmen and women. For example, the issue of 'black' (copper) money in the early 1480s, which was intended to supply the need for small change in retail transactions, caused problems for retailers who did not want to receive payment for their goods in the base coin. An ordinance made on 11 July 1482 told Aberdeen's fleshers, brewsters and bakers that, if they did not set to and supply the community, they would be expelled from their craft for a year and a day.[4]

By far the largest part of the regulations concerning crafts relates to those involving provision of household necessities, most obviously foodstuffs.[5] But the authorities' control was by no means limited to these. Indeed, as time went on, the scope of the rules widened. We find prescriptions about the cost and quality of shoes,[6] gloves,[7] horseshoes,[8] and salmon barrels.[9] The detailed mechanisms for this control varied from craft to craft. A loaf of bread had to be of a certain weight to sell for a penny and twice that to sell for two pence. Candle was also sold by weight (usually a pound of made candle for three pence in the later fifteenth century, rising to six pence per pound by the early 1530s) and had to be available in different sizes. Provision was made to deal with things that varied in quality, such as meat and ale, by setting several different prices. Special appraisers were also appointed to examine carcasses or taste ale before it was sold. They then scored the price on the carcass or on the alewife's board for all to see.[10] The sale of cleaned fish was controlled differently again, certainly from the mid fifteenth century. Instead of the flesher actually selling the fish, he was allowed to charge a fee – a penny per shilling's worth of fish – for cutting up and cleaning the larger varieties.[11]

The detailed requirements for goods manufactured by town craftsmen and women varied, of course, according to the product. The overall principles were that those who exercised the privilege of trading in the town had to make their finished products available to all townspeople when they needed them. Craftsmanship had to be of good quality; and the price had to be no more than that of the raw materials, plus an allowance for a reasonable profit. There were a variety of penalties for failure to keep to the rules, some of them monetary, some involving escheat of the manufactured goods or destruction of equipment. Beyond doubt, however, the worst punishment was to be excluded from the craft – denied the privilege of making a living by it.

The notion of a reasonable profit is fundamental in any concept of fair trade, and the authorities in medieval Aberdeen were quick to take action when they found people charging what were thought to be entirely unreasonable prices for their goods. In March 1473, for example, three hucksters were fined for selling figs and raisins for enormous prices, although we are not told how huge these actually were.[12] In April 1482, fleshers were fined for buying fish before the proper time and for taking an unreasonable profit ('wynning') for breaking fish.[13] By and large, however, it was not so much a question of extortion, as one of finding the balance between the craftsman's need to make money in return for his work, and of the customer's ability and willingness to pay for it. Put another way, it was how much the craftsman's work was worth, especially when some kinds of work could, in practice, be done by the consumer. Crafts such as candlemaking, brewing ale, and baking oatcakes were not exclusive to those who made a living by them, for they required a minimum of equipment. The raw materials required to make them – tallow, malt, and oatmeal – were readily available in the market place.[14] Indeed, in many cases these simpler crafts were carried on by women baking or brewing or candlemaking for their own household and then selling the surplus. In times of scarcity, this sort of trading was forbidden because it was felt unfair to allow a few people to purchase scarce raw materials which everyone needed and then to sell the finished article at a profit.[15]

By contrast, when there was a boost in demand, even humble traders were enjoined to ply their craft. Prior to the arrival of James IV (1488–1513) for the Christmas festivities of 1497, the alderman, bailies and council gave anxious instructions to bakers, brewsters, fleshers, fishers, stablers, candlemakers, cordiners (shoemakers), tailors, skinners and suppliers of fuel to be well-prepared to meet the needs of the king and his entourage for twenty days or more – in case the king stayed longer. Merchants were told to have wax, wine, and spices and other merchandise ready.[16] The royal visit certainly stimulated added business – sellers of elding (fuel) were told, in particular, to bring their supplies daily, indeed hourly, to the market. (It was, after all, winter.) Even so, the royal visit may not have been welcomed unequivocally by the craftsmen. Quite apart from the pressure they were under to supply the royal entourage, they may well have had worries about how generously or promptly they were to be paid for their goods. This point was not explicitly covered in the instructions given to them and the medieval royal custom of taking prises and of purveyance was a perennial source of grievance for the subjects of Scottish, as well as English, kings.[17] Interestingly, money (£40) was set aside from the town's anticipated income from its fishing 'grassums' (entry fines). This was to pay for the wine, spices and wax which the town was to offer to the king by way of a propine, the term used for a gift in kind made to the king or to a noble. But these were items supplied by the merchants rather than the town's craftsmen.[18]

Local craftsmen and the whole town depended on a supply of raw materials, particularly food, coming from the countryside.[19] Medieval towns were more rural in character than their modern counterparts. Townspeople had their own back yards in which to grow vegetables, and many owned their own pigs, as we know from the town authorities' repeated attempts to prevent animals from wandering un-checked.[20] In addition, corn was grown in the vicinity of the burgh, and there was common land for grazing.[21] In May 1490, a town herdsman was appointed to keep the whole town's cattle until All Saints' Day, at about which time they would have been slaughtered to avoid the cost of winter fodder. (Cattle are very often referred to as 'marts' because their destiny was sometimes to be slaughtered at the feast of Martinmas, on 11 November.) The herdsman's fee per cow was to be 6d and per stirk 2d.[22] But small-scale urban husbandry cannot have been on a scale sufficient to support the town's needs for food and it would have been only the wealthier burgesses who owned much land or many beasts.

The town depended to a considerable extent on foreign imports of food.[23] Inventories of the cargoes of ships entering Aberdeen in the mid 1460s, mainly from various ports in the Low Countries, show that large quantities of grain were being imported, although, of course, this is not to say that all of it was consumed in the burgh itself.[24] By the sixteenth century, the reliance on supplies from abroad is evidenced by the large consignments of grain bought up by the authorities for distribution within the town.[25] As well as grain, fruit and vegetables were imported for the local market and were much in demand. Impatient hucksters sometimes hurried down to meet incoming vessels to buy apples, onions, figs and raisins straight from the mariners, even before they reached the quay and the customs were paid.[26]

Nonetheless, the reliance of the town on supplies from the Scottish countryside was, without doubt, considerable. When setting the assize of bread in January 1517, the provost, bailies and council took into consideration the price of locally grown wheat, the weight of the 2d loaf in Edinburgh, Dundee, Perth and other parts of Lothian and Angus, and the quality of Lothian and Angus wheat compared with that grown in the countryside around Aberdeen.[27] The price and quality of local (as opposed to imported) wheat was seemingly the determining factor, suggesting that local wheat was the main source of supply. If this was so, then the preponderance of local supplies of oats, oatmeal, bere (barley) and malt (generally referred to as victual), which were more obviously traditional Scottish cereals, must have been at least as great.

The goods which came to town from the countryside were supposed to come first to the market on the Castlegate, the symbol of the burgh's privileged trading position in the region. The burgh and burgesses of Aberdeen had been granted a weekly market by charter of Alexander II (of c.1214x1222) and its merchants were given exclusive trading privileges.[28] Alexander III granted the burgesses a yearly fair in 1273.[29] In the first place, all goods produced in the sheriffdom which were intended for export – mostly obviously wool, woolfells, hides and fish – had to be channelled through Aberdeen and customs paid on them.[30] Moreover, all goods intended for consumption within the burgh which had come from the countryside – most obviously grain, fish, dairy produce and eggs – also had to come first to the market where dues were collected. Once these things had been done, the 'landmen' – the people who came from the country to sell their wares in the market place – and townspeople could trade with one another. For many townspeople, the most important thing on sale in the market was victual – the commonly used term for grain – meal which they made into oatcakes and porridge and malt which they brewed into ale. Detailed rules controlled the conduct of transactions in the market. It was not permitted to buy at a higher price than the going rate, or to offer more for a particular set of goods than other inhabitants had already agreed to give. Offering generous measures of grain in order to secure a sale was forbidden. Townspeople were ordered to commit themselves to the purchase of the particular item once they had given their earnest-money, and they were supposed to take their goods away as soon as they had been bought.[31]

The apparent need to force people to leave the market place once their shopping was done – their poke had been filled with meal or malt, their keling (cod) had been cut and cleaned, and their eggs and apples or pears chosen – suggests that it was natural for them to linger. Of course, people did not go to market only to spend their money – they went to meet their fellows and to gossip and to see the spectacle of the town about its business. We may imagine that Bruegel drew inspiration for this paintings, such as *Netherlandish Proverbs* or *The Fight between Carnival and Lent*, from the colour and variety he saw in the Flemish market places of his day. And because the market was a recognised public place – a forum to which people were known to visit, as well as being the focus for buying and selling – it made sense for it to be where royal and burghal proclamations were made. Here, too, offenders against the burgh laws were humiliated in front of the community, while goods which had been distrained for debt, such as horses, plate, jewellery or cloth, were publicly valued. Cakes and ale, pies and sweetmeats were sold and the town's common minstrels doubtless provided additional entertainment.[32] So, the market was a most interesting and exciting event – the townsman's equivalent of the social gatherings of the tournament or the pilgrimage – even though the actual purchases were often limited and the market place itself was frequently bleak and its provisions meagre.

The town provided modest commercial facilities in the market place. The tollbooth was maintained and repaired at the town's expense,[33] and standard grain measures were available for general use.[34] In bad weather, grain was supposed to be measured either underneath stairs, or in the tollbooth.[35] Providing trustworthy measures, especially for grain, was important if arguments between traders were to be avoided. The town also sought to guard against unreliable townspeople who failed to pay their debts. In January 1532, the bailies were told to hold an inquiry into irresponsible women who bought victuals 'in great' (that is, wholesale) in the market place, without the means to pay for them. The bailies were instructed to make a list of such women and read the names aloud at the market cross and forewarn the landmen. The proclamation was also to make clear that any man who sold victuals to these women in future did so at his own risk and that purchasers should expect no help from the provost and bailies.[36]

Because the market was in a fixed place – the Castlegate – and was held at fixed times, the urban community knew when and where to come. To draw particular attention to what was on sale, the town's handbell man would walk through the town ringing the common handbell to advertise what was there. Of course, it was important that the man possessed accurate information. In February 1513, the bell man, Philip Clerk, did not have the facts right. He was fined and had to beg the owners' forgiveness for having gone through the town without authority, telling all and sundry to come and buy oysters at 4d the hundred – when the boatmen who had brought them to town were selling them at 6d.[37]

The market was the place where families went to buy their food and other supplies, and where craftsmen bought their raw materials. Craftsmen were not given preferential treatment, nor any exemption from the rules about forestalling, just because they were in business.[38] Hucksters – petty retailers – were expected to wait to make their purchases until the townspeople as a whole had had their turn.[39] In times of scarcity, the authorities restricted the amount of victual which individuals were allowed to buy, allowing them only so much as was needed for their own households. The idea behind this decree was to prevent people, and particularly the unfree, from retailing victual or brewing and baking for sale.[40] Women were prominent as purchasers of malt and meal for their families' needs. Often they also made ale and cakes for sale. In October 1522, for example, eight townswomen (two from each of the town's quarters) were given the exclusive task of agreeing victual prices with the landmen before anyone else was allowed to go to market. Some of the women were to go to the malt market and some to the meal market, suggesting that the sale of each was located in a different place.[41]

There is little evidence about the landmen – the people who came from the country to sell their wares in the market place. Some were humble farmers acting on their own account, trudging to market with a sack of meal slung on their back; and some were probably estate officers, representing local lairds or religious houses. There is much more information to be gleaned about local nobles and other landed men and the town seems to have had rather ambivalent relations with them. On the one hand, it was naturally concerned to stay on good terms with them. We know, for example, that the town often gave presents of wine to people of rank, because these are included as items in the occasional surviving accounts of the deans of the guild or as propines recorded in the council registers.[42] In addition, goods for export were allowed a higher purchase price when the vendors were persons or rank. In a ruling of 1400 or 1409 (the year is not certain), the council and the majority of the burgh merchants ordained that no one was to buy Buchan wool for more than 2s (or 24d) per stone, except that of lords and free tenants who might be offered up to 30d for theirs, the same price as was permitted for the wool of Mar and Garioch.[43] By the same token, lairds and townspeople who bought salt or iron in bulk were to be given concessionary rates.[44] On the other hand, the town was clearly concerned lest nobles should exercise too great an influence in its affairs or corner the supply of export goods. A statute of the guild court in 1467 forbade merchants from encouraging lords to take wool from their tenants in part-exchange for their rents, thereby undercutting the market price.[45] Another ordinance, made in October 1411, decreed that no one was to procure the help of lairds against their neighbours or the inhabitants of the town. People were to help officials and their neighbours when they saw them in need of assistance, especially against outsiders.[46] The kind of anti-social behaviour they anticipated may have been the sort of crimes with which Margaret Balcromy was charged much later. She was convicted of a number of offences against the rules for buying and selling victual in January 1493, harbouring an unlawful person, and 'for conspiracioun in the inbrynging off gentill men be senistir informacion upoun the officiaris off the toun' and 'for the lychlyng (slandering) off the offyciaris'.[47]

The issue of the town's highly distinctive economic relationship with local nobles is related to the more general question of the extent of its reliance on the surrounding countryside for essential goods, and most obviously foodstuffs. It is possible, when we are looking at a medieval town, to think of it as a sort of enclave, separate from its environs. This is partly because the records, as well as quite naturally dealing with the town's own affairs, tend also to be preoccupied with defining the town's privileges and, by definition, excluding those outside from enjoying these rights. Yet there was, in practice, a regular and steady flow of traffic into the town from the country. There is increasing evidence by the sixteenth century of chapmen – pedlars carrying their wares on their backs – who were allowed to pass through the burgh on their way.[48] Also by the sixteenth century, the local government was encouraging landmen to come into town to augment the supply of food.[49]

The existence of this interchange is evident, paradoxically, from what had to be done to prevent movement in times of insecurity and danger. Fear of epidemic disease spreading from outside made the town shut its gates, even against commercial traffic. The guild court in 1507 was worried by the strange 'sickness of Naples',[50] and more sustained evidence of a severe episode of plague blights the records in the years 1513–15. The town did everything it could to protect itself against this contagion. In October 1513, there had been reports of a plague which had struck various burghs and other parts of Scotland and a statute forbade anyone in the burgh to receive, without permission, strangers and vagrants from beyond the Mounth or elsewhere where the plague was suspected to be.[51] In January 1514, a further measure forbade those without licence to receive anyone or any cloths or other goods from suspect places. No landmen from suspect places were to come into the burgh.[52] The efforts seem to have been in vain. Despite repeated further measures, many townspeople seem to have perished in this period. Yet, the town persisted. In July 1515, the four gates of the town were to be guarded against persons suspected of having the disease, and especially people from Old Aberdeen, where plague was evidently suspected.[53]

The records do not tell us very much about the provenance within the region of goods sold in the market place, although in a few cases a dispute between purchaser and vendor reveals where one of them came from. In October 1509, for example, Thomas Lammyntoun was ordered to pay twelve shillings to Andrew Criste in Cottown ('Corcoftoun'), which the former owed for a cow.[54] There is also a case in August 1400 in which one Lord Robert, a monk of the abbey of Old Deer, was a claimant for debt.[55] In addition, the entries in the records about forestallers – those who infringed the town's trading privileges and customs by buying up goods before they came to market – show such persons operating at a variety of locations within the sheriffdom and sometimes at a considerable distance from Aberdeen.[56] Highly valued goods largely intended for export, such as wool, skins and hides, were the most common feature of forestalling.[57] Less valuable goods, most obviously foodstuffs for the town's consumption which would not keep, probably travelled much shorter distances. Indeed, the authorities even had trouble ensuring that fish caught locally at Futty, Cove Bay, and Findon were brought to market. White fish was a particularly important source of food, especially for the poorer people in the town who needed to be able to buy it for themselves in small quantities. Measures were repeatedly taken to ensure that fish was not sold at the shore or to landmen, or in large quantities to retailers, but that it came to market and was available to everyone.[58]

These regulations were designed to make sure that the townspeople had enough food and other necessities. Of course, the availability of food varied and there were certainly times when supplies were scarce. Yet, the expectations that people had are surely an important indication of what was generally available, and those of townspeople in medieval Aberdeen were, in many ways, rather high. The evidence suggests that the commons expected to eat white fish on a regular basis, and we also know that ordinary people commonly ate meat.[59] This leads on to a further question, whether ordinary people in Aberdeen were relatively well-off. The evidence on this point is highly equivocal. We know that the wives of craftsmen often worked to supplement their husband's income. The guild court record of 1507 shows that the wives of dyers and cordiners were sometimes brewsters: the ordinance instructed that they must have one vat to brew in and another for their (husband's) craft.[60] The rules thus prevented the wives of cordiners and dyers from engaging in the cost-cutting exercise of using their husband's equipment. In their case, it was probably on grounds of hygiene but, when fleshers' wives were forbidden to make candles to sell in 1506, it seems likely that this was to stop them from having an unfair advantage in terms of a free supply of tallow.[61]

Despite restrictions such as these, it does seem clear that in many households there were two breadwinners. A further question is whether married women merely supplemented an adequate income earned by their husband, or if their activities were absolutely necessary in order to make ends meet. And, if that was the case, what of women who were the sole breadwinners in the household, as many undoubtedly were? There is evidence from other towns that about one householder in every five was a single or widowed woman.[62] The vast bulk of brewsters in Aberdeen were women and they often fell foul of the regulations. But it is not clear whether they did so because it was, more often than not, impossible to trade within the rules, or because breaking the rules, in order to make a little extra profit, was not greatly feared. No fewer than eighty-eight women were fined in 1472, and a further fifty were amerced in 1520, for breaking the assize of ale.[63] Both cases represented a large proportion of the total number of brewsters in Aberdeen for a list of 1509 included just over 150 names.[64]

Of course, not all the brewsters brewed only for sale, nor relied solely on brewing for their livelihood. The numbers of brewsters are much larger than those involved in any other single occupation in medieval Aberdeen. In particular, the numbers of bakers and fleshers are very small by comparison, for these were exclusive crafts, confined to free, male burgesses. In their case, of course, the master baker or flesher also had servants and apprentices working under him. The point that applies to the domestic 'crafts' taken as a whole, however, is that they do seem to have had a substantial market of customers – the poor, their fellow artisans, merchants and visiting grandees. The authorities took the view that their work had to be supervised, to ensure that those who relied upon them would not be let down. The close regulation of trade can be contrasted with the contemporary practice of allowing the market to determine supply. But, because of the detailed rules and their enforcement, we know a great deal more than we otherwise might about the daily working lives of very ordinary people in medieval Aberdeen.

NOTES

1 This section is based substantially on research carried out by Elizabeth Gemmill, developing work done in connection with a study of prices in medieval Scotland, published as E. Gemmill and N. Mayhew, *Changing Values in Medieval Scotland* (Cambridge, 1995). Just as the chapter on Aberdeen in that work was substantially the work of Dr Gemmill, so this part-chapter was written by her with minor additions by Mr Mayhew. Nevertheless, both authors subscribe to, and endorse, the whole.

2 E. Ewan, *Townlife in Fourteenth Century Scotland* (Edinburgh, 1990), 66–7, speaks of two possible market sites at Aberdeen and of the importance of the fair from the late thirteenth century. See also E. Ewan, 'The age of Bon Accord: Aberdeen in the fourteenth century', in J. S. Smith (ed.), *New Light on Medieval Aberdeen* (Aberdeen, 1985), 37–8.

3 *Ancient Laws and Customs of the Burghs of Scotland, 1124–1424 and 1427–1707*, ed. C. Innes, i, esp. 4–58 ('Leges Burgorum'), 60–2, ('Assise Willelmi Regis'), 64–88 ('Statuta Gilde'), 114–26 ('Articuli Inquirendi in Itinere Camerarii'), 132–54 ('Modus Procedendi in Itinere Camerarii'), and 160–86 ('Fragmenta Collecta').

4 Aberdeen City Archives [ACA], Council Register [CR], vi, 742; and see Gemmill and Mayhew, *Changing Values*, 45–6, 125–8.

5 See Gemmill and Mayhew, *Changing Values*, esp. 3–57, for a discussion of these regulations.

6 There were fixed maximum prices for shoes by the 16th century: see ACA, CR, viii, 25; x, 17.

7 E.g. in Nov. 1511 a statute for skinners, to which four of them gave their explicit consent, required them to have good, sufficiently made gloves, well-sewed and 'querelit', for all those who wanted to buy for a great or small price and especially to supply the university. All gloves were to be marked with the skinner's own mark so that the workmanship and the material would be guaranteed: ACA, CR, ix, 55.

8 A statute made in Oct 1503 forbade smiths to sell horseshoes for more than 2d, 3d, or 4d each; they were to make a horseshoe for a penny and put it on the horse's foot. The fee for removing a horseshoe was to be a penny: ACA, CR, viii, 266.

9 See Gemmill and Mayhew, *Changing Values*, esp. 103–7.

10 It is interesting that maximum prices were frequently set for lamb and mutton but that beef never seems to have been subject to such an assize: Gemmill and Mayhew, *Changing Values*, 44.

11 *Ibid.*, 47–8.

12 ACA, CR, vi, 227.

13 ACA, CR, vi, 733.

14 See N. J. Mayhew, 'The status of women and the brewing of ale in medieval Aberdeen', *Review of Scottish Culture*, 10 (1996–7), 17, for the equipment needed for brewing.

People sometimes handed over their possessions instead of paying a monetary fine, and these were often cooking pots of various kinds, eg *Abdn Recs.*, 220–1.

15 Gemmill and Mayhew, *Changing Values*, 54, 63–4.

16 ACA, CR, vii, 846.

17 See R. Nicholson, *Scotland: The Later Middle Ages* (Edinburgh, 1975), 115, 367; J. R. Maddicott, *The English Peasantry and the Demands of the Crown, 1294–1341* (*Past and Present*, Supplement, 1975).

18 ACA, CR, vii, 851. On the issue of whether there was endemic rivalry between merchants and craftsmen, see M. Lynch, 'Social and economic structure of the larger towns, 1450–1600', in Lynch, *Medieval Town*, 261–86.

19 On Aberdeen's reliance on regional produce, see also H. W. Booton, 'Inland trade: a study of Aberdeen in the later Middle Ages', in Lynch, *Medieval Town*, esp. 154–5.

20 Examples are in ACA, CR, vi, 758; viii, 615, 752 (printed above); ix, 35. For England, see also R. H. Hilton, 'The small town as part of peasant society', in *idem*, *The English Peasantry in the Later Middle Ages* (Oxford, 1975).

21 E.g. in a statute of March 1505, it was confirmed that all corn growing in the freedom of the burgh must be brought to the burgh's common mill: ACA, CR, viii, 427.

22 ACA, CR, vii, 183; see also ix, 38.

23 On medieval Scotland's imports of food and raw materials, see Ditchburn, 'Trade with northern Europe', esp. 168–9; Stevenson, 'Trade with the south', esp 183–4, 189, 193, and 201–2; and P. G. B. McNeill and H. L. MacQueen (eds.), *Atlas of Scottish History to 1707* (Edinburgh, 1996), esp. 264–5.

24 ACA, CR, v (1), 642–4. The ships, or in some cases their masters, were said to be from Dordrecht, Delft, Veere, 'Armove' in Zeeland, Antwerp, and 'Hundfleit'. Their cargoes included wheat, rye, muslin, malt, bere, meal, butter, cheese, salt, onions, apples, wine, and rice, as well as linen cloth, iron, timber products, soap, lint, and other goods.

25 Gemmill and Mayhew, *Changing Values*, 72–6.

26 ACA, CR, vii, 99–100.

27 ACA, CR, ix, 659.

28 *Aberdeen Charters and Other Writs Illustrating the History of the Royal Burgh of Aberdeen*, ed. P. J. Anderson (Aberdeen, 1890), 5–8. By the late 15th[29] century, however, there is evidence that there was a twice-weekly market. In Nov 1489, the bailies were ordered to supervise the market on Wednesdays and Saturdays, in a rota: see ACA, CR, vii, 150.

30 ACA, CR, vii, 8–9

31 Gemmill and Mayhew, *Changing Values*, 66–8.

32 For a detailed discussion of the operation of the corn market in medieval Aberdeen, see Gemmill and Mayhew, *Changing Values*, 57–65.

33 The town made an arrangement in Jan 1493 that John and Robert, their common minstrels, should have their board from the neighbours of the town. If anyone refused to receive them they were to pay them instead 12d per day for meat, drink and wage: ACA, CR, vii, 386.

34 The account of William Rolland of the costs of repairing the tollbooth in 1522, including full details of the costs of materials and of wages, was received by the provost and council on 17 April 1523 and was copied into the register: ACA, CR, xi, 280. For other examples of payments for the upkeep of the tollbooth, see ACA, CR, vii, 478; viii, 750–1, ix, 210.

35 E.g. ACA, CR, vii, 12; viii, 519.

36 ACA, CR, xiii, 439.

37 ACA, CR, xiii, 330.

38 ACA, CR, ix, 197–8.

39 E.g. ACA, CR, vi, 502, 527–8. In 1477 and 1478, bakers were fined for buying wheat at home before it was presented to the market, and in the countryside: ACA, CR, vi, 727. In 1482, fleshers were amerced for buying fish before they were allowed to do so, that is, before the burgesses and the community had been served: ACA, CR, xi, 458. In 1524, fleshers and their servants were forbidden to buy lambs coming to market until they had been presented to the cross and had remained there for sufficient time to enable the neighbours to be served.

40 E.g. ACA, CR, I, 326; vii, 653; xii, 355, 396, xiii, 139.

41 Gemmill and Mayhew, *Changing Values*, 60–4.

42 ACA, CR, xi, 187. See N. J. Mayhew, 'Women in Aberdeen at the end of the Middle Ages', in T. Brotherstone, D. Simonton and O. Walsh (eds.), *Gendering Scottish History: An International Approach*, (Glasgow, 1999), 142–55, and references cited there.

43 ACA, MSS Guildry Accounts, I 1453; Acc 100/7 (photocopy from Gordon of Gordonstoun MSS in Yale University Library) (1470–1). See also ACA, CR, vii, 839: an entry recording the king's propine in Oct 1497 included sums for gifts of wine to the earl of Huntly, Lord Oliphant, and Lord Gordon.

44 ACA, CR, ii, 52.

45 *Extracts from the Council Register of the Burgh of* Aberdeen, ed. J. Stuart (Spalding Club and Scottish Burgh Record Society, 1844–72), i, 380; see Gemmill and Mayhew, *Changing Values*, 69.

46 ACA, CR, vi, 35. The manuscript is torn and some letters of the word 'wool' are missing, but this is the word that seems to be intended. For further examples of Aberdeen's economic links with local nobles, see Booton, 'Inland trade', 148–60.

47 ACA, CR, ii, 113.

48 ACA, CR, vii, 392.

49 See ACA, CR, vii, 670; viii, 753; ix, 35; but cf. CR, xii, 47–8: it was made clear in Oct 1526 that chapmen's ability to sell in town was limited, as was that of the unfree, to one day per week.

50 Gemmill and Mayhew, *Changing Values*, 64–5.

51 See Appendix 1.

52 ACA, CR, ix, 268.

53 ACA, CR, ix, 305.

54 ACA, CR, ix, 468. For other examples of the effects of plague on Aberdeen's commerce, see Booton, 'Inland trade', 156.

55 ACA, CR, viii, 1027.

56 *Early Records of the Burgh of Aberdeen, 1317, 1399–1407*, ed. W. C. Dickinson (Scottish History Society, 1957) [*Abdn Recs.*], 156.

57 E.g. *Abdn Recs.*, 222–31; ACA, CR, ii, 11–14.

58 *Abdn Recs.*, 224.

59 A series of fines were levied on fishermen, boatmen and women from Futty, Cove Bay and Findon between 1499 and 1511 for various offences regarding the selling of fish: ACA, CR, vii, 933; viii, 805–06, 1035; ix, 37.

60 Gemmill and Mayhew, *Changing Values*, 42–3.

61 See Appendix.

62 ACA, CR, viii, 614.

63 As in Stirling, where they made up 18.7% of householders in 1550: *Scottish Antiquary*, 6 (1892), 175–8.

64 ACA, CR, vi, 27; x, 207. See E. Ewan, ' "For whatever ales ye": women as consumers and producers in late medieval Scottish towns', in E. Ewan and M. Meikle (eds.), *Women in Scotland, c1100–c1750* (East Linton, 1999), 129.

65 ACA, CR, viii, 1205–9. The list is printed with a discussion by N. J. Mayhew in 'The brewsters of Aberdeen in 1509', *Northern Studies*, 32 (1997), 71–81. See also Mayhew 'The status of women and the brewing of ale', 16–21.

The People in the Towns

Extracted from EP Dennison and GG Simpson 2000 'Scotland', in D Palliser (ed), *The Cambridge Urban History of Britain. Volume 1, 600–1540*, Cambridge (Cambridge University Press), 730–736, 736–737.

In attempting to analyse who the town dwellers were we must confront several basic issues. How many were they, for example? Guess-work figures have suggested that in the later middle ages only about 10 per cent of a national population of around 700,000 were townspeople.[1] Firm population figures for individual towns are non-existent, but it is entirely clear that all Scottish urban units were small by European city standards, most of them very small. In the thirteenth century Berwick was the wealthiest town in Scotland and some documentation from 1302 has been used to produce a population estimate as low as 1,500, while exaggerated figures in chronicle accounts of the sack of the town in 1296 might be adjusted downwards to suggest at least 3,000.[2] Dunfermline, a significant ecclesiastical burgh, has been reckoned to have about 1,000–1,100 inhabitants by 1500; and Edinburgh in 1560 (by then the capital) may have held about 12,500.[3] A few detailed town censuses emerge in the seventeenth century: Old Aberdeen, for example, again under ecclesiastical authority, had in 1636 precisely 832 inhabitants, excluding the staff, students and servants of King's College.[4] In the later middle ages only a few major towns, such as Edinburgh, Perth, Dundee and Aberdeen would have had more than 2,000 people; and, since small burghs were numerous, the average town must have held less than 1,000: by modern standards, a mere village. What follows is that these towns were tiny, close-knit structures where intimate neighbourhood contacts and interrelationships were all at the core of daily existence.

Equally fundamental is the question of who the townspeople were in terms of their origins: social, familial and locational. The answers vary not only from place to place, but also over periods of time. Early medieval burgesses, as already indicated, were often incomers, either in themselves or in their family background: persons named 'of King's Lynn', 'of Leicester', and 'of Winchester' betray English roots, while Scottish town or countryside names also occur: 'of Berwick', 'of Haddington', 'of Fingask', 'of the Mearns'. Although it is difficult to trace in detail, there was a continuing process of immigration into towns, from both urban and rural sources of population. The origins of many inhabitants remain obscure, since their names are either simple patronymics or are, apparently, descriptive of the possessor's trade or craft. It has been said of those named in the earliest Aberdeen records, around 1500, that ' "surnames" . . . appear merely to designate the individual's trade'.[5] And at a lower level there were those who remain largely or totally invisible to us. Historians often say 'little enough about the luckless weaver and fuller, and nothing at all about the really poor and destitute, for those men never put their names to parchment'.[6] Yet at the upper levels of town society elite groupings were developing, at least in larger towns, before the twelfth century ended. It has been noted that, 'although the prominent burgesses of Perth were of cosmopolitan origin, by the early thirteen century they were forming a number of small dynasties or clans within the town'.[7] Society in later medieval Aberdeen, for example, was dominated, both socially and politically, by eleven outstanding families, whose internal relationships can be displayed in family trees, often with a good deal of details.[8]

Origins and the nature of social unity can be further illuminated if we touch on the use of languages in the towns. Immigrants brought their own tongues and 'Scandinavianized Northern English, or Anglo-Danish, was certainly the principal, though probably not the only, language of the early Scottish burghs.'[9] From Old Norse *gata* derived *gate*, meaning a street; from Flemings who visited or settled came their word *caland* which became *callan*, a customer, merchant or youth: a significant term in a trading context. Down to roughly about 1200 Gaelic was still the commonest tongue in Scotland and must have been heard then in the streets of towns within reach of the Highland line, such as Inverness, Elgin, Aberdeen, Perth and Dumbarton. Even in some border towns Gaelic may not have been unknown in that era. We cannot know how many town clergy actually spoke in Latin to one another, but the daily services in the parish church were in that language. But the linguistic pattern in the towns does not retain this varied structure as we move into the later middle ages. Before the end of the fourteenth century the northern English mentioned above 'had become the dominant spoken tongue of all ranks of Scots east and south of the Highland line, except in Galloway where a form of Gaelic appears to have survived'.[10] This 'Inglis', or 'Scottis' as it was also named from the late fifteenth century, became the pre-eminent speech in towns. That position is reflected also in the various burgh records which survive, at first patchily, from about 1400. Some of the earliest of them are in Latin, but 'from the 1450s, Scots is increasingly the language of record', in the practice of town clerks.[11] The forward march of Scots usage was 'perhaps in part influenced by an impulse towards national solidarity when the nation was beleaguered in the War of Independence'.[12] By the end of the middle ages a commonality of language in towns was the norm, and that language – Scots – was one of the two national tongues, Gaelic being the other. A travelling merchant, a royal administrator or a bishop on visitation would find the same tongue predominantly in use in every town he reached; and that tongue gave cohesion to the Lowland regions of the kingdom, within which the towns had a significant place.

The life of the Scots-speaking town dwellers can be characterised best by looking at four abstract elements and attaching the practicalities of existence to each of them. The daily round involved for them all: proximity, community, hierarchy and variety. The fact of your proximity to other people was probably the single most obvious physical feature of urban living. This closeness has emerged already in comments on population size, on visible town boundaries, whether defences or end-of-rig walling, and on the horizontally occupied flats in the urban skyscrapers of some larger Scottish towns. But the consistent form of house-and-street relationship tells the same story. The crowding of houses on the street frontages, with long, narrow rigs behind, indicates an urgent desire to make contact with the customers who thronged that street. The open market area of every burgh also betokens not only the centrality of trading, but also the frequent public intermingling of folk. As a medieval town inhabitant, your neighbour mattered greatly to you: his house and garden lay immediately alongside yours, his noise and activity intruded on your life, his midden smells invaded your space, his plague infected you and your family.

This physical contiguity links too with social cohesion, which can be illustrated in several ways. Intermarriage of burghal families is frequently documented and the economic and social significance of heiresses in burgh life is very evident. In Aberdeen from the start to the end of the fifteenth century it had become twice as common for a non-burgess to marry the daughter of a burgess of guild.[13] The negative side of close social relationships emerges too from recorded details of the quite frequent personal disputes, including both verbal and physical attacks. Catherine Lyne, an inhabitant of Old Aberdeen, for example, miscalled one of the town bailies by addressing him as 'swetie hatt, clipit brecis and blottit hippis' (sweaty hat, short trousers and bloated hips). She gives a vivid picture of a fat official but she suffered for her invective, since as punishment she was banished from the town.[14] On a more positive and pleasurable note, days of festivity and merriment must have brought most of the community together in commingling relaxation. The list of recorded public entertainments is long and varied: Corpus Christi plays, processions and pageants; plays involving Robin Hood and the Abbot of Unreason; morris dancing; summer bonfires – all were elements of the occasional social whirl.[15]

A sense of community is conveyed to us at every turn. In the records the phrase 'community of the burgh' occurs as early as the thirteenth century and in later times becomes very common. From that century onwards burghs frequently possessed seals and the legend on each refers to 'the common seal of . . .' or 'the seal of the community of . . .'. 'The common profit of the town' was also a favourite piece of wording. It can be readily argued that such phraseology must quite often have represented in practice the wishes of some elite group or clique: the dominantly wealthy or politically powerful.[16] But stated duties were at least formally attached to the position of any burgess, as a full member of the community: for example, attendance at the three head or principal courts of the burgh each year was officially expected, and defaulters were fined for absence. That rule may well have been breached at times and may have been less prominent in the later middle ages, but at least the ideal of common responsibility was visible. And in a more practical way the feeling of community emerges particularly strongly in later medieval times, when care for the urban parish church is prominently on record. This was achieved in many towns, for example, by appointment of one or more kirk-masters, who were secular officials, not churchmen, charged with supervision of the building work on and around the church, and maintenance of its fabric. These masters of works display the concern of the community for its own religious observances. And strong support for services in a local church can be noted too in the active processes of founding altarages (*anglice* chantires): by the Reformation in 1560 the parish church of St Giles in Edinburgh had at least forty of these and Holy Trinity parish church in St Andrews had about thirty.[17] The frequency of services within any such major urban church displays that building and that institution as a focus for community activity to a degree utterly unlike the habits of urban populations in present-day Britain.

It was well recognised that within the community a functioning hierarchy existed: John Ireland, a fifteenth-century Scottish intellectual, remarked that 'thar is gret ordoure and dignitie ascendand fra the lauborare ore sempil persoune to the hier stag mare and mare'.[18] Above the level of burgh society itself was the legal superior of the burgh: the king as formal overlord of every royal burgh, and the baron, bishop or abbot, by royal permission, as possessor of his own baronial burgh. The degree of authority exercised by superiors varied, but each burgh usually had its own principal officer, the *prepositus* (later provost), sometimes called alderman, aided by some form of council, plus a group of bailies or magistrates. The community and the jurisdictional power structure here merged together, for, by law, every new burgess had to swear fealty to the bailies and to the community of the burgh. The significance of hierarchy can be observed when its operation occasionally breaks down, as in the frequent disputes, for example, among the craft guilds of Aberdeen about their positions in the Corpus Christi processions, the organising of which was the responsibility of the bailies.[19] Yet although political and social hierarchy leaps at us from the records, the inner workings of the structure are not yet sufficiently explored. It is not enough to say, in the words of one recent historian, that 'much of the history of the medieval town can properly be explained in terms of its institutions'.[20] There is truth in the comment, but where a sufficient quantity of late medieval and early modern records exists, as it does for Aberdeen, for example, the activities and interrelationships of families will be found to be of striking interest. The formalities of power and public office are readily visible, but within the interstices of that apparatus families are visible rising and falling, and households can be observed in operation as the social units which must often have meant more in the lives of the town inhabitants than the formal decisions of the officials who caused the hierarchy itself to tick over. The tensions between public authority and personal attitude are visible in the comment of an Aberdeen inhabitant in 1545 directed against Thomas Menzies of Pitfoddels, landed gentleman and frequently provost of the town, to the effect that the protestor 'did not care for all his power or his stane house'.[21]

The French historian Jacques le Goff has rightly remarked that 'for the men from the fields, the forest, and the moors, the town was at once an object of attractions and repulsion'.[22] Within its boundaries lay both variety and excitement. In a simple physical sense it was remarkable, as we have noted, on account of its density of buildings and of people. Yet it included within its operations agricultural activities too: in the long rigs behind the burgess frontages there were garden crops and orchards, as well as smaller domestic animals such as pigs and fowls. Many a burgess was in part a farmer also, hence the dung-heaps on the public streets which town councils frequently attempted to prohibit or remove. And the social mix of the town was also varied and complex. In addition to the hierarchical range from the significantly wealthy to the poverty-stricken, others intermingled. Kings and their households visited, living in the nearby royal castle, or at a religious house, or even in the house of a burgess or at an inn. From the twelfth century onwards aristocrats owned town properties: in a charter of about 1161, King Malcolm IV granted the royal steward 'one full toft [house site] for his lodging in every burgh of the king'.[23] Religious houses, too, purchased town tenements and used them as bases for business and as stopping points for their abbots when travelling.[24] The major towns at least, therefore, welcomed occasional important visitors whose main concerns in life were centred elsewhere. Town inhabitants were accustomed to rubbing shoulders with, or at least gazing at, a changing kaleidoscope of great persons and their numerous hangers-on.

In addition to mixing with non-burgess figures passing through, a few burgesses, even as early as the thirteenth century, can be seen turning their eyes to ownership of rural properties and so becoming an element in the laird or gentry class. This trend in the later middle ages has been briefly investigated in print and deserves careful attention.[25] Only a small minority followed this route of non-urban land acquisition. But a change of focus is involved and, for a tiny group at least, capital acquired through trade and burgh rents was evidently available to permit purchase of rural estates. The motivation may have been partly economic, but the increased status gained by a burgess-laird must also have counted for much. By the later fourteenth century we meet, for example, the figure of John Mercer, burgess of Perth, rich enough to impress an English chronicler by his 'inestimable wealth'; trusted sufficiently to be engaged on diplomatic missions in David II's reign; and powerful enough to acquire land by marrying into the family of Murray of Tullibardine, in Perthshire, and so to create a niche in landed society for his descendants, as the Mercers of Aldie and Meikleour.[26] In the words of Nicholson, 'investment in land was a stepping-stone to gentility'.[27]

To those outside the town walls the inhabitants within them looked different: in personal aims, social attitudes and institutional functioning. But the walls did not create rigidly defined enclaves. Scottish medieval town dwellers interacted with those in their hinterlands and far beyond. Integration within the kingdom was a primary keynote of all that was done by the people in the towns.

NOTES

1 R. Nicholson, *Scotland: The Later Middle Ages* (Edinburgh, 1974), p. 2; S. G. E. Lythe and J. Butt, *An Economic History of Scotland, 1100–1939* (Glasgow, 1975), p. 4.

2 W. C. Dickinson, *Scotland from the Earliest Times to 1603*, 3rd edn. (Oxford, 1977), p. 114; H. Maxwell, trans., *Chronicle of Lanercost* (Glasgow, 1913) p. 115.

3 E. P. D. Torrie, *Medieval Dundee: A Town and its People* (Dundee, 1990), p. 59; M. Lynch, 'The social and economic structure of the larger towns, 1450–1600', in M. Lynch, M. Spearman and G. Stell, eds., *The Scottish Medieval Town* (Edinburgh, 1988), p. 279.

4 G. G. Simpson, *Old Aberdeen in the Early Seventeenth Century: A Community Study* (Aberdeen, 1975), p. 5.

5 W. C. Dickinson, ed., *Early Records of the Burgh of Aberdeen, 1317, 1389–1407* (Scottish History Society, 1957), p. 247.

6 A. A. M. Duncan, 'Perth: the first century of the burgh', *Transactions of the Perthshire Society of Natural Science*, Special Issue (1974), 48.

7 A. A. M. Duncan, *Scotland: The Making of the Kingdom* (Edinburgh, 1975), p. 493.

8 H. W. Booton, 'Burgesses and Landed Men in North-East Scotland in the later Middle Ages: A Study in Social Interaction' (PhD thesis, University of Aberdeen, 1987), chapters I and II and appendix A.

9 M. Robinson, ed., *Concise Scots Dictionary* (Aberdeen, 1985), p. ix.

10 *Ibid*.

11 Lynch, Spearman and Stell, eds., *The Scottish Medieval Town*, p. 25, esp. nos. 35, 37 above.

12 Robinson, ed., *Dictionary*, pp. ix–x.

13 Booton, *Burgesses and Landed Men*, pp. 158ff.

14 Simpson, *Old Aberdeen*, p. 7.

15 A. J. Mill, *Medieval Plays in Scotland* (Edinburgh, 1927); see also above, p. 338.

16 J. H. Stevenson and M. Wood, *Scottish Heraldic Seals* (Glasgow, 1940), I, pp. 52–82; see also above, p. 306.

17 M. Lynch, *Edinburgh and the Reformation* (Edinburgh, 1981), p. 28; R. G. Cant, *The Parish Church of the Holy Trinity, St Andrews* (St Andrews, 1992), p. 7.

18 Johannis de Irlandia, *The Meroure of Wyssdome*, III, ed. C. McDonald (Scottish Text Society, 4th series, xix, 1990), p. 92.

19 Mill, *Medieval Plays*, p. 64.

20 Lynch, 'Social and economic structure', p. 267.

21 J. Robertson, *The Book of Bon-Accord: A Guide to the City of Aberdeen* (Aberdeen, 1839), p. 105.

22 J. Le Goff, *Medieval Civilization* (Oxford, 1988), p. 29.

23 G. W. S. Barrow, ed., *Acts of Malcolm IV, King of Scots, 1153–65* (RRS, I, no. 184).

24 W. Stevenson, 'The monastic presence in Scottish burghs in the twelfth and thirteenth centuries', *SHR*, 60 (1981), 97–118.

25 R. Nicholson, 'Feudal developments in late medieval Scotland', *Juridical Review* (1973), 9–16; Ewan, *Townlife*, pp. 100–16.

26 Nicholson, *The Later Middle Ages*, pp. 153, 194–5; Ewan, *Townlife*, p. 127.

27 Nicholson, *The Later Middle Ages*, p. 457.

The Scottish Medieval Pottery Industry

Extracted from DW Hall 1998, 'The Scottish Medieval Pottery Industry: A Pilot Study', *Tayside and Fife Archaeological Journal*, 4, 170–176.

INTRODUCTION

Since the start of the urban development boom of the late 1970s, the opportunity for rescue excavation in Scotland's medieval burghs has resulted in a large database of information. Included amongst this is a very large assemblage of medieval pottery which has been identified as being of native origin. This identification is based on this material dominating the excavated assemblages and not matching any known imported fabric.

As already discussed in a previous paper excavation and field-work in Scotland has had limited success when it comes to the identification and excavation of medieval kiln sites and it was for this reason that it was felt that the time was ripe for an initial survey of the subject with a view to formulating a considered project design. This pilot study will consider the existing evidence, examine possible routes of research and in targeting one specific area (the Carse of Gowrie, Perthshire) will analyse the results.

BACKGROUND AND CURRENT STATE OF KNOWLEDGE

The Scottish Medieval Pottery Industry

The current state of knowledge of the medieval pottery industry in Scotland is based purely on the analysis of fabrics recovered from urban excavation and kiln sites at Colstoun, Stenhouse, Throsk and Rattray. Another suggested kiln site at Kinnoull, Perth remains unproven.

The earliest native fabric that has been identified is White Gritty Ware, which is recovered from 12th-century deposits in Perth in association with imported fabrics from England, the Low Countries and Germany and in the Borders has been dated by thermoluminescence to 1065+140 and 1175+120AD respectively. The study of this fabric has largely concentrated on the identification of regional differences in vessel type, as any attempt at a sensible visual analysis of the fabrics has proved meaningless due to their similarities.

On current analysis a native Redware industry begins production in about the mid-13th century, and so far every east coast Scottish burgh from Stirling to

Dornoch has produced its own version of this fabric. It is currently assumed that these Redware fabrics are being produced in the vicinity of each burgh rather than at one or two major east coast pottery production centres. This assumption is based on the fact that although they belong to a single tradition, each of these fabrics is slightly different in terms of surface finish and amount of inclusions. The sourcing project recently undertaken by the British Geological Survey using inductively coupled mass spectroscopy (ICPMS) has proved to be remarkably effective in identifying different chemical trace elements in the Redwares. When coupled with thin section analysis it has even enabled the identification of differences between pottery fabrics that come from the same river valley. This new technique promises to help greatly in the search for kiln sites.

If major production centres were involved then these probably would be referred to in the documentary record and some physical remains would still be extant. Although it has been argued that the medieval road system in Scotland may have been better than had been previously supposed, surely the transportation of large consignments of pottery over a long distance would have been less cost-effective than a local supply.

The only kiln sites excavated which may have been producing such Redware fabrics are at Stenhouse and Rattray. The apparent presence of a widespread Redware tradition in Scotland has led to this pilot study, and it is on this fabric type rather than the gritty wares that this paper will concentrate.

Clay Sources

By using the MacAulay Institute Soil Survey map for eastern Scotland one is able to locate the position of both lacustrine and alluvial clays which will have been available for the manufacture of pottery in the medieval period (Soil Survey of Scotland 1982 sheet 5). There is one alluvial soil association in particular, the Stirling/Duffus/Pow/Carbrook, which appears in the close vicinity of the burghs of Stirling, Perth, Dundee, Montrose and Elgin, and it is tempting to consider that this association may indicate a clay source that could have been utilised in the medieval period.

It has already been suggested that the lacustrine clays were used for the White Gritty industries of the Borders and Fife. These white clays appear to be more suitable for producing higher fired fabrics and it is for this reason that they were used for the gritty wares, while the iron-rich alluvial clays appear more suitable for producing fabrics that were fired at lower temperatures. The use of the two different clays may also indicate differences in kiln technology, a possibility that cannot be resolved until further sites have been located and excavated.

An example of the tantalising glimpses that can be gained of the subject can be found amongst the documentary evidence (discussed below) in an entry for 1474 in the Lord High Treasurer's Accounts which says 'Item to ane passand to perth to Wil Turing, to get him to send clay to Edinburgh'; unfortunately it does not specify where this clay will come from or what it will be used for!

Fuel Sources

The lack of excavated kiln sites means that it is not known what they were fuelled with. It is not unlikely that some of the White Gritty kilns may have been coal fired, particularly in Lothian where the monks of Newbattle Abbey were given rights to extract coal as early as 1184. Elsewhere wood and peat would seem to have been the most likely fuel sources and their availability when also coupled with a water source may have been significant as regards site location. There is limited documentary evidence for the existence of 'peatarys' which were under monastic control. Jean Le Patourel has suggested that there is evidence in England that peat was used as a fuel source for firing, and given its ready availability this may have also been the case in Scotland.

Documentary Sources

As part of this pilot study the author has searched a mixture of both ecclesiastical and secular sources specifically for references to medieval potters or potting. In general it has proved very difficult to find any references to either, apart from a document of 1488 which mentions a 'Patrik Machane, potter' in a property location in the Borders.

There is a particular problem of terminology in the Scottish context. An entry in the Exchequer Rolls of Scotland dated to 1380 refers to clay pots by their Latin description 'ollis luteis'. In Old Scots it would appear that the most common term for an earthenware vessel is a 'pig'. The term 'pot (potties)' can also be used usually with a defining adjective such as 'lame' which specifically means earthenware. For example in 1502 an entry in the Lord High Treasurer's Accounts refers directly to money given to 'the pottair of Linlithgow for lame pottis'.

The differences in terminology mean that great care must be taken when the records are being examined that the right sort of potter is being identified. It has been argued that it was more common for someone who cast bronze pots to be called a 'potter', whereas a clay potter would be called a 'pigmaker'. This means that the early 16th-century references to 'pottairs' in Stirling may actually be referring to those connected with the gunmaking industry.

It is, however, also likely that these 'pottairs' may have actually been making the clay moulds for the guns, as is suggested in an entry of 1508 which records payment 'for bringing of the furm (form) of the gwn fra the potteris hous to the castell'. If this is accepted then the main trade of these 'pottairs' may have been the manufacture of earthenware vessels, and therefore their houses may prove to be the locations of some of our missing kiln sites.

The absence of potters from both the Perth Guildry Book and the burgess rolls of Dundee may suggest that the industry was not located within the burgh limits. An entry in the Book of Scone refers to one of the abbey's landholdings as 'Lamepottis' in 1452 and 'Leimpottis' in 1585. This name, when translated from Old Scots, means 'earthenware pots', the 'lame' element being Old Scots for earthenware. A search of valuation rolls has shown that a farm, a house and garden and a piece of land were all called Limepot(t)s until 1862–63. From this date onward these landholdings slowly changed their name to Parkfield, which is how they are known today (NO 1470 2502). There is no record in the local Sites and Monuments Record of any finds from this area but there would seem to be a strong case for future field-work and research if the opportunity ever arose.

Place-names with the 'potter' element do exist, but all are of 17th-century date or later, for example Potterhil in Stirling in 1615 and Potterflattis in Annandale in 1670; Potterhill in Perth is known by this name from 1577. The origin of the Perth Potterhill is not known and the author has been unable to trace it back any further than the 16th century. As discussed above these late 'potter' names may indicate the presence of metal potters, and this is certainly true of the Stirling reference.

Surnames with the 'potter' element also appear, for example Simon Potter of Dumbarton, who was one of those appointed to treat for the ransom of David II in 1357; however, it is not clear if this was his trade.

THE CARSE OF GOWRIE, PERTHSHIRE: A CASE STUDY

Introduction

It was decided to concentrate on this part of Perthshire simply because it lies in close proximity to two major medieval burghs, Perth and Dundee, and a readily available source of clay is known to exist particularly in the vicinity of Errol. This material was exploited from the late 19th century and was used for making bricks and tile at Pitfour, and is still used for bricks at Inchcoonans. The Carse of Gowrie also contains numerous examples of clay-walled buildings which were built using the same clay source.

Aerial Photographic Evidence

The author examined the aerial photographic cover for the area around Errol specifically to see if it was possible to identify anything that might be classified as crop marks of former clay pits. On a vertical photograph taken in May 1974 a series of sub-circular features are visible to the south and south-west of Errol Park (NMR ref no 2416111). These all show up as dark ringed areas in the crop and are at least 150 m in diameter. Several of these features are visible on the early editions of the Ordnance Survey where they are shown as being planted with trees and are sometimes given names, for example two of the crop marks beside Port Allen are named Murie Clay North Oval and Murie Clay South Oval. The position of these features whether planted or not is still marked on the modern Ordnance Survey Pathfinder series (OS sheet NO 22/32).

From a preliminary field visit, some of these features such as the Silvermuir Ovals (NO 2490 2180) are currently under cultivation. These distinctive features are all located around Errol on the clay source and the author wonders if they may indicate the position of early clay pits. It is tempting to wonder whether these features are the planted versions of the 'many large pools of water' which are said to have 'disfigured' the district prior to 1735.

Brick and Tile Works

The clay fields around Cottown became the site of a major tile and brick works in the 1830s. The local landlord Sir John Stewart Richardson had recognised the need for efficiently draining his farmlands in order to be able to increase his farm yields. Finding that the cost of transporting tile from other parts of Scotland was very prohibitive he began to make tiles from the clay on his own land from 1837–38. This developed into a major tile and brick factory until 1912 when it was bought out by a rival, one Alexander Bell, who had his own manufactory at Inchcoonans (to the north of Errol). There is absolutely no evidence that this clay was being exploited at a much earlier period although there is a tantalising reference to 'the flooded remains of very early clay excavation on the site' which apparently pre-date any works by the tile and brick factories. In passing it is worth pointing out that recent field-walking by TAFAC in the vicinity of another former tile works at Marlehall near Newmill, Perthshire (NO 0880 3220) located sherds of medieval Redware pottery.

CONCLUSIONS

The apparent absence of references to potters in the 13th and 14th centuries in the documentary record for Scotland is surprising as this surely must have been a major industry for several hundred years. Admittedly this may be due to the destruction of relevant documents either by invading English armies or the Reformers but one would have expected something to survive. Part of the problem may be due to the fact that the potters were never part of the burgh guildry and carried out their trade beyond the burgh limits. It is a point of some interest that the medieval trade that is best represented in the archaeological record may have been considered so lowly that it is virtually invisible in the historical record.

It has been suggested that it was the advent of new monasticism from the continent in 12th-century Scotland that may have promoted the foundation of a Scottish pottery industry. This is worth further exploration particularly when one notes the proximity of 12th-century monastic foundations to those burghs which have produced Redware fabrics.

One of the first things to do is to define exactly where a kiln site would be and what surface finds might be recovered to identify it. A combination of workable clay, water and fuel supply and adequate means of transport (either by road or water) are the four governing factors for site location. At least two of the features located on aerial photographs in the Carse of Gowrie match these definitions on all counts.

One would assume that the most obvious surface indicator of a kiln site would be pottery wasters from misfirings in the kiln. However, from a cursory search of three Sites and Monument Records from Perth and Kinross, Stirlingshire and the Scottish Borders the only pottery finds listed are all stray finds of sherds. Maybe one should be searching for large groups of pottery from rural locations that cannot be explained away by the manuring of the field; one such assemblage exists from the Low Parks in Hamilton but on recent examination by the author proved to contain no obvious kiln waste.

As with much rural medieval archaeology in Scotland, it is only by undertaking some closely targeted field-work that the questions will start to be answered. The first part of the problem is hopefully in the process of being answered through the work currently being undertaken by the British Geological Survey on clay sourcing. If this confirms that the Carse clays described above could have been used to make the Redwares found in Perth and Dundee then this will allow the targeting of some of the sites discussed.

RECOMMENDATIONS FOR FURTHER WORK

1 Further detailed study of the documentary evidence to confirm that there are no early references to potters or potting.
2 A programme of intensive field-walking of the identified crop marks in the Carse of Gowrie to see if it is possible to identify that they actually relate to clay extraction at all.
3 Field-walking of the lands of Parkfield (formerly Limepotts) Farm near Scone may also prove productive.
4 The two excavated kiln sites at Colstoun and Stenhouse will also repay some further investigation and research. The Stenhouse archive is on the point of being assessed and this will hopefully lead to full publication of this important Redware production site. The Colstoun material has been published but this only really concentrated on the pottery assemblage and very little was said about the kilns or the evidence for how they were fired. Full publication of the Colstoun excavations would be of great benefit to future research. An initial assessment of what exists in the way of excavation records and drawings for Colstoun would seem to be the first step.

Even from this limited amount of research it is clear that once the various pitfalls of terminology and apparent absence of record have been overcome there is a route to formulating a workable project design.

Dogs, Cats and Horses in the Scottish Medieval Town

Extracted from C Smith 1998, *Proceedings of the Society of Antiquaries of Scotland*, 128, 859–882.

INTRODUCTION

Over the last two decades, many town sites in Scotland have been the subject of rescue excavations, in advance of building developments. Such excavations have produced a wealth of evidence relating to the development of urban centres in the medieval period. Where waterlogging has occurred, for example in Perth, which is still periodically affected by local flooding, preservation of organic remains can be particularly good. These remains, of both animal and plant origin, can provide a rich source of information as to the diet and living conditions of the medieval urban population. Analysis of animal bone assemblages can reveal not only evidence about the beasts themselves, but also about the humans who exploited and lived alongside them. Hodgson has reviewed and summarized the evidence for domestic animals at sites on the eastern Scottish seaboard; this paper focuses on, and updates, the evidence for dogs, cats and horses, three species long associated with man, and their place in the Scottish medieval town.

THE SITES

The sites which have produced the most well-preserved and fruitful faunal assemblages, to date, are generally located in Scotland's more easterly burghs, such as Perth, Dundee, St Andrews, Aberdeen, Elgin and Inverness, although, in the west, Ayr has also been the subject of archaeological investigation. The character of the sites includes prestige frontage properties (eg 75–77 High Street in Perth, excavated in 1975–7 and hereafter referred to as PHSE), industrial backlands (Meal Vennel in Perth) and monastic foundations (Carmelite friaries of Aberdeen and Perth). A single castle site, Ladyhill, now enclosed by the modern town of Elgin, also deserves inclusion in this study, since its location places it close to, if not within, the medieval burgh. Because Ladyhill provides evidence of medieval hunting it is also a useful contrast to the burgh sites where remains of game animals are seldom seen.

The sites and appropriate references are listed in Table 1. Dates chosen for this review fall within the 12th to 16th centuries; site phases which are later than the 16th century have been omitted.

SPECIES IDENTIFICATION

It would be easy to assume that all the canine bones come from domesticated species, but of course there is the possibility of confusing post-cranial bones of wolves with those of large dogs. Wolves (*Canis lupus*) were driven to extinction in northern Scotland by the mid 18th century, but were certainly found throughout the country before that time, as numerous documentary records and evidence of place-names show. Aybes & Yalden list 69 Scottish place-names with a 'wolf' element, both Gaelic and English, from the Borders to the Highlands. Gracile dog bones may also be confused with those of fox (*Vulpes vulpes*). However, no fox skulls, which are diagnostic of the species, have been found at any of the sites. Long bones which were identified in the original site reports as 'dog/fox' have therefore been omitted here.

Similarly, one cannot always be sure that all feline bones found in towns are from domestic cats, since wild cat skins with the feet attached may have been imported into the burghs. The native Scottish wild cat (*Felis silvestris*), while generally larger than its domestic relative (*Felis catus*), is probably morphologically indistinguishable from it, at least as regards the skeleton. Features in the skull have been claimed to differ, but it has been noted that 'skulls of domestic cats show great variation in form and size, and there is not a single feature in the skull of *F silvestris* which cannot be found in certain skulls of the Domestic Cat'. Besides, as cat skulls are relatively delicate, they do not always survive well under burial conditions. Since all the cat skulls and long bones reviewed were of a relatively small size it was decided to treat them as the domestic species (*Felis catus*).

As for equids, while it is believed that all the specimens seen were from horses (*Equus caballus*), there is a possibility of previous archaeozoological workers having failed to recognize remains of donkeys (*Equus asinus*). Perhaps for this reason, reports of equids other than horses are rare in Britain, although mules (crosses between horses and donkeys) have been reported from Roman London. The Romans are thought to be responsible for the introduction of the donkey and the mule throughout Europe. A donkey tooth has been tentatively identified from Burgess Street, Leith, although this is of recent date (18th- or 19th-century date).

RELATIVE ABUNDANCE OF DOGS, CATS AND HORSES

All of the animal bone assemblages from sites considered in this review contain relatively large quantities of the bones of cattle and sheep, mainly because these were the animals on which the Scottish medieval export economy of hides, wool and woolfells was based. This heavy reliance on both cattle and sheep results in their predominance in medieval faunal assemblages, to the relative exclusion of other species. Thus, although the remains of dogs, cats and horses are retrieved from urban sites where bones are preserved, almost without fail, their numbers are fairly small with respect to those of the ubiquitous hide and wool producers.

In Table 1, the numbers of bones from dogs, cats and horses are shown alongside the 'minimum numbers of individuals' calculated from the most frequent bone from each species, at each site. These 'minimum numbers' are undoubtedly an under-estimate, but have the advantage of indicating relative abundance. For example, at 12–18 New Bridge Street, Ayr, 95 dog bones represented only two individuals, while by contrast, at PHSE, 218 dog bones (just over twice the number from Ayr) represented 17 individuals. This is because the majority of the bones at 12–18 New Bridge Street came from a single canine skeleton, while most of those from PHSE represented many single stray bones not associated with articulated skeletons.

The pattern of distribution seems to show that the bones of dogs were more commonly recovered than those of cats, with the notable exception of the two Perth High Street sites. This may be because dogs were genuinely more numerous than cats, or because cat bones, being small, may have been missed during excavation.

Bones of horses, however, are as large as those of cattle and should therefore show less bias in recovery than bones of cats and small dogs. It thus appears that horses may have been relatively uncommon in the medieval burghs, or at least that they rarely died there. Perhaps surprisingly, comparison with the deserted medieval burgh site of Rattray in Aberdeenshire indicates that here, also, horses were scarce.

TYPES OF DOGS: HUNDIS, MESSANS AND TOWNE TYKIS

Both Harcourt and Clutton-Brock, the former an authority on early domestic dogs and the latter on domesticated mammals, have cautioned against identifying the remains of animals from archaeological sites with distinct, named, modern breeds. Harcourt argued that the modern concept of 'breed' relies on such characteristics as colour and nature of the coat, carriage of ears and tail and even the temperament of the animals. It is notable that there is a resistance within the sheepdog fraternity to following such standards of appearance, preferring the attributes of the dogs which make them valuable working animals.

'Types', based on the evidence of size and head shape provided by the bones themselves, are therefore described in archaeological literature. Where semi-complete skeletons have been preserved, shoulder heights can be estimated from the lengths of the limb bones with reasonable accuracy. A further method has also been devised in which the bones of the feet, the metapodials, are used to estimate canine shoulder height. However, results do not always agree with those obtained by Harcourt's method for the same skeleton. As the margin of error for the long bones appears to be less than that for the metapodials, shoulder heights based on the former method are shown (Table 2).

The smallest dog was found at PHSE. This animal was only 23.4 cm (or 9.2 in) high. Another notably small individual, found at Castle Street in Inverness, was estimated to be about 26.5 cm (10.4 in) high. The three tallest individuals were found at Meal Vennel in Perth, Ladyhill in Elgin, and 45–47 Gallowgate in Aberdeen, standing at 63.7 cm, 62.9 cm and 61.5 cm respectively. But the majority of the dogs fell into a middle range, standing between about 30 cm and 50 cm and averaging about 43 cm. To give an impression of what this means in the live animal, the smallest dog at PHSE was about the same size as a modern Cairn terrier, and the middle range perhaps about the same size as a Border collie, based on heights quoted in modern breed descriptions. The tallest archaeological specimens were not, surprisingly, as large as might be expected, and were certainly much shorter than, say, the modern greyhound breed, which stands at between 71 and 76 cm.

In general, the canine long bones were slim with respect to their length. However, one animal from PHSE was noticeably stouter limbed, and probably slightly bow-legged. The impression gained was of a far more 'butch' individual than the typically fine-limbed dog which appears to be the medieval norm. This animal was about 39 cm high. (Despite the injunction to avoid relating the bones to modern breeds, taken alongside the shape of the skull, the temptation to compare this animal with a bull terrier is irresistible.) Only three other bow-legged individuals were seen: one was represented by the humerus, radius and ulna from Castle Street, Inverness, which gave the estimate of 26.5 cm shoulder height; another came from 120–1 Market Street in St Andrews, and was approximately 29 cm high at the shoulder; the third came from a late medieval deposit from Burgess Street in Leith. This last dog was represented by a single, 's' curved tibia, and had a shoulder height of approximately 35 cm. It should be noted for all these dogs, however, that shoulder heights based on bowed limbs are probably less accurate than those estimated from straighter legs.

Further evidence of dog type is provided by the shape of the head. Unfortunately, animal skulls are often in a damaged condition when found on archaeological sites, as a result of being crushed by pressure from overlying soil deposits. For example, a dog skeleton was found in a pit at Meal Vennel in Perth, but, although the spinal column was visible, disappointment ensued, when it was found on excavation to disappear under a large stone which had crushed the head. However, in other cases where the skulls were well preserved, the measurement indices devised by Harcourt were used to describe the shape of the head. These indices are based on comparisons of the features which contribute to the shape of the skull, that is, the width of the zygomatic arch (the 'cheek bones'), the length of the snout and the width of the muzzle. Thus, the cephalic index (CI) related the width of the skull to its overall length, the snout index (SI) shows the length of the snout relative to the whole head and the snout width index (SWI) shows the width of the muzzle relative to the width of the nose. Amongst the medieval Scottish dogs reviewed here, there was a surprising uniformity of shape. Skulls from Perth, Elgin and Inverness, although varying in overall length, appeared to come mainly from wide-headed dogs with long, fairly narrow muzzles, although one from Ladyhill, Elgin, was broader in the muzzle. Thus, with relatively few exceptions, on the basis of cephalic indices, most medieval Scottish dog skulls show little modification from the type described as 'plain dog' by Harcourt.

One skull variation which is not accounted for in these measurements, however, is that of the sagittal crest. This is a bony ridge at the back of the head which provides the attachment point for the muscles involved in closing the mouth, and which also serves to protect the roof of the cranium from injuries, such as blows to the head. A well-developed sagittal crest and associated temporal muscles are thus important in a dog, which must catch and forcibly grip its prey. However, at PHSE, one small domed skull represented a good example of a type lacking the well-developed sagittal crest present in most of the other medieval examples. Because this specimen had its upper molar teeth fully erupted and the sutures of the skull were closed, it was thought to come from an adult dog rather than a juvenile which had not reached full development. Thus, there were at least three distinct types of dog present in the material examined: the 'plain dog' type, by far the most common, with a broad face and long snout, probably of slim build, though of varying height; second, a strong, bow-legged type, with a very strongly developed, downward-angled sagittal crest to its skull, accompanied by heavy mandibles; and third, a small, fine-boned animal with which the round, domed skulls probably corresponded.

How do these dog types compare with evidence from historical sources? Early descriptions of dogs tend to concentrate on animals used in hunting, since this was the sport of kings, the nobility and higher clergy, and descriptions of common working dogs are omitted. Although appearing to originate from several independent sources, these accounts can usually be traced back to only a few authors, most particularly to Gaston Phoebus, Count of Foix (1331–91) author of *Livre de chasse*, a treatise on the art of hunting. According to Froissart, who enjoyed Gaston's hospitality, he loved dogs above all other animals and in his writing describes their good qualities as well as how to provide for their welfare. His work was later translated into English as the *Master of Game* by Edward, Duke of York, another *aficionado* of hunting. For later medieval Scottish dogs in particular, there are 16th-century descriptions by Bishop Lesley and Boece. None of these accounts exactly agrees with another, and the confusion has been compounded by more modern writers who seem determined to find a Roman or Greek origin (or even an ancient Egyptian one in the case of the greyhound and the mastiff) for almost every British dog breed. There is no doubt that dogs resembling greyhounds and mastiffs did inhabit the ancient world, but Clutton-Brock sounds a timeous note of caution when she points out the difficulty in deciding whether these dogs 'are really breeds with an unbroken line of 4000 years, or whether the genetic diversity inherent in the species causes similar characteristics to re-combine so that the same type of dog is bred in different regions and at different periods when selective breeding is carried out for the same purpose'.

However, to return to the medieval record, from illustrations and descriptions in the *Livre de chasse* it is possible to pick out the main varieties of dog known in medieval hunting. These were defined by their function rather than their appearance, or even what we would call 'breed'. The point is illustrated by a clause in the medieval Forest Laws of Scotland, whereby the owner of a mastiff found unchained in the forest would be penalized. In order to recognize the mastiff (*canes mastivos*) again, the forester should record 'what the dog was like'. If all mastiffs were of a single breed and almost exactly the same, this would be exceptionally difficult to do, but if the mastiff was of a mixed origin, the individual animal would be far more distinctive.

The main types of hound, therefore, were either those which hunted by sight, or those which hunted by scent. Of the sight, or 'gaze' hounds, the greyhound, also know as the *grewhound* or simply *grew*, was paramount, because of the speed with which it followed its prey. In the Roman period, Scotland was famed for her greyhounds, which despite the name need not necessarily have been grey. Unfortunately, no medieval Scottish skulls have been found to bear more than a passing resemblance to the greyhound; the attributes of the modern breed are a long narrow head with a rather straight zygomatic arch, well-developed sagittal crest and long jaws. The medieval dog skulls all appear to have relatively wide zygomatic arches; it may be that the exaggerated, elongated facial features of the modern greyhound were less well developed in the medieval period. Some of the larger limb bones (from, for example, Meal Vennel in Perth) may be candidates for the greyhound type. It is interesting to note that the *Livre de chasse* illustrates two distinct types of greyhound: a larger, rough-coated variety, and a smaller, smooth-coated type. Both coat types are also known from Pictish stones which depict hunting scenes, for example the Burghead stone, in which, in the opinion of Gilbert, one of each type is shown bringing a red deer stag to the ground. The modern Irish wolfhound is thought to have developed from the large rough-coated variety and this is also a likely origin for the Scottish deerhound. Both of these animals stand at over 71cm, which is somewhat larger than any of the dogs found at medieval sites.

As well as the greyhound, the chase also employed dogs known as *alaunts*, reckless dogs whose job was to seize the running stag or boar and bring it down, a role also taken by the heavy mastiff. The alaunt was a powerfully built dog, shown in contemporary illustrations as prick-eared, and with a square bull terrier head. But this dog was notorious for its uncertain temperament, 'prickly and nasty-tempered, and altogether giddier and madder than other kinds of hounds'. Since the height of the alaunt probably varied greatly, it is not too far-fetched to suggest that the sturdy, bull-headed individual from PHSE might have been just such a dog.

However, the hound responsible for scenting the game was the *chien courant* or running dog – the *canis currens* of the Forest Laws of Scotland. For Gaston Phoebus, the favourite hounds above all other were the '*chiens courants* which hunt on all day long bawling and giving tongue, and shouting all sorts of insults at the beasts which they are after'. Sadly, there can be no archaeological evidence for the noise which they must have set up, any more than there is for some of their other admired attributes, viz 'a small pair of ballocks well trussed together'. The running hound of the chase may have evolved into a type similar to the modern fox-hound. The head proportions of the larger medieval dogs studied here bear more than a passing resemblance to this type. Allied to the *chiens courants* were the dogs known as *raches* (sometimes spelt *rauches*, *rachets* or even *brachets*) although the Scots preferred them to be silent rather than noisy. Raches were usually coupled together in pairs; thus an entry in the Rental Book of Coupar Angus Abbey, dating to the 16th century, states that the tenants of Glenisla 'sall nwrice [nourish/keep] ane leiche [leash] of gud howndis, with ane cuppill or rachis, for tod and wolf'.

Another hunting dog, the *harrier*, was also known in Scotland as the *kennet* (probably from the Old French, *chienet*). Of smaller size than the alaunts and raches, the kennets were run in packs and used for lesser game, such as hares. A litany of

'kennet' names is given by the late 15th-century makar poet, Robert Henryson, in
'The Cock and the Fox':

> this wedow . . . on hir kennettis cryde:
> How! Berkye, Berrie, Bawsie Broun
> Ripe-Schaw, Rin-Weil, Curtes, Nuttieclyde
> Togidder all but grunching furth ye glyde!

Possible evidence of hounds kept in a pack comes from the castle site of Ladyhill in
Elgin. Here a single deposit contained six mandibles from at least four different dogs.
These mandibles were of medium size with a basal length ranging from 99.4–119.5
mm. There is a strong possibility that these dogs were of the same type, or were
otherwise closely related: the mandibles were all of a similar size and appearance and
in three cases showed congenital absence of the third molar tooth, as well as
crowding of the first molar against the fourth premolar. Developmental defects such
as these suggest a degree of inbreeding, such as may be seen in a closely related pack.
The size of these jaws indicates they may have been kennets.

One other medieval hound which hunted by scent deserves mention: this is the
strecour, or *sleuth hound* mentioned by Bishop Lesley, also known as a *lymer* in
English texts. As well as hunting deer, these dogs hunted men: during a period of
lawlessness in south-west Scotland, a 'sleuth hound dog' was used to track down the
Armstrong band responsible for stealing 240 sheep from Lanarkshire. Sleuth hounds
were of medium to large size and again it is not possible to relate this type to any of
the bones which have been found. They seem to have developed into the type known
as bloodhounds.

Besides these hunting dogs, which were of relatively high value, there were also
present in the medieval period the common-or-garden dogs which have gone almost
unrecorded in the literature of the time. However, some are listed in *The Boke of St
Albans*: butcher's hound, midden dog, trundle-trail, prick-eared cur and 'smale
ladies popis that beere away the flees' have come from just such a motley collection.
Indeed some dogs must have lived a semi-feral existence on the fringes of human
society. Presumably these are the ones described as 'myddyng dogges' or the 'towne
tykes [that] yowles' (Montgomerie's 'Answer to Polwart'). There was certainly scope
for rich pickings on the burgh middens, the contents of some of these having
survived, particularly at Queen Street in Aberdeen and at PHSE. The butchers' dogs
were also known as 'alaunts of the butcheries' so that some of the bow-legged
individuals from PHSE, Inverness, St Andrews and Leith mentioned above may just
as well have been the sort of proletarian animals which herded cattle on their way to
market, as those which accompanied the nobility in the chase.

However, although there is little specific evidence to say whether the remains were
of scavengers, working dogs or indeed the middling size of hounds, the last kind, the
'ladies popis' or lap-dogs may be represented by at least one example. At PHSE, an
incomplete skeleton, alas, minus the head, was found in a pit. As described above,
this is Scotland's smallest known medieval example, at only about 23 cm high at the

shoulder. This dog might as well have been a terrier as a lap-dog, but for the fact that the skeleton displayed traces of pathology, showing it to have been an elderly, perhaps decrepit individual, which indicated it may have been a cosseted pet. In medieval Scotland, such lap-dogs were known as *messans*, an appellation which could also be used as a term of abuse, as in 'a crabbit, scabbit, evill facit messan tyke'. There are oblique references to both messans and mastiffs in another satirical poem of Dunbar, in which the Queen's Wardrobe official, James Doig (or Dog) is likened to 'an mastive, mekle of mycht' and 'over mekle to be your messan', in other words, too big to be a pet ('The wardraipper of Venus boure'). By the time of Burns, the name also seems to have been applied to common small dogs, presumably of the terrier type. Thus in his tale of 'The twa dogs', the laird's dog had nae pride, 'But wad hae spent an hour caressing', Ev'n wi' a tinkler-gipsey's messan'. The term *tyke* on its own seems to signify a common mongrel from at least the late 15th century onwards, in Scotland, although originally the name came from an Old Norse word meaning only a female, a bitch. The tyke, then, is the most likely origin for the skulls referred to as 'plain dog' from urban sites.

HORSES

Complete horse skeletons are a rare find on archaeological sites and unfortunately, with the exception of the incomplete remains of a foal from the Gallowgate Middle School site in Aberdeen, none has been recovered from the medieval period. In addition, horse bones are often damaged by butchery or the depredations of burial conditions. Where intact long bones have survived, however, they can provide evidence of the stature of the animal. Kieswalter, working in the 19th century, produced a set of multiplication factors which can be applied to the lateral length measurements of limb bones in order to estimate the withers height, or highest point at the shoulders of the live animals. Lateral length measurements were available for horses in Perth, Aberdeen, Stirling and Dunfermline, and are shown alongside the withers heights, in centimetres, estimated from them in Table 3; the height in hands (a unit of 4 in) has also been included. (Although the convention is to use a full stop in the notation of height, as in eg '14.2 hands', meaning 14 hands and 2 in, this may be confused with a decimal point, therefore a colon has been used here; thus 14:2 hands.) What emerges from these data is the conclusion that all of the medieval animals are under, or equal to 14:2 hands height (58 in, or 147.3 cm). Since a pony is defined as any horse standing under 14:2 hands, the conclusion must be that all of the medieval animals encountered are best described as ponies. The smallest pony, standing at about 12 hands, was found at Stirling Broad Street, while the tallest, as just 14:2 hands, was found at Abbot's House, Dunfermline. From 15:2 to 16 hands is thought of nowadays as a good height for a riding horse, while Shire horses and modern police horses stand at around 17 to 18 hands. Horses from sites in medieval London have been found to range in height from 10:1 hands to nearly 16 hands, although most seem to be in the same range as those from Scotland. Elsewhere in medieval Britain, at

Flaxengate in Lincoln, Coppergate in York and Hamwih in Southampton, horses also tend to cluster around 13 to 14 hands height.

John Major, in his 16th-century *History of Greater Britain*, refers to horse markets held at Perth, which he refers to by its alternative name of St John's Town. Of these animals he says 'they are of no great size, and are thus not fitted to carry a man in heavy armour to the wars, but a light-armed man may ride them at any speed where he will. More hardy horses of so small a size you shall nowhere find'. This description would appear to fit the physical evidence from the Scottish sites very well indeed. The descendant of this medieval type may well be found in the sturdy garron of the Highlands, renowned for its activity and stamina. The ideal height for the modern garron is about 14:1 hands, although it can be smaller, and shortness of metapodials (cannon bones) is preferred because of the rough terrain in which they often work. The horse metapodials found at urban Scottish sites are indeed sturdy as regards their mid-shaft width, as well as being fairly short. A Pictish representation of such a small pony and its rider (possibly rendered with more than a touch of burlesque) was found at Bullionfield, near Dundee.

The name garron itself is Gaelic in origin and strictly applied only to geldings, although the term now applies to all Highland ponies whether gelded or not. Major also asserted that 'in Scotland for the most part the horses are gelded' but that 'some stallions are kept by great men in stables . . . but in the matter of riding they are neither swifter than more willing' than the geldings which he says will 'travel further in a day, and for a longer time, than a horse which has not been gelded'. There is, however, little archaeological evidence allowing the determination of sex in horses. Even the presence of a canine or 'wolf tooth', seen in one specimen, does not prove maleness, since it also occurs as a variation in some females; thus, one such specimen from PHSE might be from either sex.

Size is also indicated by the small dimension of articles of horse 'furniture'. For example a horse shoe found at Ladyhill, Elgin, was of very small size indeed; and a horse shoe from Queen Street, Aberdeen, although fragmentary, is of a size not inconsistent with a pony or small horse. As well as horse shoes, bits are occasionally found. Because the size of the bit is necessarily related to the size of the mouth into which it fits, an estimate of the animal's size can be made. One horse bit found in a 14th-century deposit at Lochmaben Castle was thus thought to come from an animal of between 13 and 14 hands height, which agrees very well with the evidence of the equine bones.

At first sight then, there would appear to be little evidence for the large war horses ridden by knights, which, according to documentary sources, existed in the medieval period. Recent work on contemporary pictorial evidence shows that it was customary for the height of the shoulder of the rider to equal the horse's withers height. Knowing the average heights of medieval men and women from excavated skeletons, it has been estimated that the average horse, even the noble 'great horses', probably stood no higher than about 15 hands; thus in Barbour's poem 'The Bruce', the king, riding to the battle of Bannockburn, 'raid apon a *litill* palfray'. In later centuries, the term 'palfrey' was used to describe a lady's small riding horse, rather than a man's. During the battle of Bannockburn, many of the English 'great horses' were killed or captured by the Scots; in the years that followed, until the Union of the Crowns, it became a felony to sell horses to the Scots, for fear of improving their stock.

Other references to the horses of the Scots army at this time are made by the chronicler, Froissart. Although he himself was writing some years after the events which he describes, he used an eyewitness account of the Scots invasion of England of 1327. Froissart did indeed visit Scotland himself in 1365 and there is no reason to doubt that he wrote accurately of his everyday surroundings. In Froissart's account of the events of 1327, 'the knights and squires are mounted on fine, strong horses and the commoners on small ponies'. Elsewhere he describes the knights' horses as 'good rounseys and coursers' while the other men ride 'those little ponies which they neither groom nor tether, but turn loose to graze freely wherever they dismount'. The archaeological evidence from town sites in Scotland, then, confirms the presence of small sturdy horses. Even those ridden by knights do not seem to have been much larger. Efforts made by the Scots to improve the size of their war horses by importing new, large animals from the continent were continually thwarted by the English, although some were smuggled over the Border in the mid 15th century.

CATS

Unlike dogs, which were present in Britain from at least the Neolithic period, cats do not appear in the archaeological record until the Iron Age. In Scotland, they have been found at the broch of Howe in Orkney, in secure contexts pre-dating the Roman conquest of Britain. The arrival of the cat in the islands, if indeed the bones represent the domestic rather than the wild species, must therefore have come about through trade. After the Roman colonization of Britain, cats began to spread from the south, but by the Roman withdrawal in the fifth century, cats were becoming feral and the population increased. The cat's value to humans was as a controller of rodents, and this is reflected in the ninth-century Welsh laws of *Hywel Dda*, which valued the animal at four pence (incidentally the same as a 'dunghill dog'). The cat's qualities are 'to see, to hear, to kill mice, to have her claws whole, to nurse and not devour her kittens'. Alcock comments on the extraordinary proliferation of cats (as well as mice) throughout the illuminated pages of the *Book of Kells*.

Sadly, and probably because they were of lesser value than the horse and hound, there is much less documentary evidence for the medieval cat. One of the few late medieval appearances of the cat in Scottish literature is found in Henryson's fable of 'The two mice'. Here the cat is referred to as 'Gib Hunter, our jolie cat' and 'Bawdronis', the second being an affectionate feline name, sometimes also applied to the hare. Although there is no archaeological evidence that cats were neutered, some reference is made to it in the cat-name 'Gib' (the short form of Gilbert) which referred to a tom-cat, and more specifically a neutered male. Thus Shakespeare's Falstaff can say 'I am as melancholy as a gib-cat' (*Henry, the Fourth*, Part 1, Act 1). In recounting the animals kept as pets in medieval monasteries, Gordon notes also that 'S[aint] Gregory kept a gelded Tom Cat, and was very fond of him'. Neutering the male cat makes him less likely to fight and of course keeps the cat population under control. However, it was probably only practised occasionally, since a large cat population could be exploited for the monetary value of the skins.

As to the physical attributes of medieval cats, there are no documentary clues. Cat bones from archaeological sites, however, indicate that the typical Scottish animal was smaller than the modern domestic feline, with altogether slimmer mid-shaft dimensions. This size difference may be due to better nutrition at the present day. McCormick found that medieval urban cats in Ireland were smaller than those from Early Christian period rural sites, perhaps indicating that town cats were left to fend for themselves in the matter of food and shelter. That existence in the medieval burgh was precarious is indicated by the presence of cat bones showing the evidence of traumatic damage. For example, three tibiae and a radius from PHSE (representing 0.9% of the total cat bones from this site) showed evidence of fracture or other lesions caused by trauma. The age distribution of cat bones at PHSE, where as many juveniles as adult cats died, also indicates a hard life.

THE ROLE OF DOGS, CATS AND HORSES IN THE MEDIEVAL TOWN

From the evidence of documentary sources and the bones of the beasts themselves it can be seen that the animals fulfilled several different functions in life. Dogs, in particular, were necessary servants of man, especially in the hunting field. A good hunting dog was a valuable asset, well-fed and cared for. Some of the larger dogs from urban Scotland could well have belonged to the hunting fraternity. However, others found within the town were more likely to have been herders' dogs, or 'alaunts of the butcheries'. Given that trade in the burghs was heavily reliant on the by-products of sheep and cattle, with the towns filled with herds of livestock on market and fair days, dogs would have been needed to exercise some sort of control. Smaller dogs, known as *heelers*, were used in relatively recent times to persuade recalcitrant livestock to move on, usually by nipping at the heels of the cattle, and it is not unlikely that some small medieval dogs were also used in this way. A reference is made to butchers' dogs in records of the Flesher Incorporation of Perth in 1717: the burgh magistrates obliged the fleshers to 'keep [their] dogs ty'd in the night time and muzl'd in the day time in all time thereafter under the penalty of five hundred merks Scots money'. However, the fleshers objected to keeping their dogs and 'bicks' muzzled on the grounds that it was 'altogether impracticable and what would render them entirely useless' to them and were successful in having the ruling altered to merely keeping their 'dogs and bicks ty'd in the night time'. Although this dispute took place in the early 18th century, the situation was probably similar to that in the medieval period, and illustrates the need for the dogs to nip at the heels of the cattle, which they certainly could not do if muzzled.

A related function to that of the butcher's or drover's dog was that of the shepherd's dog. Livestock was too valuable to lose to the wolf or other predators, and the 16th-century shepherd of Dunkeld who was enjoined to guard his sheep 'faithfully and diligently from common danger, excepting the bites of wolves [and] foxes' would have required some canine assistance. Ironically, in shepherding, man has merely exploited the natural behaviour of the dog's wild ancestor, the wolf, an animal which it may be argued has an unjustifiably bad reputation. In the 18th century the best shepherd's dog could be described by Burns as 'a gash and faithfu' tyke, As ever lap a sheugh or dyke' ('The twa dogs') and intelligent animals with these attributes must also have been preferred in earlier times.

As now, there must also have been a problem of sheep-worrying by unwatched or stray dogs. In the records of the burgh of Elgin, an act of 1658 which sought to limit the numbers of dogs in the countryside, forbade 'kearters [carters] and uthers that caries dogs alongs with them unneccessarlie to the country for peatts and turffs'.

Another important function of the dog was in guarding property from theft or vandalism. Presumably these animals would have been chosen for their fierceness and ability to bark loudly. They may have been a danger to passers-by, but were regarded as of such value that it is recorded in the Acts of Parliament of Scotland that any man who 'slais a mannis [house] hund thruch villany . . . sal wak apon that mannis myddin for a tuelf moneth and a day'.

The fortunes of the town dog were not always so favourable, however. With the passage of time, the dog population of the burghs may have become unmanageable, and attempts must have been made to control canine numbers. By the late 18th century, legal means were employed, and an annual tax of 2s 6d (a half crown) was levied on each animal, but 'from this tax . . . shepherd's and butcher's dogs are very properly exempted'. The exclusion of working dogs from this tax emphasizes their continuing importance to a society still tied to the economics of livestock keeping. Another method of control was to ban all bitches from the town, as in an act recorded in the Town Council minutes of Elgin in the year 1683, 'siclyk that no bitches be keipid within burgh'. However, this evidently met with little success, as in the year 1690, the act was widened to exclude 'cur dogges' from the town. Several archaeological sites in Elgin have produced deposits containing significant numbers of dog bones. One such deposit was recorded in a 16th-century well at Lazarus Lane, which contained a minimum number of seven dogs as well as three cats. Surprisingly, these were not puppies; only one of the skeletons came from an immature animal, while the rest were fully adult, and one was definitely male. Perhaps these were 'cur dogges' and bitches, dumped in the well, in order to avoid a penalty such as that imposed by the Town Council in the 17th century.

Horses were also employed in a variety of ways. Until the advent of the horse collar, oxen, rather than horses, were used to pull the plough. Horses, however, were employed otherwise as beasts of burden. Several references are made in the late 15th-century literature to a type of pack-horse known as a *capill*, often in poetical conjunction with the 'creillis' or panniers, which they carried. The capill also pulled carts, 'sa curtasly the cart drawes and kennis na plungeing'. The term capill is also known in Gaelic, spelled 'capull' by MacBain, and derives from the Latin *caballus*, a pack-horse. Another, possibly less valuable type of work horse known in Scotland in the medieval period was the *aiver*, sometimes averill, corresponding to the English affer or stott, which was the peasant's plough or harrow animal. The word 'aiver' eventually came to mean an old or worthless nag in Scots. The most valuable horse, however, was the one reserved for riding. In Scotland, this type was the *coursour*, a charger or stallion, but was of course the mount of the king and the nobility. James IV (1488–1513) rode such an animal. In the 15th century 'Taill of Rauf Coilyear', the capill and the coursour are contrasted, but the first carries 'twa creillis', presumably full of coal, and belongs to the collier, while the second is the property of the king, incognito. Another horse type known in 16th-century Scotland was the *jonet*, known in English as the *jennet*. This was a small animal of Spanish extraction and is mentioned in Lindsay's *Satyre of the Thrie Estaitis*: 'I wad gif baith my coat and bonet, To get my Lord Lindesayis brown jonet'.

From the evidence of Scottish medieval horse bones, however, it has not been possible to differentiate between these different types of horses, excepting that a range of heights, from 12 to 14:2 hands has been recorded. Of a study carried out on medieval horses in London, only one (out of a total of nine tibia specimens) had the slender leg proportions which indicated it may have come from a riding horse. In comparison, the Scottish animals were probably all sturdy-legged, perhaps indicating they were pack or cart-horses.

The excrement of horses and dogs was also of value, the equine variety as fertilizer for the plots of garden land within the burghs, and the canine variety as a preparation used in leather tanning, a process known as baiting or puering. Hides were an important source of revenue to the medieval economy, and the tan-pits in which they were steeped have been found at several Scottish sites. Ironically, a butchered dog skeleton was found in a tanning pit at 45–75 Gallowgate, in Aberdeen, after the pit had gone out of use in leather preparation.

The value of the cat in the medieval burgh lay chiefly in keeping the rodent population under control. While the black rat (*Rattus rattus*) has yet to be found in Scottish medieval deposits, bones of other small mammals such as house mouse (*Mus musculus*) and field vole (*Microtus agrestis*) have been recovered from sites in Elgin. Bones of brown rat (*Rattus norvegicus*) (or evidence of rodent gnawing in the form of tooth-marks on bones) are found regularly in post-medieval deposits, for example in Perth and Dunfermline. Rodents can seriously deplete stored grain and other foodstuffs, and what they do not eat, they contaminate with their excreta. In the medieval period this must have been a great problem and could have dire consequences for the human population. Periods of dearth occurred regularly as a result of poor harvests, and cats must have been of practical use in defending the stores, both in the town meal girnals and in the home. Birds, as well as mice, were seen as a problem, eating the crops of grain before they could be harvested. Here too the cat could find itself useful employment, as well as a source of food and entertainment.

The foregoing uses of cats, dogs and horses, of course apply only to the live animals. As usual, in the medieval period, few natural resources were wasted, and these animals, even when dead, continued to serve the communities in which they had lived. Possibly the most valuable in this respect was the horse, which could provide a good-sized hide. Evidence that horses were indeed skinned is plentiful at Scottish medieval sites. This usually takes the form of thin knife cuts on the shafts of the long bones, which are otherwise left intact. Where the covering of musculature and connective tissue is relatively thin under the skin, it is easy for the skinner's knife to penetrate through the periosteal membrane covering the bone and leave cut marks there. The proximal end of the metapodial and the phalanges of the feet are common sites for such cuts.

Butchery marks, indistinguishable from those on cattle bones, are also found in the form of hacks left by butchers' axes on the bones of horses. In some cases the meat has undoubtedly been removed, for example, at Castle Street, Aberdeen, where knife cuts were found on the ventral border of a horse ilium (part of the pelvis). Horse bones were sometimes split open lengthwise (in the sagittal plane) to obtain the marrow, a procedure frequently carried out on cattle bones also. Examples of horse bone marrow-splitting were found at 30–46 Upperkirkgate, Aberdeen. Obviously, the meat and marrow was removed from such bones, but it is not easy to determine whether it was intended as dog food, or for human consumption. Dogs, perhaps, would have been left to get on with the job by themselves, but they were not responsible for marrow splitting. Although gnawing marks made by dogs are often found on horse bones, they seem to appear equally frequently on the bones of cattle, sheep and pigs.

There is some documentary evidence that worn-out horses were sometimes fed to dogs. Hunting dogs in particular were well fed and cared for, principally because of their value. Documentary evidence from the 14th-century French Royal Hunting Accounts shows that '4 carcasses of old, worn-out horses' were bought at market to feed 'several thin and ailing hounds kennelled at Fontainebleau'. There is also evidence from Witney Palace in Oxford, where a hunting kennel was kept in the late medieval and post-medieval period, of butchered horse bones which are presumed to have come from dog food. In early 18th-century England such 'dog horses' were bought to feed kennelled hounds on country estates in Derbyshire, Norfolk and Worcestershire.

The Early Christian Church frowned upon the human consumption of horseflesh, which was considered by Pope Gregory III in 732 to be 'an unclean and detestable practice'. None the less, it appears that early communities, such as the Anglian settlement at Dunbar, were either unaware of the proscription on consuming horseflesh, or wilfully ignored it, for here there was plentiful evidence for horse butchery, and very little osteological evidence of dogs. Indeed, butchery of horses at Dunbar continued throughout the occupation of the site, from the Anglian to the post-medieval periods. At the medieval Carmelite site of Whitefriars, Perth, butchered horse bones were found in both pre- and post-Reformation deposits, perhaps indicating that the religious proscription of the eighth century had been forgotten. At the medieval leper hospital of St Nicholas, just outside the burgh of St Andrews, horse bones with knife cuts may represent meat donated to the lepers; rotten meat and fish left over from the burgh markets was disposed of in this way and it is possible that horse flesh was also thought to be acceptable.

In summary then, the butchered horse bones found at urban medieval sites in Perth, Inverness, Inverkeithing, St Andrews and Aberdeen may represent the waste from knackering of meat for human consumption as well as for dog food.

Horses, however, were not alone in being skinned or butchered. Examination of the bones of cats and dogs from medieval Scottish sites reveals that knife cuts, indicative of skinning, are common. A common site for such knife cuts is on the frontal bone of the skull of cats, in the region of the orbits of the eyes. The reason for this is that when skinning a cat, the convenient way to proceed is from the feet up: the paws are cut off to free the skin, the pelt is then removed from the back and neck and pulled up and over the head (rather like removing a pullover when undressing) to the point where the layers of skin over the nose is at its thinnest. Here the skin would be cut free from the head, releasing the whole pelt from the carcass, and it is here that the knife would cut into the frontal bone, leaving tell-tale marks behind. Close scrutiny of 12 cat skulls from PHSE in which the snout was present showed that seven of them had multiple knife cuts in the supra-orbital region. Other sites where cuts were observed in an identical position on the skull were 80–86 High Street, Perth and Canal Street III, Perth, as well as at 16–18 Netherkirkgate, Aberdeen. McCormick notes that cat skulls from 13th-century Wood Quay in Dublin, displayed cut marks on the orbits, evidence of a remarkably similar technique. Evidence of skinning of the paws comes from a metatarsal from PHSE which displayed knife cuts on the shaft of the bone.

A further common position for knife cuts associated with skinning is the basal border of the mandible; these marks were found on some of the cat jaws at PHSE and 80–86 High Street, Perth. By contrast with the other sites in Perth, where dog bones were more numerous than those of cat, at the two High Street sites cats were more abundant. These factors lead to the suspicion that a cottage industry in cat skinning had flourished in the High Street during the medieval period.

Dogs were also regularly skinned in Scotland in the medieval period. Bones with typical skinning cuts were found at PHSE, Meal Vennel and Whitefriars in Perth, 53–59 Gallowgate and Castle Street in Aberdeen, 106–110 Nethergate in Dundee, and Lossie Wynd in Elgin. In a dog skull from PHSE, the cut marks were found across the snout rather than between the orbits, but at least one dog mandible had cuts on the basal border, as in the feline examples.

There is some evidence that dog skins were exported from Scotland to England and France in the 17th century. With the hair, they were used in muffs or 'made into a kind of buskins for persons in the gout'; without the hair, they were used for ladies gloves and the linings of masks 'being thought to make the skin peculiarly white and smooth'.

A further, more mundane, but ultimately more useful way of employing dog skins was in the making of fishing floats, or bowies. These were traditionally made in east coast fishing communities, first recorded in the 19th century, and used the whole, inflated skin, scraped, oiled and tarred to make it float. There seems to have been no effort made to breed an ideal 'bowie dog', although a large skin was preferred for herring nets, and a smaller size for lines.

Cat skins were also traded within Scotland. An entry in the records of the Guild Merchant of Perth for the year 1552 details a list of skins, which includes 'cattis', although it is not clear whether this refers to the domestic breed or to the wild cat. Skins of cat were also exported from the port of Youghal in Ireland in the 14th century, and dog skins in the mid 16th century. An intriguing illustration of a cat skin, dating to c 1510 is incorporated in the painting now known as *The Prodigal Son* by Hieronymus Bosch, where the pelt is shown attached to the basket carried by the figure in the foreground. The skin probably has an allegorical meaning, but the painting (now in the Museum Boymans van Beuningen, Rotterdam) none the less illustrates a real facet of ordinary 16th-century life.

Some marks found on the bones of dogs and cats at archaeological sites were far more reminiscent of butchery than of skinning. For example, a dog humerus from 16–18 Netherkirkgate, Aberdeen, had cut marks around its distal articulation identical to those commonly seen on dismembered sheep bones. These cuts indicate that the meat was cut off the bone. At PHSE, also, bones of both dogs and cats showed far deeper cuts than would be necessary merely to remove the animal's pelt. Cuts on both the cranial edge and blade of a dog scapula are far more likely to be associated with removal of the musculature, that is, the flesh, than with skinning. Similarly, deep knife cuts on the head or greater trochanter of four different dog femora, as well as one from a cat, at PHSE, indicate that the hip was disjointed. This seems excessive if the main aim was only to get the skin off the animal, not its meat. Also at PHSE, two cat innominates had parallel knife cuts around the acetabulum, as well as on the ilium and ischium, which are also highly suspicious. Urban sites are not, however, the only ones at which dogs were thought to have been eaten. McCormick found that a dog skeleton recovered from a stone-lined pit at Pluscarden Priory, Moray, had knife marks around the acetabulum of the pelvis (the hip articulation). In addition, a cat skeleton from the same pit had also been dismembered.

Eating the meat of dogs and cats was probably only practised during periods of dearth or food shortage. Perhaps the most influential source of prejudices or taboos regarding food animals has come from the biblical notion, in the books of Leviticus and Deuteronomy, of ritually 'clean' and 'unclean' beasts; 'animals that go on their paws' must not be eaten, and this probably refers to fissipedes such as dogs and cats.

As well as using the meat, skins and hair of dogs and horses, the people of the medieval period also found uses for the bones. The favourite bone was the horse metapodial or cannon bone, which was sought after for the manufacture of ice skates. These can be made with only a few simple modifications, mainly by trimming the bone at its proximal end to give an upswept 'toe', and flattening the posterior aspect of the shaft and the distal articulation to give a smooth surface which will glide along the ice. A hole was sometimes added at the toe or heel to attach the metapodial skate to the foot, and with the help of a pole, the skater could propel himself along, without lifting the feet. Bone skates were common throughout Europe in the medieval period and have been recovered from sites in Aberdeen and Perth. Other favoured horse bones were the accessory metapodials known as splints, which have a long, tapering shaft and are easily modified into awls and points. Dog bones do not seem to have been used regularly, as they do not have the special features of the horse metapodial or splint which make it easy to adopt the morphology of the bone to a specific function. Thus, a dog humerus from a 13th- to 15th-century context at 106–110 Nethergate, Dundee, which was used as a mortar mixer, was probably just a stray bone picked up from the midden; this type of tool could just as easily have been made from a long bone of sheep. The snapped-off shaft of the bone was surrounded and filled with mortar, indicating a rough-and-ready tool, but in addition, the bone also had knife cuts on the distal articulation which may have related either to skinning or meat removal.

EVIDENCE OF DISEASE AND INJURY

The rate and type of bone pathologies in animal bone assemblages can sometimes be related to the success of husbandry practices. Although medieval Scottish horses occasionally suffered from relatively minor arthritic changes to their joints (for example at St Nicholas Farm, St Andrews), no gross pathologies or evidence of trauma were seen. The health of the horses, as shown by the evidence of their bones, was no worse, and possibly better than that of contemporary plough oxen in Scotland. However, it must be remembered that only a small number of diseases leave traces on the skeleton. In addition, there is very little evidence that young horses died, with the exception of two bones from a very young, possibly newborn, foal at Gallowgate Middle School. The presence of butchered adult horse bones in the same context indicates that a pregnant mare may have died or been killed. At the other sites where horse remains were found, the evidence of both bones and teeth indicates the animals had reached adulthood when they died. The oldest animal (from PHSE) was at least 11 years old at death, on dental evidence.

Amongst dogs, the evidence suggests that dental problems, such as ante-mortem tooth loss, occurred fairly infrequently. Loss of the first lower premolar teeth was noted in one dog mandible at PHSE; another example from the well deposit at Lazarus Lane, Elgin, had lost the lower fourth premolar. These teeth may have been lost through damage caused by hard food, or alternatively, through periodontal disease caused by food impaction around the teeth. Another site where breakage or complete loss was noted was in the upper canine tooth; in the dog found in the cesspit at Mill Street, Perth, this tooth suffered only breakage, but in another individual from Lazarus Lane, Elgin, the tooth was long gone, with the result that the natural infilling of the root-holes (alveoli) with new bone had occurred by the time of death. Otherwise, dog dental health was fairly good amongst the known examples.

Likewise, dog long bones were found to be relatively free of visible signs of disease. Where it did occur, pathologies were either mainly of the arthritic variety, or had been caused by trauma. The most interesting example of arthritic change occurred in the smallest dog in the sample, the 'messan' from PHSE. The long bones, vertebrae and ribs showed various symptoms of osteoarthritis, including lipping, grooving and eburnation of articular surfaces, particularly in the spine. There was also evidence of localized osteoporosis, most noticeable in the lower fore limbs.

Unfortunately the animal's skull and teeth were not retrieved, but it seems likely that it had reached old age. The small size of this dog, together with its somewhat decrepit condition, and the fact that it was disposed of in a pit rather than on the ever-available open midden, seem to indicate this was a cosseted pet rather than a working terrier, as suggested above. It was extremely unlikely to have been a feral animal.

By contrast, the dog from a cesspit at Mill Street in Perth seems to have led a less sheltered life. The skull of this animal showed evidence of a healed fracture, as well as traumatic damage to both the upper and lower canine teeth and loss of several of the upper incisors resulting in a complete reshaping of the animal's muzzle. In addition to this, there was a large healed oval lesion, passing completely through the bone, on the dog's right shoulder blade, as well as various other small lesions and evidence of swelling. Such damage was probably caused by a piercing injury of some kind, such as the bite of another dog. Taken along with the evidence of blows to the head, the suggestion that this may have been a guard dog is attractive, although other possible explanations must include organized dog-fighting. Had the dog been a stray it is unlikely to have been deliberately buried in the cesspit; feral animals usually find somewhere far away from people, perhaps sheltered by a hay-stack or wall, in which to curl up and die.

It is worth mentioning here that there was no evidence on the bones of dogs' feet for the brutal practices of 'knee cutting' (*genuiscissio*) and 'expeditioning', which were operations carried out on dogs' feet and legs during the Norman period in England. The purpose of these mutilations was to ensure that no commoners' dogs were capable of the speed required to catch the King's deer. In the Assize of the Forest of 1184 it is stated that 'mastiffs shall be lawed', referring to the removal of the claws and three toes of the forefeet. The Forest Laws of Scotland, although including some borrowings from English sources, never enforced 'lawing' of dogs.

Cats found at medieval sites showed only infrequent evidence of disease. One femur specimen, found at PHSE, had a grossly misshapen proximal end, which must have resulted in a defective hip joint and associated lameness. Other abnormalities seen at PHSE were associated with trauma, for example one radius, from an incomplete skeleton, showed a probably healed fracture, while three tibiae displayed bony lumps on the shaft which were probably caused by injury to the soft tissue and periosteum overlying the bone. Injuries like these perhaps reflect the precarious existence of urban felines.

As with dogs, cat dental health was good on the whole, although in the case of the site where cat bones were most frequent (PHSE) this may be related to the young age at which they died. On the basis of both epiphyseal fusion and dental evidence, roughly equal numbers of kittens and adult cats died. By contrast, few puppies or juvenile dogs were found at the same site.

MEDIEVAL ATTITUDES TO DOGS, CATS AND HORSES

In the medieval period, some animals, particularly those from which good financial returns could be made or which performed functions indispensable to their owners, were well cared for. Probably the only animal retrieved from a medieval Scottish excavation which can be said with any degree of conviction to have been one of the privileged minority treated as pets, was the small messan-dog found at PHSE. Others, such as the dog found in the cesspit at Mill Street, Perth, were not so fortunate. The grand total of seven dogs and three cats found in the well at Lazarus Lane in Elgin, two more cats dropped into a well at Canal Street III in Perth, five adult cats and five kittens launched into a disused garderobe chute at Dairsie Castle in Fife, and three adult dogs, a puppy and two cats interred in a pit at Meal Vennel in Perth, all seem to have met similar fates. Disposal in pits need not mean these animals were given some semblance of 'decent' burial, however; one of the dogs from the Meal Vennel pit showed evidence of skinning cuts, and it is very likely that all of the dogs and cats found there were first stripped of their pelts.

Skinning, however, was not seen as abuse, but simply as an opportunity for economic gain, in some circumstances even a necessity, in the same way as the slaughter of animals for food. It was accepted that these things were part of God's providence, or as Henryson explains in 'The preaching of the swallow': 'All creature he maid for the behufe, Of man and his supportatioun'. Even where animals were exploited by people in their leisure activities, for example in bear-baiting and dog- or cock-fighting, there was no guilt attached to the acts themselves. The only danger which was perceived came from the possibility that acts of cruelty to animals would lead inexorably to similar actions against other members of the human species. Archaeological evidence of both cock-fighting and bear-baiting is thought to have been found in medieval Scotland. At PHSE, in a 15th-century context, the bony spur of a cockerel's leg was sawn off in order that a sharper, artificial spur could be attached. At Castle Park, Dunbar, a scapula of brown bear (*Ursus arctos*) was found in a 14th- or 15th-century context, where it had no natural business, since bears are thought to have been extinct in Scotland since at least the 10th century. Only human amusement can explain this animal's presence. In addition, the pathetic condition of the dog found in a cesspit at Mill Street in Perth indicated injuries caused by dog-bites, as described above. This dog, too, may have been a trained fighting animal.

Apart from pitting animal against animal for the purposes of entertainment, there were other kinds of amusement to be had from brute beasts. One such required the services of a live cat, and persisted in the towns of Perth and Kelso until the 18th century at least. In Perth, the game coincided with the Midsummer Market held on the town's South Inch. Penny, a 19th-century historian of the town, described the scene:

> a small barrel inclosing a cat and a quantity of soot, was hung up . . . [the men] rode through, giving the barrel a stroke; and the man that broke the barrel and let out the cat (by which he received a plentiful quantity of soot about his ears)

gained the prize. The poor cat was then tossed about amongst the mob, which put an end to its future usefulness. Its remains afforded rude sport to the youths.

In Kelso, too, the sport, as recorded in 1789, also required a cat and a bag of soot. This custom seems to be a survival from earlier times and is presumably similar to one Shakespeare makes allusion to in *Much Ado About Nothing*, when Benedick says 'if I do, hang me in a bottle like a cat, and shoot at me'. Cat-torturing feasts are also known from medieval France and the Low Countries, often taking place on St John's Eve (Midsummer, as in the Perth survival) and involving the entire population of the town; in France a large pyre was erected and not one but several dozen cats in bags were placed on it. A variant of this practice involved throwing the cats from a tower. St John's Eve festivities contained many traditional elements originating from folklore rather than Christianity, despite being held in honour of the saint, and the involvement of cats may also be of some antiquity.

The evidence from medieval Scotland has shown that although animals which were treated as pets or privileged companions undoubtedly existed, these were probably in the minority. Rather, species such as dogs, cats and horses, were exploited for their hides, fur and their meat in the same way as other domesticated beasts such as cattle, sheep and pigs. Cruelty to the 'brutall beistis' was not unknown, but probably did not result in the same feelings of sentimentality, abhorrence and guilt as we experience today. Instead, as their remains show, most animals were a means to an economic end. The teachings of the Christian Church allowed human communities to exploit all of creation for their own benefit. Animals, in this scheme of thought, were created so that 'every living thing may be meat for you' (Genesis IX, 3) and according to Thomas Aquinas possessed no immortal souls. This philosophy conveniently allowed animals to be treated in a variety of ways, depending on the ends which they were bred to serve, thus justifying both cruelty and indulgence towards the same species, as circumstances required.

TABLE I: NUMBERS OF BONES AND MINIMUM NUMBERS OF DOGS, CATS AND HORSES (MNI) AT SCOTTISH URBAN SITES (12TH–16TH CENTURIES)

		DOG		CAT		HORSE	
Site	Date	n	MNI	n	MNI	n	MNI
Perth							
PHSE1	12th–14th cent	218	17	413	31	200	11
Canal Street I	14th–15th cent	27	2	1	1	19	3
Canal Street II	12th–15th cent	7	1	17	1	14	1
Canal Street III	13th–15th cent	9	1	28	3	18	1
St Ann's Lane	13th–14th cent	20	3	26	3	6	1
Kirk Close	13th–15th cent	22	2	23	2	8	3
Methven Street	Medieval	1	1				
Mill Street	12th–16th cent	47	5	4	1	35	5
Kinnoull Street	Medieval–post-medieval	2	1			1	1
Whitefriars (Carmelite Friary)	Medieval–post-medieval	4	1	2	1	7	1
80–86 High Street	12th–14th cent	8	2	131	7	4	1

		n	MNI	n	MNI	n	MNI
Scott Street	14th–15th cent	3	1	1	1	13	1
Meal Vennel	14th–15th cent	27	3	13	3	27	3
Meal Vennel	15th–16th cent	95	5	17	2	54	2
Aberdeen							
Queen Street	13th–14th cent	15	2	11	1	2	1
42 St Paul Street	12th–14th cent	11	2	28	3	23	3
45–47 Gallowgate	13th–14th cent	2	1			3	1
45–75 Gallowgate	13th–16th cent	32	3	38	2	16	3
Gallowgate Middle School	Medieval–post-medieval	4	1	3	2	9	2
Castle Street Areas A, B, C	13th/14th–15th cent	28	1	10	2	4	1
Castle Street Area H	13th/14th–15th cent	1	12	8	1	5	1
16–18 Netherkirkgate	Medieval	21	2	49	4	5	1
30–46 Upperkirkgate	12th cent and later	1	N/A	8	N/A	9	N/A
Carmelite Friary	13th/14th–15th cent	1	1	6		4	
Elgin							
High Street (HS 77)	13th–14th/15th cent	14	3	10	3	8	2
Lazarus Lane	16th cent	111	7	34	3	7	1
Lossie Wynd	15th–16th cent	4	1			6	1
Ladyhill	12th–15th cent	36	1			8	1
Inverness							
Castle Street	13th–15th cent	35	3	7	2	31	2
Inverkeithing							
5/7 Townhall Street	13th–15th cent	7	1	2	1	14	2
Dundee							
106–110 Nethergate	13th–16th cent	32	3	2	1	3	1
Stirling							
Broad Street (1978)	Medieval	41	3			10	1
Dunfermline							
Abbot House	12th/13th–15th/16th cent	92	3	94	5	35	2
St Andrews							
St Nicholas Farm	Medieval–post-medieval	24	3	3	1	34	2
120–4 Market Street	Medieval	24	1				
134 Market Street	12th–13th cent	3	1	2	1	4	1
Cinema House, North Street	12th/13th–14th cent	2	1	4	1	8	1
Ayr							
Harbour Street (6C)	13th/14th–15th cent	10	1	1	1	1	1
12–18 New Bridge Street	Medieval–post-medieval	95	2	2	1	14	1

NOTES

Only those site phases dating up to, and including, the 16th century have been included in this table. Later phases from these sites have in some cases been omitted. Where the site has been described only as medieval, this may be taken to mean the period from the 12th to the 15th centuries.

KEY

n number of bones
MNI minimum number of individuals
N/A not available

TABLE 2: SUMMARY OF DOG SHOULDER HEIGHTS

Site	Shoulder height (cm) based on:				
	Humerus	Radius	Ulna	Femur	Tibia
Perth					
PHSE: 'Messan' skeleton				234	
Bow-legged skeleton				391	
Others	31.3 – 58.7	34.4 – 60.5	32.6 – 54.6	25.4 – 57.4	24.7 – 57.2
Canal Street I: skeleton				53.7	
St Ann's Lane	48.9			48.9	48.5 – 49.1
Mill Street: skeleton				50.4	
Others				40.8	45.3 – 48.5
Meal Vennel	54.2 – 63.7				
Aberdeen					
Queen Street	31.3	31.8			35.1
42 St Paul Street				34.5	
45–75 Gallowgate				38.3 – 61.5	61.1
16–18 Netherkirkgate			51.2		
Elgin					
High Street	45.6				
		54.4			
Lazarus Lane				45.3	
Skeleton 084					
Skeleton 090				34.9	
Other		44.6			
Ladyhill	50.2 – 62.9				
Inverness					
Castle Street: bowed					
humerus and ulna	26.5		27.3		
Other	44.7	44.9 – 45.2	45.8		
Inverkeithing					
5/7 Townhall Street				43.6	
Dundee					
106–110 Nethergate:					
skeleton	313				30.0
Stirling					
Broad Street	40.6			41.1	40.0
St Andrews					
120–4 Market Street: bow-legged skeleton				29.1	

NOTE
Measurement of individual bones are available in the site archives

TABLE 3: WITHERS HEIGHTS OF HORSES

Site	Bone	Lateral length (mm)	Shoulder height (cm)	Hands height
Perth				
Whitefriars	Metacarpal	207	132.7	13
Meal Vennel, Phases 1–5	Radius	333	144.2	14:1
	Metatarsal	247	131.65	13
Meal Vennel, Phases 6–7	Tibia	296	129.1	12:3
80–86 High Street	Metatarsal	253	134.85	13:1
	Metatarsal (ice skate)	Est	133.25	13:1
Aberdeen				
45–75 Gallowgate	Tibia	314	126.9	13:2
	Metatarsal	244	130.05	12:3
Stirling				
Broad Street	Radius	282	122.1	12
	Metacarpal	191	122.4	12
Dunfermline				
Abbot's House	Metacarpal	228	146.1	14:2

NOTE
A pony is a horse of under 14:2 hands (58 in or 147.32 cm)

The Nobility

Extracted from A Grant 1991, *Independence and Nationhood: Scotland 1306–1469*, London (Edward Arnold 1984; reprinted by Edinburgh University Press), 120–143.

I

Medieval society's other special group was of course the nobility. That, however, is a surprisingly elusive concept, and despite the obvious prominence of 'the nobles' in Scottish history, the late-medieval Scottish nobility is much harder to define than the churchmen. The first thing to stress is that our modern British concept, equating nobles with parliamentary peerage, does not apply. There was no Scottish peerage until the mid fifteenth century, and even after then the Scottish nobility clearly contained many individuals who were not peers of parliament. The Scottish concept of nobility, therefore, was probably akin to the Continental one, which included those who in England would be called gentry and in Scotland lairds.

What was the Scottish dividing-line between nobles and non-nobles? Contemporaries probably thought in terms of noble birth – as in the anti-English joke related by Bower (see chap 2: viii) – and the right to bear coats-of-arms, but in practice these ideas were too vague to be helpful in defining the nobility. Nor is the distinctive feature of Continental nobility, exemption from war taxation (because nobles were expected to fight personally) applicable here, for war taxation never developed in Scotland. Indeed the only clear-cut division between ordinary people and their social betters is the tenurial one between the mass of the peasantry who rented land from year to year, and the freeholders, who had security of tenure and generally held their land in perpetuity. Now since, in this context, free means privileged or honourable, and since all obvious nobles were freeholders, there is at least a case for equating the late-medieval Scottish nobility with the freeholders, at least at its widest. This issue requires further research, but certainly no better cut-off point is evident higher up the Scottish social scale.

The difficulty of definition is itself significant. The absence of such a clear division within the landowning class as in England (where the parliamentary peerage developed earlier and took over the concept of nobility) probably helped inhibit the growth among the lairds of the strong, even aggressive, self-consciousness visible among the English gentry, both nationally in the House of Commons and locally in the shire communities. Scots lairds could be just as assertive individually as English gentlemen, but did not exhibit the same collective sense of identity. Similarly because there was not the same division between nobles and non-nobles as in France (where tax-exemption privileges meant entrance to the nobility became more strictly regulated), Scottish nobles' sense of social supremacy was less institutionalized – especially the idea of their status as the exclusive military elite, an important cause of social tension in France. Although late-medieval Scottish society was not totally fluid, class-consciousness was probably relatively slight, while upward social mobility, depending on the acquisition of freeholdings and open to anyone with sufficient wealth, would have been fairly straightforward. The only real social barriers seem to have been economic ones.

Even with this extremely wide definition, the Scottish nobility was still only a small proportion of the population. Countless surviving charters give the impression that most of Scotland's thousand or so parishes contained at least one and often several families of freeholders. Therefore we can probably think in terms of around 2,000 heads of families, or some 10,000 nobles: probably little more than 1 per cent of the pre-plague population. This very rough estimate corresponds with figures for early-fourteenth-century France, where the nobility appears to have been between 1 and 1 ½ per cent of the population. It also fits well with the fact that in August 1296 Edward I's officials recorded homages from some 1,500 Scottish landowners. Their list is not exhaustive – its most famous omission is William Wallace – but it probably gives a reasonable idea of the Scottish 'upper class' at that time. Thereafter the Scottish nobility presumably shrank and grew again following the general demographic trends; but unfortunately there is no data for estimating its size satisfactorily until the later sixteenth century.

Of this noble body, the vast majority were insignificant as individuals. The laymen who mattered in national affairs – the magnates or higher nobility – usually numbered around 50: for instance 48 are named in the Declaration of Arbroath,[1] 56 are listed as doing personal homage at Robert II's coronation in 1371, and 44 belonged to the peerage at the end of James II's reign. Beyond these, it is likely that there were only a few hundred substantial lairds with any great local importance. The rest of the Scottish nobility would simply have consisted of petty country gentry – 'bonnet lairds' is an apt later term – who often had no more land than wealthy peasants. These were the poorer gentlemen who just had to be armed 'at thare gudly power', according to 1426 legislation. Little wonder that well-off husbandmen probably had more in common with these small lairds than with cottars and rural labourers. Collectively, however, the small lairds, like the husbandmen, made a great contribution to the cause of Scottish independence – as the long English lists of forfeited freeholdings demonstrate. And despite their individual insignificance, they also provided the core of the followings essential to magnate power. The great nobles, on whom so much Scottish history focuses, could never have had the importance they had without the lesser nobility behind them.

II

At the top of noble society, one striking feature was the survival into the late Middle Ages of the earldoms and 'provincial lordships' of earlier medieval Scotland. There were 29 of these in Robert I's reign, ranging from Caithness in the north to Annandale in the south, and from Mar in the east to the Isles in the west; 14 carried the special status of earldom. In the late 1320s they belonged to 13 earls and five 'provincial lords' (the greatest magnates, Thomas Randolph, James Douglas and Robert Stewart each had several, while three were in crown hands). They all covered huge stretches of territory, containing hundreds of square miles and (as their names indicate) corresponding to provinces of the country; within them their earls and lords virtually acted as provincial rulers. Generally they dated back to the eleventh and twelfth centuries, and in some cases beyond, but perhaps the most typical was the earldom of Moray, created in 1312 for Thomas Randolph out of the shires of Moray, Nairn and Inverness, and held with full vice-regal powers. That creation, and the fact that nearly every earldom and lordship that came into the king's possession was granted out again, demonstrate that the continuation (and perhaps reinvigoration) of this centuries-old territorial pattern was the deliberate, conservative policy of Robert I – himself formerly earl of Carrick, lord of Annandale and part of Garioch.

The pattern of earldoms and lordships lasted throughout the fourteenth century, although there was considerable turnover in ownership. Well before 1400, however, the beginnings of change can be seen. In an increasing number of earldoms the association between the provinces and the lands actually held or supervised by the earl was dissolving. An act of 1401 institutionalized this by stating that whenever earldoms or lordships came into crown hands, any baronies within them must in future be held directly of the crown. And when two new earldoms were created – Douglas for William lord of Douglas in 1348 and Crawford for David Lindsay of Glenesk in 1398 – each was merely a personal promotion in rank, with no 'provincial' connotations (except that Douglas possessed several 'provincial lordships'). The same is true of the dukedoms of Rothesay and Albany, also created in 1398 for Robert III's son and brother. Honorific dignities – as the rank of earl had been in England for centuries – had appeared in Scotland.

There was also a trend towards the accumulation of territory. The Stewart possessions grew most, especially after Robert II became king. In the 1390s 12 earldoms and lordships were held by members of the royal family. This build-up of territory was unequalled, but the Douglases and Dunbars were also following suit. The result was the concentration of earldoms and lordships in the hands of fewer magnate families: 31 were now shared among 15 magnates from 10 different families – with the Stewarts, Douglases and Dunbars having 22 of them. Moreover, only three provincial lordships were held independently of earldoms.

Fifty years later the top of noble society appears radically different. The families which had accumulated most fell foul of either James I or James II, and their lands were forfeited. Several other earldoms and lordships reverted to the crown through natural causes. In a reversal of fourteenth-century royal policy, James I and James II mostly kept possession of territory which came into the crown's hands (doubtless for fiscal reasons, following the fall in customs revenues). So by 1455 – after the great Douglas forfeiture – the crown held no fewer than nine of the old 'provincial' earldoms and eight of the lordships.

Thereafter, although James II granted some out again, especially to his young sons, the former pattern was never recreated. In the 1460s there were only five 'provincial' earls or lords of the old type: the earl of Angus (who had part of Angus plus Liddesdale and Jedburgh lordships), the lord of the Isles (also earl of Ross), the earl of Sutherland, the earl of Atholl (James II's half-brother, given the earldom in *c* 1452), and the earl of Huntly (who although a new – 1445 – honorific creation, had the lordships of Strathbogie and Badenoch). Moreover five new personal earldoms had been created by James II: Errol for Lord Hay, Morton for Lord Douglas of Dalkeith, Rothes for Lord Leslie, Argyll for Lord Campbell, and Marischal for Lord Keith. All, like Crawford, were honorific dignities – especially Marischal, where the title derived from an office. The top of late-medieval Scottish society had been completely restructured.

III

The dukes, earls and 'provincial lords' were not the only nobles prominent in Scotland's national affairs. Throughout the period, some 20 or 30 others were also always important enough to count within the higher nobility. When the Scottish peerage emerged in the 1440s, these were the lords of parliament – the peerage's bottom rank. Like English parliamentary barons, whom they copied, lords of parliament had special titles (William Lord Hay rather than William Hay lord of Errol) and the right to personal summonses to parliament. Thereafter the Scottish higher nobility is an institutionalized, easily identifiable group: the 'lords' as opposed to the 'lairds'.

Earlier, however, it is much harder to identify this part of the higher nobility. The problem arises over the term 'baron'. In the earlier Middle Ages it meant an important lord, and 'the baronage' could be equated with the higher nobility – as remained so in England. But in Scotland 'baron' evolved differently. In the twelfth and thirteenth centuries, important lords possessed many 'multiple estates' – the basic units of Scottish landlordship above the individual toun, roughly equivalent to parishes – and these apparently came to be called baronies. Moreover barons had special powers; being important lords, close to the king, they were trusted to have criminals caught and dealt with on their estates. This jurisdiction, over theft, assault, and accidental homicide, became known as 'baronial jurisdiction', and probably spread to most baronies. Robert I developed the concept further, restricting baronial jurisdiction to estates which the crown permitted to be held 'in free (privileged) barony'. That reduced the number of baronies, but there were over 200 at the end of his reign, and subsequent grants of baronial privileges – a useful form of crown patronage, giving status and a significant boost to seigniorial revenues – increased their number to over 350 in the later fourteenth century and over 1,000 (more fragmented ones) in the sixteenth. These baronies were shared among many nobles – more than 100 in the fourteenth century – who, since they held free baronies with baronial powers, were known as barons.

By the fourteenth century, therefore, baron was a tenurial, not a personal, concept, extending far beyond the higher nobility. Most barons were local lairds. Some, however, who possessed several baronies or were prominent in other ways, were important nationally and must be counted within the higher nobility. But there is no obvious dividing-line between these – whom we can call 'greater barons' – and the rest. As with the nobility as a whole, this in itself is significant. Ambitious nobles could easily enter at least the 'second division' of the higher nobility – as John Lyon (ancestor of Queen Elizabeth the queen-mother) did spectacularly, rising from king's clerk in the late 1360s to be chamberlain of Scotland, lord of five baronies, and husband of one of Robert II's daughters, before being murdered, perhaps by a jealous rival, in 1382. Conversely, once-prominent families could sink out of the second division – as happened with the descendants of Robert Lauder of the Bass or William Dishington of Ardross, close councillors of Robert I and David II respectively.

Compared with the earls and 'provincial lords', the territory held by 'greater barons' was not impressive; John Lyon probably had more than most. The Setons and Hays (both prominent throughout the period) appear more typical. The Setons' ancestral lands were the baronies of Seton in East and Winchburgh in West Lothian. Robert I granted Alexander Seton (whose career is outlined in chapter 1:ix) several territories, including Tranent, Elphinstone and 'the Barns' beside Haddington as baronies; but Seton, Tranent and Elphinstone were all in Seton parish, and at most his lands seem the equivalent of two or three parishes. His descendants made no more substantial acquisitions during the late Middle Ages. The chief estates of Gilbert Hay, Robert I's constable, were his ancestral barony of Errol in Perthshire, and the Aberdeenshire barony of Slains, granted by Robert I; Errol probably covered two parishes, Slains one. His descendants added the barony of Caputh, near Dunkeld, and in 1415 brought the former thanage of Cowie in Kincardineshire; even so, these four baronies were not a huge estate.

The only 'greater barons' to acquire significantly more were David Lindsay of Glenesk and James Douglas of Dalkeith, who in the later fourteenth century amassed complexes of a dozen or so baronies through inheritances and personal acquisition; these, though scattered over the country, probably did approach the earldoms in area, and Lindsay became earl of Crawford in 1398. But they were exceptional. In the early fourteenth century many of those who can reasonably be counted as 'greater barons' only had one or two baronies. At the end of the century, three or four baronies seem the norm, although some important men had less. This remains much the same in the mid fifteenth century, when the 'greater barons' became lords of parliament: James Hamilton's main estates, erected into the 'lord-ship of parliament of Hamilton' in 1445, consisted of the baronies of Cadzow and Machan in Lanarkshire and Kinneil in West Lothian.

Lord Hamilton's three baronies had been granted to his fore-father Walter, son of Gilbert (who had changed sides advantageously after Bannockburn), by Robert I. That is typical of the 20 or so early lords of parliament. Most headed long-established families, like Douglas of Dalkeith, Lyon, and Erskine, whose prominence went back to the mid fourteenth century; at least a dozen were descendants of leading barons in Robert I's reign; and five – Lords Hay, Keith, Graham, Seton, and Somerville – were from families important even in the twelfth century.

Why, then, did the new rank emerge? In the highly status-conscious fifteenth century, barons who were the greatest nobles below the dukes and earls, who were accustomed to having a voice in parliaments, and who doubtless equated themselves with the English parliamentary barons, presumably wanted some means of distinguishing themselves from the lesser landowners who were barons too. The English usage of baron was unsuitable, so the term lord of parliament was employed instead. The pressure went back to the 1410s, when peerage-type titles occur, but intensified after 1427, because by then the disappearance of so many earls had left both a political and a social vacuum. In the 1440s the greater barons included all but a handful of the most important nobles. Hardly surprisingly, their virtual takeover of the higher nobility was followed by the establishment of the new rank.

Thus the new lords of parliament did not so much rise into the peerage as remain within the higher nobility while those above them disappeared. They were not a new nobility. But these developments made the top of Scottish noble society look very different. Compared with the old earls and provincial lords, most mid-fifteenth-century magnates were not such great landowners. And when James II promoted some lords of parliament to the rank of earl without giving them much extra land, the higher nobility's transformation was complete. Thenceforward it was a relatively homogeneous body, containing few really large landowners. The earls were no longer significantly different from the others; in early-modern Scotland, indeed, there were several with less power and influence than neighbouring lords of parliament.

IV

Late-medieval noble estates were normally heritable. With luck, they would pass to their owners' sons; but sons can never be guaranteed. Among the late-medieval French and English nobilities father–son succession was remarkably precarious, with noble families dying out in the direct male line on average once every three or four generations, and few surviving much beyond a century. Failing sons the estate might go to daughters – generally being partitioned when a father left two or more – and thence to their husbands, usually themselves landowners. Or if the increasingly common entails to male heirs applied, brother, cousins or more distant collaterals would inherit; again they would often be landowners already. Sometimes, when there were no heirs, estates reverted to the overlord or the crown. Over several generations, therefore, family territory was likely to be either dispersed, or (if it survived) to be enlarged by inheritance through entails or through marriages to heiresses. This is obviously important for the history of noble societies; inheritance patterns, indeed, were as influential as royal policies.

The most spectacular Scottish example of the process is the complicated build-up of the vast Douglas territories. The duke of Albany's earldoms of Fife and Menteith also came from heiresses; and both entails and heiresses helped produce the estates of the Lindsays, earls of Crawford. Among the earls as a whole, the French and English pattern of extinction is repeated almost exactly. In 1300 there were 13 families of earls; 43 more appeared between then and 1469;[2] but in 1469 there were only 19, mostly James II's creations. In this period, every 25-year generation except one saw at least a quarter of the families fail in the direct male line; the failure rate was as high as 47 per cent in 1350–74.

The difficulty of definition makes the other magnates harder to analyse. But for the 1320s, the names in the Declaration of Arbroath plus those of other obviously important nobles give a list of 42 families; by 1350 14 had died out in the direct male line. And for the 1350s and 1360s 47 important families (those surviving from the 1320s, their successors, and others which were prominent then) can be examined: 13 had died out by 1400. Although more detailed study is needed, in the fourteenth century the rest of the Scottish higher nobility apparently conforms to the general pattern too.

Conversely, 16 – over a third – of the important baronial families of the 1320s survived beyond 1469 in direct father–son succession. Such survival is much less common elsewhere. And even more remarkably, out of the leading 40 baronial families of early-fifteenth-century Scotland (those which had peerages by 1450, plus others which were prominent earlier in the century), no fewer than 28 survived the entire fifteenth century in the direct male line, while 18 survived past 1600. That completely contradicts the experience of the English and French late-medieval nobilities.

One reason might be that the chances of untimely death were smaller for Scotland's fifteenth-century nobles. There was little civil war after 1340, and the wars with England slackened off, whereas in England and France civil and inter-national war intensified; plague perhaps receded more quickly in Scotland too. The longer a noble lived, the more sons he could beget (though his wife's age obviously mattered too). Certainly longevity is another marked feature of the late-medieval Scottish nobility. The earls (for whom there is most evidence) lived on average to around 50; many nobles passed 70, and over a dozen reached 80 – including three successive earls of March. Also, since Scotland was less urbanized, nobles would have spent little time in the unhealthy conditions of large towns. Yet why did the barons' demographic pattern differ so much from the earls'? It is not simply a question of the latter's political vulnerability; for instance Duncan earl of Lennox was over 80 when he was executed in 1425, but only left two daughters. The explanation for the striking demographic resilience of the greater barons' families remains unclear; but it is an extremely important aspect of late-medieval Scottish noble society.

It meant that, despite the nobility's general fluidity, there was an increasingly large core of families who were continuously prominent. These, of course, have been encountered several times already: the Lindsays, Hays, Keiths, Setons, Hamiltons, Erskines, and so on. They were a major part of the 'Bruce establishment' of the 1320s, they made up the bulk of the greater barons of the fourteenth and early fifteenth centuries, they dominated the new peerage, and for hundreds of years after the 1450s their names reverberated through Scotland's history.

These remarkably durable families, moreover, produced not only heirs but a multiplicity of sons. Many greater barons of the later part of the period had several each, and many of their younger sons established lasting families of their own. But that is not true of the entire period. It seems that in the mid fourteenth century the greater barons were not, collectively, producing enough sons to replace themselves; only in the 1380s did male replacement rates apparently become positive. That suggests that the numerous cadet branches of the leading families of late-fifteenth-century Scotland were a relatively new phenomenon; certainly it is difficult to find anything similar in earlier centuries. This doubtless helps to explain the prominent of magnates' surname or kinship groups in the later fifteenth century.

The important families also had daughters. But because so many sons were produced, heiresses – very important in other medieval societies – are rare at this level of the Scottish nobility, especially in the fifteenth century. And since the greater barons generally inter-married, they rarely married heiresses; among the top 40 baronial families of the early fifteenth century, there are only six instances of marriages to significant heiresses during the entire century. Similarly, although most Scottish magnate families established entails to male heirs, these seldom needed to come into operation. Therefore among the greater barons, particularly after about 1400, accumulation and dispersal of territory were much less striking than among their English counterparts, or indeed among their Scottish predecessors. Also there was less occasion for property disputes (frequent in England) arising out of such indirect inheritances. These can be found – for instance over the Douglas inheritance in 1388, or in 1369 when James Douglas of Dalkeith and Thomas Erskine fought a judicial duel – but they seem at least relatively uncommon in late-medieval Scotland.

V

What happened to noble finances in late-medieval Scotland? This question is particularly hard to answer, since the available sources are scantier than for other aspects of noble society. Scottish medieval landlords did not preserve old estate records, perhaps because of the system of short, variable leases. In general, however, we have already seen that late-medieval trends were unfavourable to landlords; the most striking evidence is the near halving of national land valuations in 1366. Thereafter, although rents and valuations rose, they probably lagged behind inflation, especially in the fifteenth century. The brief boom in wool and leather exports would only have given temporary compensation from landlords' flocks and herds. Only in seigniorial dues, particularly those involved in baronies, may there have been growth: the amount of land held in free barony expanded steadily during the period, and also several magnates received grants of regality, giving them jurisdiction over major crimes, and thus the fines and forfeitures from the criminals.

It has however been demonstrated for England that similar financial pressures were countered in various ways: through accumulating larger estates, as more territory came into fewer hands through obtaining a share of royal revenues in annuities or other forms of patronage; and through war profits, in wages, ransoms, booty, and conquered lands. All these points applied in Scotland, but to a lesser extent. First, the Scottish inheritance patterns meant that large-scale accumulations of territory were less common, especially in the fifteenth century. Secondly, the Scottish crown could not provide great subsidies. Annuities were granted, particularly by Robert II and Robert III, but the peak of £1,300 paid to the nobility in the early 1400s hardly compares with the £30,000 then being paid by Henry IV of England. Little more than a quarter of the higher nobility enjoyed annuities; these varied from £13 to £340 (a brief, exceptional case), but generally were around £40–£50 – useful, but not huge, amounts. And many annuities were cancelled in the fifteenth century. The only other significant diversion of royal revenue was in the 1410s, when the earl of Douglas and his followers took large sums from the customs. Thirdly, Scots nobles had no opportunities for embezzlement, because Scots armies were unpaid; they suffered as much as gained from cross-border raiding; the balance of ransoms probably went against them; and there was no territory to be conquered.

The late-medieval economic contraction ought therefore to have affected Scottish nobles relatively badly. This is supported by evidence that they did not have large amounts of cash at their disposal; big payments were made by instalments, and occasionally magnates had to sell land to meet demands such as their reliefs (death, or inheritance, duties). On the other hand, only one or two magnates ever sold out altogether; sales of land were invariably to other magnates; and contemporary mortgages show greater nobles lending money to lesser ones. At the top of noble society examples of impoverishment are balanced by examples of wealth.

Moreover between about 1380 and 1500 – just the period of apparent financial pressure – there was a building boom. Almost every family of any importance had money to spend on their residences. Mostly they built tower-houses. These generally appear stark, even primitive, nowadays, and are sometimes taken to indicate their builders' poverty. But the starkest is probably Threave in Galloway, built by Archibald 'the Grim', third earl of Douglas; since he was rich enough to build what he liked, Threave's style was obviously not dictated by cost. The same is also true of the tower-houses constructed by David II at Edinburgh and Robert II at Dundonald in Ayrshire. The style was perhaps influenced by the realization that large curtain-wall castles were undesirable during Anglo-Scottish wars; they tended to be taken over by English forces, and were usually slighted on their recapture. Tower-houses were also relatively comfortable – certainly warmer, for the lord's apartments were above the main hall and fireplace. And most were splendid when inhabited, as those which have survived in something close to their original states, like Neidpath near Peebles or the highly sophisticated Borthwick near Dalkeith, demonstrate. No figures are available for the cost of noble tower-houses, but 'David's Tower' at Edinburgh castle cost £758 between 1367 and 1383 – under £50 a year – which was probably reasonably typical, and also quite within the means of many nobles.

What the nobility wanted from castles was prestige, comfort, and somewhere 'for the safe-keeping of his people and his goods', as William Keith the marischal stated in 1394 when building Dunnottar, near Stonehaven: functions the tower-houses fulfilled well. The possessions kept in them certainly needed safe-keeping. The will of James Douglas of Dalkeith, dated 1392, shows what a leading noble would have had. The bequests included: four sets of armour (the rest were to stay in the new Dalkeith castle), three jewelled gold clasps, two gold circlets, a gold collar, four gilt belts, several brooches and other jewels, eight rings, a cross made from the True Cross, a gilt reliquary containing St Mary Magdalene's hair, many silver and gilt utensils, including his best gilt cup weighing 18lb troy, a large quantity of cloth-of-gold, silk and fur clothing, and his books of the statutes of Scotland, romances, grammar and logic. The total was worth £1,559. Whatever the economic trends, James Douglas clearly lived in considerable splendour.

James Douglas of Dalkeith is also one of two magnates for whom financial details have survived: the value of the 1376–7 rental, which covered roughly half his estates, was £483, suggesting a total income from rents of over £900. David earl of Strathearn, Robert II's fourth son, is the other: in 1380 Strathearn's rents came to £273. It also appears that the earldom of Mar and lordship of Garioch were together worth between £1,000 and £1,300. To put the figures in perspective, an earl's minimum yearly income in fourteenth-century England was reckoned at 1,000 marks, or £667, sterling. While the Strathearn rents were much less (though Earl David had other income), the revenues of the lord of Dalkeith and the earl of Mar were both above that minimum.

There is one other set of figures, for James I's hostages. The 1423–4 negotiations give incomes for 35 nobles: six earls, 14 from families which had peerages by 1450, and 15 others. The earls' incomes average around 850 marks, the future peers' 770, and the others' 400. Unfortunately, some assessments are much less plausible than others. Moreover, are they in sterling (they come from English documents, and the ransom was in sterling) or Scots money, worth only half sterling? Either currency causes problems. And do they denote rents, Scottish 'extents' or valuations, or total incomes? If they are taken at face-value and assumed to be in sterling, they correspond quite well with the 1436 income-tax returns for 51 English peers, which average £768: the Scottish magnates have about a third less, which seems reasonable. But whether that is a safe conclusion remains unclear.

Since, however, the assessments for Douglas of Dalkeith and Strathearn are 1,500 marks and 500 marks, both close to those from the 1376–80 rentals, perhaps the 1423–4 figures give a rough guide to incomes in the later fourteenth century, before currency debasement complicated matters. At that period £10 a year appears a comfortable income for ordinary people: so we can probably multiply the figures by 1,000 or more to gain some idea of modern terms, over £500,000 (tax-free) a year, while the greatest men like the Albanies and Douglases (not assessed in 1423–4) had many times more. The exercise is crude, but it helps demonstrate how very well off the Scottish magnates were compared with the rest of the population. And they continued to enjoy great wealth, irrespective of the economic trends, throughout the late Middle Ages.

VI

Whatever happened to incomes, one point remains constant: noble estates were generally held from landlords 'in feu and heredity and in perpetuity', for honourable obligations. This kind of landowner-ship is nowadays described as 'feudal'. The king was the ultimate landlord. Those holding directly of him were 'tenants-in-chief'; their estates were divided into parts providing them with steady revenue (peasant holdings and demesnes) and parts held of them by other landowners as feudal sub-tenants. The latter's land might be similarly divided, and so on. Feudal tenants, in return, had to be faithful to their lord, give him good counsel, and warn him of dangers. In addition they owed either personal service, mostly military, or a sum of money (sometimes substantial, sometimes nominal: called 'feu-farm' and 'blench-farm') in lieu. Feudal tenure was thus not merely a system of landownership, but involved reciprocal relationships between lords and followers within the nobility. It helped provide local government, too: feudal landowners were entitled to hold courts for settling disputes between inhabitants of their lands, while the barons (almost always tenants-in-chief) had baronial powers of criminal jurisdiction and sometimes the vice-regal powers of regality.

Feudalism – as this form of social organization is usually called – was never a static system. It was merely one stage in a process of social evolution beginning long before and ending long after the 'classic' feudal period of the eleventh and twelfth centuries. The evolution differed greatly from country to country, depending on particular circumstances. For instance the administrative–jurisdictional side of feudal society survived much longer in Scotland – where baronies and regalities flourished – than in England. That is partly because Scottish kings and adminis-trators (mostly barons themselves) did not feel threatened by seigniorial jurisdiction, and so did not try to undermine it. But the main reason is probably medieval Scotland's relatively neat territorial pattern. Since most disputes were between neighbours and most crime was local, the common, if rough, equation of local community with parish and with barony meant that barony courts were able to deal with the majority of cases. The point applies particularly strongly to the provincial earldoms and lordships. In England, where the territorial pattern was infinitely more fragmented, seigniorial jurisdiction could not operate so well, and gradually withered away.

The tenurial side of feudal society also evolved differently in Scotland. There was no equivalent to the English statute of *Quia Emptores* ('Whereas buyers . . .') of 1290, which severely restricted the creation of feudal subtenancies. By then English land grants were generally commercial transactions, maintaining the feudal form chiefly to give the vendor the right to the 'incidents' of feudal tenure like relief (inheritance duty) and wardship (when the lord took over the holding during the minority of an under-age heir). But when a tenant sold most of a holding, the overlord often could not assert *his* rights. Therefore after 1290 the purchaser of land had to replace the vendor as the overlord's tenant. Although to the magnates' economic advantage, that stopped them making typical feudal grants for service. In late-medieval Scotland, in contrast, the magnates had the best of both worlds. Scottish overlords were always entitled to vet their tenants' grants, and in the late Middle Ages they mostly insisted on the purchaser replacing the vendor. Yet they themselves continued to grant land in straightforward feudal tenure. Feudal sub-tenancies thus continued, but normally only at one level below the tenant-in-chief; this again may be linked to the survival of the fairly neat early-medieval territorial pattern.

Few late-medieval Scottish land grants, however, were specifically for knight-service and incidents; the majority merely stipulate 'service used and wont', which may or may not indicate knight-service. And many were for money renders, either feu-farm (common since the twelfth century) or more usually its variant blench-farm, in which a penny or a token (such as a pair of spurs) was rendered to denote superiority, while the knight-service and incidents were waived. Monetary feudal tenure eventually replaced tenure by military service altogether in Scotland, and proved so convenient that it remained until recently the standard way of holding land: subject-superiors and feu duties (modern equivalents of tenants-in-chief and feu-farms) were only abolished in 1976. Until then, strictly speaking, Scotland was a feudal country! Modern Scottish 'feudalism', of course, was merely a legal fiction within which a purely commercial conveyancing system operated. And that was largely true of the late Middle Ages too: most property transactions were probably sales, especially grants in blench-farm. In that respect Scotland was like England, although their conveyancing practices developed differently.

On the other hand, straightforward grants of land in return for service were still being made. Moreover several blench-farm grants were made to men described as the donor's knight or esquire; the specific knight-service and incidents were being waived, presumably as a favour, but the basic, imprecise obligations of general fidelity, service and counsel were still expected. One of the most 'feudal' grants of all in Scottish history was made in the late 1380s, when the second earl of Douglas gave his illegitimate son Drumlanrig, in feu and heredity and 'in blench-farm [*sic*], . . . by performing the service of one knight in [the earl's] army in place of all other obligations'. The fiscal part of feudal tenure is set aside; Douglas simply wanted personal service. This remarkable charter shows the flexibility of late-medieval Scottish tenurial practice – and also the difficulty of generalizing about it.

VII

Feudal tenure probably explains why earls' incomes seem little higher than greater barons'. In Strathearn, for instance, the five Highland parishes west of Crieff produced as much rent as the 12 easterly, more Lowland ones; but the latter supported at least 15 feudal tenancies and land held by Dunblane cathedral and Inchaffray abbey. The other provincial earldoms and lordships had similar patterns. This originated in Scotland's early feudal period, when power and prestige were measured more through knightly followers than wealth. Nobles had always kept sufficient land to finance their splendid life-styles, but had used the surplus to endow their followings. Earls and provincial lords had naturally been able to create most sub-tenancies, either from scratch or by converting pre-feudal arrangements. That reduced their revenues to much the same level as the more important barons', but their regional power would not have been significantly affected, for feudal tenants had always had to acknowledge their overlords' superiority and jurisdiction. And while in the fourteenth century not all the landowners in earldoms and lordships counted as the straightforward followers of the earls and lords (two of the Strathearn tenants were the earl of Douglas and James Douglas of Dalkeith), that probably would still apply to the local lairds whose main estates lay within those earldoms or lordships.

The relationship, however, was not simply feudal. Past endowment of younger sons meant that earls and provincial lords often had kinship ties with local lairds. Intermarriage among local lairds often led to the construction of large kinship groups focussed on the earls and lords. These may have been reinforced by concepts stemming from pre-feudal, kin-based, Gaelic society: the office of earl derives from Gaelic provincial governors and ultimately from tribal leaders. That is seen in the 'law of Clan MacDuff', by which the kindred of 'Macduff' (the family of the original earls of Fife) could claim that only the earl of Fife had jurisdiction over them; it still operated even when Fife belonged to the Stewarts. Another consequence of the earls' pre-feudal origins was the 'army of the earldom'; until the late fourteenth century the earl was the automatic military leader of all the earldom's inhabitants. Also, in the twelfth century, earldom courts seem to have been held in gatherings of the armies presided over by the earls; these later presumably developed into the earls' barony and regality courts, through which the earldoms were formally run. There were of course similar barony or regality courts in the provincial lordships.

None of the ties of lordship, kinship and jurisdiction was necessarily very cohesive. The complexity of inheritance patterns and the land market often weakened purely feudal relationships. Kinship ties which included cognatic relationships through females (as in fourteenth-century Scotland) could easily become over-extended and diffuse. And the mere possession of a seignorial court did not guarantee effective jurisdiction. But in medieval Scotland the simple yet extremely potent geographical connections between the earls and lords, the earldoms and lordships, and the local land-owning communities pulled the various ties together. The forces of lordship, kinship and jurisdiction became complementary, directing the general loyalty of the local communities towards the earls and provincial lords, and making these extremely powerful.

Their power, moreover, probably extended beyond the bounds of their earldoms and lordships. Although those did not cover medieval Scotland entirely – there were many gaps between them, containing lands held by barons and lesser tenants-in-chief – nevertheless in the fourteenth century they lay at the centre of all the major regions, except the Edinburgh–Stirling–Perth triangle where the crown was the regional lord. Within most regions an earl or lord would naturally be the leading magnate, easily able to outface other regional tenants-in-chief. Earls and lords can thus be seen as maintaining clear-cut spheres of influence, based on the earldoms and lordships but stretching beyond them. Admittedly the situation was never quite so neat in practice. Nevertheless it does appear that the provincial earldoms and lordships gave medieval Scotland extremely regionalized power-structures – much more so than in England – which, after their reconstruction by Robert I, survived at least until the end of the fourteenth century.

VIII

The mechanisms of lord–man relations within Scottish noble society were never static. The classic feudal tie was bound to evolve, because (except in the special circumstances of the provincial earldoms and lordships) it would not satisfy the inherently contradictory forces of hereditary landownership and personal service. We have seen part of the Scottish evolution in the fourteenth-century tendency for land to be granted simply for general, unspecified service, with the fiscal elements of feudal tenure being waived. These grants, although feudal, emphasize general, personal service. At the same time there are many instances of lords giving their followers money, usually annuities, instead of lands in return for service; such grants were attractive when rents were stagnating (at least until inflation started), but were easily withheld if the service was unsatisfactory. The follower might be appointed to an office, such as steward of part of the lord's estates, and given a fee. Sometimes, too, grants of land or money were accompanied by bonds of retinue recording the reciprocal obligations of lord and man. Although few survive, these were probably quite common in the later fourteenth century; in 1399 it was enacted that everyone had to obey the king's lieutenant, 'nocht agaynstandande ony condiciounis of retenewis'. They are like the indentures of retinue, the standard institution of lord–man relationships in late-medieval England. But in Scotland – where there was no restriction on granting land, and where ready cash was probably comparatively scarce – money grants never really replaced land grants; the earls of Douglas, for example, generally gave their followers land. Similarly bonds of retinue never completely replaced formal charters. For most of the late Middle Ages there was absolutely no standardization to Scottish lord–man relationships.

Then in the mid fifteenth century the institution of the 'bond of manrent' appeared. This was a written, witnessed contract given by the follower to the lord, in which he promised to accompany his lord when required, support him in all actions and disputes, give counsel and warning of danger, and help protect him from harm – all on the understanding (though a reverse contract was not automatically given) that the lord would maintain the follower's interests. The earliest known example dates from 1442, and thereafter bonds of manrent became common. Etymologically 'manrent' means the same as 'homage', and the reciprocal lord–man obligations are the same as the primary ones of the feudal relationship. But bonds of manrent concentrate on intangible human ties; it is unusual for them to be accompanied by grants of land or money. Thus they are the final Scottish stage of the general trend dissolving the 'classic' feudal connection between personal service and land tenure.

The other main tie, kinship, also changed significantly in late-medieval Scotland. Kinship ties, in which a magnate's family was expected to show special loyalty to him, were commonplace in medieval Europe. They are similar to lordship ties – indeed lordship is nowadays seen as a kinship substitute, with the symbolism of even the typically feudal act of homage being interpreted as creating an artificial father–son relationship. In practice the two kinds of tie were often combined, as when the fourth earl of Douglas granted Herbert Maxwell of Caerlaverock 40 marks a year in 1407, and obliged himself 'to suppowelle and defende the forsayde Syr Harbarte in all his ryghtwys cause, als we awe to do to our man and our kosyn'. But – as in this example – for much of the Middle Ages the concept of kinship in Scotland as elsewhere was mostly cognatic, including relationships through females. That produced very large kinship groups, with several potential heads – resulting in inherently weak ties (unless the special geographical conditions of the Scottish earldoms and lordships applied). And this was probably exacerbated in late-medieval Scotland by the fact that magnates married each other's daughters or the kings' daughters (between them Robert II and Robert III had 11 daughters, who had 16 husbands), and so were all interrelated. In those circumstances cognatic kinship was hardly an effective form of social organization.

By the later fifteenth century, however, typical Scottish kinship ties were no longer cognatic. They were male – agnatic – relationships, which linked all who had the same surname to the head of the family, producing a much more effective kinship group. The change is one reason why kinship remained a major force in Scottish noble society much longer than in other countries. Since agnatic kinship was predominant in Celtic societies, this was perhaps a legacy from Scotland's Gaelic past. But that cannot fully explain its re-emergence during the fifteenth century. There is probably a connection with the establishment in this period of the male entail, by which magnates stipulated that their estates should go to sons, brothers and other male heirs in preference to heiresses. This demonstrates growing aware-ness of agnatic relationships – and once entails had existed for a few generations they in effect created agnatic kinship groups linked by the prospect (however remote) of inheriting the family estates. Yet male entails were common elsewhere. In Scotland, however, the consciousness of male relationships shown in entails must have been accentuated by the fact that the main families creating them were also those which were so abnormally successful at producing sons and durable cadet branches. They were the families who dominated Scottish noble society from the mid fifteenth century, and it was their kindreds who became so prominent. The sheer demo-graphic vitality of these families is almost certainly the major factor behind the flourishing of agnatic kinship within the late medieval Scottish nobility.

IX

One striking feature of these new social relationships is that they usually operated within limited geographical areas. While later-fifteenth-century magnates often had scattered estates, their interests tended to focus on particular parts of the country –

north-east Aberdeenshire with the Hays (despite their title earl of Errol), central Lanarkshire with the Hamiltons, and so on. These were their spheres of influence, within which local lairds gave them bonds of manrent, and where many of their cadet branches were established. Geographical proximity strengthened both the agnatic kinship ties and the bonds of manrent – just as it strengthened the provincial earldoms and lordships. Indeed the new power structures of the later fifteenth century were probably as highly regionalized as the old ones had been, even if the actual areas of power were not the same.

In a way continuity was inevitable. The provincial earldoms and lordships disappeared haphazardly, leaving a separate power vacuum in each region, which tended to be filled separately by one or more magnates within the general pattern of regionalized local power. But, again, the demography of fifteenth-century noble families is also very important. Usually in late-medieval Europe marriage to heiresses was the common means of acquiring lands, and so family estates and interests varied considerably from generation to generation.[3] In Scotland, however, heiresses were extremely rare among major fifteenth-century families. Therefore successive generations of magnates possessed much the same lands, and were concerned with the same spheres of influence. Also, they could not endow younger sons from their wives' lands (a common practice elsewhere); they either had to use their own estates, or marry them into the families of local lairds. As a result, the stability and durability of the new regional power structures were greatly enhanced.

Another striking feature is that the new social relationships were almost always exclusive. A later-fifteenth-century magnate's followers were associated with him and no one else. That was axiomatic with the kinship ties, because agnatic family groupings can only have single heads. But instances of a man giving bonds of manrent to more than one lord are rare, which makes bonds of manrent different from – and much stronger than – their precursors, especially those of the early feudal era when men were usually the vassals of several lords. It also makes them appear even more obviously a substitute for kinship, in which the lord's exclusive relationships with his followers are the same as those between the head and members of a family.

But while it was assumed in bonds of manrent that the lord, like a father, would maintain his followers' interests, in practice the institution possibly favoured the lord more than the followers. Not only did it require exclusive loyalty, but the legal contract was commonly just one-way, from follower to lord, and lords (while promising protection and patronage) rarely granted material rewards of land or money in return. It is hardly surprising that the institution became so popular with fifteenth-century magnates. Moreover, bonds of manrent were not necessarily given to lords voluntarily: they are sometimes found at the culmination of disputes between neighbouring landowners, being exacted by the victor from the loser.

These points suggest that the emergence of bonds of manrent in the mid fifteenth century was connected with the territorial reordering of that period. The disappearance of the old pattern of provincial earldoms and lordships must have caused local tension and strife – in the north-east competition to fill the vacuum left when the earldom of Mar came into crown possession in 1435 was an important aspect of James II's reign. In addition to the battle of Brechin, there were several cases of local violence elsewhere. More commonly, perhaps, local landowners simply faced up to each other – and then the weaker (with the smaller resources, kindreds and following) backed down peaceably. But whether or not violence took place, whoever emerged as the dominant lord in a particular area generally formalized his position by obtaining bonds of manrent. Thus the institution did not simply evolve by chance from the earlier social ties; it was probably consciously developed – perhaps even invented – to fulfil a particular function. This is akin to the near-simultaneous emergence of the lordships of parliament (again marks of social superiority) developed by the same magnates who employed the early bonds of manrent. Both were consequences of the transformation of the top layer of Scottish noble society during the middle years of the fifteenth century.

What happened when a region contained two or more equally powerful nobles? One possible consequence was local feuding – which was certainly not absent from late-medieval Scotland. But there are also several instances of bonds of friendship between magnates, in which they agreed that disputes between them or their kindreds and followers should be settled jointly and amicably. One early example is an indenture between the duke of Albany and the fourth earl of Douglas in 1409. Similar agreements are quite common after the mid fifteenth century; they include bonds between the earl of Errol and the eldest son of the earl of Huntly (potential rivals in the north-east) in 1466, and Lords Graham and Oliphant in 1500. Such bonds indicate that local rivalries did not cause insurmountable problems. Perhaps the magnates were content to parcel regions out among themselves rather than challenge each other's spheres of influence (as seems more common a century later, when demographic expansion among noble kindreds may have made demarcation disputes harder to avoid).

The significance of these points is highlighted by a comparison with late-medieval England. There lord–man relationships were almost entirely based on the indenture of retinue, which was a two-way contract, was generally supported by a money-grant from the lord, and did not provide such exclusive loyalty, for a man could have indentures with more than one lord. Agnatic kinship ties never developed so strongly in England (except possibly in the far north), and kinship was an ineffective force outside the immediate family. And magnate power, in general, was not so regio-nalized; in most areas interlocking and conflicting interests are evident, rather than clear-cut spheres of influence – partly the result of long-term fragmentation of estates, accentuated by the effects of frequent succession by heiresses. Therefore although individual English magnates were very powerful, their local positions were often insecure. They needed gentry support, as all medieval magnates did every-where, but were often unable to insist on it unequivocally. Moreover it could be fairly easy for gentry to play off one magnate in a region against a rival – thereby increasing the instability of local power structures and the tension of local politics.

For later medieval Scotland – although the argument remains theoretical at present – it appears that there was less likelihood of such instability and tension.

It would be wrong to say that local lairds were generally under magnates' thumbs, or that magnates usually rode roughshod over lairds' interests. Yet the balance of power in the mutual relationships seems to have tilted towards the magnates, whereas in England it tilted towards the gentry. As a rule, Scottish lairds would probably have found themselves with little alternative but to accept the regional dominance of a particular magnate; if they quarrelled with him, there was rarely anyone else they could turn to to uphold their interests – let alone protect them in their quarrel. Thus despite the personal, institutional, and territorial upheavals within the higher nobility, the exercise of fairly clear-cut, unchallenged regional power by most magnates continued to be the most important characteristic of the Scottish nobility throughout the late Middle Ages. It was, indeed, not until the Reformation introduced the additional, disruptive factor of personal religious beliefs into the lord–man relationships that the highly regionalized power structures of Scottish noble society started to disintegrate.

NOTES

1 Thirty-nine in the text, another nine on seals or seal-tags; see A. A. M. Duncan, *The Nation of Scots and the Declaration of Arbroath* (Historical Association pamphlet, 1970), p. 34.

2 Following the guidelines in K. B. McFarlane, *The Nobility of Late Medieval England* (Oxford, 1973), p. 172, inheritance through an entail (as with the 3rd earl of Douglas) is counted as the appearance of a new family.

3 Landowners generally tried to stop lands going to heiresses by establishing male entails; but the difficulty of producing sons in the fourteenth and fifteenth centuries meant that, in England and France at any rate, succession by heiresses was usually merely postponed, not eliminated.

Early Church Architecture in Scotland

Extracted from E Fernie 1986, *Proceedings of the Society of Antiquaries of Scotland*, 116, 393–411.

Scottish church architecture in stone before the middle of the 12th century is characterized by a wide variety of building types. There are, for example, the separate round towers at Abernethy and Brechin, the round tower attached to the west end of the church at Egilsay, the square western porch and tower surviving at Restenneth, the two-cell chapel of St Margaret in Edinburgh Castle and the three-cell church of St Rule in St Andrews. The dates of these monuments have conventionally been related to the southern categories of Anglo-Saxon, Saxo-Norman and Anglo-Norman, and hence attributed to periods from the eighth century to the 12th. It is my view that these brackets are far too wide and that the buildings in question should all be dated to the late 11th and early 12th centuries and possibly entirely into the 12th.

The round tower at Abernethy is a free-standing structure with a single doorway some six courses above ground level and four bell openings near the top. Its date is a matter of dispute between the 10th or early 11th centuries, and the late 11th or early 12th centuries. The Irish round towers, to which family Abernethy obviously belongs, cover the period from the 10th century to the 13th, and hence do not as a group resolve the disagreement. There is, however, clear evidence of Norman influence in the form of the angle-rolls and the features like nook-shafts on the bell openings. This implies a date after the 1070s and probably after 1100, as the earliest angle-rolls in Normandy are of the 1060s, at St Stephen's in Caen (Calvados) and in England of the 1090s, at Durham Cathedral. The doorway is different, with flat stripwork instead of mouldings and shafts bordering the opening. This is a much older or at least simpler type of design, like the stripwork of the late Anglo-Saxon period or the continuous band found on Irish buildings, yet the masonry of the tower indicates that the doorway was built at the same time as the bell openings. There are two kinds of stone, a greyish one in the first courses excepting the doorway, and a yellowish one for everything else, including both the doorway and the bell openings. As subsequent examples will show, this contemporaneous use of forms of apparently different dates is characteristic of Scottish architecture around 1100.

The tower at Brechin, now attached to the south-west corner of the cathedral but originally free-standing, is very like that at Abernethy in shape and in the number and position of its openings. Its construction has been linked to the statement in the Pictish *Chronicle* that Kenneth II (971–995) gave the great city of Brechin to the

Lord while others have claimed it as Norman or specifically of the 12th century. The later dating is supported, once again, by the form of one of the openings as the flat, unbroken and edged band surrounding the doorway occurs on the churches of Killeshin and St Peakan's in Ireland, both dated to the 12th century. Given the date of these comparisons it is not impossible that the tower was occasioned by the establishing of a see at Brechin, which probably took place in the reign of David I.

The church at St Magnus on Egilsay in the Orkneys has a round tower attached to its western face which has on occasion been ascribed to the same family of Irish towers as Abernethy and Brechin. There are, however, a number of features which suggest that the tower does not belong to the Irish group. First, it is not free-standing and there is no sign of a break in the masonry between it and the nave. The fact that it is built of smaller stones is due not to it being a separate construction, but to the restrictions imposed by its cylindrical form, as the large, long blocks which occur in the walls of the nave would have required shaping to avoid them forming a broken and uneven surface. Secondly, the dimensions and proportions are different from those of the Irish type. The tower at Egilsay narrows more quickly and is squatter in its proportions (17 feet by 64 feet (5.18 x 19.50 m) at Egilsay, 16 feet by 72 feet (4.87 x 21.94 m) at Abernethy and 16 feet by 85 feet (4.87 x 25.90 m) at Brechin). Thirdly, its position on the axis of the western face of the church is unparalleled in Ireland. While there are a few Irish examples of round towers attached to a church they are positioned along one of the sides, as at Temple Finghin, Clonmacnois, of the middle of the 12th century. Fourthly, the tower at Egilsay was not designed for defence. It is entered through a doorway from the nave at ground level and by another under the gable, while the nave itself is easily accessible through two doorways, not to mention the roof.

If the source is not Irish, to which tradition does St Magnus belong? The three-cell church consisting of chancel, nave and western tower is ubiquitous in England and Scotland from the 10th century onwards; within this type St Magnus is related in particular to the group of three-cell churches with round western towers, of which the overwhelming majority are in Norfolk. These in turn point to a wider family as they show a marked similarity to a group of churches in north Germany, with one or two outliers in Sweden. Hales in Norfolk, St Julian's in Norwich, Johannisberg in Hesse and Ratekau in Schleswig-Holstein exemplify the type, into which Egilsay fits with ease. St Magnus is thus a member of a far-flung group of buildings set around the North Sea in a way which suggests that they were connected by water rather than by land.

St Magnus must have been built between the late 10th century and the early 13th because on the one hand Egilsay was in pagan hands from 876 to 998 and because on the other the church contains nothing of a Gothic character. There is little evidence which might enable one to narrow the date down within these brackets. The earliest dated example of a round-towered church is that at Heeslingen near Bremen (Niedersachsen), where Abbess Hatui (973–1013) is recorded as having built a church of stone and excavations have established that the earliest church on the site had a round western tower. Other examples in Germany can be dated to the

11th, 12th and 13th centuries. It is likely that a few of the churches of this type in Norfolk were built before 1066, but the great majority can be dated with certainty to the Norman period, most of them into the 12th century and a few into the 13th. A possible indication of the date of construction is provided by the murder of Magnus on Egilsay in 1117. He is reported as having spent the night in a church on the eve of his death, and if that is taken to be the present building then 1117 is the *terminus ante quem* for its construction. On the other hand, given his subsequent canonization and the dedication of St Magnus, one might expect the church to have been rebuilt in his honour. The start of work in a decorated Norman style at Dunfermline in the 1120s and Kirkwall in the 1130s is no bar to a similar date for Egilsay, as dozens of the East Anglian round towers appear to have been built with minimal decoration at the same time as the great Norman priories at Castle Acre, Binham and Wymondham. However, while a date after 1117 seems likely for St Magnus, it has to be acknowledged that there is no certainty to the matter.

The chamber at the base of the tower in the church of Restennet near Forfar has been related by a number of scholars to the request of Nechtan King of the Picts, in or around 710, to Ceolfrith, abbot of Monkwearmouth, for '*architectos . . . qui iuxta morem Romanorum ecclesiam de lapide in gente ipsius facerent*' (Bede, *Hist Eccles v*, 21). Despite this there is little doubt that the structure belongs to the late 11th century or the early 12th. The stripwork on the south doorway has been taken as an indication of Anglo-Saxon workmanship and hence of a possible eighth-century date, but while the feature is common in Anglo-Saxon churches it does not occur on any monument securely dated before the Viking invasions of the ninth century, and is on the contrary confined to those which are normally dated to the 10th and 11th centuries. St Peter's at Barton-on-Humber of around the year 1000 has strip-work comparable to that at Restennet, but the closest parallel is provided by the doorway to the tower of Abernethy which, according to the arguments presented above, should be dated around 1100. This parallel also calls attention to the important fact that the stripwork at Restennet lies flush with the through face of the jamb, whereas in the Anglo-Saxon examples it is set out a few inches. This placing makes the Restennet arch comparable with the continuous band used not only at Abernethy but also at Brechin and in Ireland, though, because the sill lies level with the ground, there is no face across the bottom.

Despite the indication of a late date from Abernethy the stripwork does not of itself permit one to place the chamber more accurately than between the late ninth century and the early 12th, but the imposts on the eastern arch narrow these brackets dramatically. The large archway opening eastwards into the nave is an original part of the fabric. Along with the south doorway it forms part of the first build, as that is distinguished by the less evenly cut and laid masonry which rises some 14 feet (4.26 m) to the top of the chamber before giving way to the better cut stone of the later tower. The imposts which carry the arch of this opening have a distinctive profile consisting of a concave chamfer separated by a quirk from the vertical face of the block. This is a formula common in Norman buildings of the 11th century at, for instance, the abbeys of Bernay (Eure, first half of the 11th century), and St Stephen's in Caen (Calvados, 1060s to 1080s). In the British Isles the earliest surviving example appears to be in the monastic buildings erected at Jarrow after the re-settlement from Winchcombe in 1074. This evidence corroborates a date around 1100 already suggested by the comparison of the stripwork with Abernethy.

The building known as St Margaret's Chapel in Edinburgh Castle is a small rectangular structure consisting of an apsed sanctuary and a nave separated by a chancel arch decorated with chevron moulding. The interior is whitewashed but the tooling indicates that the walls are original and the vaults modern work. On the exterior squared masonry like that of the walls on the interior runs in a reddish and grey band round all sides except the north. It would be unusual if the original building had not had a vault over the apse, but there is no agreement over whether there was one on the nave. The argument has see-sawed: the vault gives no indication of the original arrangement as it is obviously modern, whether of the mid 19th-century restoration or of the preceding period when the building was used as a powder magazine; but the heads of the windows curve forward as part of the vault, therefore a vault was originally intended; but the heads of the windows are themselves in restored stone and are therefore inadmissible as evidence for the original form. It is likely that this will remain an open question.

The form of the east end, a curved apse set into a rectangular exterior, is common in a flanking position in Norman buildings, as on the ends of the choir aisles of St Stephen's in Caen of the 1060s, or Lincoln Cathedral in the 1070s, but it is unknown in Normandy or Britain as the culmination of a single or main liturgical space. The nearest examples of this type are the axial chapels of the cathedrals of Auxerre in northern Burgundy (Yonne, 1031ff) and Santiago in north-west Spain (Galicia, 1077ff). While the form of these examples is similar to that of St Margaret's, the context (radiating off an ambulatory at the east end of a great church) could hardly be more different, and an alternative explanation is offered by the likelihood that the chapel formed part of a larger secular structure such as a house or tower. This is suggested by the lack of parallels for a free-standing chapel on this small scale and by the complete lack of original masonry along the entire north face, including the north-west and north-east corners. The structure could not have been very large since there is only 40 feet (12.19 m) between the north face of the chapel and the edge of the platform on which it stands, but numerous parallels suggest themselves in contemporary castles. The castle at Rochester, of the 1120s, has a chapel on the second floor of its entrance block attached to the main building on one side only, it is similar in size to St Margaret's and consists of a sanctuary (albeit rectangular within) and a nave with a chancel arch between the two. More directly relevant, the keep at Bamburgh, which may date from before the siege by David I in 1138, has on the first floor a chapel with an enclosed apse like that of St Margaret's. In both of these examples the chapel is situated above ground level, but the ground-floor setting at Edinburgh could be explained by what must have been the small size of the whole building and by its secure situation near the top of the Castle rock.

Despite its apparent simplicity the dimensions of St Margaret's Chapel reveal it as a design of some sophistication, with a handful of lengths repeated and interwoven on different axes, as follows. Allowing for irregularities, the interior is 10 feet wide, the sanctuary 10 feet long, the nave 16 feet long, and the whole 28 feet long. The exterior (allowing the same thickness for the lost north wall as the 2-foot thickness of the south wall) is 14 feet wide, the sanctuary 14 feet long, the nave 20 feet long and the whole 32 feet. Thus in tabulated form:

- the interior length of the whole = twice the exterior width
- the exterior length of the whole = twice the interior length of the nave
- the exterior length of the nave = twice the interior width of the whole

In addition the apse has a radius of 5 feet (making it half a circle inscribed in the 10-foot square of the sanctuary), the chancel arch is 5 feet wide, and the chancel wall, like the three surviving outer walls, is 2 feet thick.

The date of the chapel is disputed. It has traditionally been identified as the *oratorium* mentioned in Margaret's *Life*, which would place it earlier than her death in 1093 (*Vita* xiii, 252). The chevron decoration on the chancel arch is not, however, compatible with an 11th-century date since the first dated occurrence of the motif in the British Isles is in the later parts of Durham Cathedral, begun in 1093 and completed in 1133, suggesting c 1110–15 for its introduction there. It also occurs, in a form very like that on the chapel, on the south doorway into the nave of Holyrood Abbey, which was founded in 1128. Since David I (1124–53) was responsible for Holyrood it seems likely that St Margaret's was built in the second quarter of the 12th century.

One or two writers have conducted a rearguard action in defence of the traditional date by arguing that the chancel arch is an insertion, because it is not properly bonded to the flanking walls and because it is set off the centre of the apse. There are, however, four reasons for disagreeing with this conclusion. First, while bonding between two walls is an almost sure sign that they were built together, lack of bonding cannot be taken as a sign that the two parts are not contemporary. Secondly, other aspects of the layout are slightly irregular, so the placing of the arch does not set it apart from the rest of the building. Thirdly, the dimensions of the building suggest that the chancel arch is an integral part of the design. Finally, one should beware of the proposal that, if part of a building does not fit one's argument, one removes it by defining it as an insertion. In arguing against an 11th-century date, however, it is worth reflecting that if a connection had not been drawn between the chapel and Margaret in the first place, there would not have been sufficient interest to ensure its survival after its discovery by David Wilson in 1846 nor its restoration by the War Office (largely at the instigation of this Society) in the early 1850s. It is, in other words, open to doubt whether the Society would have been so successful if it had been defending 'an interesting piece of 12th-century Norman work'. In this sense it may be legitimate to see the building as enjoying the special protection of Margaret herself.

The standing remains of St Rule's chapel consist of a rectangular nave and a tall western tower, with three large arches, one at the east end of the nave, one in the middle between the nave and the tower, and one in the western face of the tower. (I shall refer to these as the chancel arch, the tower arch and the western arch respectively). There is evidence of two lost parts: to the east a chancel, with the roots of its walls visible flanking the chancel arch and with foundations seen in the 18th and late 19th centuries; to the west a new, larger nave indicated by an added roof-line and by signs that the western arch is an insertion.

Before the middle of the 19th century the dates proposed for this building were romantic guesses, like the attribution to one Hergustus, fourth-century king of the Picts. Serious analysis of the monument began with the work of Joseph Robertson who, in 1849, linked it to a description in the Legend of St Andrew of the building activity of Robert, bishop of St Andrews from 1127 to 1159. In 1912 Gaetano Rivoira concluded that the nave, the tower and the chancel and tower arches were all built at the same time, while the western arch had clearly been broken through to link the original church with an added (but now lost) new nave. He also noted the close similarity between the rich mouldings of the chancel arch and the inserted western arch and concluded that the western alteration must have been carried out very close in date to the original construction. Finally, John Bilson, in a brilliant paper, pointed out the close similarities between the mouldings of the chancel arch and the western arch to those at Wharram-le-Street in Yorkshire, sealing the connection by noting that Bishop Robert was an Augustinian from Nostell Priory in Yorkshire, and that Nostell had acquired Wharram-le-Street in the early 12th century.

This traditional view was challenged by the Taylors in 1965. They argued that the chancel arch was also an insertion, so that the 12th-century Norman arches comparable to those at Wharram-le-Street were Robert's additions to an older fabric consisting only of the tower and the attached rectangular cell. They dated this building to the first half of the 11th century because of the archaic qualities of the plan and details such as the arched lintels over the windows. This analysis, with dates proposed at various points in the 11th century, is the currently accepted view in the literature.

Despite this consensus the argument from the material evidence in favour of an attribution of the whole fabric to Bishop Robert appears to me to be incontrovertible. The status of the eastern arch is pivotal: if it is an insertion as the Taylors claim then the basic structure is earlier than Robert; if it was built with the wall then the structure was raised by Robert. A close examination of the fabric leaves no doubt that the arch was built with the wall, since, 1) the rectangular jambs (as opposed to the shafts, which are often treated differently) course perfectly with the walls, by contrast with the arch inserted into the western face of the tower, and 2) the north plinth course returns eastwards without a break.

These two observations are sufficient in themselves to establish that the arch was not inserted, but there are many other supports for the contention, in particular a comparison with the tower arch (that between the tower and the nave). No one has argued that this is inserted. The Taylors contrast it with the richly moulded eastern arch and conclude that the two must be of different dates. Yet there is no basis for the view that all arches of a particular date must have the same degree of decoration; on the contrary arches at all periods are made plain or decorated because of differences in their position, which makes it entirely fitting that the arch into the chancel is more heavily decorated than that into the tower. When the new nave was added to the west the arch then inserted into the west face of the tower would have become the new chancel arch, which explains why it has an almost identical moulding to the old one. Much more important than that, however, is the fact that the chancel arch is simply a version of the tower arch (ie the middle arch) with decorative mouldings in addition. If one removes the angle rolls and concave mouldings the form which remains is indistinguishable from that of the tower arch. Further, as Bilson pointed out, the tower arch of St Rule's is virtually identical to that at Wharram-le-Street. They share the following features:

- inclined jambs with nook shafts and tall capitals,
- a horseshoe-shaped arch with both radial and non-radial voussoirs,
- the arch composed of two square-edged orders constructed in two separate layers,
- abaci with a hollow chamfer except on the north-south face of the inner order, which is flat.

Abaci with a flat section on the inner order are known only in these two buildings, constituting a 'Morellian detail' which almost amounts to proof that the two arches were built by the same mason. Thus, if the arches at Wharram-le-Street are 12th-century (and everyone including the Taylors agrees that they are) then the tower arch at St Rule's is 12th-century and the fabric is 12th-century. Further, since the mouldings of the chancel arch are all but identical to those of the inserted western arch, the initial construction and the enlargement cannot be many years apart, and since Robert is both the link with Wharram-le-Street and the person responsible for enlarging the church it seems clear that the two building operations should have taken place in his period of office, between 1127 (or 1124) and 1159.

There remains the objection, often raised in this and similar contexts, that buildings of very different form and character cannot be contemporary, that St Rule's for instance, cannot be contemporary with David's abbey at Dunfermline. Yet such contemporaneity is not a problem so much as a demonstration of the fact that historical events are nearly always less disciplined than the typologies constructed for them, as with the examples of varied but contemporary architectural detail at Abernethy and Restennet already discussed. There is, more importantly, the possibility of a difference of function, that St Rule's was designed with a different purpose in mind from Dunfermline Abbey.

St Rule's is very small beside Dunfermline (76 feet (23.16 m) in total external length against 120 feet (36.57 m) internal length of the nave alone at the abbey), indeed so small that one may ask whether we are comparing like with like. David's building is a great church, a basilica designed for monastic services and royal burials; St Rule's has a nave internally 26 feet (7.92 m) long, which it is hard to believe would have been considered adequate at any date for the central space of a country's premier cathedral.

If St Rule's was not a cathedral, what was it? Ronald Cant has described 'the old church of St Andrews' (as it was known before the 15th century) as first and foremost a shrine for St Andrew's relics – the three fingers of his right hand, an arm bone, a knee cap and one of his teeth – with the tower serving as a landmark for pilgrims. Seen in this light St Rule's appears more as a martyrium than a congregational church, a container for things rather than people (or for one person, St Andrew, rather than a congregation). It is thus not an undersized cathedral but a huge casket.

This notion is underlined by the quality of the workmanship evident in the fabric. The foundations are much more impressive than is usual with buildings of this size, consisting of boulders packed with clay extending to a depth of 6 feet (1.83 m) over the whole site. The dimensions indicate great care both in the regularity of the setting out (the north wall of the nave, for example, is exactly the same length as the south wall), and, it can be argued, in the proportional relationships divised between the different parts of the building. The masonry is of a standard which will stand comparison with anything of the 11th and 12th centuries in the British Isles. In so far as the blocks have beds rather than nodes, a number of them are laid against the bed, making their excellent state of preservation somewhat ironic given the deleterious effects which such laying is supposed to produce. One can contrast St Rule's with, for example, Wharram-le-Street, which looks third-rate in comparison or even more tellingly with the much less regular masonry of the nearby cathedral of the second half of the 12th century, at which point one is forced to ask, what price typology as a means of determining date?

All this material evidence needs to be examined in conjunction with the documentary sources, in order to establish whether Robert might have built one type of church – the reliquary casket – shortly after his election in 1124, and abandoned it by enlarging it into another – a eucharistic church – shortly after the establishing of the priory in 1144. The earlier building, Robert's first conception, deserves such clarification, since it is an architectural gem, a first-class piece of construction worthy of housing St Andrew's relics.

According to conclusions proposed here the six buildings analysed in this paper should all be dated in the four decades between c 1090 and c 1130. If these dates are correct then the chief characteristic of the period is its extraordinary diversity, a diversity which can be seen as a reflection of the variety of views of the people who built the buildings, whom they were trying to impress, and how best they thought they could achieve their aims.

St Rule's Church, St Andrews, and Early Stone-Built Churches in Scotland

Extracted from N Cameron 1994, *Proceedings of the Society of Antiquaries of Scotland*, 124, 367–378.

The magnificent ruin of St Rule's Church at St Andrews consists of a western tower and a rectangular main chamber to the east. The tower, which is square on plan, rises some 33m in height and has round-headed arches in its eastern and western walls. The main chamber has a round-headed arch in its east wall. This arch gave access to a smaller eastern chamber which does not survive. Although the tower is of exceptional height for a church of the earlier Middle Ages, the most remarkable aspect of the building is the exceptional quality of its masonry construction, which is unsurpassed by any early Romanesque church in the British Isles.

The building contains three main arches. For clarity, they may be called the west, the central and the east arches. The dating of the building really hinges on the east arch, the roll-and-hollow mouldings of which are evidently of early or mid-12th-century date, as has recently been emphasized. If this arch is integral with the rest of the building, the church has to be consigned to the 12th century. If viewed as a secondary alteration, however, then the original period of building can be extended back into the 11th century, which accords with surviving historical evidence.

There is general agreement on the curious disjunction between the form of the mouldings of the east and west arches and the other stylistic features of the building. Unconvincing explanations have been provided for this, most recently that this style may have emanated from a disparate group of insecurely dated minor parish churches in Yorkshire and Lincolnshire and, unprovably, from the lost buildings of Nostell Priory.

Previous discussion of the building has largely been polarized between those who believe the east arch to be integral, and those who consider that the opening of which it forms a part has been inserted. The principal point of this paper is to propose a new interpretation of the physical evidence of the east arch which explains the ambiguities which St Rule's has hitherto presented. A careful examination of the structure shows that the east arch has in fact been rebuilt.

Earlier writers generally agreed that the west arch has been inserted. This is a particular difficulty for those arguing for a later date, because it quite clearly has the same form of moulding as that of the east arch, which they argue is integral with the original period of construction. The jambs and capitals of the west arch have probably been reused: the present arch almost certainly represents rebuilding undertaken in conjunction with the construction of the later nave to the west.

The central arch, which has simple right-angled voussoirs in two-order form, is universally agreed to be original. It courses perfectly with the surrounding masonry and there are no signs of its being disrupted in any way. The arch was supported by conical capitals, one of which survives, partly damaged. Below the capital were cylindrical nook-shafts, the bases of which survive.

It has been proposed that St Rule's was built in two phases in the early-to-mid 12th century. This argument regards both the west and east arches as insertions made shortly after the original campaign finished, the arches having been 'cut through the west wall of the tower and the east wall of the eastern compartment'. This analysis of the east arch can, however, be discounted for there is incontrovertible physical evidence that there were originally two chambers to the east of the tower, not one. This is provided by the return of the massive plinth course at the east end of the main chamber which, most obviously on the north side, lies below original masonry. This demonstrated conclusively that an eastern chamber was part of the original layout. It has been argued that the demolished eastern chamber was original and that the east arch, which linked it to the main chamber, is also original. This contrasts with the view that the east and west arches are complete insertions of 12th-century date in an earlier fabric.

The jambs of the east arch are undoubtedly original. They course perfectly with the surrounding masonry, up to a height of some two courses below the level of the capitals. The jambs, however, rest on platforms of roughly coursed masonry some 0.6 m in height which contrast strongly with the neatness of the base course in the rest of the building. Most significant, however, is the disrupted masonry around the arch, which provides a striking contrast to that of the unaltered central arch. Indeed, a number of small blocks of stone have been packed around the head of the east arch, a masonry technique that is inconceivable in a normal campaign of construction but which fully accords with the insertion of a new element into an existing structure.

The interpretation here proposed is that the east arch has been partly rebuilt. The original jambs and capitals have been retained but the opening has been heightened and the arch reconstructed. The capitals have probably been reused unaltered, but close analysis of the abaci reveals compelling evidence that they have been recut. Their roughly pecked surface, which contrasts with the finely wrought abaci of the central arch, is evidently the result of pragmatic recutting from square to rounded plan to correspond with the rebuilding of the stepped angular form of the original arch with the heavy roll-and-hollow mouldings of its later replacement.

The observation that the east arch has been heightened allows the ambiguities of the construction to be explained. The confusion regarding this element, reflected in the different interpretations previously offered in the literature, is to be explained in terms of its partial rebuilding subsequent to the original campaign of construction of the church. This analysis allows a more flexible approach to be taken to the dating, which is no longer constrained by the need to base the date on the Anglo-Norman arch mouldings, which could not conceivably be dated to before the 12th century.

Indeed, this interpretation accords with the documentary evidence, used in a selective manner by Bilson to substantiate his late dating of the monument and subsequently accepted by others. Bilson proposed that the 13th-century 'Legend of St Andrew' supported his view that Bishop Robert built the church following his consecration as Bishop of St Andrews in 1127. In fact, the text relates that he 'set himself zealously to accomplish what he had much at heart – the enlargement of his church and its dedication to divine worship' (Chron Picts-Scots, 191). That the church was mostly complete is unequivocally referred to in the very significant and conclusive phrase *basilica . . . ex majori jam parte consummata*, which has not before been referred to in the secondary literature (Chron Picts-Scots, 191). There is therefore nothing in the text to substantiate the idea that Bishop Robert built the church anew. That he did not rebuild the church in its entirety when he came to St Andrews can probably be attributed to his great difficulties in raising revenue, referred to in the Legend (*Sed quoniam impensa erant modica, modice erigebatur et fabrica*, 'But since funds were small, building was also carried out in a limited way'). He found it necessary to raise funds by using his own share of altar revenues and by reclaiming *oblationes* from various lay recipients (Chron Picts-Scots, 191).

Bilson suggested that the design of St Rule's was derived from the parish church of Wharram-le-Street in the East Riding of Yorkshire, the link between the two churches being provided by Bishop Robert; he had first been brought to Scotland from Wharram-le-Street's probable mother house, Noestell Priory, to which the church of Wharram-le-Street was appropriated in the early 12th century. Unfortunately, Wharram-le-Street cannot be securely dated by documentary evidence. A further difficulty is presented by the features Bilson sought to compare with St Rule's. The arch of the west doorway at Wharram-le-Street which Bilson compares with the west and east arch profiles of St Rule's, appears to have been inserted. Other points which Bilson relates to St Rule's, such as the form of the Wharram-le-Street tower-arch and its capitals, also present a less than clear-cut analogy. Unlike the St Rule capitals, which have the unusual details of necking raised above the lowest edge of the capital, those at Wharram-le-Street have no necking. In addition, the Wharram-le-Street capitals have the distinctive element of pendant triangles carved in high relief. A far closer comparison for these features is provided, for example, by the tower arch at Broughton Parish Church, Lincolnshire, which is not considered by Bilson.

A major feature of the towers of St Rule's and Wharram-le-Street is the use of twin belfry openings. A superficial examination of these suggests they are similar, as Bilson suggested. In reality, there are very strong differences. It is important to emphasize that the tower of Wharram-le-Street has been reduced in height, and that the projecting shafts to each side of the belfry openings almost certainly supported a projecting round-headed hoodmould. At St Rule's, there was no such feature. Furthermore, St Rule's has recesses for nook shafts to each side of the openings; the Yorkshire church has simple right-angled surrounds. Twin belfry openings are, of course, one of the most common features of Anglo-Saxon towers, and the form of those used at Wharram-le-Street is typical of a large number of towers across the north of England. Particularly close analogies to Wharram-le-Street exist at St Peter's Monkwearmouth (County Durham), St Mary's Bishophill Junior, in York, and St Cuthbert's, Billingham (County Durham).

Even accepting the idea that there was an architectural connection between Wharram-le-Street and St Rule's, there is an uncritical assumption that the process of influence is from Wharram-le-Street to St Andrews, perhaps based on the unstated idea of south to north diffusionism, despite the great difference in architectural quality and functional status which divides these two buildings. In the case of St Rule's, the idea that Bishop Robert might have included Yorkshire masons in his retinue on his way north is undermined by the fact that he did not go directly to St Andrews but spent a number of years at Scone. Moreover, the link with Nostell could obviously have worked both ways, and as Wharram-le-Street is not securely dated it cannot even be assumed that it predates St Rule's. It is also unlikely that a small and poorly constructed minor parish church in the East Riding should have acted as the model for a great pilgrimage church which represents such an extraordinary level of technical sophistication. In addition, there are no significant points of comparison between St Rule's and the surviving fragments from Scone Abbey, and almost nothing is known of the original appearance of Nostell Priory.

The enlargement and rebuilding by Bishop Robert was probably undertaken to provide a more elaborate setting for the shrine of St Andrew. The building of a substantial nave to the west, considerably wider than the original church, as suggested by the existing wall-line, would have been the most conspicuous enlargement. By so doing, Bishop Robert may have tried to create a functioning cathedral from what was effectively a pilgrimage church. Although St Rule's was a most conspicuous landmark, and must have acted like a beacon for pilgrims from the south, its ground area was evidently extremely limited for the seat of a bishopric of the importance of St Andrews. This was an issue, indeed, in the time of Bishop Fothad II (c 1059–93), when the relics of the Apostle St Andrew were attracting such a volume of pilgrims that Queen Margaret endowed a ferry across the Forth and hostels on either bank. The constrained east end of the church must have made the procession of large numbers of pilgrims very difficult. It is tempting to consider the possibility that Bishop Robert's recasting of the west and east arches – the corbels supporting the string-course above the west arch have been cut away at the arch-head – would have allowed the shrine of St Andrew, raised on a *feretrum*, to have been viewed properly from the new nave through the line of three arches. This would accord with general liturgical practice in the early 12th century, when there was a growing tendency to limit direct access to shrines to pilgrims of privileged status.

The existence of the church before the second quarter of the 12th century is also suggested by the status of the church of St Andrew as a centre of royal patronage. Queen Margaret and King Malcolm III buried their son Etheldred there. The description of this is of considerable significance, as it refers specifically to the building: '*Etheldredus sepultus est in antiqua ecclesia Sancti Andree de Kilrymonth sub arcuali testudine lateris chori australis; tercio natus Sancte Margarete*' ('Etheldred was buried in the old church of Saint Andrew at Kinrimund on the south side of the choir below the arch; the third born of Saint Margaret'). In the reign of Alexander I, the king's Arab steed was led up to the high altar in confirmation of the nearby lands of the Boar's Raik being assigned to the church. The church was also the centre of a bishopric which attracted major ecclesiastical figures such as Turgot of Durham and Eadmer of Canterbury, bishops in 1109–15 and 1120–1 respectively.

There is also a wider architectural context for St Rule's in a group of early ecclesiastical buildings in Scotland which includes Restenneth Priory, Brechin Round Tower and Abernethy Round Tower. Abernethy and Brechin are now the only surviving free-standing round towers in Scotland. Their age has been the subject of much debate, and recently a date of c 1100 or later has been assigned to them. It was noted that the tower at Abernethy has Anglo-Norman angle rolls and hook shafts around the belfry openings, indicating a post-Conquest date. This evidence was used to suggest that the doorway, with its stripwork surround, is therefore also of 12th-century date. A further examination of the masonry reveals a more complicated story. There is clear evidence of a masonry break which steps down to each side of the doorway; the lower courses are of long, narrow reddish blocks while above the break more square and regular blocks of yellow stone are employed. Moreover, the fact that the break descends to the base of the doorway also confirms that rebuilding has been carried out. This raises doubts as to whether Fernie's 12th-century dating of the whole building can be accepted. Historically, also, there is no doubt that by c 1100 Abernethy was a major ecclesiastical centre of some five centuries standing with important communities of Culdee and regular clerics. In 1089 it was the place at which King Malcolm of Scotland paid fealty to William the Conqueror, again implying a settlement of some significance.

The round tower at Brechin also raises difficult questions about dating. It has been ascribed to the 12th century on the basis of comparisons with the windows of two churches in Ireland, at Killeshin, County Laois, and St Peakan's, County Tipperary, but these churches are not themselves securely dated by documentary evidence. Brechin was an important ecclesiastical centre as early as the late 10th century, when Kenneth II gave the great *civitas* of Brechin to the church. Most importantly, according to Boece – in a little-known reference which was excluded from later translations of his history of Scotland (Boece 1526) – when the Danes sacked Brechin c 1017 they left standing only *turrim quondam rotundam mira arte constructam*. The carved decoration of the doorway is of very high technical quality, but the zoomorphic motifs are more analogous to Pictish carving, such as that of the carved stones at Meigle (Perthshire), than anything from the Romanesque period. Moreover, the high-quality cyclopean masonry of which the tower is constructed, extremely untypical of post-Conquest architecture, has close analogies with some pre-Romanesque stone-built Irish monuments such as Gallarus Oratory, County Kerry, and St Macdara's Isle church, County Galway, and the overall appearance is similar to Irish round towers such as Glendalough in County Wicklow. There is also a close comparison between the *christus triumphans* figure at the head of the doorway and that on the Maghera lintel in Derry, usually dated to the ninth or 10th century. Strangely, the unusual pelleted border around the Brechin doorway has not previously been compared with that around the roundel of the cross-slab carved with the Virgin and Child in the cathedral at Brechin, normally dated to the 10th or early 11th century, which is also carved with zoomorphic motifs. This evidence would tend to suggest that a pre-12th-century date and possibly a late 10th-century date would be appropriate for the tower at Brechin.

Also crucial to the discussion of early ecclesiastical architecture in Scotland is the tower of Restenneth Priory near Forfar. A foundation of Early Christian date, it has often been associated, arguably on limited evidence, with the church built c 710 at the instance of Nechtan, King of the Picts, who sought advice from Abbot Ceolfrith of Jarrow regarding *architectos . . . qui iuxta morem Romanorum ecclesiam de lapide in gente ipsius facerent* (Bede, *Hist Eccles*, v 21). The lowest portion of the tower has been ascribed a variety of dates, a 12th-century date having been assigned on the questionable basis of comparison with the stripwork doorway at Abernethy dated to c 1100, and on the form of the north-east arch impost. The form of this impost would rightly indicate a post-Conquest date, but there is evidence to suggest that the tower has been rebuilt on a number of occasions, and there is a masonry break running east/west at roughly the height of the springing-point of the arches. In an English context, for example at Kirk Hammerton and Middleton, both in Yorkshire, and at Barton-on-Humber in Lincolnshire, stripwork similar to that used at Restenneth would normally be ascribed to the late 10th or early 11th century. There seems to be no reason to assume that Restenneth represents a building style over a century out of date by northern English standards.

Further evidence of a pre-Conquest stone church tradition in Scotland is provided by the arched stone lintel from Forteviot in Perthshire, now in the collection of the National Museums of Scotland. Forteviot was closely associated with the Pictish kings, a church having been founded there by King Angus I or II as early as the seventh or eighth century. The arch, of double-curved form, was most probably that of a doorway, and that it is carved with a cross indicates that it was of ecclesiastical origin. This interpretation is enhanced by what appears to be a lamb, probably intended as Pascal, beside the cross. The style of carving is hard to place in a Romanesque context, but it shows close affinities with late Pictish relief carving, for example that of the standing stones at Aberlemno in Angus. Also perhaps indicative of church building in stone before the 12th century are the foundations of the church at Brough of Birsay in the Orkney islands which have been identified with the church built c 1060 for Thorfinn, Earl of Orkney, as seat for the bishop of his earldom, although this has been subject to debate. With an apsed east end, which may be an addition, it is broadly similar in plan to the additional church built at Dunfermline by Queen Margaret in about 1070, the foundations of which survive below the floor of the present abbey nave.

By the second quarter of the 12th century, the date of the present Dunfermline nave, the architectural influence of Durham Cathedral, begun in 1093, was extensive in east-central Scotland. As well as Dunfermline Abbey, it included the parish churches of Leuchars in Fife and Dalmeny in West Lothian, their mature Romanesque forms quite different in character to those of the group of monuments described above. There is, therefore, substantial evidence that there was a rich pre-12th-century tradition in stone-built church architecture in Scotland, the nature of which has by no means exhausted debate.

REFERENCES

Bede, *Ecclesiastical History of the English People*, ed B Collgrave (Oxford, 1969).
Boece, H, *Scotorum Historiae*, lib IX, Paris (1526).
Chronicles of the Picts: Chronicles of the Scots, ed WF Skene (Edinburgh, 1867).

Critical Historicism and Medieval Studies

Extracted from L Patterson 1990 (ed), *Literary Practice and Social Change in Britain 1380–1530*, Berkeley, Los Angeles and London (University of California Press), 1–5.

'Always historicize!' The motto that Fredric Jameson announced at the beginning of the decade as Marxism's only 'transhistorical imperative' has now, at its end, been inscribed on the banner under which literary studies as a whole seems to be marching.[1] This is perhaps most visibly the case in Renaissance Studies, where the so-called New Historicism has generated both innovative work and widespread discussions of historicist methodology. But analogous and heated debates are also taking place among Romanticists, Americanists, and intellectual historians; indeed, no area of literary study has been immune from the impulse to traverse the terrain between literary texts and a material world that constitutes the not-literature of history. These reflections have inevitably revealed different assumptions and interests, and clearly no single label can be usefully applied to the historicist enterprise as a whole, least of all the already assigned, hotly contested, and irredeemably vague 'New Historicism'.

To replace 'New Historicism', a term with which even those who coined it are now evidently uncomfortable, Howard Horwitz has recently proposed the more broadly based term 'critical historicism', on the model of Nietzsche's attack upon the uncritical objectivism of academic history.[2] The term also recalls Horkheimer's classic essay on 'Traditional and Critical Theory', which contrasts the critical thinking that attempts to grasp the historical contingencies of its own activity to a technocratic practice that protects itself from self-reflection by appeals to scientific objectivity.[3] And since it is both capacious and as yet un-appropriated by any single group, 'critical historicism' is able to refer to a wide range of historicist initiatives while still asserting the crucial fact of initiation itself, of work that conceives of itself as something other than business as usual.

This sense of innovation is, despite the risk of presumption, worth stressing. The re-emergence of historicism in literary studies will be experienced by many medievalists as a vindication, the recovery of a practice that medieval studies was wise enough never to have left behind. But it is a return with a difference, a difference that the medieval studies of the future – and it is by no means inevitable that medieval studies will have a future – must inscribe within its practice if it is to recapture general scholarly attention. The marginalization of medieval studies within the academy is a phenomenon worthy of the reflection not only of beleaguered medievalists but of their often surprisingly ill-informed colleagues as well. The fact is that the Middle Ages has from the beginning served the post-medieval Western historical consciousness as one of the primary sites of otherness by which it has constituted itself. According to the universally accepted scheme, our world begins with what historians now call the early modern period, what cultural historians have always called the Renaissance. This is a modernity that is defined above all by its difference from the pre-modern Middle Ages: humanism, nationalism, the proliferation of competing value systems, the secure grasp of a historical consciousness, the idea of the individual, aesthetic production as an end in itself, the conception of the natural world as a site of colonial exploitation and scientific investigation, the secularization of politics and the idea of the state – all of these characteristics and many others are thought both to set the Renaissance apart from the Middle Ages and to align it definitively with the modern world. On the other hand, as the name given it by the Renaissance declares, the Middle Ages is a millennium of middleness, a space that serves to hold apart the first beginning of Antiquity and the Renaissance re-beginning. And ever since the Renaissance, medieval pre-modernity has with few exceptions been experienced by modernity as 'Gothic' – exotic and romantic, to be sure, but also esoteric and obscure. In a word, as alien. Roget's *College Thesaurus* provides the following synonyms for the word *medieval*: feudal, knightly, courtly, antiquated, old-fashioned, out-dated, quaint.

Despite the obviously prejudicial effect that follows from this definition, it has been not merely accepted but on the whole embraced by the institution of medieval studies. The reason is not far to seek. The sense of the Middle Ages as other confers upon the medievalist an unquestionably professional self-definition, no small endowment in a social world in which the utility of humanistic study is always in question. Since the object of study is so unfamiliar, so radically different, the medievalist must acquire appropriately difficult scholarly abilities: a knowledge of obscure languages, mastery of a wide range of historical techniques (palaeography, philology, codicology, diplomatics), a capacity to sustain interest in texts most readers dismiss as obvious or tedious, and an ability to attend to large stretches of writing that are, by any standard, otiose (few medieval texts are too short). A tolerance for boredom and a capacity for *Sitzfleisch* are prime requisites for the aspiring medievalist. Not surprisingly, the medievalist is professionally prepared not by being educated but by being 'trained', and the professional structure of medieval studies remains, as a consequence, remarkably hierarchical. Medieval studies is a clerisy, and the more difficult of access are its central mysteries the more authority is invested in the high priests.

What also follows from the designation of the Middle Ages as definitively other is the entrenchment of a positivist methodology. If the activity of understanding is defined as the observation of otherness, then the self that does the observing need hardly be taken into account; since the object of study is, by definition, an *object*, then the subjectivity of the observer is irrelevant. The relationship is entirely technical: medieval culture is an enigma to be solved rather than a living past with claims upon the present. Indeed, a lack of contemporary relevance stands as one of the prime indicators that an account of a medieval text is sufficiently historical – sufficiently objective – to be taken as reliable. To be sure, such a project is necessarily embarrassed both by the trans-historicity of literature – the *Canterbury Tales* is present to us in a way that the Rising of 1381 is not – and by the way in which textual interpretation confronts the critic with acts of judgment that require continual recourse to his or her own values. But the positivist response to this embarrassment is to reduce literature to an epiphenomenon: literary meaning is seen as the effect of a determinative historical context, a context that is itself reduced to homogeneity in order to provide a sufficiently straightforward interpretive grid. In medieval studies this homogenization has been particularly intense, as is evident in the concern – amounting at times to an obsession – with anachronism. For if texts can be shown to bear meanings that do not accord with what has always been taken to be authentically medieval, then the notion of a homogeneous, monolithic Middle Ages that has always provided interpretive stability to the entire project (and, not coincidentally, has answered to larger cultural and political needs) is called into question.

The otherness by which the Middle Ages was stigmatized by the Renaissance thus remains in force, supported on the one hand by a humanist master narrative that defines modernity as post-medieval and on the other by a professionalized medieval studies in quest, like all professions, of legitimacy and devoted to an objectivist methodology that privileges a knowledge of 'historical facts' over the negotiations of interpretation. In a very powerful sense, the Middle Ages is and always has been taken to be the realm of the past, of the historical. One effect of this has been to force the medievalist opposition into ahistoricity: young scholars interested in renovating medieval studies by integrating it into literary studies as a whole have tended to insist on the modernity of the Middle Ages. Arguing that medieval interests prefigure modern preoccupations, this project typically takes the form of using one of the various recent forms of theory as the agency by which to relocate medieval texts in contemporary contexts. While the results are occasionally stunning (Howard Bloch's *Etymologies and Genealogies* is an exemplary instance), the essentialist and idealist character of much recent theorizing can render this work vulnerable to the charge that Caroline Bynum has called 'presentism'.[4] As the essays in this collection demonstrate, in different ways and to different degrees, there is no desire here to stigmatize any form of theoretical thinking as, by definition, historically irrelevant. But for those who believe in a social determination of cultural production, writing must be understood as above all a social practice and therefore in need of as detailed a historical contextualization as possible. What this means for critical practice is that the insights generated by theoretical formations such as psychoanalysis, structuralism, and deconstruction need to be located within and subordinated to a social analysis.

In a larger sense, the renovation of medieval studies requires not simply the importation of theory but a sustained critique of the assumptions that underwrite the prior alienation of the Middle Ages as a whole. For these assumptions derive from the modernist effort to escape from history by absorbing it: Jurgen Habermas has explained how modernism 'discloses a longing for an undefiled, immaculate, and stable present', and Paul de Man has shown that the other by which modernity defines itself is not a particular past but the very fact of historicity itself.[5] The goal of a self-assertive medievalism must be not the denial of the historicity of the past it seeks to recover but the affirmation of the historicity of the present in which it practices: the Middle Ages is indeed the realm of the historical, but so is every other period, including our own. And since what connects the medieval past and the modern present is their historicity, it is historically focussed methods of analysis that are best able both to respect historical particularity and to reveal such socially determined continuities as class and gender.

NOTES

1 *The Political Unconscious* (Ithaca: Cornell University Press, 1981), p. 9.
2 ' "I Can't Remember': Skepticism, Sympathetic Histories, Critical Action", *South Atlantic Quarterly* 87 (1988): 790.
3 First published in 1937, the essay is included in Max Horkheimer, *Critical Theory: Selected Essays*, trans. Matthew J. O'Donnell and others (New York: Continuum, 1972), pp. 188–243.
4 R. Howard Bloch, *Etymologies and Genealogies: A Literary Anthropology of the French Middle Ages* (Chicago: University of Chicago Press, 1983); Caroline Walker Bynum, *Holy Feast and Holy Fast: The Religious Significance of Food to Medieval Women* (Berkeley and Los Angeles: University of California Press, 1987).
5 Habermas, "Modernity – An Incomplete Project", *New German Critique* 22 (1981); reprinted in Paul Rabinow and William M. Sullivan, eds., *Interpretive Social Science: A Second Look* (Berkeley and Los Angeles: University of California Press, 1987), pp. 142–44; de Man, "Literary History and Literary Modernity", in *Blindness and Insight: Essays in the Rhetoric of Contemporary Criticism* 2nd edn. (Minneapolis: University of Minnesota Press, 1983), pp. 142–65.

The Ideology of Blood: Blind Hary's *Wallace*

Extracted from RJ Goldstein 1993 *The Matter of Scotland: Historical Narrative in Medieval Scotland*, Lincoln, Nebraska and London (University of Nebraska Press), 215–222.

One of the most striking aspects of the career of William Wallace is that he became a legend in his own time. While he lived, he came to the attention of several English chroniclers, and both his presence in England during his raids into Northumberland and his execution in London enabled him to enter the popular English imagination as few individual Scots have ever done. The English government regarded him as an outlaw from the start of his career. The farther his activities led him into enemy territory, the more notorious was his reputation for violence. One chronicler, for example, lists among Wallace's many depraved acts his forcing Englishmen and women to dance naked together and his disembowelling infants while they hung at their mothers' breasts (*Chron. Rishanger* 226). When he was finally brought to justice as a traitor (a charge he steadfastly denied), his execution was gleefully celebrated by the English. Pierre Langtoft lavishes much attention on the meaning of his dismembered corpse (*The Chronicle of Pierre de Langtoft*, 1866–68, ii, 362), and a ballad preserved in Harley MS 2253, "The Execution of Sir Simon Fraser", observes

> þe waleis quarters sende to is oune contre
> On four half to honge, huere myrour to be
> þer-opon to þenche, þat monie myhten se
> Ant drede
> [The Wallace's quarters were sent to hang in four corners of his own country, to be a mirror for the Scots to think on, that many might see and fear.]

Thus Wallace's tortured body is invested with significance. Barrow has written of the "false economy" that makes "one man pay with his blood for the deeds of a whole nation". But another economy was clearly operating as well: the public execution, in Foucault's words, is "a ceremonial by which a momentarily injured sovereignty is reconstituted" in order to demonstrate "the dissymmetry between the subject who dared to violate the law and the all-powerful sovereign who displays his strength". It was Wallace's unwavering refusal ever to admit that Edward was his sovereign that most irked the king, who singled him out for the cruellest of punishments. While Wallace lived a free man, Edward's very sovereignty and the order of law that legitimized it were under challenge. It is relatively easy, therefore, to see Wallace as the prototype of the modern terrorist – and his execution as a reciprocal "exercise" of "terror" on the part of the king.

One of Wallace's most vexing traits, however, was his relatively low birth: he had taken on the leadership of the national resistance with no hereditary claim to that role. An uneasy combination of annoyance at his low status and terror of his destructiveness is well expressed by one contemporary writer who described him as "a low-life [*ribaud*] from nowhere who did very great damage to the English". In the view of many writers, then, Wallace upset the natural order of social hierarchy.

But a simple shift of ideology transforms the outlaw into a hero: "terrorist" from the point of view of the state; "freedom fighter" from the point of view of national or proletarian liberation struggles. Yet the state, medieval or modern, is also capable of acts of terror. Edward's vindictive execution of Wallace became incorporated into the fabric of the hero's life. Scots were thus possessed of a countermemory that was radically subversive from an English point of view. The transmission of this subversive memory remained, until the fifteenth century, predominantly oral, giving the Wallace legend ample time to become steadily detached from historical "accuracy". The development of an extensive discourse on "the Wallace" before the composition of Blind Hary's *Wallace* (c 1476–78) is well known and requires only the briefest of sketches here.

John of Fordun provides a short account of Wallace's career, which focuses on his rise to power, his inspiring victory at Stirling Bridge, and his devastating defeat at Falkirk. Fordun brusquely reports his resignation of the guardianship and, his main interest having shifted to the reformed Bruce, gives brief notice of Wallace's death.

Andrew of Wyntoun provides the first vernacular account of Wallace's career (*The Original Chronicle of Andrew of Wynton*, ed. F. J. Armour, 1903–14). It includes some nice touches, making the legend both more dramatic and more human than it was in Fordun's hurried annals. Andrew also provides valuable testimony to the existence of popular gestes and ballads on the Wallace:

> Off his gud deidis and his manheid
> Gret gestis and sangis ar maid;
> Bot ȝit sa mony, I trow nocht,
> As he in his dais wrocht.
> (viii 2257–60)

Moreover, Andrew senses that the possibilities have not yet been exhausted and predicts greater things to come. In his modest way, though, he leaves that task for others:

> Quha his worschip all wald write,
> He suld a mekle buke endite;
> And all his deidis to write in heire
> Thareto I want wit and laysere.
> (2262–64)

Andrew perhaps imagined someone writing a "mekle buke" after the example of *The Bruce*; if so, he realized that such a moment in the history of Scottish literature was too important to be wasted on a man of ordinary talent.

Walter Bower (1385?–1449) marks a new stage in the Wallace legend – the inflation of rhetoric. Bower's expansion of Fordun's account provides much of the spirit we later encounter in *The Wallace*, for the *Scotichronicon* presents an altogether loftier version of our hero than we have yet seen: Wallace, "the hammer and scourge of the English", has God on his side. For his unbending allegiance to his nation, he is rewarded with heavenly bliss after his martyrdom, as seen by an English hermit during a vision. Bower's work, then, transforms Wallace into a symbol for all time, a moral absolute.

With Hary's *Wallace*, the Scottish countermemory reaches its greatest sophistication, uniquely combining the most subversive elements of national hatred with a highly elaborated literary form. It must be emphasized that Hary's cultural importance lies in his remarkable ability to speak to the needs of a widely popular sentiment in the poetic language that was being fashioned at the end of the Middle Ages. It is no accident that the unique manuscript of *The Wallace* also contains the text of *The Bruce*. Although composed a hundred years later, *The Wallace* was obviously intended by its author to complement Barbour's poem – even to be read alongside it – and John Ramsey's hurriedly copied manuscript of 1488 confirms that the two works were indeed closely associated from the start. That *The Wallace* soon overtook the earlier work in popularity (to judge from the history of the early printed versions of the two poems) testifies to the poet's extraordinary success in capturing the mood of his fellow Scots even at the expense of the venerable Archdeacon. The popular success of *The Wallace* lasted through the nineteenth century – an impressive achievement by any reckoning – thanks to the Augustanization by William Hamilton of Gilbertfield, which was admired by Burns and Wordsworth.

Despite their similarities, however, *The Bruce* and *The Wallace* are vastly different poems. For now, we may allow the two endings to suggest the ideological difference between these works. The entire movement of *The Bruce* is toward the signing of the Treaty of Edinburgh, which marks the peace enabling Scot and Englishman to join under the banner of the Crusades. The impetus of *The Wallace*, on the other hand, is toward the hero's martyrdom during the bitter early stages of the war. Wallace's final words are not easily forgotten: " 'I grant', he said, 'part Inglismen I slew,/In my quarrel me thoucht not half enew [enough]'."

That *The Wallace* remained part of Scotland's living culture for so long suggests the poem's peculiar attraction as an affirmation of specifically Scottish values and as a symbolic act of resistance to England's political and cultural hegemony. At the same time, it would be difficult to overestimate the complexity and courtly sophistication of Blind Hary's poem. Although this fact should be apparent to anyone generally acquainted with Middle English or Scottish verse, it has not been sufficiently recognized in the past. There are many reasons for this failure. As the poem's most recent editor points out, the author's traditional sobriquet conditioned the responses of audiences and editors alike ever since the sixteenth-century historian John Mair (Major) gave his famous and often-quoted account of the blind-born minstrel. McDiarmid, in fact, is the first editor to take the poet's credentials as an author seriously enough to submit the poem to the critical editing it deserves. Yet if the prejudices that derive from Blind Hary's name – prejudices that McDiarmid has set in their proper place once and for all – long prevented the poem from being fully appreciated, it also suffered, paradoxically, from the opposite fate: it was appreciated all too well and by too many. If not popular in origin, the poem (or rather the discursive formation of which it provides the major statement) was, in the long run, popular by destination.

In drawing on the full potential of the violent emotions arising from Scottish nationalism, Hary ensured his poem an immense popularity long after *The Bruce* virtually ceased to be read. The lasting appeal of the original *Wallace*, its modernization, and the popular ballads derived from the original provide some indication of the effects generated by the author's perfervid patriotism and the exuberance of his narrative – qualities that lend themselves better to translation or ballad mongering than does the texture of the original language. Something of *The Wallace* thus continued to live even after the literary sophistication of the original was increasingly lost on large numbers of readers as the language and the stylistic and generic conventions of medieval literature in general grew less and less familiar.

The poem's once solid reputation has never recovered from a decline that began in the nineteenth century. Part of the reason for the current indifference is to be located both in the ideology of the poem and in shifts in taste – that is, in ideology in general – that occurred during the nineteenth century. As Scheps observes, it was only in the nineteenth century that "Harry's *moralitas* [came] to be held against him" ("Literary Nature" 183). One Victorian critic thought Hary's poem "the rude embodiment of a popular feeling", a mixture of "barbarous taste", "ludicrous prejudice", and "fierce vulgarity". Earlier in this century Neilson, in a memorable phrase, describes Hary's "arithmetic of slaughter, his unending rhetoric of victory and bloodshed". Schofield similarly observes: "The spirit of hate animates the *Wallace* throughout, and no power on earth can cast it out, so as to make its body wholly clean". These early critics clearly express their moral revulsion at Hary's glorification of bloodshed and slaughter. Indeed, Schofield finds that the poem "reeks of the shambles".

It must be admitted that to most modern sensibilities, the poem's celebration of human slaughter can be repugnant in ways that other works, equally relentless in their portrayal of violence, are not. The alliterative *Morte Arthure*, for example, is equally violent but far more congenial than Hary's glorification of slaughter. The difference clearly hinges on Hary's attitude toward violence (against the English). At times *The Wallace* is shocking, and this impression tends to stick in the mind long after the memory of specific incidents has faded. It is easy enough to see how respectable Victorian gentlemen in Edinburgh, Glasgow, or London would have taken offense at Hary's "vulgarity". It is also easy to see that they spoke for their class and not for their nation.

It is ironic, then, that Victorian critics objected to Hary's "barbaric" taste, thus rejecting as "vulgar" a work of far greater literary artifice than Barbour's *Bruce*; it is equally ironic that debased versions of Hary's poem (children's tales, ballads, translations, and popular adaptations) were so beloved of the Scottish peasantry when it had been *The Bruce*, not *The Wallace*, that was conceived with the widest possible audience in mind. Posterity has played bizarre tricks on this remarkable piece of class discourse.

It is impossible to mistake the partisan viewpoint of *The Wallace*. The first thing that strikes us about the poem is its anti-English sentiment as the poet warns the Scots of "our ald annemys cummyn of Saxonys blud" (1.7). That the poet's incendiary purpose could still achieve results after three hundred years is confirmed by a letter of Robert Burns's, in which he confesses that reading the poem as a youth made his blood "boil" to this day. Hary's propagandistic intentions were realized in part through his revisionary presentation of history or, as I shall frequently call it, his displacement of history. For now it is enough to stress that Hary consciously altered events in order to provoke his contemporaries' hatred against the English. This also leads him to skip over atrocities committed by Scots against their own kind, since the emotions these incidents would incite could distract attention from the central aim of the poem, as Hary himself suggests:

> Mony thar deit off cruell Scottis blud.
> Off this trety the mater is nocht gud,
> Tharfor I ces to tell the destruccioun.
> Pete is was, and all of a nacioun.
> (viii, 99–102)

Hary's refusal to portray this history of Scot against Scot is just one form of the suppression of an unpleasant truth that we will come to recognize as characteristic of the author. Although Barbour controls his presentation of history to lend certain effects of tidiness to his narrative, there is nothing in *The Bruce* on a scale comparable to, for instance, Hary's complete fabrication of the atrocity committed at the Barns of Ayr, one of the emotional high points of the poem. Such fictionalized events add further justification to Wallace's bloody revenge against the English.

The *Scotichronicon*'s First Readers

Extracted from S Mapstone 1999 in BE Crawford (ed), *Church, Chronicle and Learning in Medieval and Early Modern Scotland*, Edinburgh (Mercat Press), 40–46.

The *Scotichronicon* is both an important precursor of and a demonstrable influence on a large number of the literary texts produced in fifteenth- and early sixteenth-century Scotland. This is partly because as a work it contains within it so much more than historical reportage or document. Within its massive bounds we also find many of the elements that characterise the late-medieval Scottish literary corpus: advice to princes; exempla; family (particularly Douglas) encomia; anti-English excurses; pious and devotional material; fables; Boethian reflections; anti-feminism; dreams and visions; and also a certain amount of vernacular verse.

Bower was himself responsive to a considerable range of texts that cut across the uncertain boundaries of the historical and the literary. Notable Scottish examples of Scottish texts of this sort that were important to him are Barbour's *Bruce* and the anonymous chronicle also used by Wyntoun, and which for Bower was a particularly telling, if slightly ideologically tricky, source for the reigns of David II and Robert II. Stephen Boardman's fascinating article on this reminds us again of the degree to which the *Scotichronicon* was itself a complex re-reading and re-writing of a *melange* of different sources and different ideological perspectives. And still within this neo-literary ambit, Bower had ready recourse to a considerable number of the instructive and exemplary collections current across Europe during this period. This mixing of material may have frustrated some later readers who wanted a more annalistic and less digressive account of Scottish history, but it was obviously a great creative stimulus to others.

One of the earliest out of the starting blocks was the author of the vernacular poem *De Regimine Principum*, which concludes two MSS of the *Liber Pluscardensis*. The poem's opening image comparing the king's correct ruling of his kingdom to a minstrel's correct tuning of his harp, is very probably inherited from Book IV, chapter 50 of the *Scotichronicon*. The rest of the poem owes a greater debt to advisory passages in the *Liber Pluscardensis*, employing them and extending their specificity, and thus provides us with yet another example of a reader familiar with two forms of the *Scotichronicon*. This is one of the reasons why I think there is a good case for arguing that Sir Gilbert Hay is the author of the *De Regimine Principum* poem, even if he is not responsible for the *Liber Pluscardensis*.

Another Scots poem for which the *Scotichronicon* is an even more powerful source is Hary's *Wallace*, written in the late 1470s, which draws strongly on Books XI and XIII in a manner that powerfully qualifies the image still trotted out at intervals of Blind Hary as a not particularly literate minstrel-figure. Hary used the *Scotichronicon* amidst a group of sources, in which Barbour's *Bruce*, especially, and Wyntoun's *Chronicle* also figure significantly, and can qualify what he does to Bower, but there are many places where his response is directly to that text. The nationalism and hostility to the English seen in the *Scotichronicon* struck ready chords with Hary, and he found too in Bower's shaping of Wallace a figure of whom he was to make even more. Wallace is a striking but troubling focus of Bower's emphasis upon the value of strong kingship, however flawed some of its exponents may have to be seen to be, in the *Scotichronicon*. The portrayal of his person and of his actions demonstrates Scotland's need for an assertive king at a time when it does not have one. Wallace acts temporarily like a ruler, but his tragedy is that he is not a king. But however attractive a symbol Wallace is for Bower in that regard, Bower will not allow Wallace, once Bruce has entered the narrative, to become the kind of challenge to the idea of Stewart kingship that he is to become in Hary's poem. This part of the *Scotichronicon*, by contrast, charts the course that makes Bruce's famous encounter with Wallace at Falkirk a trigger for a reformation in Bruce from traitor towards ruler that ultimately leads to his endorsement as a figure of prudent wisdom – a quality that Bower admires in monarchs precisely because it endows them with a judgmental autonomy, vital in relation to a political community itself frequently viewed by him as unstable and disruptive.

As such, Bower's narrative of Wallace eventually subscribes to a further endorsement of the unifying value of Stewart monarchy. By contrast, Hary's *Wallace*, written under the patronage of two knights, Sir William Wallace of Craigie and Sir James Liddale, who formed part of a nexus of Border families firmly opposed to James III's current policy of accord with the English, approaches such matters differently, and offers a reading of the *Scotichronicon* partially if not completely at odds with its dominant ideological thrust. In so doing, Hary tellingly identifies and expands some of those moments in the *Scotichronicon* that expose some of Bower's greatest doubts about Bruce. The most memorable example here is the two scenes in Book XI of *Wallace* where Hary builds dramatically on to his sources to shape the dialogue between Bruce and Wallace on the battlefield at Falkirk and after it.

As his editors argue, Bower may have been drawing here on now-lost folklore models or popular tales, but the way in which he shapes the scene for ideological purposes may also indicate an influence from Fordun who, as James Goldstein has argued, had shown himself perfectly capable of 'transform[ing] the traditional Gaythelos into the spokesman for political attitudes current in fourteenth-century Scotland'. I have no difficulty in seeing Bower as largely responsible for the highly charged dialogue in this scene: his misogynistic remarks elsewhere in the *Scotichronicon*, for instance, provide an evocative context for Wallace's damaging charge that Bruce is guilty of a womanish cowardice. It is these sort of moments that Hary has an eye for and he makes much of their potential, so that when Bruce asks Wallace, 'Quhart art thow thar?', he pithily replies 'A man'. Hary alters the scene so that

Bruce seeks to win Wallace over to the side of the English and 'gud pes' in the first of the two encounters over which it extends in his poem. Whereas in Bower the narrative movement is towards Bruce's transformation, here it is turned into a different tenor altogether as Scotland's rightful king tries to persuade the country's defender of the lure of an English alliance. It is in this scene that Hary's feelings, and those of his patrons, about the dangers of an English peace are given the emotive dressing of association with the struggle for Scotland's fiercely fought-for independence. The contemporary pungency of this dialogue is unmistakable.

Yet when Wallace answers that he is a 'man', he is also economically pointing up another aspect of his position. He is a man, not a king or a claimant. Throughout the debate his position is unchanging: implacable resistance to the English, determination to free his country, but emphasis too upon the level of his loyalty to the Bruce – despite the fact that Wallace could take the crown from him. Indeed, this is what finally returns the *Wallace* to an ideological position not *too* far off from the *Scotichronicon*. A true kingly figure, a man actively pursuing good kingship, is absent from the *Wallace*. But if this suggests that, transferring the paradigm to their own day, Hary and his patrons felt that Scotland lacked a proper king, what also seems to have been the case is that when it came to it they did not know, or could not think of, by whom he should be replaced. However aggressively it expresses its antipathies, the *Wallace* rests finally on the hope of reform, and nor does it abandon the ideal of assertive, right-minded kingship. The strength of Stewart kingship, an underwriting theme of the *Scotichronicon*, is borne out in the ideological limits of the *Wallace*.

A revealing light is shed on these similarities and divergences in the presentation of the Wallace in the *Scotichronicon* and the *Wallace* by the use of both texts in *The Talis of the Fyve Bestes*. This is a late fifteenth-century or early sixteenth-century poem that provides yet another example of a creative reaction to both the *Scotichronicon* and a *Scotichronicon* descendant. The second of the tales, told to the lion king by a hart (II.63–125), describes the ascent into heaven of the soul of Wallace as described by an angel to a visionary hermit. The Asloan MS is partially damaged at this point, but the text can be reconstructed to tell that the hermit also sees souls descending to hell and purgatory, and two probably religious figures accompanying Wallace to heaven, all having died that day. The story survives in slightly different form in both Book XII of the *Scotichronicon* and the *Wallace*, and details in the *Fyve Bestes* suggest that its author knew and used both versions. The author claims that the imprimatur of this story is well established: 'Ane haly heremed quhar he [was]/As in autentik writ we reid' (75–6), which, if it is an allusion to the *Scotichronicon*, suggests its important validating status for some readers and writers. Yet the presentation of the Wallace in the *Fyve Bestes* internalises a strained moment of interpretation that takes us back to some of the tensions between Bower's and Wallace's readings of him, which shows up the poem's joint legacy. In the conclusion to the tale, Scottish independence, as personified by Wallace, is stressed in terms that evoke Hary's poem:

> Bot Scotland ay defend he walk
> Fra subjectioiun of Saxonis blud.
> Thus for his realme stedfast he stud. (113–15)

However the moralisation of the tale, having initially endorsed this position, then qualifies it:

> Bot nevertheless, quhat ever the pepill deme,
> The gud of pece thair can no man expreme. (125–26)

The message to a monarch in this advice to princes work is thus two-fold but problematical: Scottish independence is eminently worth fighting for, but peace is also of great value – no matter what the popular feeling may be. The poem here speaks to the national sentiments aroused particularly by Hary's *Wallace*, but tempers them by an eirenic comment that may look to the frequent statement in Bower that bringing peace to a country is one of the greatest qualities a monarch can supply. This is not to deny Bower's own nationalism, but the view here that nationalism may also involve the espousing of peace in circumstances that politically permit it, is not one inimical to the *Scotichronicon*. This quite complex political position was one that informed Scottish-English relations through the latter years of the fifteenth century and into the sixteenth. Both James III and James IV oscillated between periods of what Norman Macdougall calls 'Anglophobia' and a pragmatic pursuit of peaceful relations with England; in this respect the element of contradiction that the conclusion of the hart's tale displays has a distinctly contemporary relevance.

The interspersing of advice to princes material within the wider generic context of a chronicle makes Bower one of the influential early examples of what is one of the marked features of the Scottish advisory tradition: the insertion of advisory material in wider generic contexts. Bower has numerous forms for advice-giving: straightforward instruction; lament; encomium; fable; exempla – the example of Alexander and the pirate that he cites in chapter 39 of Book X, for instance, in order to criticise Edward I's conquesting aspirations, persistently comes up in later Scottish advisory literature such as John Ireland's *Meroure of Wyssdome*, the *Buik of King Alexander the Conquerour* and the *Buke of the Chess*. The fluid movements from these advisory strategies back into a historical narrative are an important structural precedent for later advice to princes literature. As important too, though, is the template for the identification of advice-giving with shoring up the Stewart *status quo* that is Bower's project in the *Scotichronicon*. Conscious as he is of the faults of many of the kings he portrays, including James I, Bower's position finally endorses Stewart kingship in the dead person of James I with an optimism tinged with anxiety that will become a hallmark for much later Scottish advice to princes literature.

Robert Henryson has his narrator, Aesop, say of tense relations between men and their lords in the *moralitas* to his advice to princes fable 'The Lion and the Mouse':

Mair till expound, as now I lett allane,
Bot king and lord may weill with quhat I mene:
Figure heirof oftymis hes bene sene. (1612–14)

But there is no need to go rushing off in pursuit of concealed allusions to Lauder Bridge here. Henryson is making the point that these are recurrent situations, and the carefully nuanced image he gives of kingship in this poem as ideally both strong and merciful, fallible but reformable, but with the potential still for both tyranny and temperance, has much in common with Bower's shaping of it, to which Henryson's remarks may even refer – the reference here could well be literary, within what is a very literary fable. (The case of this fable, on the advantages of granting remissions and of not encouraging your supporters to bear grievances, strikes some particular advisory resonances with Bower's judgements on the way David II dealt with the potential noble rebellion against him in 1363.) It also seems to me quite possible that Bower gave something else, still barely researched, to Henryson. A quantity of fables, from a real variety of sources and some still unidentified, are included through the *Scotichronicon*, and Bower is certainly the most extensive user of fabular material in Scottish writing before Henryson. There are no direct correspondences of fables between them, but Bower's willingness to politicise his fables (often with a sense that a particular situation reflects a recurrent advisory issue), and to give them different moralities from those traditionally assigned to them, certainly anticipates, and may well influence, Henryson's own practice in his fabular collection.

The *Scotichronicon*'s widespread popularity with its earliest readers thus had much to do with the fact that it was such an adaptable authority. That so many of its readers were also writers demonstrates the extent, still insufficiently studied, to which it was source or inspiration for vernacular as well as Latin texts. That literary process seems to have started in the very margins, or in this case, endpapers, of the Corpus MS of the *Scotichronicon* itself. Following the conclusion of the chronicle proper, there are a number of items in the hand of the main scribe including a vernacular poem now known as *Ane Ballet of the Nine Nobillis*, a piece which adds Robert the Bruce to the standard nine worthies and then demands the reader, 'Ye gude men that thir balletis redis,/Deme quha dochtyast was in dedis.' This piece seems to be related to an item that follows it dealing with the origins of the Stewarts, and claiming that Walter Stewart was with Godfrey of Boulogne when he conquered Antioch. The Corpus MS is the earliest copy of this work. The poem and some of the pieces surrounding it, such as that on the origin of the Stewarts and a pedigree of the kings of France, are clearly, in one sense, extraneous to the *Scotichronicon*, and yet they equally clearly had an accepted association with it as a general part of the matter of Scotland, since they do get copied into other MSS of the whole work. The context and date at which the *Ballet of the Nine Nobillis* first appears makes it worth floating the suggestion that this may be another work by, or closely associated with, Sir Gilbert Hay. But, more relevantly to our purpose, it seems to me that the *Ballet* does what many of the first readers of the *Scotichronicon* wanted to do; it supports the chronicle on one level but, on another, recontextualises and comments on it. The question as to where Bruce stands among the ten nobles at once endorses his status among them, a status much advocated by Bower, and yet leaves uncertain where he stands in terms of supremacy. It provides the matter of the *Scotichronicon* with a different historicising context that is momentarily more one of universal history – as in, say, Wyntoun's *Chronicle* – than that which Bower had set out to create. The poem thus stands in supportive but interrogative relation to the chronicle it follows, as one of the earliest examples of a process to be continued, with different kinds of emphasis, right down to the present day, in the production of Donald's index.

Politics and Poetry in Fifteenth- and Sixteenth-Century Scotland

Extracted from RJ Lyall *Scottish Literary Journal*, 3 (1976), 5–10.

In dealing with one or other of the numerous Middle Scots poems which are in some way concerned with politics, scholars have tended wherever possible to relate the authors' political preoccupations to the events of the reign of James III (1460–88), who has long been a text-book model of the wilful, intemperate monarch. However convincing such identifications may be in individual cases, it is remarkable that there has been very little attempt to connect these works to one another through their political content. Equally, the association of such poems with James's reign is based upon a portrayal of that monarch which itself requires – and is beginning to receive – much more critical attention than previous historians have been willing to give. The purpose of the present article is to re-evaluate the grounds on which several Middle Scots poems have been dated to, and seen to allude to, James III's reign (and particularly to its final years), and to attempt answers to three connected questions: whether such dating is justified by the literary and political evidence, how far the poets concerned are articulating specifically topical views rather than continuing long-standing medieval literary and philosophical traditions, and lastly, if there *is* substance to the link between these works and the reign of James III, what this tells us about the ideological role of the poet in the Scotland of their day.

Henryson's *Morall Fabillis* understandably enjoy a pre-eminence among the works we are to consider. But quite apart from the poems' very considerable literary merits, they provide a sensible starting-point for this discussion, since it is fairly clear that they at least were most probably written within our period. That is, we do not need to rely, as M W Stearns did, on supposed political allusions to date the *Fabillis* to 'the late seventies or the early eighties'. Two kinds of evidence combine to help us here. First, the incomplete text of the *Fabillis* in the Bannatyne MS (along with other partial versions in the earlier Makculloch and Asloan MSS) suggests that successive drafts, representing different stages of Henryson's work, existed in the sixteenth century. Now, two of the fables absent from Bannatyne's version derive from Caxton's *Aesop* (1484), and therefore cannot have been written before that date, while another which appears to come from Caxton's *Reynard the Fox* (1481) was present in Bannatyne's copy-text. These dates only give us a *terminus a quo*, of course, but it does seem probably that Henryson was working on his *Morall Fabillis* in the 1480s, and that he added some fables to his original collection after 1484. It is possible that all the *Fabillis* were written after that date, and conceivably even within the reign of James IV, but the greater likelihood is that they date from the 1480s.

It is a considerable leap, however, from that conclusion to the tracing of contemporary allusions in the *Fabillis*. That Henryson is concerned with the nature of the Christian commonwealth is undeniable, but more than any other of the Middle Scots poets, he attempts to integrate his political observations into a comprehensive vision of man's place in the universe. Much of the political comment in his poetry is conventional in any case, but it is in addition subordinated to a sense of man's miserable condition, of the transitoriness of this world, which is itself conventional. In *The Scheip and the Doig*, for example, the courts are seen to be operating in favour of the rapacious rich:

> Se how the cursit syn of cuvatys
> Exylit hes bayth lufe, lawty, and law:
> Now few or nane will execute justice,
> In falt of quhome the pure man is ourthraw.
> The verity, [suppois the Juge it] knaw,
> He is so blindit with affectioun,
> Bot dreid, for meid, [he lettis] the rycht go doun. (155–61)

By setting his narrative in a consistory court and by using contemporary legal terminology, Henryson has certainly increased the immediacy of his fable, but his real concerns are wider than the present political situation: like the author of *Piers Plowman* he sees that there are fundamental moral, even eschatological reasons for the miseries of this world, and he acknowledges that they are the consequences of man's sinful state, 'our grit offens' (1.169). It follows, of course, that although Henryson does not explicitly make the point, he did not see contemporary injustices primarily as the consequence of an individual's actions or of a particular set of circumstances. It is part of the human condition.

The *moralitas* of *The Wolf and the Lamb* again discusses the plight of the poor, this time from an economic rather than a legal standpoint:

> The pure peple this lamb may signify
> As malemen, merchandise, and pure lauboreris,
> Off quhome the lyfe is half a purgatory,
> To wyn with lawty, leving as effeiris.
> The wolf betakynis fals extorceneiris
> And oppressouris of pure men, as we se,
> Be violens, be craft, or sutelte. (92–8)

Henryson goes on to elaborate on the three kinds of 'extorceneiris': crooked lawyers, the greedy rich, and grasping lairds. In various versions of this fable throughout the Middle Ages, however, the wolf's oppression of the lamb had stood for the oppression of the innocent (and especially of the poor but honest), and even the specific kinds of tyrants Henryson attacks are commonly the objects of medieval satire and complaint. The situation of the poor commons is both a manifestation of that post-lapsarian condition I have just referred to, and the reflex of the medieval ideal of the interdependence of social classes, and as such it provides a constant theme in political literature. We cannot assume, *a priori*, that Henryson's discussion of the issue means that the position was worse in late fifteenth-century Scotland than at other times and places, though of course it may have been, and we must recognise that Henryson stands clearly within a medieval tradition of social protest.

If these are examples of political poetry, then that is true only in a rather general sense. More limited applications have been suggested, however, for *The Lyoun and Mous*, where the lion, which

> May signify a prince or empriour,
> A potestat, or yit a king with croun, (254–5)

is captured in a net and rescued by a horde of mice, led by one which he has previously spared. M W Stearns has suggested that this story might allude to the imprisonment of James III by the Boyds and their allies: he defends his topical application of the fable by reference to Henryson's cryptic remark in the *moralitas*:

> Bot king and Lord may weill with quhat I mene;
> Fegour heirof oftymis hes bene sene. (293–4)

Stearns glosses these lines as 'the king and lords may well know what he means since examples have frequently been seen hereabouts', an interpretation which distorts the passage, since 'heirof' cannot mean 'hereabouts' and since 'king' and 'lord', which might at first glance seem to be singular, both in fact function as plural. The reference, in other words, is much less specific than Stearns would have us believe, meaning rather that the significance of the fable should be apparent to both kings and lords, since the situation has often been repeated. The lines are, if anything, pointing us away from, rather than towards, any particular application.

Although Stearns's explanation of *the Lyoun and the Mous* in terms of the events of 1466 has not won much support, other critics have been willing to pursue the idea that the poem is topical. John MacQueen goes further than Stearns:

> The lion, in fact, is probably a direct and not altogether unfriendly portrait of James III . . . The mouse represents the ordinary people of Scotland, and while Henryson does not specifically say so, it is fairly clear that the hunters who trap the lion are the Scottish nobility, whose general hostility to James III is notorious.

James's most recent biographer, while stressing that the poem is not 'a disguised history' of the reign, accepts that some such reference was intended, while the most specific interpretation so far offered has come from Ranald Nicholson, who detects a very 'precise' allegory in which the mice are the Edinburgh burgesses who apparently helped Alexander Stewart, Duke of Albany, obtain his brother the king's release from Edinburgh Castle on 29 September 1482, after the coup at Lauder in August, and their leader is 'doubtless' Walter Bertram, who was rewarded for his services to the king's cause. We are, thanks to the efforts of N A T Macdougall and Professor Nicholson, now in a better position than previously to understand the complex events of August–September 1482, and it is clear that James was at the centre of a major struggle for power between conflicting groups of nobles.

But it is another matter to sustain such a precise allegorisation by reference to the text of *The Lyoun and the Mouse*. Apart from a direct appeal in the *moralitas* for 'ye lordis of prudence' to consider the virtue of pity, there is nothing in the poem which explicitly refers us to Henryson's Scotland, and much of the emphasis, both in the narrative and in the *moralitas*, falls upon the initial folly of the mice, whose playing all over the lion represents the rebellion of the poor when they see the laws unenforced (in this case through the slumbering of the lion). Far from being unequivocally praiseworthy, therefore, the mice are themselves a target for criticism. The political implications of the fable are clear enough: injustice leads to further lawlessness, the great are always subject to the mutability of this world, and generosity, like our sins, comes home to roost:

> Oft tyme is sene a man of small degree
> Hes quyt [ane kinbute] baith for gude and ill,
> As lordis has done rigour or grace him till. (278–89)

In the sudden reversal of the lion's fortunes, as his lament (lines 211–22) makes apparent, the fable in fact resembles that voluminous literature *de casibus* of which Chaucer's *Monk's Tale* and Lydgate's *Fall of Princes* are the best-known English examples. It is conventional, therefore, both in its reaffirmation of the inter-dependence of the various elements of the state, and in its warning that temporal rulers cannot afford to rely on their power, since it is transitory and always vulnerable. In one important respect, Henryson pursues this general moral theme so far that he actually seems out of key with his times: whereas there is a good deal of evidence in the parliamentary records (and, as we shall see, some traces in the poetry) of opposition in the fifteenth century, and particularly in the reign of James III, to the royal policy of freely granting remissions, Henryson argues that pity dictates that rulers should 'remyt sum tyme a grit offens'. If this reveals a topical reference, it is surely in favour of rather than against royal policy, but it seems to me to be probably that Henryson is here, as elsewhere in the fable, arguing in the most general terms.

Like Henryson's other 'political' fables, *The Lyoun and the Mous* uses the weaker animal to speak on behalf of the poor commons. Whatever the demerits of the way in which the mice take liberties with the lion's person, the mouse is given a straightforward and authoritative speech expounding basic legal theory:

'In every Juge mercy and rewth suld be,
As assessoris and collaterall.
Without mercy, Justice is crewelte,
As said is in the lawis spirituall.
Quhen rigour sittis in the tribunall,
The equety of law quha may sustene?
Rycht few or nane, bot mercy go betuene.' (148–54)

This preoccupation with the administration of justice is, as we shall see, a prominent theme not only in Henryson but throughout the political literature of the fifteenth and sixteenth centuries, but again the note which Henryson strikes is a little different from that which we find most often among his near-contemporaries. All the emphasis in *The Lyoun and the Mous* is on the importance of tempering justice with mercy; while other writers are more concerned with the need for efficiency in the administration of justice. The common factor is perhaps the opposition to arbitrariness: true justice transcends the interests of any individual or party. Henryson's three political fables are all concerned with the nature of justice, and to this extent they are typical of their age. But I do not think that any of them, not even *The Lyoun and the Mous*, was intended as an allegorical portrait of the reign of James III: the themes are too conventional, the language too general.

Two more alleged references to James's reign in the *Morall Fabillis* require even stronger reservations. Stearns detected an allusion to James's favourites in *The Wolf and the Wedder*, and to the treason of Alexander Stewart, duke of Albany in *The Paddock and the Mous*. The first case is hardly probable: Henryson was writing at least two years after the event at Lauder Bridge (1482) in which the favourites are supposed to have been overthrown, and the criticism of presumptuousness and gaudy dress is in any case within another well-established tradition. It is just possible that Henryson intended the attack on excessively splendid dress to bring to mind the charges against James's courtiers, but even the language echoes Hoccleve and others so closely that we are bound to be sceptical. The real point of the *moralitas*, that everybody should accept his social lot and make the best of it, is the great political cliché of the later Middle Ages, and is echoed within the *Fabillis* (without any suggestion of a topical reference) in the *moralitas* of *The Uplandis Mous and the Borowstoun Mous*:

So intermellit is adversitie
With erdly joy, so that no stait is fre,
Without truble or sum vexatioun:
And namely thay that clymis up most he,
And nocht content of small possessioun. (207–11)

To detect political allusion in *The Paddock and the Mous* involves a greater forcing of the text; Henryson offers two explanations of his story, one a warning against plausible villains, the other an allegorical reading in which we see the soul perish through the sins of the body. The perils of flattery are a favourite Henrysonian theme, and there is certainly no verbal clue here that a more specific comment, concerning the treachery of the duke of Albany, is intended.